FLOWERS by COLOR

FLOWERS by COLOR

A Complete Guide to over 1000
Popular Garden Flowers

GENERAL EDITOR
Mary Moody

HORTICULTURAL CONSULTANTS
Ruth Rogers Clausen
Kenneth A. Beckett, VMM

MALLARD
PRESS

First published in North America in 1990 by
Mallard Press
An imprint of BDD Promotional Book Company, Inc.
666 Fifth Avenue
New York, NY 10103, USA

Mallard Press and its accompanying design and logo are
trademarks of BDD Promotional Book Company, Inc.

By arrangement with Weldon Russell Pty Ltd

Produced by Weldon Russell Pty Ltd
372 Eastern Valley Way
Willoughby NSW 2068 Australia

A member of the Weldon International Group
of Companies

Horticultural Consultants: Kenneth A. Beckett, VMM,
Ruth Rogers Clausen

Contributors: Joyce Beaumont, Cert. Hort., Cert. Land
Design; Kaye Healey; Cheryl Maddocks, Cert. Hort.; Peggy
Muntz, Assoc. Dip. Hort., MAIH; Graeme Purdy; Lorna
Rose, Assoc. Dip. Hort., MAIH; Harold Wilkes, BA,
FRHS, FAIH, Cert. Hort., past president AIH, FICM.

Principal Photographers: Nan Barbour, Gillian Beckett,
Stirling Macoboy, Lorna Rose

Project Co-ordinator: Christine Mackinnon

Editor: Shirley Jones

Design Concept: Warren Penney

Designers: Christie & Eckermann Art Design Studio,
Catherine Martin, Kathie Baxter Smith

First published in North America in 1990 by
The Mallard Press

Copyright © 1990 Weldon Russell Pty Ltd

ISBN 0 792 45267 4
Library of Congress

Typeset by Savage Type Pty Ltd, Brisbane, Qld, Australia
Produced by Mandarin Offset, Hong Kong
Printed in Hong Kong

A KEVIN WELDON PRODUCTION

ACKNOWLEDGMENTS

Weldon Russell Pty Ltd would like to thank the following people for their
assistance in the production of this book:

Picture research: Joanna Collard; Jane Lewis; Rosemary Wilkinson

Horticultural advisers: Ross Bond; Tony Rodd; Jan Wilson

Photographers: Adelaide Botanic Gardens; Heather Angel; Ardea London Ltd;
Australian Picture Library; A–Z Collection; Bay Books; Ross Bond; Eric
Crichton; Garden Picture Library; Pamela Harper; Shirley Jones; Tania
Midgley; Photos Horticultural; Pamela Polglase; Graeme Purdy; Tony Rodd;
Royal Botanic Gardens, Melbourne; Don Schofield; Harry Smith Collection;
Smith Polunin Collection; Peter Valder; Weldon Trannies.

Front cover: left to right; top to bottom
Hydrangea macrophylla
Thunbergia grandiflora
Ceratostigma willmottianum
Ranunculus asiaticus
Narcissus (daffodil)
Laburnum anagyroides
Dahlia
Zinnia elegans
Rosa 'Bloomfield Courage'

Endpapers:
Wisteria and *Rhododendrons*, Nooroo,
Mt Wilson, N.S.W.

Page 1:
Cottage garden, Sissinghurst, U.K.

Page 2:
Iris germanica 'Amethyst Flame'

CONTENTS

Rosa 'Cecile Brunner'

HOW TO USE THIS BOOK

This book has been divided into five color groups: orange-red, pink, purple-blue, white and yellow. Each color group is further divided into six plant types: annuals, bulbs, climbers, perennials, shrubs and trees. Within each of these groups entries are listed alphabetically by botanical name. A comprehensive Index of Botanical Names will help you to locate the entry within these major groupings.

If you are unsure of the botanical name of the plant species refer to the Index of Common Names. Where a plant is known by more than one botanical name refer to the Index of Synonyms.

Sample entry

All entries in the book contain the following information.

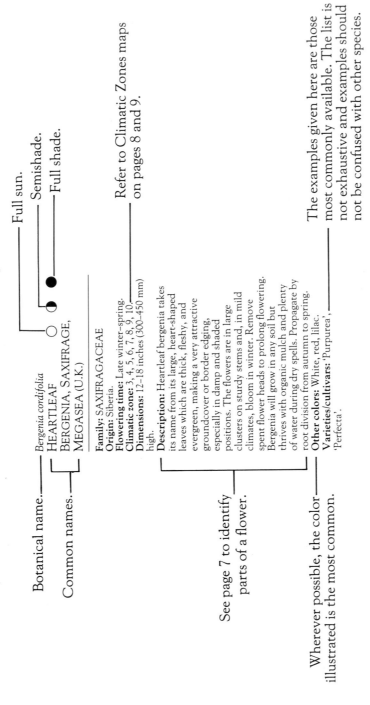

Full sun.
Semishade.
Full shade.

Refer to Climatic Zones maps on pages 8 and 9.

Botanical name.
Common names.

Bergenia cordifolia
HEARTLEAF
BERGENIA, SAXIFRAGE,
MEGASEA (U.K.)

Family: SAXIFRAGACEAE
Origin: Siberia.
Flowering time: Late winter-spring.
Climatic zone: 3, 4, 5, 6, 7, 8, 9, 10.
Dimensions: 12–18 inches (300–450 mm) high.
Description: Heartleaf bergenia takes its name from its large, heart-shaped leaves which are thick, fleshy, and evergreen, making a very attractive groundcover or border edging, especially in damp and shaded positions. The flowers are in large clusters on sturdy stems and, in mild climates, bloom in winter. Remove spent flower heads to prolong flowering. Bergenia will grow in any soil but thrives with organic mulch and plenty of water during dry spells. Propagate by root division from autumn to spring.
Other colors: White, red, lilac.
Varieties/cultivars: 'Purpurea', 'Perfecta'.

See page 7 to identify parts of a flower.

Wherever possible, the color illustrated is the most common.

The examples given here are those most commonly available. The list is not exhaustive and examples should not be confused with other species.

pages 8 and 9. These maps are based on average annual minimum temperatures provided by the United States Department of Agriculture (U.S.D.A.). Regions indicated by the dark areas on the maps on page 9 are, in most cases, suitable for growing plants from zones 8, 9 and 10. Each zone covers a large area and does not take into account changes in altitude, varying rainfall, soil conditions or microclimates. Therefore the zonings should be used as a guide only, with the understanding that most species will adapt to slighter warmer (one zone above) or slightly cooler (one zone below) conditions than those listed. Readers should check with their local garden center to ensure that species are suited to cultivation in a specific area.

Using color in your garden

Before consulting the individual entries in this book, it will be helpful to read the 'Introduction to Using 'Color in Your Garden'. Color is one of the most striking

Parts of a flower

To enable you to plan your garden using color every entry is illustrated. To help identify the parts of a flower and their distinguishing features, see the diagrams on page 7.

Glossary

The glossary on page 298 explains many of the horticultural terms readers may not be familiar with and defines some of the more general descriptive terms; for example,

Raceme: a group of flowers arranged along an unbranched stem, each floret having a distinct stalk.

Climatic zones

Each entry lists the climatic zones in which the flowers can be grown. The climatic zones are outlined on the maps on

elements in a garden and can reflect happiness and vitality, which factors affect the appearance of color, how to use create peace and harmony or result in disarray and discord. color when designing your garden; for example, how to It is, therefore, important to understand the effects that accentuate space, how to complement the environment, color can have when planning your garden. and how to establish particular types of gardens, such as a The introduction explains briefly the symbolism of color, cottage garden, a rockery, or a more formal garden.

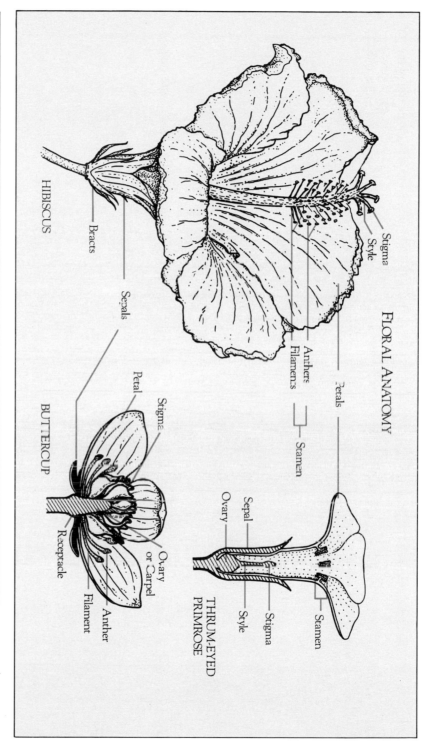

FLORAL ANATOMY

HIBISCUS

Stigma
Style

Bracts

Sepals

Anthers
Filaments

Petals

Stamen

BUTTERCUP

Stigma

Petal

Receptacle

Ovary
or Carpel

Anther

Filament

THRUM-EYED
PRIMROSE

Sepal

Ovary

Style

Stigma

Stamen

7

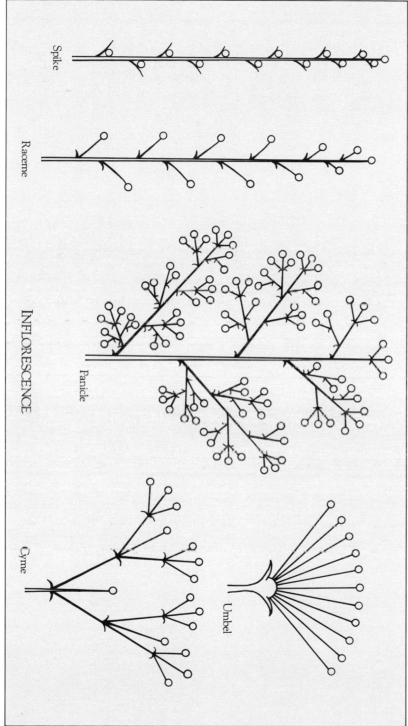

INFLORESCENCE

Spike

Raceme

Panicle

Cyme

Umbel

— CLIMATIC (U.S.D.A) ZONES —

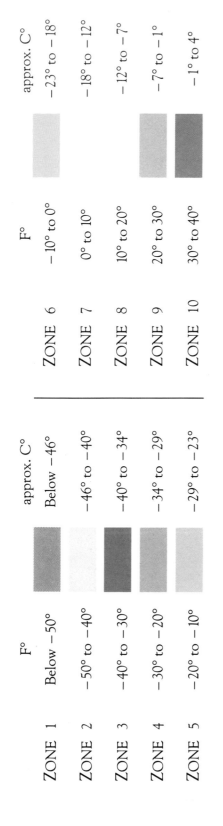

	F°	approx. C°
ZONE 1	Below −50°	Below −46°
ZONE 2	−50° to −40°	−46° to −40°
ZONE 3	−40° to −30°	−40° to −34°
ZONE 4	−30° to −20°	−34° to −29°
ZONE 5	−20° to −10°	−29° to −23°

	F°	approx. C°
ZONE 6	−10° to 0°	−23° to −18°
ZONE 7	0° to 10°	−18° to −12°
ZONE 8	10° to 20°	−12° to −7°
ZONE 9	20° to 30°	−7° to −1°
ZONE 10	30° to 40°	−1° to 4°

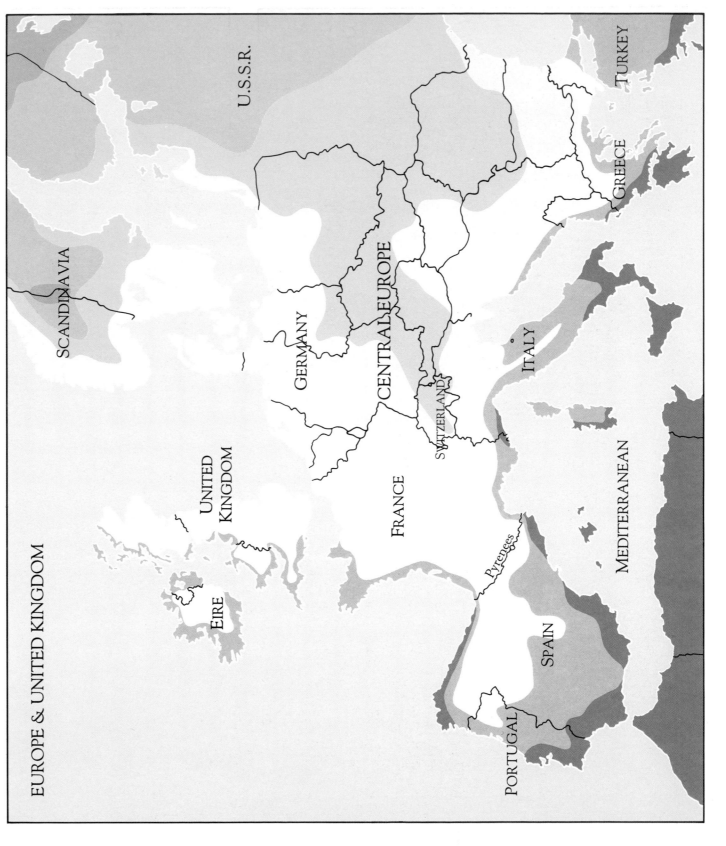

EUROPE & UNITED KINGDOM

SCANDINAVIA

U.S.S.R.

UNITED KINGDOM

EIRE

GERMANY

CENTRAL EUROPE

FRANCE

SWITZERLAND

ITALY

TURKEY

GREECE

Pyrenees

PORTUGAL

SPAIN

MEDITERRANEAN

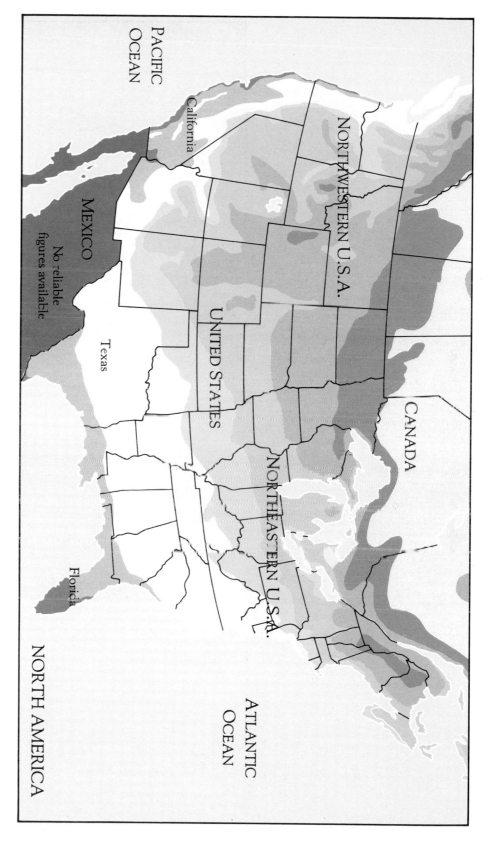

PACIFIC
OCEAN

California

MEXICO
No reliable
figures available

Texas

Florida

NORTHWESTERN U.S.A.

UNITED STATES

CANADA

NORTHEASTERN U.S.A.

ATLANTIC
OCEAN

NORTH AMERICA

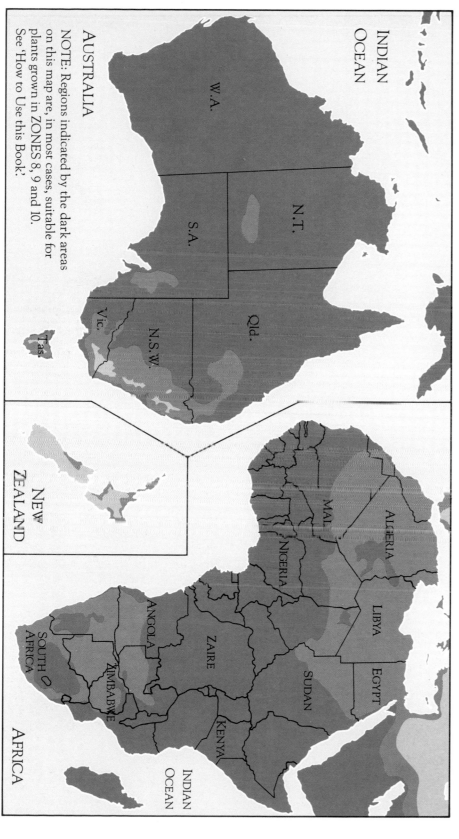

INDIAN
OCEAN

W.A.

N.T.

S.A.

Qld.

Vic.

N.S.W.

Tas.

AUSTRALIA

NOTE: Regions indicated by the dark areas
on this map are, in most cases, suitable for
plants grown in ZONES 8, 9 and 10.
See 'How to Use this Book.'

NEW
ZEALAND

ALGERIA

MALI

NIGERIA

LIBYA

EGYPT

SUDAN

ANGOLA

ZAIRE

KENYA

ZIMBABWE

SOUTH
AFRICA

INDIAN
OCEAN

AFRICA

9

INTRODUCTION TO USING COLOR IN YOUR GARDEN

No other feature in the garden is as important as color. We use color to shape the garden, to create a mood, to add interest, to impose an effect of distance and to create a particular atmosphere in a particular space. Color can be used in many different ways, sometimes to establish a natural effect, sometimes to establish a personal touch.

Color has always had symbolic significance. Bright, vivid colors suggest happiness and vitality. They tend to excite responses and to lead the eye from one area to another in the landscape. Subdued and cool colors suggest reflection and contemplation and can be used to produce a relaxing and peaceful effect.

Flower color is the most striking of the elements used in designing gardens and is often the least understood. We can't really say that gardens are an extension of nature and that therefore all colors 'go' together. In the same way as we can have a clash of color in the garments we wear, we can also have a clash of color in the garden. It is therefore important to understand how color works and how it can be used to create different effects and moods when we are planning a garden.

What is Color?

We have special color receptors in the retina of the eye that react to the wavelength of light. The brain interprets this as color. Unreflected daylight appears more or less white. White light is a combination of all the colors of the spectrum, that is, of the rainbow. If the surface of an object reflects back all wavelengths of light reaching it, the object appears to be white. If the pigment at the surface absorbs all wavelengths except green, then that object appears green.

White Strictly speaking, white is not a color in itself, but a combination of all the other colors of the rainbow. White is a symbol of purity and peace. Because it is light and delicate, it reduces the intensity of adjacent colors and is often used to soften them or to blend in with them.

Yellow One of the brightest of the colors, yellow suggests cheerfulness and liveliness. It has strong associations with the sun and energy and in primitive cultures was used to portray sunlight and signify divine glory. Yellow is associated with emotions such as jealousy and treachery and denotes cowardice. In the garden, yellow can be used to lighten dark corners.

Green Green is the most common color in the landscape. Like blue, it is regarded more as a passive than an active color and suggests contemplative moods. In the environment, green is associated with freshness. Because there are so many different shades of green in nature, it never becomes a boring or dominant color. Green, like yellow, is associated with jealousy.

Because color plays such a very important part in the design of the modern garden, we tend to forget that in earlier times color was not considered at all when gardens were planned. We tend to forget, too, that until recently few ordinary people in the Western world had gardens attached to their houses, although there were possibly cottage gardens around the smaller homes. Most gardens were in public parks, or attached to the larger manor houses or the chateaux and castles of the period. These gardens depended for their effect on the use of form and mass, the three-dimensional shapes of trees, shrubs and small hedges being used in the spatial layout of the grounds. This is particularly the case with the Renaissance gardens. When the gardens at Versailles were designed, the added flower color within the specially landscaped layout was coincidental to the architecture.

Color was not consciously introduced into the design of gardens until the eighteenth century. William Chambers in England is said to have been the first person to plant an area in flowers of the same color.

The use of form and symmetry for effect.

The primary colors
Red, yellow and blue are described as the primary colors, because by mixing one or more of these colors in different proportions, all the other colors can be produced. The color wheel shown illustrates the relationship between colors. The three larger segments show the primary colors of light. Adjacent to each primary color are shades of its secondary color.

Purple
This color is associated with royalty and the church. Monarchs, and cardinals who can be regarded as 'princes' of the church, both wore purple for ceremonial robes. To Christians, purple symbolizes penitence and celibacy and suggests moods of resignation, melancholia and affliction.

Blue
Blue is the classical symbol of serenity, coolness and passivity, and is often used to suggest loneliness. Because blue does not force its presence upon the eye, it is often used to create an effect of distance and to suggest spaciousness. It can be used as a unifying element in the landscape.

Factors Affecting the Appearance of Color

Many different factors can affect the color of a flower. These fall into three categories: the effects of different sorts of light; the treatment the plants receive; and the actual characteristics of the plants themselves.

Natural phenomena and conditions
Distance affects the appearance of a color. The further away from the viewer a color is, the less impact it has. If a flowering tree, such as a crab apple, is to be viewed from the kitchen window, for example, then it should be planted fairly close to it. The further away it is from this viewing point, the more likely its color is to become diffused by lights and shadows and thus to lose its effect.

Sunlight and shade
The angle of the sun, the humidity, the amount of cloud cover and the temperature will all, separately or together, have an effect on the color of flowers. In regions like Florida, the Mediterranean and the tropical areas of Australia, the light is very much more intense than in the cooler temperate regions of the northern hemisphere, like Britain. This strong light tends to wash out color. The degree of shade will also affect plant color, very vivid colors being softened by shade. Shade can also affect flowers in another way. Flowers such as agapanthus are normally grown in full sun. They will grow in shaded areas, but may not flower so prolifically. Because of this, the flowers do not form such a mass of color and lose much of their visual impact.

Geographical location
Because temperature affects the way we see color, a particular flower will have a different intensity of color in

Symbolism of color
Red
Red is a popular color in the garden. In early times, peoples such as North American Indians colored their totem poles red, the early African tribes used red clay to fashion their figurines and the Australian Aborigines used red in their rock paintings to contrast with the vegetation. Red symbolises anger, passion, danger and strife. In the garden, the color red draws the eye and is often used to call attention to a specific area. Large expanses of red, however, are tiring to look at.

Pink
Pink is a softer, gentler color than red but, like it, signifies warmth and welcome. It is a color that is affected by adjacent colors and is therefore considered to be neutral. It shows up well at dusk in the half-light and is seen to best effect against silver and gray foliage. Mixing different tones of pink gives the illusion of distance, the colors softening into a gentle blur.

different geographical zones. In warm temperate zones, such as Florida, plants may flower for a longer period than in colder climates, but the color may be less intense. Conversely, in colder climates, as in Britain, for example, the flowering period may be short, but the color more intense.

Intensity of light

We must realize that the quality of the light differs in different parts of the world. In the northern hemisphere, the light is soft, while in the Mediterranean regions, it is brighter, producing harsh contrasts and throwing dark shadows. Time of day also affects light intensity and the way we see color. In the early morning and at dusk, pastel colors appear more vivid than at noon. Colors such as red are difficult to discern in the late evening, but white flowers will shine like beacons. The warm colors such as reds, oranges and yellows have a tendency to appear closer to the viewer than the cooler colors like green and blue.

Treatment

Types of soil

Soil conditions will affect flower color. It is often important to know the pH of the soil (how acid or alkaline it is), but the degree of acidity or alkalinity can be easily controlled by digging in certain substances such as peat or lime, which means that gardeners can adjust soil conditions to suit the plants they want to grow.

The pH of the soil will often affect the color of particular flowers. Hydrangeas, for example, have blue flowers if the soil is acid, and pink flowers if it is alkaline. This is why gardeners add lime to the soil if they want hydrangeas to retain their pink color.

Methods of propagation

The way in which a plant propagates itself may influence its color. A nursery may sell seedlings of pink forget-me-nots. If a gardener plants these near blue-flowering forget-me-nots, the two species may be cross-pollinated. The seeds produced by the pink flowers as the result of this cross-fertilization will produce seedlings that have blue flowers, not pink.

A similar situation can arise with plants that are cultivars. If seeds are taken from an orange-flowering nasturtium cultivar, for instance, there is no guarantee that the seedlings produced will have flowers of the same color as the plant they came from.

Pruning

Pruning can be used to help rectify color 'errors', as, for example, when a plant of a particular color has been inadvertently grown where its color clashes with its neighbors. Heavy pruning can prevent it from flowering until it can be transplanted to a more appropriate position in the garden. In some instances, pruning is used to stop the plants from flowering altogether. In Japan, azaleas are grown purely for their foliage, and have to be constantly pruned so that they do not flower.

Plant characteristics

Shape

The form or shape of a plant will also affect the appearance of its color. The arrangements of its branches, the thickness of its foliage, its shape, will all affect how much light penetrates it. This in turn affects how intense the color of the leaves and flowers appears to the eye. The angles of the branches and stems throw certain shadows that also affect color intensity. Height and width are further factors in the way we see the color of a plant. Flowers growing thickly on a low-growing, spreading plant appear much more vivid and colorful than flowers borne here and there on a tall tree high above the line of sight.

The arrangement of flowers on a plant will intensify or weaken the effect of their color. Dogwood flowers prolifically along the full length of the branches. This makes it appear a much more colorful tree than one like horse chestnut, which bears flowers at the ends of the branches only.

Texture

The texture of the parts of a plant will alter the appearance of color. If both leaves and petals are finely textured, their color appears softer and less intense than in those plants that have dark, glossy leaves and vivid, bold flowers. Dark, glossy surfaces reflect more light than rough-textured ones. This makes the shiny surfaces appear lighter in color than the rough-textured ones that are not so highly reflective. On the other hand, the light reflected from shiny surfaces can make colors round about appear more intense. The dark, glossy leaves of the evergreen magnolia reflect light onto the flowers, which intensifies their whiteness.

There is a strong link between color and texture in plants. Soft pastel colors are associated with fine texture, and bright, vivid colors with coarse textures.

Use of Color in Designing a Garden

We can produce many different effects in the garden by careful use of color. By itself it does little to enhance an area. It is the way it is used, and its association with the other elements in garden design such as line, unity, symmetry, shape and texture, that give color its effect. It is important to have some overall plan or theme.

Psychologists have demonstrated that both our physical and mental well-being can be influenced by color. A disorganized and chaotic mass of color in the garden can produce an unsettling and disturbing effect; well-planned use of color can give a sense of peace and calm.

Color composition

There are three types of color composition that we can employ when designing a garden — (a) the use of one color only; (b) the use of complementary colors; (c) or the use of a variety of colors.

Tone of one color.

(c) In this type of composition, colors are used at random to create a colorful picture. The cottage garden is a good example of such a composition.

A variegated color composition.

Use of Color to Create Special Effects

Creating the effect of space

When designing a garden, the distance at which particular plants will be viewed is an important consideration. Careful use of color can alter perspective. If, for instance, you wish to make a long, narrow space appear shorter, flowers of warm, solid colors like reds and oranges, planted at the far end of the space, can foreshorten it. Alternatively, the cooler, more subdued colors like greens and blues, appropriately used, can appear to extend it.

Color should not be regarded as merely a decorative medium. It can be used to shape the landscape, enrich the view and disguise unwanted elements. It can be used to produce a relaxing, peaceful atmosphere or a vibrant, busy atmosphere.

Scale

Gardens should be designed so that their scale is appropriate for the size of the grounds they occupy and the size of the buildings they complement. A garden surrounding a two-storey home will need some taller shrubs and trees in it and perhaps a high wall or fence, if it is not to appear too small for the area. As many of today's gardens are small, color can be used to make them appear larger.

Color can be used also to break up areas that appear too solid. If the garden has a boundary wall that is often in shadow, placing pale-colored plants nearby will make the area appear less solid, and this illusion can be heightened by adding a strongly colored mass in the foreground.

(a) In a monochromatic composition, we use only the one color, or tones of it, throughout the garden. An example of this is a silver and white garden, using plants that have white flowers and plants that have silver foliage.

(b) Here the dominant color chosen is one of the primary ones, and other flowers grown for accent are mixtures of its opposite, or complementary color. If, for example, in a perennial border we grow yellow flowers as the dominant ones, the others in the mixture would be shades of mauves and violets.

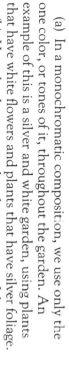

Complementary colors.

Use of color in the natural background area enhances the garden.

Color can be used to break up areas that appear too solid.

Background color

The background to a garden may be within the garden itself, or it may lie outside it. It can be composed of trees, shrubs, a neighboring house wall, or features in a neighboring garden or in adjoining open, natural areas. We need to establish whether we wish the background to appear either further back or further forward. This naturally depends on the size of the garden and the spaces within it. In some circumstances, a neutral tone acts as a foil for the range of colors in the foreground. Sometimes it is necessary to plant subdued colors in the background to create an illusion of distance, or finely textured plants can be grown there for the same effect.

Color as accent

An accent color is one that highlights certain areas in the garden. We often wish to draw attention to a particular section of the garden. This can be done by the dramatic use of color. Flowers with a strong, vibrant color can be planted

and a contrasting range of flowers, either in the complementary color or of an entirely different color, planted alongside. The strong, bright colors attract the eye and draw attention to the area. The eye will be drawn from one section of bright color to the next, creating a sense of movement through the garden. Often accent color can be used to induce a sense of excitement or happiness, but if it is overused it will tend to have the opposite effect and defeat its purpose.

Color harmony

Strategic use of color is an important way of achieving harmony in the garden. The intimate areas of the garden should harmonize with one another and the whole garden should also harmonize with the surrounding landscape to avoid a sense of confusion. Restricting the number of colors used will create not only harmony, but a sense of calm as well.

One way of balancing color and creating harmony is to use shadow and the foliage of plants as neutralizing agents to subdue color. Interspersing white flowers and gray or green foliage between color masses tones down the brightness of the masses.

Another way of achieving harmony is to use a sequence of color to give a sense of continuity and to draw the eye in a calm and orderly manner through the garden space. The sequence could move gradually from dark tones of a particular color, through to medium and then light creating a rhythmic pattern of color. Sharp breaks in the visual link will upset this sequential effect.

Cut flowers

Many people use their gardens as a source of cut flowers. Choosing to plant flowers whose colors will harmonize with the different rooms to be decorated and whose blooms, when cut, last well indoors can give the gardener a keen sense of enjoyment.

Accent color draws attention to a particular section of the garden.

Color and neutral foliage are used to create harmony.

Planning the Garden

The seasons

Different flowers are produced at different seasons and gardens can be planned around these seasonal changes. In the milder climates where winter flowerers grow well, we can plan the garden so that there are always some flowers in bloom, creating areas of color. Seasons, however, are not always consistent. Variations in temperature and rainfall can result in flowers being produced either earlier or later than normal and in some cases the flowering period can be foreshortened or brought to a sudden conclusion. Nature can prove to be very perverse and we must make allowances for this.

Climate

Climate is, of course, closely connected to geographic location. The color of a flower which is blooming in the snow appears very different from that same flower blooming against a different background. Helleborus and crocus look

far more striking flowering in the snow than in areas where it does not snow. Climate also determines, to a large extent, the length of the flowering period. In England, forsythia is recognized as the first of the spring flowering shrubs, while in Australia it is a winter flowerer. When planning a garden we must take climate into account and choose only those plants which will show to best advantage in our own particular geographic location.

Color to Complement the Environment

The manufactured environment

We must consider the color and texture of the hard landscape elements when we select plants that are going to grow near them. We must choose plants that harmonize with such things as paving surfaces, the texture of a wall, and the nearby garden furniture. Often it is not possible to change materials or the manufactured structures in the

garden when desired, and in this case plants can be carefully selected so that the colors neither highlight the undesirable structure, nor clash with it.

Surrounding architecture

When choosing color schemes, the architectural style of the surrounding buildings and the age of the garden are both important considerations. If we want to make a faithful reconstruction of an earlier-style garden, then we will select those species of plant that were available at that particular time. If we merely wish to approximate the style, we will select colors that suit the color scheme of the building, rather than attempt a faithful restoration. This is adaptation rather than restoration. Because of the large number of hybrids on sale today, there is a much greater range of color to choose from than there was in earlier times.

Surrounding landscape

When planning a garden, the surrounding environment

A color scheme to suit the surrounding buildings.

16

A cottage garden — a place of relaxation.

must be given careful consideration. This is particularly important where a garden adjoins a natural landscape, when flowers should be chosen, not only for their color, but also to harmonize with the landscape. There is an overwhelming desire today to grow the rare and exotic plants, simply because they *are* rare and exotic, rather than to choose what is appropriate for the landscape. If the garden has no natural landscape surrounding it, the choice of flowers is not so important.

Types of Gardens

The cottage garden

A cottage garden is one that provides the owner with all his or her needs in the way of flowers and vegetables. Usually, the space is limited, so plants are crowded together. Vegetables, herbs, fruit trees and flowers are mixed in together, and there is always something ready for picking, whether it is flowers or fruit. The nature of the layout makes this type of garden a happy place to be in; it is not only productive, but also provides a place of relaxation and recreation for the owner-gardener.

The formal garden

The formal garden is characterized by a strong emphasis on line, on symmetry in layout and on the shape of the plants used. It reflects the architectural style of the buildings it encompasses by, perhaps, using plant species that were characteristic of that particular era. The layout is stylized and the plants are set out so that they follow the lines of the paths. The old-fashioned rose garden is a good example of a formal garden.

The wild garden

The wild garden can be simply part of an undisturbed natural environment, or it can be created to simulate such an environment. Regeneration occurs because the plants seed themselves naturally. In general, the plants are massed

17

A formal garden — the emphasis is on line and symmetry.

and grow at random with no concern for neatness of the garden, the beds are not clearly defined and it is the trees and their canopies that determine the layout. The wild garden, like a wilderness, is a place to lose yourself in.

The rockery

The rockery originated from the gardener's desire to grow the rare and fragile alpine plants. Today, rocks are often brought into the garden to make a suitable environment for such plants. In a garden where there are changes in level, you can retain soil with the aid of rocks, and grow suitable plants in the space between them. If you are lucky enough to have a garden which has natural rock areas in it, it is important not to remove them. Design the garden around them, rather than digging them up to make a rock garden.

• • • •

There are numerous different styles of garden, usually designed to suit the style of the architecture, the size of the grounds and individual taste. Today we place great emphasis on color in the design of the garden.

Color should not be regarded as merely a decorative medium. It can be used to shape the landscape, to enrich the view and to disguise unwanted elements. With proper thought and planning it is possible to use color to achieve many different effects in the garden and to produce many different sorts of atmosphere from the relaxing and peaceful to the vibrant and busy. By discriminating use of color, we can make our gardens functional and aesthetic retreats from the hurly-burly of the modern world.

JAN WILSON

A wild garden — plants are massed and grow at random.

A rockery — a place for rare or fragile plants, or to utilize different levels in the garden.

ORANGE-RED
FLOWERS

ANNUALS

Antirrhinum majus

Antirrhinum majus
COMMON SNAPDRAGON, TOAD'S MOUTH

Family: SCROPHULARIACEAE
Origin: Southwestern Europe.
Flowering time: Late summer–autumn.
Climatic zone: 6, 7, 8, 9, 10.
Dimensions: Up to 3 feet (1 meter) high.
Description: Snapdragon is usually classed as an annual, but may persist as a short-lived perennial. Its tall stems, well-clothed with foliage, are topped by racemes of showy, tubular flowers. The strong stems and long-lasting flowers make snapdragon ideal for tall floral arrangements. Although old-fashioned, it is still popular in the garden because of its height and versatility. The dwarf varieties available in segregated or mixed colors make it an excellent massing or border flower. Plant seedlings in an open, sunny position in moderately rich and well-drained soil.
Other colors: White, cream, yellow, pink, purple.
Varieties/cultivars: 'Tetraploid', 'Guardsman', 'Floral Carpet' (dwarf), 'Little Darling,' (semidwarf).

yellow, orange, and red. Protect from snails while seedlings are young, and water well during hot weather.
Varieties/cultivars: 'Splendens' (red foliage, red flowers), var. *salicifolius* (narrow leaves).

Alonsoa warscewiczii

Alonsoa warscewiczii
MASK FLOWER

Family: SCROPHULARIACEAE
Origin: Peru.
Flowering time: Summer.
Climatic zone: 6, 7, 8, 9, 10.
Dimensions: Up to 2 feet (600 mm) high.
Description: This subtropical plant produces its small, individual flowers in terminal racemes. It is usually well-branched which shows off its bright, flat flowers, whose petals curl slightly outwards at the extremities. Mask flower may be grown in any well-drained soil, outdoors as an annual or in a greenhouse.
Varieties/cultivars: There is a compact form *A. compacta* growing to 12 inches (300 mm) high.

Amaranthus caudatus

Amaranthus caudatus
KISS-ME-OVER-THE-GARDEN-GATE (U.S.A.), LOVE-LIES-BLEEDING (U.K.), TASSEL-FLOWER

Family: AMARANTHACEAE
Origin: Tropical Africa, South America.
Flowering time: Summer.
Climatic zone: 6, 7, 8, 9, 10.
Dimensions: Up to 3 feet (1 meter) high.
Description: This tall, annual plant is eye-catching with its minute, red flowers clustered in dense, pendant tails which are sometimes more than 15 inches (400 mm) long. Grow in any well-drained garden soil but add compost or well-rotted manure prior to planting. Best suited to large spaces where it can be displayed as a feature. It needs plenty of sunshine.
Varieties/cultivars: 'Viridis' (green flowers).

Amaranthus tricolor

Amaranthus tricolor
JOSEPH'S-COAT, FOUNTAIN PLANT

Family: AMARANTHACEAE
Origin: Tropical Africa.
Flowering time: Summer.
Climatic zone: 9, 10.
Dimensions: Up to 4 feet (over 1 meter) high.
Description: Joseph's-coat, as its name indicates, has multi-colored foliage which is most striking in massed plantings. The flowers are red and, although tiny, appear in dense spike-like clusters hidden among the foliage which is flushed or striped with many shades of

22

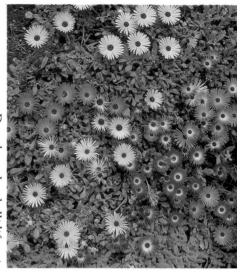

Dorotheanthus bellidiformis

Dorotheanthus bellidiformis syn. *Mesembryanthemum criniflorum*

LIVINGSTONE DAISY

Family: AIZOACEAE
Origin: South Africa.
Flowering time: Early summer–autumn.
Climatic zone: 6, 7, 8, 9, 10.
Dimensions: Up to 3 inches (75 mm) high.
Description: A dwarf plant, Livingstone daisy is frost-tender, preferring warmer weather. It has succulent foliage, a mat-forming habit, and short, spreading, flat, daisy-like flowers up to 2 inches (50 mm) in diameter. The original flower was rosy-red with white centers but the plant is now available in mauve, orange, and yellow, usually with a ring of white near the center. The colors are iridescent and the flowers make an excellent annual border in hot, dry climates. In dull or wet conditions, they will close, as they also do at night. It tolerates poor, dry soil, but prefers a well-drained, sunny site.
Other colors: See Description.
Varieties/cultivars: 'El Cerrito'.

Eschscholzia californica

CALIFORNIAN POPPY

Family: PAPAVERACEAE
Origin: United States (west coast).
Flowering time: Summer–autumn.
Climatic zone: 6, 7, 8, 9, 10.
Dimensions: Up to 12 inches (300 mm) high.
Description: Californian poppy, the official floral emblem of California, is a hardy annual or short-lived perennial that seeds prolifically, so it is wise to locate it where it can spread without interference. The brilliant open flowers,

Eschscholzia californica

which are complemented by the fine, fern-like, gray-green foliage, fold at dusk, but make a vivid show in strong sunlight. They are not suitable for indoor decoration. The plant tolerates a wide range of soils, but dislikes continued dampness.
Other colors: Creamy-white, yellow, gold, pink.
Varieties/cultivars: Among many varieties are 'Alba', 'Crocea', 'Rosea', 'Mission Bells', 'Ballerina', 'Double Mixed'.

Mirabilis jalapa

FOUR-O'CLOCK, MARVEL-OF-PERU

Family: NYCTAGINACEAE
Origin: Central South America.
Flowering time: Summer.
Climatic zone: 6, 7, 8, 9, 10.
Dimensions: Up to 3 feet (1 meter) high.
Description: This is a perennial plant

Mirabilis jalapa

which may be grown as an annual. It is soft-wooded, of bushy habit, and produces terminal flowers. It is called four-o'clock because its flowers open in the late afternoon and may even remain open through the night. The fragrant flowers, which cover the outside of the plant, are tubular and flare out to about 1 inch (25 mm) across. They seed prolifically. The foliage is easily bruised but recovers quickly from damage. Plant in full sun, in light, well-drained soil. Water regularly or they will droop in hot weather. Feed monthly from spring through summer.
Other colors: Pink, white, yellow.

Papaver nudicaule

ICELAND POPPY

Family: PAPAVERACEAE
Origin: Sub-arctic region in Europe, Asia, North America.
Flowering time: Late winter–early spring.
Climatic zone: 5, 6, 7, 8, 9, 10.
Dimensions: Between 10 and 18 inches (250–450 mm) high.
Description: Iceland poppies make a distinctive floral display, with their cup-shaped flowers on naked, hairy stems. They like a sunny aspect where they are protected from the wind. The showy, papery flowers emanate from pairs of boat-shaped, hairy sepals. Poppies are very suitable for mass planting as well as for harvesting as cut flowers. They may be picked in bud to open later indoors. Iceland poppies prefer cool climates and light, well-drained soil. The plants should be sustained on complete fertilizer, but should not be allowed to produce flowers too early.
Other colors: White, cream, yellow, pink.
Varieties/cultivars: 'Spring Song', 'Coonara', 'Artists Glory', 'Rimfire'.

Papaver nudicaule

Salvia splendens

and bouquets. Penstemons require full sun or at least four hours of sunlight daily. They may be propagated by cuttings in late summer. Penstemon prefers a loose, gravelly soil with excellent drainage. Ensure there is some wind protection.

Other colors: Pink, mauve, blue, white.

Penstemon x *gloxinioides*

Papaver rhoeas

Papaver rhoeas
FLANDERS POPPY, SHIRLEY OR CORN POPPY (U.K.)

Family: PAPAVERACEAE
Origin: Europe, Asia.
Flowering time: Summer.
Climatic zone: 4, 5, 6, 7, 8, 9, 10.
Dimensions: Up to 3 feet (1 meter) high.
Description: This is the common European poppy, seen often among the fields of wheat (corn) in Europe where it is regarded as a weed. In cultivation, it becomes a hardy, colorful annual with wiry stems and sparse foliage. The short-lived flowers are borne singly at the top of each stem well above the foliage; they are mostly single red, with very noticeable black stamens. Removing the spent blooms encourages flowering. Shirley poppies like full sun, rich soil, and good drainage. Seed may be sown directly into the ground after adequate preparation. They are best displayed in the landscape as a mass planting or at the back of a perennial border.

Other colors: White, pink, and bicolors.

Penstemon x *gloxinioides*
PENSTEMON

Family: SCROPHULARIACEAE
Origin: Hybrid.
Flowering time: Spring–summer.
Climatic zone: 5, 6, 7, 8, 9, 10.
Dimensions: Up to 3 feet (1 meter) high.
Description: Penstemon is a hardy perennial which may be grown as an annual. It produces several sturdy stems from the base, with flowers covering the terminal racemes. The plant is stiff and erect and lends charm to the cottage garden. As a vase flower, it is long-lasting and because of its long stems, is a favorite in large flower arrangements

Salpiglossis sinuata
PAINTED-TONGUE (U.K.), VELVET TRUMPET FLOWER

Family: SOLANACEAE
Origin: Chile, Peru.
Flowering time: Summer.
Climatic zone: 4, 5, 6, 7, 8, 9, 10.
Dimensions: Up to 2 feet (600 mm) high.
Description: This is a hardy annual which grows into a many-branched, rather slender plant, bearing brightly-colored flowers each 2 inches (50 mm) in diameter. Most colors have a herringbone marking on the petal, but this is not as noticeable with the reds and purples. Its profusion of blooms makes *Salpiglossis* ideal for cutting and indoor use. Good drainage is important as root rot is a problem. Add plenty of well-rotted compost to the ground prior to planting.

Other colors: Yellow, mauve, cream.

Salvia splendens
SCARLET SAGE

Family: LABIATAE
Origin: Brazil.
Flowering time: Summer, autumn, winter.
Climatic zone: 4, 5, 6, 7, 8, 9, 10.
Dimensions: Up to 2 feet (600 mm) high.
Description: *Salvias*, with their strong, upright, shrubby growth habit, provide a vivid display of scarlet flowers. They are best used in borders or in association with perennials where a focal point is required. *Salvias* flower about four months after sowing and in cool climates require a heated glasshouse for germination. They need a sunny location and are tolerant of a wide range of soils.

Other colors: White, pink, dark-purple.
Varieties/cultivars: 'Blaze of Fire', 'Salmon Pigmy', 'White Fire', 'Purple Blaze', 'Tom Thumb' (dwarf).

Salpiglossis sinuata cultivar

Senecio x hybridus
CINERARIA

Family: COMPOSITAE
Origin: Hybrid.
Climatic zone: 9, 10.
Flowering time: Late winter-spring.
Dimensions: Up to 3 feet (1 meter) high.
Description: Cineraria is a perennial, but is best grown as an annual. It is slow to develop from seed, but the floral display makes the wait worthwhile. The flower clusters are up to 12 inches (300 mm) across and are composed of numerous daisy-like flowers, about 2 inches (50 mm) wide, many having a white circle towards the center. The color range, though wide, does not include yellow or gold. The plant requires protection from full sun, frosts, and strong wind. Apart from its use as a mass bedding display, cineraria may be potted to provide vivid color indoors. This is especially so in cold climates where it does best under glass.
Other colors: Brown, pink, blue, purple, bicolors.
Varieties/cultivars: 'Stellata', 'Multiflora', 'Californian Giant', 'Grandiflora Nana', 'Prized Mixed', 'Exhibition', 'Berliner Market'.

Senecio x hybridus cultivar

Ursinia anthemoides

Ursinia anthemoides
DILL LEAF

Family: COMPOSITAE
Origin: South Africa.
Flowering time: Summer.
Climatic zone: 4, 5, 6, 7, 8, 9, 10.
Dimensions: Up to 12 inches (300 mm) high.
Description: This charming low-growing annual is similar to arctotis, except for its delightfully fine, feathery foliage. The flowers are prolific and daisy-like, with purple centers and bright yellow-orange petals. Seeds for this annual should be sown in late winter or spring in average soil with good drainage. In cold climates, sow under glass. Over-rich soil encourages foliage production at the expense of flowers. Choose a sunny position and water daily until germination, which is usually rapid. When established, the plants require little or no maintenance. Dill leaf is an excellent border specimen.
Other colors: Various shades of orange.
Varieties/cultivars: Some hybrid forms

Zinnia elegans
ZINNIA

Family: COMPOSITAE
Origin: Mexico.
Flowering time: Summer.
Climatic zone: 5, 6, 7, 8, 9, 10.
Dimensions: Up to 2½ feet (750 mm) high.
Description: Zinnias prefer a warm, sheltered position in the garden, where they can enjoy full sun and protection from the wind. Their tall, erect stems with clasping foliage can often be brittle. The showy, single or double, daisy-like flowers, which are about 4 inches (100 mm) across, make a striking display in the garden as well as being suitable for cutting. Zinnias take twelve weeks to flower from seed and in cooler climates should be sown later than in warmer ones. The plants are subject to fungal diseases in unusually wet periods.
Other colors: White, yellow, rose-pink, apricot, lavender, purple.
Varieties/cultivars: Many cultivars available including 'Happy Talk' (unusual petals), 'Envy' (lime-green), 'Lilliput' (2½ inches (30 mm) wide — pompom), 'Thumbelina' (dwarf).

Zinnia elegans cultivar

Zinnia haageana
PERSIAN CARPET, MEXICAN ZINNIA (U.S.A.), CHIPPENDALE DAISY

Family: COMPOSITAE
Origin: Mexico.
Flowering time: Summer.
Climatic zone: 5, 6, 7, 8, 9, 10.
Dimensions: Up to 2 feet (600 mm) high.
Description: This is a warm-climate bedding plant, producing masses of flowers above deep-green, spear-shaped leaves. The blooms are 2½ inches (60 mm) wide and the layers of ray florets are bright red, with yellow to orange tips. Since the stems are soft, the flowers are not suitable for floral work. The plant flowers for over three months in the garden. Moderately rich soils and shelter from winds are essential.
Other colors: Bicolors.
Varieties/cultivars: 'Old Mexico', 'Persian Carpet', 'Dazzler'.

Zinnia haageana 'Dazzler'

○

Crocosmia masonorum
MONTBRETIA (U.K.), GOLDEN SWAN

Family: IRIDACEAE
Origin: South Africa.
Flowering time: Summer.
Climatic zone: 7, 8, 9.
Dimensions: Up to 4 feet (approx. 1 meter) high.
Description: As the common name "golden swan" suggests, this plant has a graceful, arching quality. Its stems of bright orange flowers bend like the neck of a bird. It is a good companion plant with *Gladiolus* as its foliage and growth habit are similar, and they require the same conditions — full sunlight and a well-drained position in deeply prepared soil. The flowers are ideal for cut flower arrangements.

Canna indica

○

Canna indica
INDIAN-SHOT, CANNA

Family: CANNACEAE
Origin: Central and South America.
Flowering time: Summer.
Climatic zone: 9, 10.
Dimensions: Up to 5 feet (approx. 2 meters) high.
Description: Indian-Shot was first introduced into Europe in 1846 by a French consular agent who planted his "souvenirs" in a garden near Paris. The leaves of this versatile plant were formerly used for wrapping food and its seeds for ammunition and rosary beads. Often seen gracing public parks, it makes a lofty statement amidst lower shrubs. Indian-Shot forms a lush backdrop against a wall and with its small tubular flowers looks especially effective with the foreground planted with zinnia and salvia. It prefers fertile, deep soil in full sun and should be watered regularly. It is one parent of many popular garden hybrids known as *Canna* x *generalis*.

and use the dwarf varieties for borders. Dahlias are much favored by florists during their flowering season. They prefer moist soil, well-dug and fertilized. These sun worshippers were termed "water-pipe" by the Mexicans.
Other colors: Red, orange, pink, purple, white, yellow.
Varieties/cultivars: Single, anemone flowered, collerette, paeony flowered, decorative, ball, pompom, cactus and semi-cactus.

Gloriosa rothschildiana
CLIMBING LILY, GLORY LILY ◑

Family: LILIACEAE
Origin: Tropical Africa.
Flowering time: Spring-summer, northern hemisphere; spring-autumn, southern hemisphere.
Climatic zone: 9, 10.
Dimensions: Up to 5 feet (approx. 2 meters) high.
Description: This is a spectacular lily, which climbs using fingertip tendrils at the tops of its leaves. The bright yellow and red flame-like petals turning to orange and claret curve backwards while the flower stalk itself arches down. A tropical plant, it needs plenty of water and leaf mold. A well-drained but moisture-retaining potting mix is beneficial. Plant it as a backdrop to orchids or train it along a trellis or wall that is partially shaded and protected from the winds. Prune it to ground level when the plant dies back.

Gloriosa rothschildiana

○

Dahlia hybrids
DAHLIA

Family: COMPOSITAE
Origin: Hybrid.
Flowering time: Summer-autumn.
Climatic zone: 3, 4, 5, 6, 7, 8, 9, 10.
Dimensions: Up to 6 feet (2 meters) high.
Description: Dahlias, which were cultivated by the Aztecs, were introduced into Europe in 1789. A favorite of the Empress Josephine of France, these members of the daisy family were reserved for the royal gardens. Grow them in large beds with their sisters, aster and chrysanthemum,

Dahlia hybrids

Crocosmia masonorum

Haemanthus multiflorus

Haemanthus multiflorus
FIREBALL LILY, BLOOD LILY, SCARLET STARBURST (U.S.A.)

Family: AMARYLLIDACEAE
Origin: Tropical and southern Africa.
Flowering time: Spring-summer.
Climatic zone: 9.
Dimensions: Up to 18 inches (450 mm) high.
Description: This exotic member of the amaryllis family has broad leaves and deep-red flowers, followed by scarlet berries. Unable to withstand frost, it is best grown in clumps, in warm but shady nooks. In colder climates, it prefers greenhouse conditions. Ginger lily (*Hedychium gardnerianum*) can be used as a companion for color accent and perfume. The neck of the bulb should be planted just below the surface of well-drained soil. Flower spikes last for one to two weeks.
Other colors: White, orange.

Hippeastrum puniceum
BARBADOS LILY, GIANT AMARYLLIS

Family: AMARYLLIDACEAE
Origin: South America.
Flowering time: Spring, northern hemisphere; spring-summer, southern hemisphere.
Climatic zone: 9,10.
Dimensions: Up to 3 feet (1 meter) high.
Description: These exotic specimens make ideal pot plants. Up to three or four red trumpet-like blooms are borne on long stems, the strap-like leaves appearing after the flowers. In tropical climates they can be grown outdoors, but in cooler climates they must be grown indoors near a sunny window. The bulb should be two-thirds buried in potting mixture and moved into the sunlight when it sprouts. Feed monthly with weak liquid fertilizer. This lily may be induced to flower in mid-winter.
Other colors: White, purple, orange.

Hippeastrum puniceum

Lachenalia aloides
CAPE COWSLIP, SOLDIERS

Family: LILIACEAE
Origin: South Africa.
Flowering time: Spring.
Climatic zone: 9, 10.
Dimensions: 9–12 inches (225–300 mm) high.
Description: When these hardy plants are mass-planted, their bright flowers look like marching soldiers. Because of their size, lachenalias are especially suited to borders and rock gardens, providing good cut flowers which retain their color even after drying. The foliage is spotted at the base and attractive. The plants may also be grown in pots or hanging baskets and like a seaside environment. Lachenalias attract birds and are almost disease- and pest-free. They grow in any good garden loam. In very cold climates, a greenhouse environment is preferred.
Other colors: Red, orange, white, blue, pink.

Lachenalia aloides

Lapeirousia cruenta syn. *Anomatheca cruenta*
FLAME FREESIA, PAINTED PETALS (U.S.A.)

Family: IRIDACEAE
Origin: South Africa.
Flowering time: Late spring-summer, northern hemisphere; spring, southern hemisphere.
Climatic zone: 9, 10.
Dimensions: Up to 10 inches (250 mm) high.
Description: These pretty ornamental flowers look well in rock gardens and as pot plants and provide good blooms for cut floral arrangements. Grow them in pots of sandy soil or well-drained pockets in sheltered or warm situations. In cold climates, they prefer a greenhouse. The bright coral-red blooms on long spikes will flower for extensive periods. They resemble miniature gladioli and plants will often self-sow. Divide the bulbs every few years to prevent overcrowding. If placed in a woodland setting, they can be allowed to naturalize.
Other colors: Blue-purple, yellow, white.

Lapeirousia cruenta

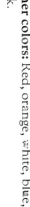

Sparaxis tricolor

Schizostylis coccinea 'Major'

Lilium pardalinum

Sprekelia formosissima

Sprekelia formosissima

arrangements. It can be grown successfully outdoors in northern Europe and North America though it cannot tolerate severe winters, and likes positions in or near shallow water, which makes it an ideal ornamental pond plant. A site protected from winds but affording full sun is preferable. It may be propagated by seed or root division.

Other colors: Pink.
Varieties/cultivars: 'Mrs Hegarty', 'Viscountess Byng', 'Major'.

Lilium pardalinum
PANTHER OR LEOPARD LILY

Family: LILIACEAE
Origin: California.
Flowering time: Summer, northern hemisphere; spring–summer, southern hemisphere.
Climatic zone: 7, 8, 9, 10.
Dimensions: 4–6 feet (1.2–2 meters) high.
Description: Belonging to the Turk's Cap group, one of the two main groups of *Lilium*, this is an erect bulb with red and yellow drooping waxy flowers. The tips of the spotted petals curve back almost to the stem. This quick-growing lily bears flowers for many weeks. It does not like being overcrowded nor being disturbed once it is established, but tolerates groundcovers because they give protection to its roots. It is best planted as a feature on its own. Water well.

Other colors: Purple.

Schizostylis coccinea
KAFFIR LILY (U.K.),
CRIMSON FLAG, RIVER LILY

Family: IRIDACEAE
Origin: South Africa.
Flowering time: Autumn.
Climatic zone: 8, 9.
Dimensions: Up to 2 feet (600 mm) high.
Description: Renowned for its long spikes of four to six crimson, star-shaped flowers, this lily is a vigorous grower. The flower spikes last well in floral

Sprekelia formosissima
AZTEC LILY (U.S.A.),
JACOBEAN LILY (U.K.)

Family: AMARYLLIDACEAE
Origin: Mexico.
Flowering time: Summer.
Climatic zone: 9, 10.
Dimensions: Up to 12 inches (300 mm) high.
Description: These striking crimson flowers resemble fleur-de-lys, the deep-green, ribbon-like leaves developing as the flower dies. The plant was introduced into Europe by the German botanist, von Sprekelsen, in the 18th century. It can be grown in pots or the greenhouse and brought indoors for flowering. If grown in the garden it merits a feature position. Plant the bulbs in light fertile soil mixed with compost, with the neck just below ground level.

Sparaxis tricolor
HARLEQUIN FLOWER
(U.K.), VELVET FLOWER

Family: IRIDACEAE
Origin: South Africa.
Flowering time: Summer.
Climatic zone: 6, 7, 8, 9.
Dimensions: Up to 18 inches (450 mm) high.
Description: The name *sparaxis* comes from the Greek for "torn" and refers to the torn spathe , or pair of bracts, that encloses the flowers of this species. Several flowers grow on each stem. Borders, large tubs, or indoor containers are all suitable for this sun-loving plant. It will grow successfully in partial shade, but the flowers close in dull weather. Ordinary garden soil mixed with compost gives good results. Protect from frost by lifting the corms when they die down in autumn. Plant again in spring.
Other colors: Red, orange, pink, white.

28

Tritonia crocata
BLAZING STAR (U.K.),
WEATHERCOCK, MONTBRETIA
(U.K., U.S.A.)

Other common names: FLAME
FREESIA
Family: IRIDACEAE
Origin: South Africa.
Flowering time: Spring-summer.
Climatic zone: 9.
Dimensions: Up to 18 inches (450 mm)
high.
Description: A showy herbaceous
perennial, *Tritonia* bears orange or
yellow, bell-shaped flowers for several
weeks. Suited to pot-plantings, borders
or massed plantings with freesias or
other bulbs. It is called *Tritonia*,
meaning weathercock, because of the
variable directions of the stamens.
Although there are about fifty species,
this is the only one commonly
cultivated. A hardy grower, it likes a
sunny situation in ordinary garden soil
and should be treated like its near
relative, the gladiolus. In cold climates,
a greenhouse environment is preferred.
Other colors: Red, pink, yellow.

Vallota speciosa

Tritonia crocata

Tulipa hybrid cultivars
TULIP

Family: LILIACEAE
Origin: Turkey.
Flowering time: Spring.
Climatic zone: 5, 6, 7, 8, 9.
Dimensions: 6–30 inches (150–750 mm)
high.
Description: The tulip was first
introduced into Europe in 1554 by the
Austrian Ambassador to the Sultan of
Turkey. By 1634 the tulip craze had
swept the Netherlands. Fortunes were
made and lost and rare bulbs
commanded high prices. Tulips provide
magnificent color in massed plantings.
In cooler climates they can be grown
indoors in pots and make pretty
window displays. Bulbs should be grown
in slightly alkaline, rich, well-drained
soil. They respond well to fertilizing and
are sensitive to windy areas.
Other colors: Red, white, pink, yellow.

Tulipa hybrid cultivars

Vallota speciosa
SCARBOROUGH LILY,
GEORGE LILY

Family: AMARYLLIDACEAE
Origin: South Africa.
Flowering time: Summer.
Climatic zone: 9, 10.
Dimensions: Up to 2 feet (600 mm) high.
Description: Clusters of scarlet,
trumpet-shaped blooms accompany
leaves up to 2 feet (600 mm) long.
Planting the lily in clumps with white
amaryllis provides dramatic contrast. It
is well-suited to pot-planting or in
garden beds where full sun is available.
In colder climates, the protection of a
greenhouse or warm window sill is
necessary. It thrives in deeply dug, well-
drained soil which has been fertilized.
Other colors: White.
Varieties/cultivars: *V. alba*.

Berberidopsis corallina
CHILEAN CORAL VINE,
CORAL PLANT (U.K.)

Family: FLACOURTIACEAE
Origin: Coastal forests of Chile.
Flowering time: Summer.
Climatic zone: 8, 9.
Description: The leaves of this scrambling, twining shrub are oblong, 2–3 inches long (50–70 mm), glossy dark-green, and sharply-toothed. Crimson rounded flowers hang in drooping clusters, and are followed by small berries. It is not an easy plant to grow, but it will do best in a cool, lime-free soil with protection from wind and frost. Severe winters can damage or kill it. Unless trained onto a trellis or frame, this evergreen plant will grow as a sprawling mound.

Bougainvillea x buttiana

cooler zones, but only the mature plant can withstand even moderate cold. Usually grown on a sunny wall, bougainvillea can be kept in pots if limited in size, and it can also be trained to a "standard" tree shape.

Campsis grandiflora syn. *C. chinensis*
TRUMPET VINE,
TRUMPET CREEPER (U.K.)

Family: BIGNONIACEAE
Origin: China.
Flowering time: Summer.
Climatic zone: 7, 8, 9.

Bougainvillea x buttiana 'Scarlet O'Hara' syn. 'San Diego' (U.S.A.)
BOUGAINVILLEA

Family: NYCTAGINACEAE
Origin: Hybrid.
Flowering time: Summer.
Climatic zone: 9, 10.
Description: This is one of the most spectacular tropical vines in cultivation, its vivid color being due to the three prominent bracts that surround the small, insignificant flowers. The strong branches have sharp spines. The plant requires sun, heat, and good drainage. Do not overwater. Hard pruning is necessary to control the size of the vine and to promote flowering. Although an evergreen in warm climates, it can become semideciduous or deciduous in

Description: Sprays of brilliant orange-red, trumpet-shaped flowers open out to five rounded lobes. *Campsis* is a strong, deciduous vine with heavy, woody growth, and with aerial rootlets which cling to rough surfaces. In hot climates, hard pruning in winter will promote new vigorous growth for the following year. In cooler climates, pruning is unnecessary. Grow in full sun and give average watering to produce a quick-growing vine. It can withstand salty winds and is a good choice for coastal areas.

Campsis radicans
COMMON TRUMPET
CREEPER

Family: BIGNONIACEAE
Origin: Southeastern United States.
Flowering time: Midsummer–late summer.
Climatic zone: 5, 6, 7, 8, 9.
Description: A larger and more vigorous vine than *Campsis grandiflora*, this plant will quickly cover a brick, stone, or timber wall. Its attractive foliage has nine to eleven toothed leaflets, and flowers are 3 inch (75 mm) long, orange tubes. Use it for large-scale effects, and quick summer screens, but keep it under control as it can become top-heavy. A cold winter can kill the stem tips, but new growth appears quickly in spring.
Other colors: Yellow.
Varieties/cultivars: 'Flava'.

Campsis grandiflora

Berberidopsis corallina

Clerodendrum splendens
GLORY-BOWER

Family: VERBENACEAE
Origin: Tropical West Africa.
Flowering time: Spring and autumn.
Climatic zone: 9, 10.
Description: Scarlet flowers hang in large clusters on this evergreen shrubby scrambler. Shiny, corrugated, leathery leaves up to 6 inches (150 mm) long give it an attractive appearance. It may be short-lived if not given good drainage

Clerodendrum splendens

and protection from the wind. To grow as a climber, it will need to be tied and trained to a trellis or wire frame, but can be grown as a rounded shrub. Use it where a light vine is required; it will not become large or invasive. In cold climates, a greenhouse is necessary.

Distictis buccinatoria syn. Phaedranthus buccinatorius
MEXICAN BLOOD TRUMPET, BLOOD-RED TRUMPET VINE

Family: BIGNONIACEAE
Origin: Mexico.
Flowering time: Bursts of flower throughout the year.

Distictis buccinatoria

Campsis radicans

Climatic zone: 9, 10.
Description: The trumpet-shaped, waxy flowers, 4 inches (100 mm) long, have flaring lobes. They are crimson red, with a scarlet sheen and an orange-yellow throat, and are conspicuous because they stand out beyond the foliage. This is a very vigorous vine with rough, leathery, oval leaflets, and needs annual pruning to keep it under control. It will attach itself by tendrils to walls, fences, and sheds. For a quick-growing, dense, evergreen cover, this is a good choice, especially with the added bonus of spectacular flowers. In a cold climate, a greenhouse environment is essential.

Eccremocarpus scaber
CHILEAN GLORY FLOWER

Family: BIGNONIACEAE
Origin: Chile.
Flowering time: Late summer and early autumn.
Climatic zone: 8, 9.
Dimensions: Up to 10 feet (3 meters) high.
Description: This charming climber is rather delicate in appearance, with dainty foliage and bright orange-red, tubular flowers. By no means a vigorous grower, it requires a deep, rich, and well-drained soil, and a sunny, open position. Encourage the young plant to grow on a trellis, and water and feed it frequently, especially during summer. In cool climates, where frosts are a problem, it can be grown as an annual.
Other colors: Yellow, carmine.
Varieties/cultivars: *E. s. aureus*, *E. s. carmineus*.

Eccremocarpus scaber

Kennedia rubicunda

Climatic zone: 8, 9.
Description: One of the most strikingly beautiful flowers, the Chilean bellflower is a highly prized climbing plant for cool districts. A cool mountain zone with rich soil is its preference. The roots should be well mulched to retain moisture and keep an even temperature. The growth is slender, never dense, and the vine needs support to grow up against a wall. Given the right conditions, this is a beautiful plant with trumpet-shaped, waxy flowers, 2 inches (50 mm) long. It is the national flower of Chile.
Other colors: White.
Varieties/cultivars: *L. r.* var. *albiflora.*

○

Kennedia rubicunda
DUSKY CORAL PEA

Family: LEGUMINOSAE
Origin: Eastern Australia.
Flowering time: Spring and early summer.
Climatic zone: 9, 10.
Description: An excellent evergreen plant for a quick screen on a fence or trellis, the dusky coral pea is also a very good groundcover. It needs sun and warmth, and once established is drought-tolerant. The oval leaves are in groups of three, tough and leathery, with the new growth an interesting silky brown. The red pea-shaped flowers hang down, usually in pairs, and are 1½ inches (40 mm) long. This is a hardy and vigorous vine, but not invasive.

○

Lapageria rosea
CHILEAN BELLFLOWER,
CHILE-BELLS

Family: PHILESIACEAE
Origin: Chile.
Flowering time: Late spring–autumn.

Climatic zone: 7, 8, 9.
Description: With smaller leaves than *L. latifolius,* but larger flowers, this hardy, herbaceous, climbing perennial is a popular plant for cut flowers. It is easily grown and long-lived if given adequate water and fertilizer. After it dies down each year, a good mulch over the roots is advisable, and it will produce new shoots from the root clump in spring. It prefers cool conditions, but a sunny position. The flowers, although not fragrant, are charming and useful in floral arrangements.

○

Lathyrus grandiflorus
TWO-FLOWERED PEA,
EVERLASTING PEA

Family: LEGUMINOSAE
Origin: Southern Europe.
Flowering time: Midsummer.

Lathyrus grandiflorus

Lonicera sempervirens
TRUMPET
HONEYSUCKLE,
CORAL HONEYSUCKLE

○ ◐ ●

Family: CAPRIFOLIACEAE
Origin: Southeastern United States.
Flowering time: Summer.
Climatic zone: 7, 8, 9.
Description: This robust, fast-growing climber is evergreen in mild climates, and will tolerate a shady position. Rich orange-scarlet flowers with yellow inside appear at the ends of branchlets, usually in groups of six. The upper leaves are joined in pairs. The flowers are not fragrant but are large, 2 inches (50 mm) long, and rich in color. Good soil and cool roots will result in a handsome vine which should be thinned out occasionally. A support should be provided for its twining habit.
Other colors: Yellow.
Varieties/cultivars: 'Sulphurea'.

Lapageria rosea

Lonicera sempervirens

32

Manettia bicolor

Passiflora coccinea

Manettia bicolor syn. *M. inflata*
FIRECRACKER PLANT, FIRECRACKER FLOWER (U.K.)

Family: RUBIACEAE
Origin: Paraguay, Uruguay.
Flowering time: Spring, summer, autumn.
Climatic zone: 9, 10.
Description: An evergreen, small, dainty twiner, *Manettia* is an easily managed little plant. The 1 inch (25 mm) long, waxy, tubular flowers are yellow-tipped, and the lower half is covered with bright scarlet bristles. The flowers give a delightful sprinkling of color for many months. It is useful as cover for pillars, and to produce light shade over pergolas. Rich soil and a sheltered position are preferred, and it can be grown among shrubs for protection from cool winters. In cold climates, a greenhouse environment is essential.

Passiflora coccinea
RED PASSIONFLOWER (U.K.); SCARLET PASSIONFLOWER

Family: PASSIFLORACEAE
Origin: Venezuela–Brazil.
Flowering time: Summer.
Climatic zone: 9, 10.
Description: The startlingly beautiful flowers gave the name to this genus of tendril-climbers. It was believed that features of the flower were representations of the suffering of Jesus Christ. The red passionflower has shiny, wide scarlet petals, 4 inches (100 mm) across. The very free-blooming habit in summer makes it desirable as a cover over pergolas or on fences or, in a cooler climate, it can be grown in large pots and brought indoors in the winter months. It may not flower until two or three years old, but removing old wood in the winter will promote flowering.

Pyrostegia venusta

Pyrostegia venusta

Pyrostegia venusta
FLAME VINE, FLAMING TRUMPET, APRICOT BELLS

Other common names: GOLDEN SHOWER
Family: BIGNONIACEAE
Origin: Brazil, Paraguay.
Flowering time: Winter, spring.
Climatic zone: 9, 10.
Description: In full flower, the flame vine has clusters of slender-tubed flowers hanging like a dense curtain from a woody, evergreen vine. It is an exceptionally vigorous grower, and will cover high walls or roof tops. It produces its best growth when planted in a very sunny position. A strong support is necessary, as new growth drapes over the previous growth, and eventually the vine becomes very thick and dense. It will tolerate wind and mild frost when established, and is improved with regular watering. Adaptable to a greenhouse in cooler areas.

Quisqualis indica
RANGOON CREEPER

Family: COMBRETACEAE
Origin: Burma to the Philippines and New Guinea.
Flowering time: Summer.
Climatic zone: 9, 10.
Description: The slender, dainty flower tubes of the rangoon creeper are 3 inches (75 mm) long, and change from white to pink and crimson. The delicious and unusual fragrance resembles apricots, and is very pervasive at night. Support is needed to train this shrubby vine up over a wall or fence, and it can make climbing stems up to 3 feet (1 meter) long each year. Although it will tolerate some shade, a warm protected site is best. Plant it near an open window to gain the benefit of its distinctive perfume.

Quisqualis indica

6 inches (150 mm) above the prostrate branches. It is a very useful plant as a groundcover, to cover low walls, or to train up pillars. It is sufficiently vigorous to train up house walls and even over sheds or out-house buildings. Prune after flowering.

Rosa 'Albertine'
ALBERTINE ROSE

Family: ROSACEAE
Origin: Cultivar.
Flowering time: Summer.
Climatic zone: 5, 6, 7, 8, 9.
Description: Grown as a rather lax shrub, or trained as a climber, this popular rose has loosely double, large, and richly-fragrant, coppery-pink blooms. The flowers are in clusters of six to ten, and are carried on upright stems

Rosa 'Albertine'

Rosa 'Bloomfield Courage'
BLOOMFIELD COURAGE

Family: ROSACEAE
Origin: Cultivar.
Flowering time: Midsummer.
Climatic zone: 5, 6, 7, 8, 9.
Description: A trailing plant which can grow stems 10 to 12 feet (3 to 4 meters) long in one season, this rose can be used

Rosa 'Excelsa'
EXCELSA ROSE

Family: ROSACEAE
Origin: Cultivar.
Flowering time: Spring.
Climatic zone: 6, 7, 8, 9.
Description: The small, bright crimson flowers on this supple-stemmed climber are double, and produced in great abundance in springtime. It will grow up to 12 to 15 feet (4 to 5 meters), and is often grafted onto the top of a tall stem to create a weeping standard rose. It also

as a good groundcover, even in fairly poor soil. As it has a habit of taking root from the stems which are in contact with the soil, it can spread over a wide area. It is often grafted to a tall standard to produce a weeping standard rose. The flowers, which are single, deep-red with white centers and yellow stamens, and are about 1½ inches (40 mm) across, hang in clusters.

Rosa 'Bloomfield Courage'

Rosa 'Excelsa'

Tecomaria capensis
CAPE HONEYSUCKLE ○ ◑

Family: BIGNONIACEAE
Origin: South Africa.
Flowering time: Autumn and winter.
Climatic zone: 9, 10.
Description: Best used as a clipped hedge, this *Tecomaria* is a rambling, scrambling, shrubby plant with evergreen foliage. It is easily grown in warm districts, but needs to be controlled. New growth comes from the base each year, so the width increases quite significantly. It can be used to cover a bank, or be trained up through a wire frame as a free-standing hedge, or supported against a fence or wall. The orange flowers are prolific, but are reduced with regular clipping.
Other colors: Orange-yellow, pink, yellow.

Tecomaria capensis

makes an excellent groundcover, or can be grown over a tree stump, or low wall, or trained up a post or pillar. Pruning in the winter is needed to remove old wood and selectively shorten some of the branches.

Thunbergia alata

Climatic zone: 7, 8, 9, 10.
Description: From five to seven leaflets make up the small circular leaves of this climbing perennial herb. The fleshy tubers produce new growth each year. The curious-looking flowers have a scarlet spur and yellow petals, and look like little, tailed balloons. This is a very pretty summer-flowering twiner, and should have support to hold it in place. Wire frames can be used, which will be quickly covered, or it can be grown in a hanging basket for summer display. In cold areas, it will flower in spring under glass.

Tropaeolum speciosum
FLAME CREEPER ○

Family: TROPAEOLACEAE
Origin: Chilean Andes.
Flowering time: Summer.

leaves on little winged stems. The slender stems and light appearance are deceptive. It is able to cover a shed or a sloping bank very quickly. The funnel-shaped orange flowers are a colorful addition to a dreary corner. It is easily kept under control if grown as an annual (especially in cooler districts). It prefers a sunny position and foliage will be thicker and more attractive if adequate water is provided.
Other colors: Creamy-yellow, white.

Tropaeolum speciosum

35

Thunbergia alata
ORANGE CLOCK VINE, BLACK-EYED SUSAN VINE ○ (U.S.A.)

Family: ACANTHACEAE
Origin: Tropical Africa.
Flowering time: Late summer–autumn.
Climatic zone: 5, 6, 7, 8, 9, 10.
Description: This well-known twining perennial vine has toothed, triangular

---

Tropaeolum tricolorum
CLIMBING NASTURTIUM, TRICOLORED INDIAN CRESS ○

Family: TROPAEOLACEAE
Origin: Chile.
Flowering time: Spring–summer.
Climatic zone: 9.
Description: Unusual, beautiful flowers appear on this herbaceous climbing perennial. It has a fast-growing habit, with the fleshy roots producing new growth in the spring. The flowers are about 1½ inches (40 mm) wide with little "stemmed" petals which give an open, delicate appearance. They are vivid scarlet with yellow at the base. The vine itself likes the sun, but the roots should be kept cool and moist, and protected from temperature changes. Neutral to acid soil is essential. Severe winters can kill this plant.

Tropaeolum tricolorum

Climatic zone: 3, 4, 5, 6, 7, 8, 9.
Dimensions: Up to 18 inches (450 mm) high.
Description: Aquilegias are one of the loveliest of perennials for the spring border. C. *canadensis* has yellow petals with red sepals and spurs and looks well planted with the strong blue of *cynoglossum* and the white of *Anemone sylvestris*. It prefers a well-drained, sandy loam and liquid fertilizer during its growth period. In hot climates a semi-shaded aspect is preferable and plants will be short-lived if allowed to become waterlogged. It self-sows modestly in cold climates and is a good cut flower.

Aquilegia hybrids
COLUMBINE

Family: RANUNCULACEAE
Origin: U.K.
Flowering time: Early summer.
Climatic zone: 3, 4, 5, 6, 7, 8.

Aquilegia hybrids

it is susceptible to cold, high humidity, and fungal disease, it is worth growing for its unusual and exotically colored flowers and its red woolly stems. It prefers sandy, well-drained soil and requires manure and plenty of water in spring. With its narrow strap-like foliage and interesting flowers it makes an impressive show. It is a good cut flower, fresh or dried.
Other colors: Yellow, green, pink.

Anigozanthos manglesii

Aquilegia canadensis
COMMON
COLUMBINE, CANADIAN
COLUMBINE (U.K.)

Family: RANUNCULACEAE
Origin: North America.
Flowering time: Early summer.

Aquilegia canadensis

Alstroemeria aurantiaca

Alstroemeria aurantiaca
PERUVIAN LILY,
CHILEAN LILY

Family: ALSTROEMERIACEAE
Origin: South America.
Flowering time: Summer.
Climatic zone: 8, 9.
Dimensions: Up to 3 feet (1 meter) high.
Description: Although the Peruvian lily is quite hardy, it is both drought- and frost-susceptible, and requires well-drained, moist soil and shelter. Its showy flowers are valued as pot specimens and for cut flower arrangements. It can be naturalized under trees or grown in cool greenhouse conditions, but it is best in an open, sunny, sheltered site. Propagate it from root division in autumn after the rapid root increase of summer, or propagate from seed. Peruvian lily is a handsome companion for agapanthus and scabiosa in a sheltered border.
Other colors: Pink, yellow.
Varieties/cultivars: 'Dover Orange', 'Moerhaim Orange', 'Lutea'.

Anigozanthos manglesii
KANGAROO-PAW

Family: HAEMODORACEAE
Origin: Western Australia.
Flowering time: Late spring–summer.
Climatic zone: 9.
Dimensions: Up to 6 feet (2 meters) high.
Description: A. *manglesii* is an easy species of kangaroo paw to grow. Although

36

Dimensions: Up to 2½ feet (750 mm) high.

Description: Aquilegias come in myriad colors and in single and double varieties. Their foliage is dainty and rather like coarse maidenhair fern. The taller cultivars are most suited to the herbaceous border and the smaller ones for rockeries. Some aquilegias are propagated by root division in spring; others are best left to self-sow, which they do profusely in cool, moist conditions. They are frost-resistant, but drought-susceptible, and are best grown in well-drained, sandy loam. They look attractive if left to naturalize under deciduous trees, and are good as cut flowers.

Other colors: Pink, blue, white, yellow, purple.

Varieties/cultivars: 'Snow Queen', 'Nora Barlow', 'McKana Hybrids', 'Laudham Strain'.

Astilbe x arendsii

Astilbe x arendsii
ASTILBE, FALSE SPIREA

Family: SAXIFRAGACEAE
Origin: Hybrid.
Flowering time: Summer.
Climatic zone: 4, 5, 6, 7, 8, 9.
Dimensions: Up to 4 feet (approx. 1 meter) high.
Description: Astilbes are seen at their best in partial shade. Naturalized under trees and beside ponds they are spectacular. However, they will grow in the herbaceous border provided they have rich, moist soil. Their foliage is as pretty as their feathery flowers and often has a coppery-pink tinge. The plants are best propagated from root division in autumn and early spring. Astilbes are heavy feeders, so fertilize well in spring and summer. Cut back in autumn and divide every three years. They are a showy cut flower.

Other colors: White, pink.

Varieties/cultivars: 'Feuer', 'Bressingham Charm'.

Astilbe x crispa
GOATSBEARD

Family: SAXIFRAGACEAE
Origin: Hybrid.
Flowering time: Summer.
Climatic zone: 5.
Dimensions: Up to 10 inches (250 mm) high.
Description: Astilbe x crispa, with its salmon-pink, feathery flowers, is an excellent choice for rockeries, especially those surrounding small ponds. It is also lovely when grown edging pathways beneath established deciduous trees. Its requirements are moist soil and semishade. As plants reproduce rapidly, division every few years is advisable. Propagate from root division in autumn and early spring.

Varieties/cultivars: 'Perkeo', 'Peter Pan', 'Gnome', and several others.

Astilbe x crispa

Centaurea dealbata 'Steenbergii'
WILD CORNFLOWER

Family: COMPOSITAE
Origin: Caucasus.
Flowering time: Summer.
Climatic zone: 4, 5, 6, 7, 8.
Dimensions: Up to 3 feet (900 mm) high.
Description: Centaurea dealbata 'Steenbergii' is valuable in the herbaceous border, both for its foliage and its flowers. Its leaves are lobed and silvery-white on the underside, and its thistle-like flowers are a rich crimson. The plant looks showy when grown with *Lavandula angustifolia* and *Catananche caerulea*. It requires a light, dry but fertile soil, and may need to be staked. Propagate it by root division in spring or sow in autumn or spring. As a cut flower, it forms a splash of color indoors.

Other colors: Pink, purple.

Centaurea dealbata 'Steenbergii'

Centranthus ruber
RED VALERIAN (U.K.), JUPITER'S BEARD

Family: VALERIANACEAE
Origin: Mediterranean region.
Flowering time: Summer.
Climatic zone: 7, 8, 9.
Dimensions: 2–3 feet (600–900 mm) high.
Description: Red valerian is an herbaceous perennial which grows pleasantly bushy. It thrives in any well-drained soil and needs little attention apart from the cutting back of spent flowers. Often used for dry situations where other plants do not do well, it self-sows profusely and can become a problem if not contained. Propagate it from seed in spring or soft tip cuttings. Red valerian looks well planted with *Veronica spicata* and *Iberis sempervirens*, and is a good cut flower.

Centranthus ruber

Clivia miniata

Clivia miniata
KAFFIR LILY
Family: AMARYLLIDACEAE
Origin: South Africa.
Flowering time: Spring.
Climatic zone: 9, 10.
Dimensions: 1½–2 feet (450–600 mm) high.
Description: The Kaffir lily can be naturalized beneath large trees. With shelter from hot summer sun and winter frosts, good drainage, and plenty of compost, it will reward you with a dazzling floral display in spring. In cold climates it needs to be grown under glass. This is followed by a crop of deep crimson berries from late summer into winter. It needs to be kept moist in spring and summer, but needs drier conditions in autumn and winter. Propagation is by root division after spring flowering. Large clumps provide a showy effect. It is an excellent cut flower and pot specimen.
Varieties/cultivars: 'Grandiflora'.

Dianthus deltoides
MAIDEN PINK
Family: CARYOPHYLLACEAE
Origin: Europe.
Flowering time: Late spring.
Climatic zone: 4, 5, 6, 7, 8, 9.
Dimensions: Up to 10 inches (250 mm) high.
Description: Maiden pink, with its spreading habit and neat mat-like appearance, makes an excellent groundcover, border edging, and rockery plant. It requires very well-drained alkaline soil and good air

Dianthus deltoides

circulation, so do not mulch. Propagation is by cuttings in late summer, root division or seed in spring. Extend flowering by cutting back spent flowers and prune the flowering stems in autumn. As long as they do not crowd it out, it looks lovely grown with *Bellis perennis*, *Myosotis scorpioides* and *Cerastium tomentosum*. This is an excellent cut flower.
Other colors: Pink, white with crimson eye.
Varieties/cultivars: 'Albus' and some others.

Euphorbia griffithii 'Fireglow'

Euphorbia griffithii 'Fireglow'
FIREGLOW
Family: EUPHORBIACEAE
Origin: Cultivar.
Flowering time: Early summer.
Climatic zone: 5, 6, 7, 8, 9.
Dimensions: Up to 3 feet (1 meter) high.

Description: Fireglow is one of the hardier euphorbias. It is perennial, with attractive veined foliage, and produces masses of rich orange flowers for about 2 months in early summer. The color is actually in the bracts, not the petals. It prefers semishade and is easy to grow in any moderately fertile, well-drained soil. Propagation is by cuttings or root division. Care should be taken to avoid contact with the sticky, milky substance exuded by all euphorbias when cut. At best it is an irritant, at worst poisonous.

Gaillardia x grandiflora
BLANKET FLOWER
Family: COMPOSITAE
Origin: Hybrid.
Flowering time: Summer.
Climatic zone: 4, 5, 6, 7, 8, 9.
Dimensions: 1–3 feet (300–900 mm) high.
Description: Gaillardias come in dazzling shades of red and yellow and are particularly showy if planted en masse. They tend to get a bit untidy, so if this is a problem, choose the more compact dwarf variety, 'Goblin'. They are fussy about soil in that they need it to be exceptionally well-drained in autumn and winter. Any summer dryness can be counteracted with mulch. Liquid manure is beneficial at the budding stage. Propagation is by root division in autumn or spring. Gaillardias are good cut flowers.
Other colors: Yellow, deep crimson, bicolors.
Varieties/cultivars: 'Burgundy', 'Copper Beauty', 'Dazzler', 'Yellow Queen'.

Gaillardia x grandiflora

Gazania x hybrida

Gazania x hybrida
GAZANIA, TREASURE FLOWER

Family: COMPOSITAE
Origin: Hybrid.
Flowering time: Summer.
Climatic zone: 8, 9, 10.
Dimensions: Up to 12 inches (300 mm) high.
Description: Gazanias are available in trailing and clumping varieties, the trailing form being especially useful in rockery and terraced situations. They prefer light (even poor), well-drained soil in full sun and benefit from a dressing of blood and bone in spring. Propagation is by stem cuttings or seedlings in autumn. Gazanias are salt-resistant, so are good in coastal areas, but they are very frost-susceptible and in frost-prone regions should be lifted and stored over winter. The flowers, with their habit of closing in the late afternoon, have no value when picked.
Other colors: White, cream, yellow, pink, green.
Varieties/cultivars: 'Freddie', 'Sunbeam'.

Geum quellyon syn. G. chiloense
AVENS

Family: ROSACEAE
Origin: Chile.
Flowering time: Summer.

Climatic zone: 5, 6.
Dimensions: Up to 2 feet (600 mm) high.
Description: This is a charming old-fashioned perennial with pinnate, hairy, coarsely toothed leaves and tall stems topped by panicles of brilliant red flowers. Ideal as part of an herbaceous border, it can be grown successfully in any moderately rich soil with good drainage, and will propagate easily from seed.
Other colors: Yellow, orange.
Varieties/cultivars: 'Lady Stratheden', 'Mrs. Bradshaw', 'Prince of Orange', 'Red Wings', 'Starkers Magnificent'.

Geum quellyon 'Prince of Orange'

Heuchera sanguinea
CORAL BELLS

Family: SAXIFRAGACEAE
Origin: Southwestern United States, Mexico.

Heuchera sanguinea

Flowering time: Summer.
Climatic zone: 4, 5, 6, 7, 8, 9.
Dimensions: Up to 2 feet (600 mm) high.
Description: In 1885, several plants of coral bells survived a journey from Mexico to England and were later hybridized. *H. sanguinea* is at home in shaded rock gardens. Mix it in with white primula and dark-blue campanula in borders. Mulched, well-drained soil encourages it to flower freely.
Varieties/cultivars: Many cultivars are available.

Kniphofia uvaria and hybrids
RED-HOT-POKER, TORCH LILY

Family: LILIACEAE
Origin: Hybrid.
Flowering time: Spring-autumn.
Climatic zone: 6, 7, 8, 9.
Dimensions: 2–4 feet high.
Description: Red-hot-pokers, with their brightly colored, torch-like flowers erupting from large clumps of grass-like foliage, make handsome specimen plants and are a showy feature in the summer border. They need well-drained, sandy loam with the addition of compost or animal manure. Mulch to protect the crown from freezing in cold climates and to retain moisture during the flowering season. Propagation is by root division in late winter or early spring.
Other colors: Yellow (without *uvaria*).
Varieties/cultivars: 'Yellow Hammer', 'Buttercup', 'Mount Etna', 'Royal Standard' (all of hybrid origin).

Kniphofia uvaria

Lobelia cardinalis
CARDINAL FLOWER

Family: LOBELIACEAE
Origin: Eastern North America.
Flowering time: Summer.
Climatic zone: 4, 5, 6, 7, 8, 9.
Dimensions: 3–6 feet (1–2 meters) high.
Description: The cardinal flower is suitable for both the sheltered border and the cottage garden. It is sun-tolerant but will also grow in partial shade. It needs constantly moist, well-mulched, and well-drained soil, and in colder climates protection against prolonged cold and damp is essential. It can be propagated by root division and cuttings in spring. Cardinal flower looks well planted with *Artemesia lactiflora* and *Astilbe arendsii*. Its flowers are short-lived.
Other colors: White.
Varieties/cultivars: 'Alba', 'Angel Song', 'Arabella's Vision', 'Twilight Zone'.

Lobelia laxiflora

Lobelia laxiflora
PEACH-LEAVED LOBELIA, TORCH LOBELIA

Family: LOBELIACEAE
Origin: Arizona to Mexico and Colombia.
Flowering time: Summer.
Climatic zone: 9, 10.
Dimensions: From 3 feet (1 meter) high.
Description: This is a tall, shrubby

Lobelia cardinalis

member of the genus *Lobelia* with a spread equal to its height. Place it among other sun-loving, evergreen shrubs or near a wall where it will be protected from frosts. Do not plant it near gross feeders, as it likes rich, moist, well-drained soil. The red and yellow flowers, 1 inch (30 mm) across, are in terminal leafy spikes. Propagation is by seed or cuttings.

Lupinus 'Russell Hybrid'
RUSSELL HYBRID LUPIN

Family: LEGUMINOSAE
Origin: Hybrids.
Flowering time: Summer.
Climatic zone: 5, 6, 7, 8, 9.
Dimensions: 3 feet (1 meter) high.
Description: Lupins are among the showiest of the herbaceous perennials. They form handsome clumps, their gray-green foliage a perfect backdrop for their own abundantly colored blooms

and for companion plantings of *Papaver orientale*, *Phlox paniculata*, *Penstemon gloxinioides*, and *Baptista australis*. They prefer a light, neutral, sandy soil and plenty of water. Propagate them from seed sown direct in autumn or by division in early spring. Lupins are good cut flowers.
Other colors: White, cream, yellow, pink, blue, lilac, purple.
Varieties/cultivars: 'Betty Astell', 'Lilac Time', 'Fireglow', 'Gladys Cooper'.

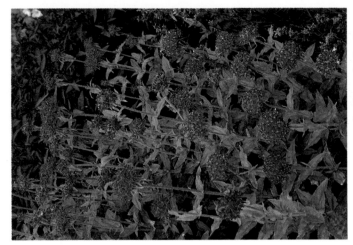

Lupinus 'Russell Hybrid'

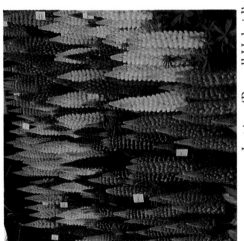

Lychnis chalcedonica

Lychnis chalcedonica
MALTESE-CROSS

Family: CARYOPHYLLACEAE
Origin: Northern Russia.
Flowering time: Summer.
Climatic zone: 4, 5, 6, 7, 8.
Dimensions: Up to 3 feet (1 meter) high.
Description: *Lychnis chalcedonica* adds vibrant color to the herbaceous border or cottage garden. It is hardy, a prolific seeder, and looks very well planted with the blues and purples of some varieties of salvia, and *Nepeta x faassenii*, offset by splashes of white from *Achillea*. It thrives in any well-drained, moist soil, but appreciates extra mulch and water in spring and summer. Propagation is by seed in spring or by division in late winter. Regular picking keeps the plant under control and prolongs flowering.
Other colors: White, rose-pink.
Varieties/cultivars: 'Alba', 'Flora Plena'.

40

Monarda didyma

Monarda didyma
BEE BALM, OSWEGO TEA

Family: LABIATAE
Origin: North America.
Flowering time: Summer.
Climatic zone: 4, 5, 6, 7, 8, 9.
Dimensions: 2–3 feet (up to 1 meter) high.
Description: *Monarda didyma* is a delight. Its colors are superb, its fragrance overwhelming, attracting bees and butterflies in profusion. It looks as well in the herbaceous border as the herb garden, particularly if care is taken with color combinations. It requires only average, well-drained soil, but benefits from good mulching and plenty of water in dry conditions, especially if planted in full sun. Its leaves can be used for potpourri. Propagate from seed or by division in spring. It is susceptible to powdery mildew.
Other colors: White, pink, mauve, purple.
Varieties/cultivars: 'Blue Stocking', 'Cambridge Scarlet', 'Snow Maiden', 'Croftway Pink'.

Paeonia officinalis 'Rubra Plena'
COMMON PEONY

Family: PAEONIACEAE
Origin: Cultivar.
Flowering time: Late spring.
Climatic zone: 5, 6, 7, 8, 9.
Dimensions: Up to 3 feet (1 meter) high.
Description: Once established, peonies will grow for decades in the cool-climate garden. They require well-drained, deep, fertile soil, enriched with plenty of animal manure, and ample water during the flowering period. They also need protection from strong winds and, in warmer areas, extra shade. Propagation is by tuber division in early autumn, but take care to disturb established clumps as little as possible. Prune by removing spent flower stems when foliage yellows. Picked at the bud stage, peonies are excellent cut flowers.

Paeonia officinalis 'Rubra Plena'

Papaver orientale
ORIENTAL POPPY

Family: PAPAVERACEAE
Origin: Southwestern Asia.
Flowering time: Early summer.
Climatic zone: 4, 5, 6, 7, 8, 9.
Dimensions: 3–4 feet (approx. 1 meter) high.
Description: The oriental poppy is a long-time favorite for the herbaceous border and cottage garden. Its large, open blooms, often early blotched at the base, come in dazzling colors and more than compensate for its foliage, which becomes very untidy after flowering. This is best disguised by surrounding poppies with perennials like *Stokesia laevis*, *Veronica virginica*, and *Anemone x hybrida*. Oriental poppy requires well-drained, deep loam with a good dressing of manure in early spring. Propagation is by division in spring or by seed. It is a good cut flower.
Other colors: Pink, rose, white, yellow.
Varieties/cultivars: 'China Boy', 'Mrs Perry', 'Grossfürst', 'Perry's White', 'Princess Victoria Louise', 'Harvest Moon'.

Papaver orientale 'Harvest Moon'

Pelargonium x domesticum
MARTHA WASHINGTON GERANIUM (U.S.A.), REGAL OR SHOW GERANIUM (U.K.)

Family: GERANIACEAE
Origin: Hybrids.
Flowering time: Spring–summer.
Climatic zone: 9, 10.
Dimensions: 18 inches (450 mm) high.
Description: *Pelargonium x domesticum* is larger in habit than *P. x hortorum* and has a shorter flowering season. Its foliage is evergreen and pleasantly aromatic when bruised, and its flowers are deeply colored and ruffled. In the northern hemisphere, it is often grown as a showy greenhouse pot specimen. It requires well-drained, light soil with a dressing of complete fertilizer in late winter to encourage flowering. Do not overwater. It is susceptible to frost and fungal disease. Remove spent flowers to prolong blooming.
Other colors: White, pink, mauve, purple.
Varieties/cultivars: 'Axminster', 'Mrs G. Morf', 'Hula', 'Carefree', 'Annie Hawkins'.

Pelargonium x domesticum

Pelargonium x hortorum
ZONAL GERANIUM

Family: GERANIACEAE
Origin: Hybrids.
Flowering time: Late spring–autumn.
Climatic zone: 9, 10.
Dimensions: 6 inches–3 feet (450 mm–1 meter) high.
Description: *Pelargonium x hortorum* is a shrubby evergreen perennial, valuable for its variable foliage as well as its flowers, which come in single, semidouble and double form. It likes well-drained, neutral, light soil and dislikes excess water. Water only in dry weather. To keep the plant thick and encourage flowering, prune regularly. Propagation is by cuttings in summer in cold climates, and year-round elsewhere. It is a good cut flower, but is susceptible to frost and fungal disease.
Other colors: White, pink, salmon, mauve.
Varieties/cultivars: 'Dagata', 'Rubin', 'Highland Queen', 'Henri Joignot'.

Pelargonium x hortorum

Penstemon barbatus
BEARDLIP PENSTEMON, PENSTEMON (U.K.)

Family: SCROPHULARIACEAE
Origin: South western United States, Mexico.
Flowering time: Summer–autumn.
Climatic zone: 4.
Dimensions: 2–3 feet (600–900 mm) high.
Description: Beardlip penstemon, formerly known as *Chelone barbatus*, takes its name from its flowers' bearded throat and lip. The species appears in several colors, but the scarlet-flowered one is the most popular. It is not particularly hardy and requires well-drained, fertile soil and shelter from wind. Excess water in winter will kill it. Propagation is from cuttings in late summer or seed sown under glass in spring. The plant needs hard pruning to ground level in spring, just as new growth begins. Beardlip penstemon is good for planting on wild, sheltered slopes.
Other colors: Pink, purple, lavender.
Varieties/cultivars: 'Carnea'.

Penstemon barbatus

Penstemon x gloxinioides 'Firebird'
PENSTEMON, GLOXINIA PENSTEMON

Family: SCROPHULARIACEAE
Origin: Hybrid.
Flowering time: Summer–autumn.

Climatic zone: 8, 9.
Dimensions: 2 feet (600 mm) high.
Description: *Penstemon x gloxinioides* 'Firebird' is similar to *P. barbatus*, but its flower is larger and unbearded, and it flowers more abundantly. Well-drained soil and a sheltered position are necessary for good growth, and it benefits from winter mulching. Partial shade will give the plant a longer life and weekly application of soluble fertilizer will extend its flowering. It is at its best in the herbaceous border with perennials like *Anthemis sancti-johannis*, *Helenium autumnale* and *Lavandula stoechas*.

Penstemon x gloxinioides 'Firebird'

Pentas lanceolata
EGYPTIAN STAR-CLUSTER

Family: RUBIACEAE
Origin: East Africa–southern Arabia.
Flowering time: Summer.
Climatic zone: 9, 10.
Dimensions: 2–5 feet (600–1500 mm) high.
Description: *Pentas lanceolata* is ideal for the sunny subtropical garden, preferring wet summers, warm winters, and no frost. In cooler climates, it can be grown under greenhouse conditions and it lends itself to pot cultivation. It requires well-drained, sandy soil with the addition of plenty of organic mulch. It is fast-growing, with a shrubby habit. To keep its shape and induce constant flowering, prune it lightly and regularly. Propagation is from seed or, more commonly, from tip cuttings taken in spring to autumn and grown in humid conditions.
Other colors: White, pink, rose, lilac.
Varieties/cultivars: 'Coccinea'.

Pentas lanceolata

Physalis alkekengi syn. *P. francheti*
BLADDER CHERRY, CHINESE LANTERN (U.K.)

Family: SOLANACEAE
Origin: Southeastern Europe–Japan.
Flowering time: Summer–autumn.
Climatic zone: 3, 4, 5, 6, 7, 8, 9, 10.
Dimensions: Up to 2 feet (600 mm) high.
Description: *Physalis* is a hardy, creeping perennial, grown largely for its showy, berry-bearing calyx that becomes brightly colored and inflated after flowering. It requires well-drained soil and plenty of summer water. Because of its creeping habit, it can be useful as a groundcover, particularly the dwarf cultivar 'Nana'. Propagation is by seed or by root division in autumn or early spring. The dried calyces make handsome winter decoration and the berries are edible.
Varieties/cultivars: 'Gigantea', 'Orbiculare', 'Monstrosa', 'Nana'.

Physalis alkekengi

Potentilla atrosanguinea
RUBY CINQUEFOIL

Family: ROSACEAE
Origin: Himalayas.
Flowering time: Summer, northern hemisphere; spring, southern hemisphere.
Climatic zone: 5, 6, 7, 8, 9.
Dimensions: Up to 18 inches (450 mm) high.
Description: A very useful plant for a small garden, ruby cinquefoil is compact and colorful, its strawberry-like blooms flowering for many months. It looks effective in a border, when complementing *Gypsophila* and *Alyssum*. This pretty perennial will thrive in moderately moist soil of average

fertility, providing it has full sun. This reason alone makes it a good choice for small, suburban gardens. Propagate it by division or seed in spring.
Other colors: Yellow.
Varieties/cultivars: 'Gibson's Scarlet', 'California'.

Potentilla atrosanguinea

Potentilla nepalensis
NEPAL CINQUEFOIL

Family: ROSACEAE
Origin: Himalayas.
Flowering time: Summer, northern hemisphere; spring, southern hemisphere.
Climatic zone: 5, 6, 7, 8, 9.
Dimensions: Up to 18 inches (450 mm) high.
Description: This is a tufted herbaceous perennial which is a good front of border plant. The deep-green, serrated leaves accompany rose-red flowers with darker centers. It will flower profusely for many months during the spring or summer. Plant it in a border among phlox and primula for a pretty, cottage-garden look. It will flourish in ordinary soil in full sun, and

is a good choice in a garden where the soil has been neglected.
Varieties/cultivars: 'Miss Willmott', 'Roxana'.

Verbena x *hybrida* 'Lawrence Johnston'

Potentilla nepalensis 'Roxana'

Verbena x *hybrida*
ROSE VERVAIN, COMMON VERBENA (U.K.)

Family: VERBENACEAE
Origin: Hybrid.
Flowering time: Summer–autumn.
Climatic zone: 9, 10.
Dimensions: Up to 2 feet (600 mm) high.
Description: This pretty, spreading, border or groundcover plant will bloom for long periods. Densely packed flower heads set amid dark-green leaves give an effective display. There are many named varieties in a wide choice of colors. Usually grown as an annual, verbena will develop a compact habit if new shoots are pinched out. Remove dead flower heads to prolong the blooming period. Lower growing varieties look attractive, spilling over rock edges or walls. Grow the plant from seed or cutting.
Varieties/cultivars: 'Lawrence Johnston'.

Bauhinia galpinii

Calliandra tweedii

Bauhinia galpinii syn. B. punctata
RED BAUHINIA (U.S.A.),
ORCHID TREE, BUTTERFLY
TREE ○

Family: LEGUMINOSAE
Origin: Tropical Africa.
Flowering time: Summer.
Climatic zone: 9, 10.
Dimensions: 6 feet (2 meters) high.
Description: During summer this shrub is a mass of brick-red flowers. The mid-green leaves have the appearance of a butterfly, hence the common name. For best results grow red bauhinia in a well-drained acid soil. A mulch of cow manure or a handful of complete plant food applied around the tree in early spring will ensure a good flower display. After flowering, the shrub is covered in masses of brown pea-like pods the seeds from which can be used for propagation.

Calliandra tweedii
RED TASSEL FLOWER,
FLAME BUSH, RED
POWDERPUFF ○ ◑

Family: LEGUMINOSAE
Origin: Brazil.
Flowering time: Summer and again in autumn.
Climatic zone: 9, 10.
Dimensions: 6 feet (2 meters) high.
Description: This dense shrub is covered in numerous short branches and finely divided dark-green, fern-like foliage. The large rich-red flowers have a pompom-like appearance. Red tassel flower prefers a well-drained soil, but is adaptable to other soil types. Apply a mulch of manure or compost in spring. Where summers are hot keep well-watered. In cold climates a glasshouse is required. Prune, if necessary, after flowering has finished in autumn. This shrub makes an ideal feature plant.

Begonia x corallina

Begonia x corallina
CORAL BEGONIA ○ ◑

Family: BEGONIACEAE
Origin: Hybrid.
Flowering time: Spring–autumn.
Climatic zone: 9, 10.
Dimensions: 8–10 feet (2–3 meters) high.
Description: A pretty free-flowering shrub having coral-red flowers and attractive foliage, coral begonia is an ideal shrub for a herbaceous garden. It can also be grown in a large tub on a patio or verandah. In cold climates, a greenhouse is required. A sheltered position is a must. Its main requirement is a well-drained soil that is enriched with animal manure or compost.

Other colors: Pink, white.

Callistemon citrinus 'Endeavour'

Flowering time: Spring–summer.
Climatic zone: 9, 10.
Dimensions: 6–13 feet (2–4 meters) high.
Description: This bushy, medium-sized shrub, which has large spikes of deep mauve-pink flowers, can be used as a specimen shrub or screen plant in a warm climate garden. The flowers last quite well when picked and brought indoors for decoration. This bottlebrush will grow in any well-drained garden soil. Mulch around the base with cow manure or compost in spring. This will not only feed the plant, but keep the soil moist. Water well during summer.

Weeping bottlebrush is tolerant of most soils and makes an excellent screen plant. It prefers a mild climate but will tolerate some frost. Organic fertilizer applied in late spring and plenty of summer water speeds growth. It makes an excellent cut flower.
Varieties/cultivars: 'Captain Cook', 'Hannah Ray', 'Gawler', 'King's Park Special'.

Callistemon citrinus
CRIMSON
BOTTLEBRUSH ○ ◑

Family: MYRTACEAE
Origin: Cultivar.
Flowering time: Spring.
Dimensions: 5 feet (approx. 2 meters) high.
Description: A hardy shrub in milder climates, crimson bottlebrush thrives in a wide range of soil types including sandy loam, clay and wet, soggy soil. Large, crimson, bottlebrush-like flowers cover it in spring. Pruning should be carried out if necessary as soon as the flowers fade and before new growth develops. Fertilize around the shrub with either an organic mixture or a mulch of cow manure. Crimson bottlebrush may be used in a shrub border or on its own as a specimen plant.

Callistemon citrinus 'Western Glory'
BOTTLEBRUSH ○

Family: MYRTACEAE
Origin: Cultivar.

Callistemon citrinus 'Western Glory'
BOTTLEBRUSH ○

Family: MYRTACEAE
Origin: Cultivar.

Callistemon viminalis

Callistemon viminalis
WEEPING OR
DROOPING BOTTLEBRUSH ○ ◑

Family: MYRTACEAE
Origin: Eastern Australia.
Flowering time: Summer and again in autumn.
Climatic zone: 9.
Dimensions: 20 feet (6 meters) high.
Description: An outstanding feature plant, this large shrub has an attractive weeping habit and during spring and autumn is covered in a profusion of bright-red flower spikes. The new leaf growth is an attractive bronze color.

Calycanthus floridus

Calycanthus floridus

Calycanthus floridus
COMMON SWEET
SHRUB (U.S.A.), CAROLINA ○ ◑
ALLSPICE (U.K.), STRAWBERRY
SHRUB

Family: CALYCANTHACEAE
Origin: North America.
Flowering time: Spring–summer.
Climatic zone: 5, 6, 7, 8, 9.
Dimensions: 8–10 feet (2–3 meters) high.
Description: This is a hardy, deciduous shrub which prefers a position in partial shade, though in cold climates full sun is necessary to ensure flowering. When flowering, it is covered in attractive reddish-brown flowers. The soil should be rich and well-drained with compost or leaf mold added to it each other spring. Pruning out the old wood after flowering has finished helps to maintain this shrub's attractive appearance. Common sweet shrub looks delightful when planted in a shrub border next to white flowering shrubs.

Cantua buxifolia
FLOWER-OF-THE-INCAS

○ ◑

Family: POLEMONIACEAE
Origin: Peru.
Flowering time: Spring–summer.
Climatic zone: 9, 10.
Dimensions: 6–10 feet (2–3 meters) high.
Description: A sparse, evergreen shrub, *Cantua buxifolia* has beautiful pendulous clusters of bright-rose or pale-red funnel-shaped flowers with an elongated tube. For best results, plant it in well-drained soil enriched with well-rotted compost or leaf mold. It requires at least half-sun and some protection from heavy frosts. In cooler climates, plant *Cantua buxifolia* against a warm sunny wall. Do not prune — this will ruin its shape.

Cestrum fasciculatum 'Newellii'

organic matter such as compost or manure. A good soil will ensure quick growth. It can be easily propagated from cuttings taken in autumn or winter. In colder areas it can be grown on a sunny wall or in a conservatory.

Chaenomeles japonica
DWARF FLOWERING QUINCE, JAPONICA, JAPANESE QUINCE (U.K.)

○ ◑ ●

Family: ROSACEAE
Origin: Japan.
Flowering time: Spring.
Climatic zone: 5, 6, 7, 8.
Dimensions: 3 feet (1 meter) high.
Description: Dwarf flowering quince is a low, spiny, deciduous shrub that spreads wider than its height. Bright orange-red flowers cover the plant before the leaves appear or just as they unfold. The hard, round apple-shaped yellow fruits are delightfully fragrant and make excellent jam or jelly. It is a very hardy shrub which will tolerate full shade or sun, and will thrive in any free-draining garden soil. It can be grown in city conditions, as it is tolerant of pollution. It is often used in hedges or in a shrub border.
Varieties/cultivars: 'Alpina'.

Chaenomeles japonica

Cantua buxifolia

Cestrum fasciculatum 'Newellii'
RED CESTRUM

○

Family: SOLANACEAE
Origin: Cultivar.
Flowering time: Spring–summer.
Climatic zone: 7, 8, 9.
Dimensions: 6–8 feet (2–3 meters) high.
Description: 'Newellii' is a seedling variant. The spectacular, bright orange-red, pitcher-shaped tubular flowers cover it in spring and summer. Grow it at the back of a shrub border or among other screening shrubs. The soil should be well-drained but enriched with

Chaenomeles speciosa
JAPONICA, ○ ◑ ●
COMMON FLOWERING QUINCE
(U.S.A.), FLOWERING OR
JAPANESE QUINCE (U.K.)

Family: ROSACEAE
Origin: China.
Flowering time: Spring.
Climatic zone: 5, 6, 7, 8.
Dimensions: 6–10 feet (2–3 meters) high.
Description: A delightful deciduous shrub, flowering quince has a wide, spreading, rounded habit with dark, glossy green foliage. When grown in milder climates it is only partly deciduous. The 2-inch (50 mm) wide flowers are scarlet to blood-red. Yellowish-green fruit, which makes excellent jam, follows the flowers. This hardy shrub will grow in any soil type as long as it is well-drained. Mulching with manure or compost in late winter ensures a good flower display.
Other colors: Deep crimson, pink and white, pink, white, orange, buff-coral, creamy-salmon, orange-red, creamy-apricot.
Varieties/cultivars: Numerous cultivars have been developed from this species.

Chorizema cordatum

Chorizema cordatum
HEART-LEAF FLAME ○ ◑
PEA, FLAME PEA, CORAL PEA

Family: LEGUMINOSAE
Origin: Western Australia.
Flowering time: Late spring and summer.

47

Climatic zone: 9, 10.
Dimensions: 3–6 feet (1–2 meters) high.
Description: An attractive low-growing shrub, flame pea is used in rockeries as a specimen plant in hot climates. In colder areas, a greenhouse may be necessary. The small red and orange pea-shaped flowers, which are very bright, attractive, and abundant, cover the plant for nearly six months. The leaves are hear-shaped. Its main requirement is a well-drained, sandy soil. It is frost- and drought-resistant. Flame pea is easily propagated from seed, but these should be soaked in water that is near boiling point before they are sown.

Chaenomeles speciosa 'Umbilicata'

Cytisus scoparius 'Crimson King'
COMMON BROOM ○

Family: LEGUMINOSAE
Origin: Hybrid.
Flowering time: Spring.
Climatic zone: 6, 7, 8, 9.
Dimensions: 4–9 feet (1–3 meters) high.
Description: 'Crimson King', a cultivar of *Cytisus scoparius* has magnificent true red flowers. It is extremely easy to cultivate, but prefers a well-drained soil. In warmer climates, pruning it back by at least half its height after flowering ensures a thicker shrub. In cool areas, pruning should be limited to avoid dieback. This is an ideal plant for a shrub or perennial border and looks magnificent if planted near white flowering plants. It is easily propagated from cuttings taken in early spring.

Cytisus scoparius 'Crimson King'

SHRUBS

Fuchsia magellanica
MAGELLAN
FUCHSIA, COMMON FUCHSIA
(U.K.)

● ● ● ◑ ○

Family: ONAGRACEAE
Origin: Southern Chile, Argentina.
Flowering time: Summer–autumn.
Climatic zone: 7, 8, 9.
Dimensions: 6–10 feet (2–3 meters) high.
Description: This is a free-flowering shrub with long, arching branches and an abundance of pendant flowers. The flower sepals are bright crimson and the petals are purplish-blue. It can be used in a shrub border or as a hedge plant. The nodding flowers are very rich in honey, making this a valuable bird-attracting plant in the garden. It is easily propagated from cuttings taken in late summer or spring. For best results plant in a rich, free-draining soil.
Other colors: Scarlet and deep violet; white and mauve; white and pink.
Varieties/cultivars: 'Alba', 'Riccardo', 'Variegata', 'Gracilis'.

Euphorbia milii

Euphorbia milii
CROWN-OF-THORNS

○

Family: EUPHORBIACEAE
Origin: Madagascar.
Flowering time: Summer.
Climatic zone: 9, 10.
Dimensions: 3 feet (1 meter) high.
Description: Crown-of-thorns is a spiny, succulent shrub with brown, almost leafless stems and long, straight, tapering spines. The leaves are very sparse and appear at the ends of branches. The flowers themselves are inconspicuous but are surrounded by showy, bright scarlet bracts. In warm climates, the best location for the crown-of-thorns is in a large rockery or against a wall. A greenhouse location is essential in cold climates. Its needs are a hot position and a well-drained soil.

Hibiscus schizopetalus
FRINGED HIBISCUS,
JAPANESE HIBISCUS

○

Family: MALVACEAE
Origin: Tropical East Africa.
Flowering time: Spring–summer.
Climatic zone: 9, 10.
Dimensions: 5–10 feet (approx. 1½–3 meters) high.
Description: Fringed hibiscus is a pretty shrub with slender stems which usually require supporting. The orange-red pendant flowers have fringed, backward curving petals with long stamens projecting beyond them. Fringed hibiscus requires a warm, sheltered position and a rich, well-drained soil. It can be trained on a wall or trellis. In spring cut away any

Fuchsia magellanica 'Gracilis'

Feijoa sellowiana

Feijoa sellowiana
FEIJOA, PINEAPPLE
GUAVA (U.S.A.), FRUIT SALAD
TREE

○

Family: MYRTACEAE
Origin: Brazil.
Flowering time: Summer.
Climatic zone: 8, 9, 10.
Dimensions: 5–20 feet (2–6 meters) high.
Description: This attractive ornamental shrub is grown for its crimson-and-white flowers and edible fruit. The leaves are gray-green with a white, felty underside. The dark-green fragrant fruits ripen in winter and, when mature, fall on the ground. They can be eaten raw or used in jam. Feijoa likes a well-drained soil but requires ample summer water for good fruit production. The fragrant petals can be eaten and look delightful sprinkled over the top of a salad. Not suited to areas where winters are severe.
Varieties/cultivars: 'Variegata', 'Gigantea', 'Coolidgei'.

48

Hibiscus schizopetalus

Dimensions: 4–7 feet (approx. 1–2 meters) high.
Description: *Leonotis* is a pretty, square-stemmed plant with downy, dull-green leaves and showy spikes of orange-scarlet flowers. The name *Leonotis*, from *leon* (lion) and *otos* (ear), was given because the flower looks like a lion's ear. This fast-growing plant thrives in well-drained soil. A mulch of manure or compost in spring will ensure good flower production. Pruning can be carried out if required after the flowers have finished.

Leonotis leonurus
LION'S EAR ◯
Family: LABIATAE
Origin: South Africa.
Flowering time: Late summer–autumn.
Climatic zone: 9, 10.

requirement is an extremely well-drained sandy soil. A rockery, especially one or a sloping site, is an ideal position, but in cooler climates a greenhouse is necessary.
Other colors: See description.
Varieties/cultivars: 'Scarlet O'Hara'.

Leonotis Leonurus

Leucospermum reflexum
ROCKET PINCUSHION ◯
Family: PROTEACEAE
Origin: South Africa.
Flowering time: Spring.
Climatic zone: 9.
Dimensions: 6–10 feet (2–3 meters) high.
Description: This eye-catching shrub has downy, bluish-gray leaves and large orange-red flowerheads about 4 inches (100 mm) across. Good drainage is essential for the plant's success. It should not be planted where there is a heavy clay subsoil, as the excessive moisture retained will eventually rot the roots, causing plant collapse. During wet spring weather the new shoots will often rot and collapse. This is not a disease and does not occur when the weather is dry and hot.

Leucospermum reflexum.

Lechenaultia formosa 'Scarlet O'Hara'

unwanted growth, and shorten the stems and branches to within 5 inches (125 mm) of the base. It can be grown in a large pot or tub. In cool climates, it grows best in a greenhouse.

Lechenaultia formosa
LECHENAULTIA ◯ ◑
Family: GOODENIACEAE
Origin: Western Australia.
Flowering time: Spring and summer.
Climatic zone: 9.
Dimensions: 11 inches (300 mm) high.
Description: This prostrate shrub is covered in small grayish-green leaves and an abundance of vermilion-red flowers in spring. It is variable in form and also flower color which can vary from white, yellow, pink, rose to any combination of these. Its main

❀

Mussaenda frondosa
MUSSAENDA

Family: RUBIACEAE
Origin: Tropical Africa, Asia, Pacific islands.
Flowering time: Summer.
Climatic zone: 9, 10.
Dimensions: 3–6 feet (1–2 meters) high.
Description: The orange-yellow flowers of this shrub are actually quite inconspicuous, but they are surrounded by large white bracts which stay on the plant for a long time after the flowers have fallen. The combination of the soft-green leaves and the white bracts is very striking. Mussaenda thrives in warm coastal districts where the soil is free-draining. Plant it in a shrub border or use as a specimen plant. In colder climates, a greenhouse location is necessary. Feed it in early spring and water well during the summer months.

Mussaenda frondosa

Odontonema strictum syn.
Thyrsacanthus, Justicia coccinea
RED JUSTICIA, FIERY SPIKE

Family: ACANTHACEAE
Origin: Tropical America.
Flowering time: Autumn.
Climatic zone: 9, 10.
Dimensions: 8 feet (2–3 meters) high.
Description: A favorite plant for hot-climate gardens, it has large, glossy green leaves and spectacular scarlet flowers which open irregularly. It is often grown on patios in a large pot. Red justicia's main cultivation requirements are a rich soil, preferably with leaf mold added, and ample summer water. It is easily propagated from spring cuttings.

Protea grandiceps

Protea spp.
PROTEA

Family: PROTEACEAE
Origin: South Africa.
Flowering time: Depends on the species, but generally winter.
Climatic zone: 9, 10.
Dimensions: 2–10 feet (approx. 1–3 meters) high.
Description: There are many species of proteas. The flowers of *Protea pulchra* vary from deep ruby-red to salmon and pink. *Protea neriifolia* 'Taylors Surprise' has brilliant salmon-red flowers and *Protea nana* is renowned for its bright rosy-crimson to orange-red flowers. Proteas strongly resent over-rich soils and thrive in rather poor slightly acid soil that contains a lot of rubble or sand. Add sulfur to the soil if it is too alkaline. Avoid using phosphates. Do not overwater.
Other colors: Pink, white, green, cream.

Odontonema strictum

Punica granatum
POMEGRANATE

Family: PUNICACEAE
Origin: Southwest Asia.
Flowering time: Summer.
Climatic zone: 8, 9.
Dimensions: 10–20 feet (3–6 meters) high.
Description: The new spring leaves of this large deciduous shrub are coppery in color before changing to a deep, shiny green. In autumn they turn a bright yellow. The orange-red flowers have a wrinkled appearance. The fruit needs a long hot summer before it develops properly. Pomegranate's main requirements are a hot position and a well-drained soil. It can be grown very successfully in large pots or tubs, or against a sunny wall. Feed with a complete plant food in spring.
Other colors: Scarlet-red, ruby-red, reddish-salmon.
Varieties/cultivars: 'Pleniflora', 'Spanish Ruby', 'Nana', 'Nana Plena', 'De Regina', 'Albo-plena'.

Punica granatum

50

Rhododendron x gandavense

Rhododendron Knap Hill

GHENT AZALEA, ◯ ◗
DECIDUOUS AZALEA, MOLLIS
AZALEA

Rhododendron x gandavense

Family: ERICACEAE
Origin: Hybrid.
Flowering time: Spring.
Climatic zone: 6, 7, 8, 9.
Dimensions: 5 feet (approx. 2 meters)
high.
Description: This is a mixed race of
hybrids, the result of crossing between
R. luteum and several other species.
Many are in the orange-red color range.
The flowers are lightly perfumed and
the shrub is slightly more twiggy than
other deciduous azaleas. Ghent azaleas
like a cool, acid soil which has been
enriched with organic matter, preferably
peat. They will grow in full sun in cool
climates, but in temperate climates
prefer partial shade.
Other colors: Pink, yellow.
Varieties/cultivars: There are
numerous cultivars throughout the
world.

DECIDUOUS AZALEA ◯ ◗

Rhododendron Knap Hill

Family: ERICACEAE
Origin: Hybrid.
Flowering time: Spring.
Climatic zone: 6, 7, 8, 9.
Dimensions: 3–9 feet (1–3 meters) high.
Description: Knap Hill hybrids
originated in England in the early
1900s. They are valued for their orange-
red color range. The leaves color in
autumn before they drop. They like cool
to cold climates and will grow in full sun

Telopea speciosissima

NEW SOUTH WALES ◯ ◗
WARATAH

Telopea speciosissima

Family: PROTEACEAE
Origin: Australia (N.S.W.).
Flowering time: Spring.
Climatic zone: 9, 10.
Dimensions: 10 feet (3 meters) high.
Description: Very large, red flowers
(3–6 inches, 80–150 mm in diameter)
appear on this shrub during spring. The
flowers are followed by long brown
pods. Waratahs tend to respond to
cultivation provided that the soil is acid
and rainfall high. They always look
more magnificent in a garden than in
the wild. For best results feed only with
organic fertilizers and prune rather hard
to shape them after flowering. Waratahs
attract birds to the garden as well as
making superb feature plants. Keep well
watered during summer.
Varieties/cultivars: 'Braidwood
Brilliant'.

in colder climates but perform just as
well or better in dappled shade. A
mulch of leaf mold or cow manure,
applied around the base of the shrubs in
spring, will keep the shallow roots moist
and cool during summer.
Other colors: Yellow, gold, orange,
scarlet, pink, white.
Varieties/cultivars: Numerous cultivars
are available throughout the world.

Brachychiton acerifolium
ILLAWARRA FLAME TREE, FLAME BOTTLE TREE (U.K.)

Family: STERCULIACEAE
Origin: Eastern Australia (coastal slopes).
Flowering time: Late spring–early summer.
Climatic zone: 9, 10.
Dimensions: 35–45 feet (11–14 meters) high.
Description: This tree is erratic in its flowering habit, but the blooms, which appear as a cloud of scarlet on bare wood, are a sight worth waiting for. Sometimes only one side of the tree will produce flowers. Good flowering seems to follow a dryish winter. It is mostly evergreen, but is deciduous on the flowering branches. The Illawarra flame tree flourishes in warm, coastal districts and is a popular garden tree. It does not suffer from any special pest or disease problems.

the Baptist is believed to have eaten in the wilderness. Although slow growing in its native lands, it is more vigorous in cultivation. The leaves are dark green and leathery in texture, while the reddish flowers appear in small clusters close to the branches. Ideal for growing in hot and dry conditions, well-drained soil produces the best results. A male and female plant are required to produce the edible pods.

Crataegus laevigata 'Paulii' syn.
C. oxyacantha 'Paul's Scarlet'
DOUBLE RED HAWTHORN, MIDLAND HAWTHORN (U.K.), SCARLET THORN

Family: ROSACEAE
Origin: Cultivar
Flowering time: Spring–early summer.
Climatic zone: 5, 6, 7, 8, 9.
Dimensions: 16–20 feet (5–6 meters) high.
Description: A hardy little tree-cum-shrub, English hawthorn is smothered in gorgeous scarlet flowers in spring. Often used in the landscape as a hedge, the leaves turn yellow in autumn, and its dense, thorny growth gives protection even in winter when the leaves have dropped. It prefers a limestone soil, performs best in a cool climate, and is problem-free.

Crataegus laevigata 'Paulii'

Delonix regia
ROYAL POINCIANA (U.S.A.), PEACOCK FLOWER, FLAME TREE

Other common names: FLAMBOYANT TREE
Family: CAESALPINACEAE
Origin: Madagascar.
Flowering time: Summer.
Climatic zone: 9, 10.

Callistemon viminalis 'Hannah Ray'

evergreen tree flowers for long periods and, like most bottlebrushes, will grow in very variable soil conditions, from poorly drained to well drained. Its long, brush-like, crimson flowers attract honey-eating birds. Young foliage is a pink color which later turns to green. Sawflies, which in some areas cluster on leaves and branches in warmer months, may be removed by hand.

Ceratonia siliqua
CAROB BEAN, LOCUST

Family: CAESALPINACEAE
Origin: Eastern Mediterranean.
Flowering time: Spring, northern hemisphere; spring–autumn, southern hemisphere.
Climatic zone: 6, 7, 8, 9.
Dimensions: 15–30 feet (5–10 meters) high.
Description: This compact-growing tree is grown chiefly for the generous shade it affords in hot climates, and for the edible beans which follow the flowers in autumn, and which St. John

Ceratonia siliqua

Brachychiton acerifolium

Callistemon viminalis 'Hannah Ray'
BOTTLEBRUSH

Family: MYRTACEAE
Origin: Cultivar
Flowering time: Spring and autumn, southern hemisphere; summer, northern hemisphere.
Climatic zone: 8, 9, 10.
Dimensions: 13 feet (4 meters) high x 6 feet (2 meters) wide.
Description: A cultivar of the weeping bottlebrush, this delightful, small,

Delonix regia

in coastal districts. It is often planted as a shade tree in large gardens, and in parks and car parks. It may also be grown in pots in a frost-free greenhouse though it does not flower in containers.
Other colors: White.
Varieties/cultivars: 'Alba', var. *orientalis*.

---

hemisphere; late spring–summer, southern hemisphere.
Climatic zone: 9, 10.
Dimensions: 15–40 feet (8–12 meters) high.
Description: If planted in full sun with excellent drainage, this small tree will reward you with masses of fluffy, red flowers each year. Large gum nuts (the fruits), which follow, hang on the tree for a long time, and can be used as dried arrangements for the house. One of the most popular small eucalypts, it has found its way into coastal gardens of both hemispheres. It needs a sheltered position and mild winter climate.
Other colors: Color is variable.

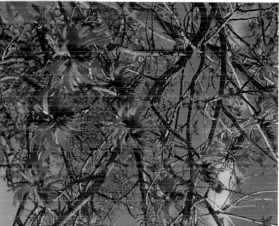

Erythrina x sykesii

Eucalyptus leucoxylon 'Rosea'
WHITE IRONBARK

Family: MYRTACEAE
Origin: Cultivar.
Flowering time: Winter–late spring.
Climatic zone: 9, 10.
Dimensions: 30–45 feet (10–15 meters) high.
Description: White ironbark, which is a winter-flowerer, is popular in many home gardens and parks for its abundant, pretty rose-pink flowers and contrasting handsome bark. Its long-stalked buds with their pointed caps, which are found in groups of three, make the tree readily identifiable. Although the bark is mainly smooth and yellowish, the tree is nevertheless classed as an ironbark rather than a smoothbark, because of the fibrous, persistent bark near the base. A medium-sized eucalypt, white ironbark adapts well to most soils and conditions.

Eucalyptus ficifolia
RED-FLOWERING GUM, SCARLET-FLOWERING GUM

Family: MYRTACEAE
Origin: Western Australia (southern coast).
Flowering time: Summer, northern

Eucalyptus ficifolia

53

Dimensions: 40–50 feet (12–15 meters) high x 50–65 feet (15–20 meters) wide.
Description: Flamboyant by name, flamboyant by nature, *Delonix regia* flowers only in the warmest of climates or in a warm microclimate, when suddenly the whole canopy of the tree is covered in showy bunches of red flowers. Grown as a beautiful shade tree, the canopy often spreads to twice the width of the height. Leaves are similar to those of the blue-flowering jacaranda — lacy and bright green, almost evergreen. This tree is widely planted in Florida and tropical towns in Australia.
Other colors: Cream (rare).

Erythrina x sykesii syn. *E. indica*, *E. variegata*
COMMON CORAL TREE, SYKES'S CORAL TREE (U.K.)

Family: LEGUMINOSAE
Origin: Hybrid.
Flowering time: Late winter–early spring, northern hemisphere; mid-winter–late spring, southern hemisphere.
Climatic zone: 9, 10.
Dimensions: 40–60 feet (12–18 meters) high.
Description: Belonging to a large genus of over 100 species, the common coral tree is a familiar sight in both northern and southern hemispheres. Its brilliant red flowers are a welcome sight in winter as they appear on bare branches, the leaves following later. Sharp, fat prickles cover trunk and branches. A tree of generous proportions, with a wide canopy and a short trunk, it flourishes

Eucalyptus leucoxylon 'Rosea'

Malus 'Profusion'

yearling. It belongs to a group of *M. niedzwetkyana* hybrids. Like most crab apples it is very hardy and is happy in most soils, given adequate humus. Mass-plant it or use along a driveway or pathway for a spectacular display of flower color in spring, and of brilliant crab apples in autumn.

Metrosideros excelsa
POHUTUKAWA (N.Z.), NEW ZEALAND CHRISTMAS TREE

Family: MYRTACEAE
Origin: New Zealand.
Flowering time: Summer, northern hemisphere; late spring–summer, southern hemisphere.
Climatic zone: 9, 10.
Dimensions: 30–60 feet (10–18 meters) high.
Description: *Metrosideros* is very much at home clinging to soil at the beach edge. This evergreen revels in salt-laden, windy, and exposed sites, and sports eye-catching, fluffy red flowers in time for Christmas in the southern hemisphere. It requires a cool, prolonged

Metrosideros excelsa

Euphorbia pulcherrima
CHRISTMAS STAR, POINSETTIA (U.K.)

Other common names: MEXICAN FLAMELEAF
Family: EUPHORBIACEAE
Origin: Tropical Mexico and Central America.
Flowering time: Winter–spring, northern hemisphere; late autumn–late spring, southern hemisphere.
Climatic zone: 9, 10.
Dimensions: 10–12 feet (3–4 meters) high.
Description: Brilliant red bracts surround the insignificant flowers of this world-popular plant. Grown outdoors, it needs a warm, sheltered position. Short days and long dark nights are necessary for good flowering. Commercial growers simulate these conditions in glasshouses to produce flowers over a very long period. Plant potted specimens outdoors in warm climates when the flowers have died.

Euphorbia pulcherrima

Cut back most of the stem after flowering and tip-prune a few weeks after new shoots appear. The stems are brittle and the milky sap is poisonous.
Other colors: Cream, pale pink.
Varieties/cultivars: 'Henrietta Eck', 'Annette Hegge' (dwarf).

Malus 'Profusion'
ORNAMENTAL CRAB APPLE, RED CRAB APPLE, FLOWERING CRAB APPLE (U.K.)

Family: ROSACEAE
Origin: Hybrid.
Flowering time: Early summer.
Climatic zone: 4, 5, 6, 7, 8, 9.
Dimensions: 6–20 feet (2–6 meters) high.
Description: As its name suggests, this delightful, small crab apple is one of the most free-flowering of all the crab apples, producing flowers when just a

winter to flower well, and needs plenty of space to develop a wide crown from the start, stout trunk. It makes a good hedge or windbreak and will stand heavy pruning. Grow new plants from cuttings or seed.
Other colors: Creamy yellow.
Varieties/cultivars: 'Aurea'.

Prunus campanulata
TAIWAN CHERRY, BELL-FLOWER CHERRY, FORMOSAN CHERRY ○

Family: ROSACEAE
Origin: Taiwan and Ryuku Archipelago.
Flowering time: Late winter–early spring.
Climatic zone: 9.
Dimensions: 20–30 feet (6–8 meters) high.
Description: Pretty, carmine, bell-shaped flowers hang in small clusters from this deciduous, ornamental tree before the leaves appear. One of the reddest-flowered cherries, it is for a warm climate only. It is seldom grown in areas with late frosts, which damage the blossom and foliage. Its single trunk and wide canopy make for a splendid garden tree under which can be grown plants that enjoy dappled shade in summer and sun in winter.

Prunus campanulata

Prunus persica 'Magnifica'
DOUBLE RED-FLOWERING PEACH ○

Family: ROSACEAE
Origin: Cultivar.
Flowering time: Spring.
Climatic zone: 5, 6, 7, 8, 9.
Dimensions: 10–20 feet (3–6 meters) high.
Description: One of the best red-flowering cultivars, this tree comes into blossom in late spring. It has large, double, bright rosy-red flowers. In wet climates the disease peach leaf curl is a problem. Spray with bordeaux mixture each spring when flower buds swell or color up, to kill over-wintering fungus, or prune back the branches to about half their length immediately after flowering. Plant this tree to provide a canopy of color over spring-flowering shrubs and perennials.

Prunus persica 'Magnifica'

Spathodea campanulata
WEST AFRICAN TULIP TREE, FOUNTAIN TREE, FLAME-OF-THE-FOREST ○

Family: BIGNONIACEAE
Origin: West Africa.
Flowering time: Early spring–late summer.
Climatic zone: 9, 10.
Dimensions: 30–60 feet (9–18 meters) high.
Description: Bold in every way, this tree will take your breath away at first sight. Handsome, evergreen, compound leaves support the magnificent, scarlet-orange flowers that are borne in spikes just above them. The display lasts a long time as flowers open one after the other instead of en masse. The tree develops a broad dome. It thrives in warm coastal areas, but should be protected from strong, salt-laden winds. Plant it in fertile soil with good drainage. It can be easily grown from seed sown in spring in the glasshouse.

Spathodea campanulata

Stenocarpus sinuatus
QUEENSLAND FIREWHEEL TREE ○

Family: PROTEACEAE
Origin: Australia (Queensland and N.S.W.).
Flowering time: Early autumn–mid-winter, southern hemisphere.
Climatic zone: 8, 9, 10.
Dimensions: 30–100 feet (10–30 meters) high.
Description: Not grown nearly as much as it deserves in Australia, it is often planted as a street tree in California, where it is well appreciated. Beautiful and interesting at every stage of its development, there is no other flower quite like this one, aptly described as a "wheel". The "spokes", or flower buds, arranged around a central hub, split open to expose the golden stamens within. A slow-growing, slender tree, it reaches in cultivation only half the height it attains in its native habitat. This evergreen can be grown in warm areas only.

Stenocarpus sinuatus

PINK FLOWERS

Agrostemma githago
CORN COCKLE

Family: CARYOPHYLLACEAE
Origin: Mediterranean region.
Flowering time: Summer.
Climatic zone: 3, 4, 5, 6, 7, 8, 9.
Dimensions: Up to 3 feet (1 meter) high.
Description: This is an erect, slender plant with narrow, grayish, hairy foliage. The rosy pink to magenta-colored flowers are on single stems and open flat to 2 inches (50 mm) wide. The corn cockle is still considered to be a weed in grain-growing areas where its flowers are prominent in the fields. In cultivation it is hardy, but it is of no use in floral work, as the flower folds towards evening. It needs a sunny, well-drained position.
Other colors: White, rose-purple, lilac-pink.
Varieties/cultivars: 'Milas' (flowers are 3 inches (75 mm) wide, 'Purple Queen'.

annual or perennial which flowers continuously in warmth. The flowers, though small — are produced in clusters on a stiff, succulent stem. Begonias are used for borders or massed bedding with contrasting colors of foliage and flowers. The leaves may be deep bronze to bright green according to variety. Plant in rich, well-drained soil, but allow soil to dry out a little between waterings.
Other colors: White, red.
Varieties/cultivars: 'Thousand Wonders', 'Comet'.

Begonia semperflorens

Dimensions: Up to 4 inches (100 mm) high.
Description: This is the original daisy. The flowers are up to 1 inch (25 mm) wide, and are double in form. They are formed on a single stem and protrude from the basal leaves, which are shiny green and in the form of a rosette. The plant may be used as an attractive edging in cooler gardens. It will not stand continued hot sun. Although usually grown as an annual, it may be perennial. Rich, moist soil conditions are essential for success.
Other colors: White, rosy-red.
Varieties/cultivars: 'Montrosa' (larger heads of flowers, red), 'Rosea' (rose-pink), 'Prolifera' (secondary heads on the stem).

Callistephus chinensis
CHINA ASTER

Family: COMPOSITAE
Origin: China, Japan.
Flowering time: Summer–early autumn.
Climatic zone: 4, 5, 6, 7, 8, 9.
Dimensions: Up to 2 feet (600 mm) high.
Description: This is one of the best garden plants for floral art. The stiff stems may branch to form up to six flowers on each. The flowers, up to 5 inches (125 mm) wide, are many-petaled and double. The plant is subject to wilt which may weaken it considerably and suddenly. For healthy asters, ensure

Bellis perennis cultivar

Bellis perennis
COMMON OR LAWN
DAISY, ENGLISH DAISY

Family: COMPOSITAE
Origin: Europe–western Asia.
Flowering time: Spring–summer.
Climatic zone: 6, 7, 8, 9.

Agrostemma githago

Begonia semperflorens
WAX BEGONIA

Family: BEGONIACEAE
Origin: Brazil.
Flowering time: Spring–summer–autumn.
Climatic zone: 4, 5, 6, 7, 8, 9, 10.
Dimensions: Up to 12 inches (300 mm) high.
Description: This is a tender summer

that soil is light and sandy. Add lime if pH levels are acid.
Other colors: White, blue, violet.
Varieties/cultivars: 'Princess' (larger than average flowers), 'King' (more branches), 'Seven Dwarfs' (low variety).

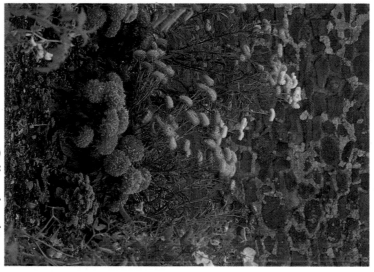

Callistephus chinensis

Celosia cristata
CRESTED CELOSIA

Family: AMARANTHACEAE
Origin: Tropical Asia.
Flowering time: Summer.
Climatic zone: 5, 6, 7, 8, 9, 10.
Dimensions: Up to 2 feet (600 mm) high.
Description: This erect plant forms

Celosia cristata

upright flowers which look like woolly feathers in terminal spikes. Their vibrant colors make them a good summer annual for hot and dry conditions. The leaves may also be variegated in red and gold colors. The flowers, in their crested shape, may be up to 6 inches (150 mm) wide and brilliant in color. They are very suitable for large displays in parks. Celosia thrives in rich, well-drained soil that is kept constantly moist.
Other colors: Yellow, orange, red, and occasionally, white and purple.
Varieties/cultivars: 'Forest Fire', 'Golden Triumph' 'Fairy Fountain' (dwarf, mixed colors, 12 inches (300 mm) high).

Cleome hassleriana syn. *C. pungens*, *C. spinosa*
SPIDER FLOWER

Family: CAPPARIDACEAE
Origin: West Indies, Brazil–Argentina.
Flowering time: Summer.
Climatic zone: 4, 5, 6, 7, 8, 9, 10.
Dimensions: Up to 5 feet (1–1½ meters) high.
Description: In the right climate, this annual can be a commanding background to lower-growing annuals. The long, clawed petals, and extended stamens of the flowers, give them their spider-like appearance. The flowers are clustered to form large heads up to 5 inches (125 mm) across, in pale pink, almost white colors, with overtones of deeper pink and mauve. Cleome is a good flower for large, open areas such as parks and needs plenty of space, as each plant is quite wide. Warm conditions are essential. Water well.

decoration. Excellent for poor, sandy soils — in fact, avoid using too much humus as flowers will be overwhelmed by foliage.
Other colors: Red, lavender, salmon, purple.
Varieties/cultivars: Single and double cultivars available.

Clarkia unguiculata

Clarkia unguiculata syn. *Clarkia elegans*
CLARKIA (U.K.), GARLAND FLOWER

Family: ONAGRACEAE
Origin: California.
Flowering time: Summer.
Climatic zone: 4, 5, 6, 7, 8, 9, 10.
Dimensions: Up to 2 feet (600 mm) high.
Description: This erect, hardy annual produces many flowers on stiff stems. The rose-pink flowers have four petals, widening at the outer edge, and up to 2 inches (50 mm) across when open. The cut flowers are good for indoor

Cleome hassleriana

Clarkia amoena
GODETIA

Family: ONAGRACEAE
Origin: Western North America, Chile.
Flowering time: Summer.
Climatic zone: 4, 5, 6, 7, 8, 9.
Dimensions: Up to 2 feet (600 mm) high.
Description: A delightful annual from California, previously classified as Godetia, this plant has graceful spikes of showy, pale pink or lavender to white flowers, measuring 2 inches (50 mm) across. Foliage is lance-shaped and toothed. The slender, erect habit of this annual makes it an ideal cut flower or useful pot plant for a cool greenhouse. Plant it in an open, sunny position in well-drained, humus-rich soil and ensure adequate water during spring growth and the summer flowering period.

Clarkia amoena

Cosmos bipinnatus
COMMON OR GARDEN COSMOS

Family: COMPOSITAE
Origin: Mexico.
Flowering time: Summer–autumn.

Climatic zone: 4, 5, 6, 7, 8, 9, 10.
Dimensions: Up to 6 feet (2 meters) high.
Description: Cosmos is a tall annual, well suited as a background in a cottage garden. The plant produces many flowers which are suitable for use indoors. The foliage is fern-like, providing an attractive background for the flowers, which are flat, open, and up to 2½ inches (65 mm) wide with yellow centers. Cosmos will thrive in most soils, preferring light, dry conditions.
Other colors: Red, white, deep mauve.
Varieties/cultivars: 'Mammoth Single', 'Bright-lights' (double flowers), 'Alba'.

Dianthus chinensis syn. *D. sinensis*
CHINA PINK, INDIAN PINK

Family: CARYOPHYLLACEAE
Origin: Eastern Asia.
Flowering time: Summer–autumn in cooler climates.
Climatic zone: 6, 7, 8, 9, 10.
Dimensions: Up to 18 inches (450 mm) high.
Description: This is a semi-hardy annual or short-lived perennial and may behave as a biennial. The semi-double flowers, which are up to 2 inches (50 mm) wide, have attractive, tooth-edged petals. They may be on single stems or loosely clustered and are only faintly fragrant. A neutral to limey soil is important and it should also be light, sandy and well-drained.
Other colors: White, lilac, red.
Varieties/cultivars: *D. c.* var. *Heddewigii*

Gomphrena globosa
GLOBE AMARANTH

Family: AMARANTHACEAE
Origin: Tropical Asia.
Flowering time: Midsummer–early autumn.
Climatic zone: 4, 5, 6, 7, 8, 9, 10.
Dimensions: Up to 18 inches (450 mm) high.
Description: This very low-growing, dense, annual plant likes a warm, dry climate. It is tough and needs no special soil conditions. It has a rounded, bushy habit, the flowers borne on slender stalks that protrude slightly from the edge of the foliage. The tight, clover-like flower heads are up to 1 inch (25 mm) in diameter. When cut, the flowers last well and are suitable for small arrangements and posies; they also dry well. Mulch in summer.
Other colors: Red, white, orange, purple. Variegated flowers are sometimes seen.
Varieties/cultivars: 'Rubra'.

Gomphrena globosa

Impatiens balsamina
COMMON OR GARDEN BALSAM

Family: BALSAMINACEAE
Origin: India–Malaya.
Flowering time: Summer.
Climatic zone: 4, 5, 6, 7, 8, 9, 10.
Dimensions: Up to 12 inches (300 mm) high.
Description: This is a tender annual that thrives in warm shade. The stiff stems are somewhat brittle and may easily suffer wind damage. The flowers are single or double and up to 2 inches (50 mm) wide. They are long-lasting on the plant and quickly replaced, but they have no value as a cut flower. Choose a good fertile soil that does not dry out and pinch back to encourage more bushy growth.

Dianthus chinensis var. *Heddewigii*

Other colors: Scarlet, yellow, white, purple. May be occasionally striped.
Varieties/cultivars: Double-flowered types are often called 'Camellia-flowered'.

Impatiens balsamina cultivar

Impatiens walleriana
BUSY LIZZY, PATIEN LUCY, SULTANA ○ ◑

Family: BALSAMINACEAE
Origin: Tanzania, Mozambique.
Flowering time: Warm months, but may flower all year.
Climatic zone: 5, 6, 7, 8, 9, 10.
Dimensions: Up to 2 feet (600 mm) high.
Description: This brittle-stemmed perennial is often grown as an annual. It thrives in warm, shaded areas where it is possible for it to flower most of the year. The flowers are up to 2 inches (50 mm) wide on single stems, and open flat. They have four petals, which are broad at the edge and curve slightly downwards. It is possible to use this plant for tubs and baskets and also to bring it indoors as a house plant. Water well in hot weather, and mulch with well-rotted compost for good results.
Other colors: Red, purple, orange, white.
Varieties/cultivars: There are double forms, also 'Nana' (dwarf-growing), and 'Variegata' (foliage variegated white).

Impatiens walleriana cultivar

Lathyrus odoratus
SWEET PEA ○

Family: LEGUMINOSAE
Origin: Southern Italy, Sicily.
Flowering time: Summer–early autumn.
Climatic zone: 6, 7, 8, 9, 10.
Dimensions: Climbing plant to 6 feet (2 m) high.
Description: The sweet pea, with its delightful fragrance, is one of the most popular of plants. Both for background planting in the garden and as a cut flower for floral use. Up to seven of the large, pea-like blooms, which are about 2 inches (50 mm) wide, are borne on a long, stiff stem. They appear in various shades of both bright and subtle colors. Being a tendril-climber, sweet pea needs the support of wires, strings, or a lattice. Add lime, and blood and bone to the soil prior to planting, and water well until plants are established.
Other colors: White, purple, red.
Varieties/cultivars: There are many cultivars of the above, some with large flowers, and very long stems. 'Bijou' is a dwarf variety, also used for bedding. Some varieties are early flowering and heat resistant.

Lathyrus odoratus cultivar

Dimensions: Up to 3 feet (1 meter) tall.
Description: This plant likes well-drained soil and flowers best in the cooler months in a warm climate. The leaves are slightly hairy and almost round in shape with clear, ribbed veins. The flowers, which are mostly solitary on the outside of the plant, are as large as the leaf — up to 4 inches (100 mm) wide — and open flat.
Other colors: Shades of red and white.
Varieties/cultivars: 'Loveliness' (satiny, rose-pink), 'Splendens' (rose-red and occasionally white), 'Silver Cup'.

Lavatera trimestris
ANNUAL MALLOW ○

Family: MALVACEAE
Origin: Mediterranean region, Portugal.
Flowering time: Early spring–autumn.
Climatic zone: 4, 5, 6, 7, 8, 9, 10.

Lavatera trimestris 'Silver Cup'

Linaria maroccana

Lunaria annua

Lunaria annua
HONESTY, MOONWORT, MONEYPLANT

Other common names:
SATINFLOWER, PENNY FLOWER, SILVER DOLLAR
Family: CRUCIFERAE
Origin: Mediterranean region.
Flowering time: Spring–summer.
Climatic zone: 7, 8, 9, 10.
Dimensions: Up to 3 feet (900 mm) high.
Description: Although this plant is grown principally for its dried seed casing, it does bear an attractive head of small purplish-pink flowers. When these flowers fall and the seed pods appear, it presents quite a different appearance. The seed pods are flat, broadly oval to almost circular, 1½–2½ inches (40–60 mm) long. When ripe, the walls of the pod fall away to reveal a central silvery membrane which glows with a pearly lustre. In this silvery pearly form, the plant lasts indefinitely indoors and is an excellent decoration. Most soils are suitable providing drainage is adequate.
Other colors: White.
Varieties/cultivars: 'Alba', 'Variegata'.

Lunaria annua

Malcolmia maritima
VIRGINIA STOCK

Family: CRUCIFERAE
Origin: Greece, Albania.
Flowering time: Early summer–autumn.
Climatic zone: 6, 7, 8, 9, 10.
Dimensions: Up to 10 inches (250 mm) high.
Description: Virginia stock is a hardy annual for cool to warm climates. The plant is low-growing and bushy which makes it ideal as an annual border for taller annuals and perennials. It is a good bedding plant for massing between shrubs. The flowers, which are only ¾ inch (19 mm) wide, are found in clusters in terminal racemes. Their sweet

Linum grandiflorum

Description: This is a slender and gracefully erect plant, which is very tolerant and produces wide, open flowers at the stem tips. It may grow in poor soil but prefers a moderately fertile one and will flower throughout the season. It will not persist in extremes of heat. Flowers are up to 1½ inches (40 mm) wide.
Other colors: Scarlet, purple, red.
Varieties/cultivars: 'Coccineum' (scarlet), 'Caeruleum' (bluish-purple), 'Roseum' (rose pink), 'Rubrum' (deep-red).

Linaria maroccana
TOADFLAX, BABY SNAPDRAGON, FAIRY FLAX

Family: SCROPHULARIACEAE
Origin: Morocco.
Flowering time: Spring.
Climatic zone: 6, 7, 8, 9, 10.
Dimensions: 12–18 inches (300–450 mm) high.
Description: This low-growing annual is mostly used as a border plant near other low-growing annuals. It should be densely planted to make a show of the delicate, small flowers, which are about 1 inch (25 mm) long and ½ inch (15 mm) wide and look like miniature snapdragons with a long spur. They are found only in soft, pastel shades and most of them have a yellow-spotted throat. Any well-drained soil will suffice, but take care not to overwater.
Other colors: Red, purple, and occasionally dark-blue.
Varieties/cultivars: 'Excelsior', 'Fairy Bouquet' (dwarf).

Linum grandiflorum
SCARLET FLAX

Family: LINACEAE
Origin: North Africa.
Flowering time: Summer.
Climatic zone: 6, 7, 8, 9, 10.
Dimensions: Up to 18 inches (450 mm) tall.

Malcolmia maritima

fragrance is reminiscent of stock. Matures quickly if planted in a warm, sunny position, in rich, well-drained soil.

Other colors: Red, purple, white.

Matthiola incana

STOCK, BROMPTON STOCK, GILLYFLOWER ○

Family: CRUCIFERAE
Origin: Mediterranean region.
Flowering time: Spring.
Climatic zone: 7, 8, 9.
Dimensions: Up to 2½ feet (750 mm) high.
Description: Stock is much sought after. With its excellent, lasting qualities, good color range, and delightful fragrance, it is ideal for floral decoration. Varieties produce long (up to 18 inches (450 mm)) stems of tight, either single or double flowers. The single flowers have the stronger perfume, but the doubles are more showy. Individual flowers are only 1 inch (25 mm) wide but there are many of them on strong upright stems. The plant may be grown as either an annual or a biennial. The soil should be enriched with lime and plenty of organic matter before planting. Water well for good results.
Other colors: White, yellow, purple, red.

Matthiola incana cultivar

Varieties/cultivars: 'Perfection', 'Hi-double' (Trisomic), 'Giant Column' (tall heads of flowers). 'Austral' (slightly dwarf to 18 inches (450 mm)), 'Dwarf' (up to 12 inches (330 mm) high).

Petunia x hybrida

PETUNIA ○

Family: SOLANACEAE
Origin: Hybrid.
Flowering time: Summer.
Climatic zone: 6, 7, 8, 9, 10.
Dimensions: Up to 18 inches (450 mm) high.
Description: The petunia in any one of its many forms is the most universally known and widely used annual in the world. It is an asset anywhere with bright summer colors in all shades. The flowers are up to 4 inches (100 mm) wide, rather flat, but sometimes fringed and frilled on the edges. They are often striped in lines from the center or in contrasting-colored circles. They may also have contrasting vein markings. The plants have soft stems and may trail, which makes them attractive in hanging baskets or bowls in good sunlight. Fertile soil and a sunny position are essential.
Other colors: All colours, including white, yellow, and mixtures of these.
Varieties/cultivars: 'Bonanza', 'Dazzler', 'Color Parade', 'Giant Victorious', 'Fringed', and many others.

Petunia x hybrida cultivar

Phlox drummondii
ANNUAL PHLOX, DRUMMOND PHLOX, TEXAN PRIDE

Family: POLEMONIACEAE
Origin: Texas.
Flowering time: Summer.
Climatic zone: 6, 7, 8, 9, 10.
Dimensions: Up to 18 inches (450 mm) high.
Description: This is a popular summer annual which grows readily in sunny situations. The separate flowers are up to 1½ inches (35 mm) wide and make a vivid show because they are closely clustered. All colors are available as well as fringed bicolors or contrasting centers. Generally phlox is not used as a cut flower, but lasts well enough to be used in small posies or bowls. Light, dry, and well-drained soils give the best results. Take care not to overwater.
Other colors: All colors and mixtures.
Varieties/cultivars: 'Compact' (dwarf form), 'Twinkle' (star-like), 'Bright Eyes', 'Derwent'.

Portulaca grandiflora
ROSE MOSS, SUN MOSS, WAX PINK

Other common names: SUN PLANT, GARDEN PORTULACA
Family: PORTULACACEAE
Origin: Brazil–Argentina.
Flowering time: Midsummer.
Climatic zone: 6, 7, 8, 9, 10.
Dimensions: Up to 5 inches (125 mm) high.
Description: Portulacas have soft, succulent stems and a trailing habit, and can be used as groundcover or a border. The flowers, which are about 1½ inches (35 mm) wide, and may be single or double, are borne on short stems and are found in bright, clear colors with, occasionally, tiny, contrasting-colored centers. They open in the heat of the day and close at night or in cloudy conditions. Portulacas prefer hot, dry climates.
Other colors: White, yellow, red, purple.
Varieties/cultivars: 'Sunglow', 'Sunnybank'.

Climatic zone: 7, 8, 9.
Dimensions: Up to 3 feet (approx. 1 meter) high.
Description: This lovely, soft-stemmed plant forms an erect, dense, compact mass of pale-green foliage which is ferny in appearance and attractive. It prefers a cool, sheltered position and produces masses of small flowers up to 1 inch (25 mm) wide in pastel tonings with vein-like markings and a contrasting-colored rim. The flowers have an upper and lower lip shaped like a small orchid. They are very decorative in hanging baskets, but are not ideal for picking. Plant in semishade in rich, moist, and well-drained soil. Pinch back new growth to encourage more blooms. Depending on the climate, this plant suits either a summer garden bed or a greenhouse.
Other colors: White, red, mauve, cream.
Varieties/cultivars: 'Dwarf Bouquet', 'Giant Hybrid', 'Hit Parade'.

Silene pendula
NODDING CATCHFLY

Family: CARYOPHYLLACEAE
Origin: Mediterranean region–Caucasus, southern U.S.S.R.
Flowering time: Summer.
Climatic zone: 6, 7, 8, 9.
Dimensions: Up to 18 inches (300 mm) high.
Description: This hardy annual is not freely grown. It forms a bushy, densely-leaved plant which bears clusters of small flowers up to 1 inch (25 mm) wide.

Portulaca grandiflora cultivar

Schizanthus pinnatus
BUTTERFLY FLOWER, POOR MAN'S ORCHID

Family: SOLANACEAE
Origin: Chile.
Flowering time: Spring–summer.

Phlox drummondii

Schizanthus pinnatus

64

The flower heads are not dense and although delicate in appearance, they are hardy. Can be grown successfully in a wide range of soils, providing drainage is good.

Other colors: Carmine, occasionally white.

Varieties/cultivars: 'Ruberrima Bonnettii', 'Compacta'.

Silene pendula ○

Viola x wittrockiana
PANSY, HEARTSEASE, LADIES' DELIGHT

Family: VIOLACEAE
Origin: Hybrid.
Flowering time: Spring-winter.
Climatic zone: 6, 7, 8, 9.
Dimensions: Up to 9 inches (225 mm) high.
Description: Pansies are one of the best known of the annual, flowering plants. The foliage spreads to about 12 inches (30 mm) wide, from which single-stemmed flowers appear face-up. They are available in all shades, in separate colors or with contrasting marks and veining. The flat flowers have four petals in opposite, overlapping pairs. They are suitable for posies or small vases and bloom for a long period. Pansies often have a very velvety texture, and prefer semishaded conditions and a moderately rich, moist soil.
Other colors: Purple, blue, maroon, red, yellow, orange, white.
Varieties/cultivars: 'Can Can', 'Roggli', 'Swiss Giants', 'Jumbo'.

Xeranthemum annuum
EVERLASTING, ANNUAL EVERLASTING, IMMORTELLE ○

Family: COMPOSITAE
Origin: Southeastern-central Europe.
Flowering time: Summer.
Climatic zone: 7, 8, 9, 10.
Dimensions: Up to 2 feet (600 mm) high.
Description: This very hardy annual will grow in poor soil, produce many single-stemmed flowers typically daisy-like in shape, but with shiny, papery petals and a firm seed center. The flowers cover the bushes although, individually, they are only up to 1½ inches (40 mm) wide. They are very useful as cut flowers and dry well also.
Other colors: White, mauve, purple.
Varieties/cultivars: 'Liguilosum'.

Viola x wittrockiana cultivar

Xeranthemum annuum

Cyclamen neapolitanum

Cyclamen neapolitanum syn. *C. hederifolium*
ROCK CYCLAMEN, COMMON CYCLAMEN (U.K.), SOWBREAD

Family: PRIMULACEAE
Origin: Southern Europe.
Flowering time: Late summer–autumn.
Climatic zone: 7, 8, 9.
Dimensions: Up to 4 inches (100 mm) high.
Description: Rock cyclamen, with its unusual rose or white petals turned backwards to resemble shuttlecocks, was used in ancient times as an ingredient in love potions. Most of the flowers are produced before the deep green and silver leaves fully expand, the first flowers appearing in late summer before any leaf shows. This cyclamen will flower for up to eight weeks. A pretty addition to a fernery it can also be grown indoors in pots. Use fertilizer sparingly. Some bulbs have been known to produce for over 100 years. Allow it to colonize in light shade beneath trees or in garden pockets. Avoid excessive use of water.
Other colors: White, purple, red.

Lilium rubellum
LILY

Family: LILIACEAE
Origin: Japan.
Flowering time: Early–midsummer.
Climatic zone: 6, 7, 8, 9.
Dimensions: Up to 2 feet (600 mm) high.
Description: This oriental hybrid produces clusters of fragrant, pink flowers. It can be planted among herbaceous perennials or in lightly wooded areas. Water settings can be enhanced by including it among stones or pebbles. Adaptable to most good,

Amaryllis belladonna

Anemone nemorosa

Amaryllis belladonna
BELLADONNA LILY, NAKED LADY

Family: AMARYLLIDACEAE
Origin: South Africa.
Flowering time: Summer–autumn.
Climatic zone: 8, 9, 10.
Dimensions: Up to 3 feet (1 meter) high.
Description: Named after a shepherdess in Greek mythology, this legendary plant has numerous fragrant trumpet-shaped flowers borne on long stems. Strap-shaped leaves usually appear after the plant blooms. If left undisturbed in a sheltered position, bulbs will multiply and give a massed display. It is suitable for borders along a gravel drive or against sunny fences. Cut flowers add elegance indoors. Water well when buds appear. Belladonna lily can be cultivated in pots for indoor display.
Varieties/cultivars: 'Rubra'.

Anemone nemorosa
WOOD ANEMONE, FAIRY'S WINDFLOWER

Family: RANUNCULACEAE
Origin: Europe including U.K.
Flowering time: Spring.
Climatic zone: 5, 6, 7, 8.
Dimensions: Up to 12 inches (300 mm) high.
Description: This pretty, pink perennial is a delightful flower to associate with ferns and primroses and will spread rapidly in woodland settings. The flowers are solitary with 6 sepals. Moist soil in a protected position suits it best. It will do well near water features in the garden.
Other colors: Blue, white.
Varieties/cultivars: 'Wilkes white', 'Flore Pleno'.

well-drained soils, it prefers an open sunny position. Light frosts will not affect it adversely, but it is sensitive to drought and excessive feeding. Large tubs of lilies look particularly effective at the entrance to a house or by the gate.

Lilium rubellum

Nerine bowdenii
SPIDER LILY

Family: AMARYLLIDACEAE
Origin: South Africa.
Flowering time: Autumn.
Climatic zone: 7, 8, 9.
Dimensions: Up to 18 inches (450 mm) high.
Description: A hardy grower with eight or more tubular flowers produced on long stems, spider lily is ideally suited for planting in rock gardens, near water, in tubs on patios or verandahs. The graceful spider-like flowers enhance trees when grown at their base. After bulbs have been planted they should be left undisturbed for several years until clumps form. They benefit from an application of general fertilizer in spring. Maintain adequate moisture.
Other colors: Red.
Varieties/cultivars: 'Pink Beauty', 'Hera', 'Fenwick's Variety'.

Nerine bowdenii

Oxalis adenophylla
MOUNTAIN SOURSOP,
WOOD SORREL (U.S.A.),
OXALIS

Family: OXALIDACEAE
Origin: Chile and Argentina.
Flowering time: Summer, outdoors; winter, indoors.
Climatic zone: 8, 9.
Dimensions: Up to 4 inches (100 mm) high.
Description: Oxalis is often overlooked as a garden flower because of its weed reputation. O. adenophylla is not a weed, but a pretty, long-flowering perennial adaptable to rock gardens, pot culture, and window boxes. Softly colored, gray-green crinkled leaves accompany pale lilac/pink flowers. Although termed wood sorrel, this is not one for making soup from. Like many of the 800 species of Oxalis, this plant has a sour juice when extracted. Grow it in a cool situation in neutral or slightly alkaline soil. It can be grown indoors in winter.
Other colors: Red, purple, yellow, white.

Oxalis adenophylla

Primula malacoides
FAIRY PRIMROSE

Family: PRIMULACEAE
Origin: China.
Flowering time: Spring.
Climatic zone: 8.
Dimensions: Up to 18 inches (450 mm) high.
Description: Associated with the arrival of spring, this plant will thrive in wooded situations or in the vicinity of water gardens and is a versatile plant for pots, edges, borders, rock gardens, and window boxes. P. malacoides flowers in various shades of rose and lavender to pure white. It prefers a moist, cool position with some sun. In colder

climates, a greenhouse is essential. Propagation is by seed or division.
Other colors: White, red, purple.

Primula malacoides

Rhodohypoxis baurii
ROSE GRASS

Family: HYPOXIDACEAE
Origin: South Africa.
Flowering time: Spring-summer.
Climatic zone: 8, 9.
Dimensions: Up to 4 inches (100 mm) high.
Description: A rhizomatous, herbaceous perennial, rose grass derived its botanical name from the Greek 'rhodon' meaning rose. The tufted foliage is hairy and masses of rose-colored flowers show pale undersides. This small, slow-growing plant is an attractive rock garden addition. A sheltered, sunny site is best. The corm-like rhizome should be located in lime-free and moist, well-drained garden soil. An easy plant to look after, it is seldom attacked by garden pests.
Other colors: White.
Varieties/cultivars: 'Apple Blossom', 'Platypetala'.

Rhodohypoxis baurii

CLIMBERS

Antigonon leptopus
CORAL VINE, CORALLITA, MOUNTAIN ROSE ○ ◐

Other common names: QUEEN'S WREATH
Family: POLYGONACEAE
Origin: Mexico.
Flowering time: Mid-summer–autumn.
Climatic zone: 9, 10.
Description: Fast-growing, *Antigonon* climbs trees, fences, or trellises by attaching itself with small, strong tendrils. Flower sprays are numerous and make a spectacular display in summer. Treat it as a perennial in cooler districts, or in very hot zones where it may burn if planted in a windy exposed position. It can be used as a groundcover for sloping banks or sunny hillsides, or as a cover over a pergola. The arrow or heart-shaped leaves are an attractive addition to the bright floral display.
Other colors: White, red.

Bauhinia corymbosa

Clematis montana 'Rubens'
PINK ANEMONE CLEMATIS (U.S.A.), TRAVELLER'S JOY ○ ◐

Family: RANUNCULACEAE
Origin: Himalayas – western China.
Flowering time: Spring–summer.
Climatic zone: 5, 6, 7, 8, 9.
Description: Pink anemone clematis has a dainty, fragrant flower with four petals in the shape of a cross. The flowers are rose-pink, fading to light pink, and are about 2 inches (50 mm) across. This deciduous vine is thin-stemmed and needs support during its spring–summer growing period when it is covered with a mass of blooms. In cold climates it flowers in early summer. It likes a warm sunny position, but does not like direct sun on the soil over the roots. Protect it by putting plenty of compost round its roots. It is best left unpruned, but if pruning is necessary, remove unwanted stems during the growing season.

Antigonon leptopus

Bauhinia corymbosa
CLIMBING BAUHINIA ○

Family: LEGUMINOSAE
Origin: South East Asia.
Flowering time: Spring and autumn.
Climatic zone: 9, 10.
Description: Orchid-like flowers with red stamens appear on this evergreen plant in spring and autumn. The typical *Bauhinia* leaves, folded in half, are small and dainty and have reddish, hairy stems. A warm and sunny spot with rich soil will help this rather slow-developing vine to reach maximum growth. Some support will be necessary to train this sprawling plant as a climber. A warm climate plant, it needs full sun, good drainage, and a protected position. It is well worth growing for its attractive appearance all year.

Lonicera x americana
HONEYSUCKLE ○

Family: CAPRIFOLIACEAE
Origin: Hybrid.
Flowering time: Summer.
Climatic zone: 7, 8, 9.
Description: A vigorous, deciduous climber, this honeysuckle has large clusters of fragrant, yellowish-white flowers that are tinged with pink when in bud. Leaves are broad, and pointed at the tip. May be pruned after flowering, or in winter, to prevent it from becoming too prolific. Well-drained, moist soil and a sunny or partially shaded position give best results.

Lonicera x americana

Clematis montana 'Rubens'

68

Mandevilla sanderi
BRAZILIAN JASMINE, DIPLADENIA (Aust.), CHILEAN JASMINE (U.K.) ○ ◑

Family: APOCYNACEAE
Origin: Brazil.
Flowering time: Almost all year.
Climatic zone: 9, 10.
Description: Unlike the white *Mandevilla*, this beautiful little vine does not have fragrant flowers, but its clear pink, 3-inch (75-mm) blooms continue nearly all year provided conditions are warm enough. Grow as a tub plant with a trellis or wire support, or train over a lattice or trellis. Protect it from harsh sun, and provide rich soil and ample water for a delightful patio plant. In very warm zones, Brazilian jasmine can be grown in full shade, but filtered light is best. In cool areas, it does well as a greenhouse or house plant.

Mandevilla sanderi

Mandevilla splendens syn. *Dipladenia splendens*
CHILEAN JASMINE ○ ◑

Family: APOCYNACEAE
Origin: Southeastern Brazil.
Flowering time: Most of the year.
Climatic zone: 9, 10.
Description: Magnificent, clear pink flowers are scattered over this lovely vine almost all year long in warm climates. In cooler areas, a greenhouse is often necessary. It is evergreen, and although it will reach 20 feet (6 meters) if grown in the best position in the ground, it is usually treated as a container plant for patios. Twining stems will climb on to a trellis or wire support. A slender pole or frame is required for container growing, or it can be pruned to a low shrubby shape. Protect it from harsh sun and give regular water and deep compost for best results.

Mandevilla splendens

Pandorea jasminoides 'Rosea'
BOWER OF BEAUTY, BOWER PLANT ○ ◑

Family: BIGNONIACEAE
Origin: Cultivar.
Flowering time: Summer–autumn.
Climatic zone: 9, 10.
Description: An evergreen, quick-growing climber, *Pandorea* has attractive, glossy, compound leaves with five to nine leaflets. The trumpet-shaped flowers are 2 inches (50 mm) long, and are pinkish-white streaked with pink or red inside the throat. Protect it from strong winds and give it adequate support for maximum cover over a fence, or train it to climb up a pillar. It is not tolerant of cold or frost, so in colder areas a greenhouse is required. It does best with regular watering and good soil. The shiny leaves make it a handsome plant when the flowers have finished.

Pandorea jasminoides 'Rosea'

Pelargonium peltatum cultivar

Pelargonium peltatum
IVY GERANIUM, IVY-
LEAVED GERANIUM (U.K.)

Family: GERANIACEAE
Origin: Eastern South Africa.
Flowering time: All year.
Climatic zone: All zones.
Description: Widely grown for its continual flowering habit and range of brightly colored flowers, the ivy geranium can tolerate sunny conditions, or partial shade. It is treated as an annual in cold districts, when it is grown just for the summer months. It can be used in hanging baskets, window boxes, pots, tubs, or can be tied to and trained up a lattice or wire frame to cover a fence or wall. The ivy-like, pointed, five-lobed leaves are shiny and attractive and ivy geranium is one of the most adaptable and versatile light trailing plants.
Other colors: White, red, purple.
Varieties/cultivars: Many including 'Amethyst', 'Galilee', 'Gardenia', 'Gloire d'Orleans', 'The Pearl'.

Podranea ricasoliana
PORT ST. JOHN CREEPER,
PINK TECOMA

Family: BIGNONIACEAE
Origin: South Africa.
Flowering time: Summer.
Climatic zone: 9, 10.
Description: The flowers appear above

Rosa 'Cecile Brunner'

the leaves on this lovely climber, and almost cover the plant. It is evergreen with glossy deep-green leaves divided into seven to eleven leaflets. The flowers are trumpet-shaped, 2 inches (50 mm) long, with rounded lobes, and are produced in large clusters. Support is needed to hold the plant against a wall or fence, or it can be allowed to grow into a wide, flowing shrub which will "lean" against a fence. It is tolerant of wind and will withstand a light frost, but in cold climates a greenhouse is essential.

Rosa 'Cecile Brunner'
PINK CLIMBING ROSE,
CLIMBING CECILE BRUNNER
(U.K.)

Family: ROSACEAE
Origin: Hybrid.
Flowering time: Summer.
Climatic zone: 5, 6, 7, 8, 9.
Description: The beautifully shaped shell-pink miniature flowers of 'Cecile Brunner' are often found among the red-colored new growth of the leaves. The plant has a tendency to be shrubby, but it can reach up to 15 feet (5 meters) or more. Give it plenty of room to spread, as the bright green foliage is attractive and will disguise an ugly corner. Even when it has become wide and thick, it still has a rather open, airy appearance. The flowers have a light, delicate fragrance.

Podranea ricasoliana

70

Rosa 'Dorothy Perkins'

Rosa 'Dorothy Perkins'
PINK CLIMBING ROSE,
PINK RAMBLER (U.K.)

○

Family: ROSACEAE
Origin: Hybrid.
Flowering time: Summer.
Climatic zone: 5, 6, 7, 8, 9.
Description: This is a beautiful little rose which has lost some popularity, due to its short blooming period and susceptibility to mildew. The non-recurrent flowers are small, dainty, double, and rosette-like. Bright pink, slightly fragrant, they are produced prolifically during early summer. Because of its vigorous growth and long, arching habit, it is often used for grafting onto a tall stem to create a weeping standard rose. The tiny buds are favorites for old-fashioned posies or small flower arrangements.

Tecomanthe hillii
PINK TRUMPET VINE

◑

Family: BIGNONIACEAE
Origin: Australia (Northeastern coast).
Flowering time: Summer.
Climatic zone: 9, 10.
Description: Rosy flowers marked with purplish lines make the pink trumpet

Tecomanthe hillii

---

vine an unusual climber. It has a vigorous twining habit, and dark-green pinnate leaves with prominent veins. The flowers are borne in drooping clusters, and are bell-shaped. Fairly humid conditions are preferred, so it is most successful in hotter climates. In other areas, a greenhouse may be necessary. It is a very showy climber on a fence or trellis in a semishaded position.

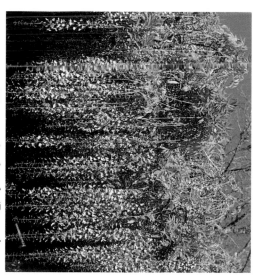

Wisteria floribunda 'Rosea'

Wisteria floribunda 'Rosea'
PINK WISTERIA

○

Family: LEGUMINOSAE
Origin: Cultivar.
Flowering time: Late spring–early summer.
Climatic zone: 4, 5, 6, 7, 8, 9.
Description: 'Rosea' is the pink form of the commonly grown Japanese wisteria. Superbly fragrant, pea flowers hang in profusion in long sprays. The flowers open progressively from the base to the tip of the spray. It differs from the Chinese wisteria in the number of leaflets (fifteen to nineteen), and in its longer flower sprays. It usually blooms a few weeks later. It is best grown over a pergola where its spectacular beauty can be seen to advantage. It needs pruning during the summer growing season, and shaping during the winter.

Acanthus mollis 'Latifolius'

Acanthus mollis 'Latifolius'
BEAR'S-BREECH, OYSTER PLANT

Family: ACANTHACEAE
Origin: Cultivar.
Flowering time: Summer.
Climatic zone: 6, 7, 8, 9.
Dimensions: Up to 4½ feet (over 1 meter) high.
Description: *Acanthus mollis* is much desired as a border and specimen plant, both for its handsome, deeply-cut and glossy foliage and its showy flowers on spikes up to 18 inches (450 mm) long. Given a sheltered, sunny position, it flowers profusely and likes a moderately rich, well-drained loam. *Acanthus* is slow to establish but forms a large clump once settled. It is propagated by seed sown in spring, or by root division in autumn or spring. Prune it by removing spent flowers and leaves. It attracts snails.
Other colors: White, lilac, purple.

Alcea rosea

Alcea rosea syn. *Althaea rosea*
HOLLYHOCK

Family: MALVACEAE
Origin: Eastern Mediterranean region.
Flowering time: Summer.
Climatic zone: 4, 5, 6, 7, 8, 9.
Dimensions: 5–9 feet (2–3 meters) high.
Description: Hollyhocks are at their best when grown as a backdrop to a profuse summer border, and given the shelter and support of a wall. They will stand sentinel to delphiniums, foxgloves, zinnias, rudbeckias, and all the other dazzling blooms of summer. They require fairly rich, well-drained soil, and plenty of water in dry periods. Short-lived, they are often treated as biennials. To promote longer life, remove flower stalks at the base as soon as the flowers fade. Hollyhocks are subject to attack by red spider and rust. They are attractive in mixed flower arrangements.
Other colors: White, purple, red, yellow.
Varieties/cultivars: 'Chater's Improved', 'Summer Carnival', 'Begonia Flowered'.

Armeria pseudarmeria

Description: *Antennaria dioica* is a useful mat-forming rockery plant because of its creeping, fast-growing habit. Its flowers are small, tubular and borne in terminal clusters, and the foliage is tufted and woolly in appearance. Although the plant grows as well in rich, moist soils as in dry, sandy conditions, it nevertheless needs good drainage. It is propagated by seed in autumn or spring or by division and looks well planted with *Achillea x lewisii* (King Edward). It has no particular value as a cut flower.
Other colors: White, rose-red.
Varieties/cultivars: 'Minima', 'Rosea', 'Rubra'.

Antennaria dioica
CAT'S FOOT, PUSSY TOES (U.S.A.), MOUNTAIN EVERLASTING

Family: COMPOSITAE
Origin: Eurasia.
Flowering time: Late spring.
Climatic zone: 4, 5, 6, 7, 8.
Dimensions: Up to 6 inches (150 mm) high.

Armeria pseudarmeria
THRIFT, PLANTAIN THRIFT

Family: PLUMBAGINACEAE
Origin: Portugal.
Flowering time: Summer.
Climatic zone: 6, 7, 8, 9.
Dimensions: 1½–2 feet (450–600 mm) high.
Description: Plantain thrift is a relatively tall variety of *Armeria* and is therefore more useful in the herbaceous border than the lower-growing common thrift, *A. maritima*. With its round flower heads borne on stiff stalks and its grass-like, tufted foliage, it is easy to grow in most soils, but thrives in well-drained, sandy loam. Removing spent blooms prolongs flowering. Easily propagated by division of clumps in autumn, plantain thrift makes a long-lasting pot specimen in cool conditions and is a good cut flower.
Other colors: White, red.
Varieties/cultivars: 'Bees Ruby'.

Antennaria dioica

Aster novae-angliae

Aster novi-belgii 'Patricia Ballard'

Astrantia maxima

Aubrieta deltoidea cultivar

Aster novae-angliae

NEW ENGLAND ASTER
(U.S.A.), MICHAELMAS DAISY
(U.K.), EASTER DAISY (Aust.) ○

Family: COMPOSITAE
Origin: Eastern North America.
Flowering time: Late summer–autumn.
Climatic zone: 4, 5, 6, 7, 8, 9.
Dimensions: 3–5 feet (nearly 2 meters) high.
Description: *Aster novae-angliae* brings a wonderful splash of color to the autumn garden. It is equally lovely as a late-flowerer in the summer border or grown in the smaller space of a city garden. Its foliage is dense and grayish-green; the flowers are large, and clustered on strong, hairy stems. It prefers well-mulched, moist, fertile soil that is well-drained and benefits from complete fertilizer in spring and summer. It has an unhappy habit of closing at night. Use it as a cut flower in indoor decorating.
Other colors: Blue, purple.
Varieties/cultivars: 'Alma Potschke', 'Barr's Pink', 'Harrington Pink', 'Ryecroft Purple'.

Aster novi-belgii 'Patricia Ballard'

NEW YORK ASTER (U.S.A.),
MICHAELMAS DAISY (U.K.),
EASTER DAISY (Aust.) ○

Family: COMPOSITAE
Origin: Cultivar.
Flowering time: Late summer–autumn.
Climatic zone: 5, 6, 7, 8, 9.
Dimensions: Up to 3 feet (900 mm) high.
Description: What color the New York aster brings to the autumn garden! Plant it against a backdrop of autumn leaves and scarlet berry colors and highlight it by the white of the Japanese windflower. It prefers well-composted, moist, and well-drained soil. Fertilizer in spring and summer, and plenty of water in dry periods are essential. Prune it by cutting spent flower stems to ground level. New York aster provides good cut flowers.

Aubrieta deltoidea

FALSE ROCK CRESS,
AUBRIETA (U.K.) ○ ◐

Family: CRUCIFERAE
Origin: Southern Greece, Sicily.
Flowering time: Spring–early summer.
Climatic zone: 5, 6, 7, 8, 9.
Dimensions: Up to 6 inches (150 mm) high.
Description: Aubrieta is a cheerful, profusely flowering rockery or border-edging plant. Its flowers appear in loose clusters, held above the foliage. They come in both single and double forms. Its grayish-green, downy leaves form a spreading mat which can be invasive if not trimmed back. Propagation is by seed sown in spring or by cuttings. Well-drained, light soil is required for best results where summers are mild.
Other colors: Mauve, lilac, purple, blue, white.
Varieties/cultivars: Several cultivars include 'Borsch's White', 'Gloriosa', 'Greencourt Purple', 'Mrs. Rodewald', 'Purple Gem', 'Variegata'.

Astrantia maxima syn. *A. helleborifolia*

MASTERWORT ○ ◐

Family: UMBELLIFERAE
Origin: Caucasus, Turkey.
Flowering time: Summer.
Climatic zone: 4, 5, 6, 7, 8, 9.
Dimensions: Up to 2 feet (600 mm) high.
Description: Masterwort, with its tall stems, numerous delicate flowers, and interesting foliage, is best suited to wild or cottage gardens. The flowers may be cut and dried for use in floral arrangements. Any ordinary garden soil suits masterwort, but it needs adequate water in summer. Propagate it by root division or by seed.

Begonia x semperflorens-cultorum

Begonia x semperflorens-cultorum syn.
B. semperflorens, B. cucculata var.
hookeri
WAX BEGONIA

Family: BEGONIACEAE
Origin: Hybrid.
Flowering time: Summer.
Climatic zone: 3, 4, 5, 6, 7, 8, 9, 10.
Dimensions: Up to 18 inches (450 mm) high.
Description: A useful perennial with fleshy foliage and showy clusters of pink flowers, *Begonia* requires a rich, moist soil and semishaded conditions. Protection from summer midday sun is essential. Often grown as a summer bedding plant among annuals and other perennials, it likes plenty of water during summer and several applications of liquid plant food to encourage good flower production. It is not difficult to propagate from stem or leaf cuttings in spring or summer, or raise from seed.
Other colors: Red, pink, white, doubles and singles, bronze and purple foliage.
Varieties/cultivars: Many cultivars are available including 'Carmen', 'Flamingo', 'Galaxy', 'Indian Maid', 'Linda', 'Organdy'.

Bergenia cordifolia
HEARTLEAF
BERGENIA, SAXIFRAGE,
MEGASEA (U.K.)

Family: SAXIFRAGACEAE
Origin: Siberia.
Flowering time: Late winter-spring.
Climatic zone: 3, 4, 5, 6, 7, 8, 9, 10.
Dimensions: 12–18 inches (300–450 mm) high.

Bergenia cordifolia hybrid cultivar

Description: Heartleaf bergenia takes its name from its large, heart-shaped leaves which are thick, fleshy, and evergreen, making a very attractive groundcover or border edging, especially in damp and shaded positions. The flowers are in large clusters on sturdy stems and, in mild climates, bloom in winter. Remove spent flower heads to prolong flowering. Bergenia will grow in any soil but thrives with organic mulch and plenty of water during dry spells. Propagate by root division from autumn to spring.
Other colors: White, red, lilac.
Varieties/cultivars: 'Purpurea', 'Perfecta'.

Bergenia x schmidtii
BERGENIA,
MEGASEA

Family: SAXIFRAGACEAE
Origin: Hybrid.
Flowering time: Late winter-late spring.

Bergenia x schmidtii

Climatic zone: 4, 5, 6, 7, 8, 9.
Dimensions: 9–18 inches (225–450 mm) high.
Description: This useful and hardy perennial has large, thick, almost leathery leaves and a showy display of pink flowers borne in nodding flower heads. It really thrives in moderately rich and well-drained soil, but can survive in less favorable conditions, including rocky and poor soils. Plant it in light shade, or in full sun if moisture is provided.

Centaurea hypoleuca 'John Coutts'

Centaurea hypoleuca 'John Coutts'
PINK CORNFLOWER

Family: COMPOSITAE
Origin: Cultivar.
Flowering time: Summer.
Climatic zone: 4, 5, 6, 7, 8, 9.
Dimensions: 1½–2 feet (450–600 mm) high.
Description: The pink cornflower, with its deep rose-colored and fringed ray flowers, looks stunning in a massed border display. Its lobed leaves, green on the surface and whitish underneath, are also attractive. It prefers dry, well-drained soil and an open position. Propagate by dividing established clumps in autumn or spring. The cut flowers are attractive in floral decorations.

Chelone lyonii
PINK TURTLEHEAD

Family: SCROPHULARIACEAE
Origin: Southeastern United States.
Flowering time: Summer-autumn.
Climatic zone: 4, 5, 6, 7, 8, 9.

Dimensions: Up to 3 feet (1 meter) high.
Description: C. lyonii is most desirable in the summer garden for both its dark, glossy foliage, and its slightly hooded, rosy-pink flowers borne on a terminal spike. It prefers partial shade and moist, humus-enriched soil. Propagate it from seed sown in spring or root division in autumn or spring.

Chelone lyonii

Coronilla varia
CROWN VETCH ○

Family: LEGUMINOSAE
Origin: Central and southern Europe.
Flowering time: Summer.
Climatic zone: 4, 5, 6, 7, 8, 9, 10.
Dimensions: Up to 18 inches (450 mm) high.
Description: This sprawling perennial can be invasive in the garden. It is ideal as a groundcover for steep, sunny banks or in borders. The long tricolored flowers of pink, rose, and white are pea-shaped. These dense clusters are most attractive against their ferny foliage, which closes up at night. Fast-growing, crown vetch will cover mounds or building rubble and control erosion if the soil is dry. Propagation is by seed.
Varieties/cultivars: 'Aurea', 'Penngift'.

Coronilla varia

Darmera peltata

Darmera peltata syn. *Peltiphyllum peltatum, Saxifraga peltatum*
UMBRELLA PLANT, ○ ◐
INDIAN RHUBARB

Family: SAXIFRAGACEAE
Origin: California, Oregon.
Flowering time: Spring.
Climatic zone: 6, 7, 8, 9.
Dimensions: Up to 4 feet (over 1 meter) high.
Description: This moisture-loving perennial has pale pink flowers that form clusters on sturdy stems about 2 feet (600 mm) high. The leaves are lotus-like and borne at the top of stems growing between 3 and 4 feet (approx. 1 meter) high. It is a suitable plant for moist areas beside ponds or streams but, because it can become very invasive, it is unsuitable for small gardens. The Californian Indians ate the peeled leaf stalks, hence the name "Indian rhubarb". Propagate it by root division or seed.
Other colors: White.
Varieties/cultivars: 'Nanum' (dwarf).

Dianthus barbatus

Dianthus barbatus
SWEET WILLIAM ○

Family: CARYOPHYLLACEAE
Origin: Southern Europe and Mediterranean region.
Flowering time: Summer.
Climatic zone: 6, 7, 8, 9.
Dimensions: Up to 16 inches (400 mm) high.
Description: Once known as the divine flower of Jupiter and Zeus, this perennial will bloom for six to ten weeks. Sweetly scented flowers are single or double and occur in a variety of colors. It is suitable for borders, edges, or potted on garden steps and decks. Related to the carnation and pinks family, *Dianthus* likes an open sunny position in sandy loam. Generous colorful heads will result from an application of lime and compost when planting.
Other colors: Red, purple, white.
Varieties/cultivars: 'Giant white', 'Dunnets dark crimson', Dwarf mixed.

Dianthus caryophyllus
CARNATION, CLOVE PINK ○

Family: CARYOPHYLLACEAE
Origin: Central Europe.
Flowering time: Summer.
Climatic zone: 7, 8, 9.
Dimensions: Up to 2 feet (600 mm) high.
Description: *Dianthus caryophyllus,* known and used as a garland flower from the time of the Norman conquest, and referred to as "the divine flower" by the ancient Greeks, is the parent of modern carnations. Commonly referred to now as "the perpetual", carnation is a perennial with multi-petaled flowers, that blooms all year round. A wide choice of colors is available. There are

Dianthus caryophyllus hybrid

also border carnations available, which flower only once a year and have a bushier growth than the perpetuals. Plant carnations in light, sandy soil mixed with compost and lime. Stakes are required for support when plants grow tall. Carnations dislike wet, sunless winters so need a greenhouse environment in these areas.
Other colors: Red, yellow, white.
Varieties/cultivars: 'Dwarf Pygmy Mixed', 'Enfant de Nice', 'Giant Chabaud'.

Dianthus plumarius
COMMON PINK, GRASS PINK, COTTAGE PINK ○

Family: CARYOPHYLLACEAE
Origin: Eastern and central Europe.
Flowering time: Early summer.
Climatic zone: 5, 6, 7, 8, 9.

Dianthus plumarius

Dimensions: Up to 18 inches (450 mm) high.
Description: *D. plumarius* is thought to be the parent of the old-fashioned and modern pinks. Similar to carnations in their foliage, pinks have simpler flowers and share a wide color range. Use them as borders in beds of carnations or sweet William. Their fragrant perfume adds an old-fashioned touch to gardens. Plant cuttings in light, sandy soil mixed with compost and lime. Provide them with a sunny position protected from wind, and water regularly. They make pretty posies indoors.
Other colors: White, red, purple.

Dianthus x allwoodii
ALLWOOD PINK ○

Family: CARYOPHYLLACEAE
Origin: Hybrid.
Flowering time: Spring–summer.
Climatic zone: 7, 8, 9.
Dimensions: Up to 18 inches (450 mm) high.
Description: Allwood pink is a hybrid whose flowers are fringed or plain-petaled and can be single, double, or semidouble. The petals spray outwards in a delicate formation from their tubular base, and are found in shades of pink, red and white, or combinations of these. Planted in front of delphiniums, they produce a cottage garden effect. Allwood pink is easy to grow in any garden soil, but requires good drainage. Alkaline soil, provided with additional humus, gives best results. Prolong the flowering period by removing spent flowers.
Other colors: White, red.
Varieties/cultivars: 'Doris', 'Lilian', 'Robin', 'Timothy'.

Dianthus x allwoodii 'Doris'

Dianthus plumarius

Dicentra eximia

FRINGED BLEEDING HEART, WILD BLEEDING HEART

○ ◑

Family: FUMARIACEAE
Origin: Eastern United States.
Flowering time: Spring–summer.
Climatic zone: 3, 4, 5, 6, 7, 8, 9, 10.
Dimensions: Approx. 12 inches (300 mm) high.
Description: Fern-like foliage and rose-purple, heart-shaped blooms that bees love make this a useful border perennial. *D. eximia* is equally at home in sun or shade, providing the soil is moist. It is a good choice for corners of the garden needing a little color. Open borders, ferneries, and rock gardens will also suit it if the soil is rich, moist, and has had humus added. Propagate by root division in early spring.
Other colors: White, red.
Varieties/cultivars: 'Alba', 'Luxuriant', 'Bountiful'.

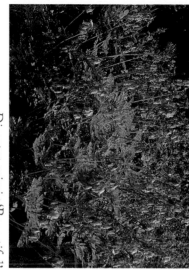

Dicentra eximia 'Bountiful'

from slugs. Lifted plants can easily be grown in a warm greenhouse.
Other colors: White.
Varieties/cultivars: 'Alba'.

Dicentra spectabilis

COMMON BLEEDING-HEART, DUTCHMAN'S BREECHES

◑ ●

Family: FUMARIACEAE
Origin: Japan, Korea, China.
Flowering time: Spring–early summer.
Climatic zone: 3, 4, 5, 6, 7, 8, 9.
Dimensions: Up to 2 feet (600 mm) high.
Description: The outstandingly elegant, heart-shaped flowers droop from arching, horizontal stems. White petals glisten at the tip of each "heart" like tears. A Japanese-style garden would suit this plant to perfection. Feature *D. spectabilis* against a cool rock wall where it will not have to compete to show its splendor. It should be planted in light sun or shade in cool, rich, well-drained soil, and protected

Digitalis x mertonensis

Digitalis x mertonensis

MERTON FOXGLOVE

◑

Family: SCROPHULARIACEAE
Origin: Hybrid.
Flowering time: Summer.
Climatic zone: 6, 7, 8, 9, 10.
Dimensions: Up to 3 feet (1 meter) high.
Description: This hybrid of *D. purpurea* is a favorite of bees and smaller insects which shelter in the drooping, rose-pink blooms. Foxglove forms a good backdrop for beds of annuals, and looks well with most cottage garden favorites. This hybrid requires frequent division in spring to maintain its perennial character. An easy plant to grow in ordinary well-drained garden soil, it benefits from an application of compost in spring.

Dodecatheon meadia

COMMON SHOOTING STAR

◑

Family: PRIMULACEAE
Origin: Eastern United States.
Flowering time: Spring–early summer.
Climatic zone: 4, 5, 6, 7, 8, 9.
Dimensions: Up to 18 inches (450 mm) high.
Description: A member of the primrose family, *D. meadia* has up to twenty rose-purple, reflexed flowers resembling shooting-stars. The yellow or purple anthers form a dart-like tip, giving the blooms their starry appearance. The foliage dies down when flowering has finished. The plant is suited to wild gardens, rock gardens, and shaded borders, and is easily grown in rich, sandy soil with plenty of organic matter. Good drainage is needed, as is moisture during the growing season. Propagate this plant by division or seed.
Other colors: Red, purple, white.
Varieties/cultivars: 'Album'.

Dicentra spectabilis

◑

Dodecatheon meadia

plenty of space to give a good display. Likes moderately rich, moist soil. Can be propagated either by division, or from seed. It benefits from an application of compost in the spring.

Eremurus robustus

Eremurus robustus
FOXTAIL LILY, DESERT CANDLES
Family: LILIACEAE
Origin: Turkestan.
Flowering time: Summer.
Climatic zone: 7, 8, 9.
Dimensions: Up to 10 feet (3 meters) high.
Description: This lofty plant, with soft-pink, closely packed flowers borne on long spikes, is a stately herbaceous perennial which can be companion-planted with delphiniums and irises. The leaves of some species of this lily are eaten in Afghanistan as a vegetable. The tubers are octopus-shaped and need to be planted 6–8 inches (150–200 mm) deep, resting on sand. Well-drained soil in an open, sunny position suits this spectacular plant best.

F. rubra looks attractive planted behind pink and white peonies in a bed. It is easy to grow in very moist garden soil, especially if humus has been added to help retain moisture. Propagate it by division of the clumps in early spring.
Other colors: Deep pink.
Varieties/cultivars: 'Venusta'.

Geranium x magnificum
CRANESBILL
Family: GERANIACEAE
Origin: Hybrid.
Flowering time: Summer.
Climatic zone: 4, 5, 6, 7, 8, 9.
Dimensions: Up to 2 feet (600 mm) high.
Description: A most successful cross between G. ibericum and G. platypetalum, this clump-forming perennial is superior to either of its parents. The wide and deeply-lobed foliage grows vigorously, while the showy violet flowers have reddish stems and bloom in profusion, measuring 1½ inches (30 mm) in diameter. It likes well-drained, moderately-rich soil and can be incorporated into a mixed bed of perennials, or grown in a large container.

Geranium x magnificum

Filipendula palmata syn. *F. multijuga*

Filipendula rubra 'Venusta'

Filipendula palmata syn. *F. multijuga*
SIBERIAN MEADOWSWEET
Family: ROSACEAE
Origin: Siberia.
Flowering time: Summer.
Climatic zone: 4, 5, 6, 7, 8, 9.
Dimensions: Up to 2½ feet (750 mm) high.
Description: A graceful perennial with large seven-lobed leaves and showy flat heads of pinkish-purple flowers. A useful addition to a mixed floral border, it has a spreading habit and requires

Filipendula rubra
QUEEN-OF-THE-PRAIRIE
Family: ROSACEAE
Origin: Eastern United States.
Flowering time: Summer.
Climatic zone: 3, 4, 5, 6, 7, 8, 9.
Dimensions: Up to 5 feet (approx. 2 meters) high.
Description: Peach-pink flowers form airy clusters on this tall, feathery border plant. Related to the rose, it needs plenty of space in a shaded part of the garden. Plant it in filtered sun under large trees or among ferns and orchids.

Geranium psilostemon.

Geranium psilostemon
ARMENIAN CRANESBILL

Family: GERANIACEAE
Origin: Turkey, Caucasus.
Flowering time: Spring–summer.
Climatic zone: 5, 6, 7, 8, 9.
Dimensions: Up to 3 feet (900 mm) high.
Description: With its brilliant magenta flowers, black-spotted at the base, and its deeply-lobed leaves, Armenian cranesbill makes an eye-catching border plant. It forms large clumps in full sun, and also looks well placed among other herbaceous perennials against a stone wall, or along pathways, or in woodland areas. It flowers freely in any light, well-drained soil, in full sun where summers are cool, but appreciates partial shade in hot areas. Propagate it by seed, cuttings, or division.
Other colors: Blue-purple.

Geranium sanguineum
BLOODY CRANESBILL

Family: GERANIACEAE
Origin: Europe, western Asia.
Flowering time: Spring–summer.
Climatic zone: 4, 5, 6, 7, 8, 9, 10.
Dimensions: Up to 18 inches (450 mm) high.
Description: An invaluable and highly adaptable plant, with flowers ranging from pale pink to reddish-purple, bloody cranesbill will tolerate full sun even in hot, dry summers. It is a good choice for open borders and sloping sites, and can also be planted among large boulders, on mounds, and in rock garden pockets. Grow it in fertile, well-drained so I mulch and water it well in summer, and give it fertilizer. Its dwarf variety, *C. sanguineum* var. *lancastrense*, forms flat carpets of large, rosy flowers.
Other colors: White, purplish-red.
Varieties/cultivars: 'Album', 'Shepherd's warning', *G. s.* var. *lancastrense*.

Gypsophila repens 'Rosea'
CREEPING BABY'S BREATH, FAIRY GRASS

Family: CARYOPHYLLACEAE
Origin: Central and southern European mountains.
Flowering time: Spring–summer.
Climatic zone: 3, 4, 5, 6, 7, 8, 9.
Dimensions: Up to 8 inches (200 mm) high.
Description: Dense mats of this dainty-flowered creeper soften sloping sites. The masses of pale pink flowers bloom profusely throughout spring and summer. It is an effective groundcover grown near paved areas or cascading over walls. Plant it in fertile, well-drained soil in a sunny position and water regularly. Apply complete fertilizer in spring and trim after flowering. Gathered in bunches, creeping baby's breath is excellent for small floral arrangements.
Other colors: White.

Geranium sanguineum

Gypsophila repens 'Rosea'

Helleborus orientalis
LENTEN ROSE, HELLEBORE

Family: RANUNCULACEAE
Origin: Greece, Turkey.
Flowering time: Late winter–spring.
Climatic zone: 4, 5, 6, 7, 8, 9.
Dimensions: Approx. 18 inches (450 mm) high.
Description: The hellebores, whose name is derived from the Greek "elein" (to injure) and "bora" (food), have been known and used since ancient times. Although the plants are poisonous, they have been used medicinally. Lenten rose is the easiest species of *Helleborus* to grow and is a popular addition to gardens. Each stem carries several cup-shaped flowers, often speckled inside. The plant grows well among trees or shrubs as a low-maintenance groundcover. Moist soil is essential.
Other colors: Pale yellow, white, green, red, maroon.
Varieties/cultivars: Several cultivars are available.

Helleborus orientalis

with large clusters of flared, trumpet-shaped flowers. Its bright purplish-pink blooms have yellow throats and together with the fern-like leaves make a good display in a sunny position in a temperate garden. It grows well in borders, rock gardens, or pots. Light soils suit it best and it needs good drainage or the roots will rot. Although it is easily propagated by seed, the seedlings take about two years to flower. In colder zones, provide winter protection. Apply a complete fertilizer in late winter.

shaped, bright green leaves accompany profuse pink flowers. Needing filtered sunlight, spanish shawl is a groundcover suited to shady edges, near ferns or in cool rock garden pockets. It prefers rich, moist, well-drained soil in a protected position. Propagation is by seed or root division. It is susceptible to drought and frost.

Heterocentron elegans

Heterocentron elegans syn. *Schizocentron elegans, Heeria elegans*
SPANISH SHAWL

Family: MELASTOMATACEAE
Origin: Mexico, Guatemala, Honduras.
Flowering time: Summer.
Climatic zone: 9, 10.
Dimensions: Up to 2 inches (50 mm) high.
Description: This perennial is shy of the sun despite its tropical origins. The stems are prostrate, with trailing or cascading branches which can reach out to 3 feet (1 meter) across. Oval or heart-

Helleborus orientalis

Liatris spicata

Liatris spicata
GAY FEATHER, BLAZING STAR

Family: COMPOSITAE
Origin: Eastern and central United States.
Flowering time: Summer–autumn.
Climatic zone: 3, 4, 5, 6, 7, 8, 9.
Dimensions: Up to 5 feet (approx. 2 meters) high.
Description: This herbaceous perennial produces tall spikes of rose-lilac flowers like fluffy feather dusters; the grass-like leaves grow in tufts. A quick-growing plant, gay feather is ideal for a mixed border and looks attractive with *Dianthus x allwoodii* in the foreground. It likes an open, sunny position and light or ordinary garden soil. Water it regularly and apply a complete fertilizer in spring. Cut it back after flowering. This plant is seldom attacked by pests or diseases.
Varieties/cultivars: *L. s. montana,* *L. s. m.* 'Kobold'.

Incarvillea delavayi

Incarvillea delavayi
HARDY GLOXINIA, PRIDE OF CHINA

Family: BIGNONIACEAE
Origin: China.
Flowering time: Summer.
Climatic zone: 5, 6, 7, 8, 9.
Dimensions: Up to 2 feet (600 mm) high.
Description: This is a showy perennial

Lychnis coronaria

Lychnis coronaria
ROSE CAMPION, DUSTY MILLER

Family: CARYOPHYLLACEAE
Origin: Southern Europe.
Flowering time: Summer.
Climatic zone: 4, 5, 6, 7, 8, 9.
Dimensions: Up to 2 feet (600 mm) high.
Description: Rose campion has wheel-like, cerise-pink flowers on pale stems. The foliage has fine, silvery hairs. A gray groundcover can be created by removing the flowers. It is a good, but short-lived, border plant, the seedlings flowering within a year. Growing either as a biennial or perennial, it likes alkaline, moist, well-drained soil and a position in sun or partial shade.
Other colors: White.
Varieties/cultivars: 'Alba', 'Abbotswood Rose', L. c. var. oculata.

Lychnis viscaria syn. Viscaria vulgaris
GERMAN CATCHFLY

Family: CARYOPHYLLACEAE
Origin: Europe.
Flowering time: Spring–summer.
Climatic zone: 4, 5, 6, 7, 8, 9.
Dimensions: Up to 18 inches (450 mm) high.
Description: The purplish-pink flowers form in clusters on top of the sticky stems that have given the common name, German catchfly, to this plant. The stickiness protects the plants from insects, particularly ants. It likes moist, sandy soil, and an open position. Propagate it by division in autumn or by sowing seed in spring. Double-flowered varieties are available.
Other colors: White, red, purple.
Varieties/cultivars: 'Splendens', 'Splendens Plena', 'Alba', 'Zulu'.

Lychnis viscaria

Description: The name Lythrum is from the Greek word for "blood", alluding to the color of the flowers. These are vibrant magenta-pink and borne in whorls around the stems, the leaves being willow-like. Marsh-loving, it is ideal planted beside ponds, near streams, or in damp places in the garden, but it also flowers freely in ground that is not especially wet. A valuable and widely grown plant, it has been used for tanning leather and in treating dysentery and blindness. L. salicaria may be invasive, but the cultivars are not.
Other colors: Red, violet.
Varieties/cultivars: 'Happy', 'Robert', 'Dropmore Purple', 'Firecandle', 'Morden's Gleam', 'Morden's Pink', 'Purple Spires'.

Lythrum salicaria

Lythrum salicaria
PURPLE LOOSESTRIFE

Family: LYTHRACEAE
Origin: Asia, Europe, North Africa.
Flowering time: Summer.
Climatic zone: 3, 4, 5, 6, 7, 8, 9.
Dimensions: Up to 4 feet (over 1 meter) high.

Malva alcea
MALLOW, HOLLYHOCK MALLOW

Family: MALVACEAE
Origin: Europe.
Flowering time: Summer–autumn.
Climatic zone: 5, 6, 7, 8, 9.
Dimensions: Up to 4 feet (over 1 meter) high.
Description: The flowers of hollyhock mallow are a delicate pink, and the cottony, heart-shaped leaves add to the plant's ornamental value in borders and beds. Related to the hibiscus, which is also a member of the mallow family, M. alcea is like a smaller version of this flower, which is probably why some consider it to be inferior. Flowers are borne in terminal spikes, and occur in great profusion. It is easy to grow in any garden soil, but prefers it dry. Propagate by dividing it in spring.
Other colors: Purple.
Varieties/cultivars: 'Fastigiata'.

Malva alcea 'Fastigiata'

Malva moschata
MUSK MALLOW,
MUSK ROSE

Family: MALVACEAE
Origin: Europe, North Africa.
Flowering time: Summer–autumn.
Climatic zone: 4, 5, 6, 7, 8, 9, 10.
Dimensions: Up to 3 feet (1 meter) high.
Description: The handsome pink flowers of musk mallow appear mostly at the top of the stems. Its leaves emit a musky fragrance when bruised. Musk mallow makes an attractive ornamental border plant among hollyhocks and lupins in cottage gardens. Drought-tolerant, it does well in most soils, but prefers a well-drained position. Propagate it from seed in spring. Musk mallow has medicinal properties.
Other colors: White.
Varieties/cultivars: 'Alba'.

only in frosty areas, but needs a position where the early morning sun will not damage the flowers after frost. The solitary, crimson flowers are saucer-shaped with yellow stamens and red filaments. It grows well in fertile, well-drained soil and must be well-watered in dry weather. A plant known to the ancients, peony was said to cure lunacy, nightmares, and nervous disorders. Ideal for low maintenance gardens, they are also excellent cut flowers.
Other colors: Red, white.
Varieties/cultivars: 'Rubra Plena', 'Alba Plena'.

Oenothera speciosa

Phlox subulata
GROUND PINK, MOSS
PINK, MOSS PHLOX (U.K.)

Family: POLEMONIACEAE
Origin: Northeastern United States.
Flowering time: Late spring, northern hemisphere; summer, southern hemisphere.
Climatic zone: 3, 4, 5, 6, 7, 8.
Dimensions: Up to 6 inches (150 mm) high.
Description: Introduced into England in the early part of the eighteenth century, ground pink is an old, easy-to-grow favorite. An evergreen creeper, it forms a thick carpet and produces dense flowers which are ¾ inch (20 mm) wide with slightly notched petals. A profuse flowerer, this alpine phlox suits rock

fading to a soft rose color, and look attractive at the front of a border or in a large rock garden. Because of its spreading habit, the plant is a good choice for a wild garden and is easy to grow in a sunny spot, in sandy or loamy soil.

Paeonia officinalis
COMMON PEONY

Family: PAEONIACEAE
Origin: Southern Europe.
Flowering time: Early summer.
Climatic zone: 3, 4, 5, 6, 7, 8, 9.
Dimensions: Up to 3 feet (1 meter) high.
Description: An extremely hardy perennial, common peony grows well

Paeonia officinalis

82

Malva moschata

Oenothera speciosa
SHOWY PRIMROSE,
EVENING PRIMROSE

Family: ONAGRACEAE
Origin: Southern United States, Mexico.
Flowering time: Summer.
Climatic zone: 5, 6, 7, 8, 9.
Dimensions: Up to 18 inches (450 mm) high.
Description: Like most evening primroses, showy primrose has flowers that open during the day. They are shallowly basin-shaped and fragrant,

Plectranthus Sp.

... gardens and sloping sites and looks attractive planted to give a spill-over effect over rocks or down stone walls. It prefers average, well-drained garden soil. Prune the stems severely after flowering to promote denser growth. Propagate it from seeds, cuttings or division of the roots.

Other colors: White, red, lavender-blue.

Varieties/cultivars: 'Alba', 'Brilliant', 'Temiscaming', 'G. F. Wilson', 'Alexander's Surprise', 'Oakington Blue Eyes', 'Red Wings', 'White Delight'.

Plectranthus Sp.
CANDLE PLANT

Family: LABIATAE
Origin: South Africa.
Flowering time: Autumn.
Climatic zone: 9, 10.
Dimensions: Up to 2 feet (600 mm) high.
Description: This plant is a most useful groundcover for shady areas, where its long branches frequently send down roots at each leaf node. The profuse spires of flowers are pale mauve when they open, fading to white, and the attractive, oval leaves are green above and deep-purple on the underside. Candle plant does not tolerate dry conditions, growing best in moist soil with plenty of leaf mold. It propagates very easily from cuttings and makes a fine hanging basket, house, or greenhouse plant.

Polygonum bistorta 'Superbum'
COMMON EUROPEAN BISTORT, EASTER LEDGES, SNAKEWEED (U.S.A.)

Family: POLYGONACEAE
Origin: Cultivar.
Flowering time: Summer.
Climatic zone: 3, 4, 5, 6, 7, 8, 9.
Dimensions: Up to 3 feet (1 meter) high.
Description: The pink flowers of this perennial appear in dense, robust spikes about 6 inches (150 mm) long, on stems well above the foliage. Its large, paddle-like leaves make it a handsome plant even when not in flower. Given the right position, it may bloom twice during the summer. Mass-plant it in full sun or shade.

Phlox subulata 'Alexander's Surprise'

long borders beside driveways and paths, or near fruit trees to attract the bees. It likes moist soil in a shaded position, although where summers are cool it will grow in full sun.

Polygonum capitatum
FLEECE FLOWER, JAPANESE KNOT-FLOWER

Family: POLYGONACEAE
Origin: Himalayas.
Flowering time: Spring-autumn.
Climatic zone: 9, 10.
Dimensions: Up to 6 inches (150 mm) high.
Description: This vigorous and quick-growing perennial has attractive, pink, globular flowers and dark-green leaves with V-shaped bands. Its low, spreading habit makes it a useful groundcover, but pruning may be necessary to control its spread. An easy-to-grow plant, it is tolerant of a wide range of soils and conditions and is seldom bothered by pests or diseases. Plant cuttings or seed in full sun or shade.

Polygonum capitatum

Polygonum bistorta 'Superbum'

Primula japonica

stems well above the foliage. It appreciates damp and shady places in rock or wild gardens. A hardy perennial, it thrives in full sun in cool climates, but in warmer areas it needs partial shade. Plant it in moist, humus-enriched soil. Propagate by division.

Primula japonica
JAPANESE PRIMROSE
Family: PRIMULACEAE
Origin: Japan.
Flowering time: Late spring–early summer.
Climatic zone: 5, 6, 7, 8, 9.
Dimensions: Up to 16 inches (400 mm) high.
Description: Primula has strong stems bearing whorled tiers of glistening flowers which look spectacular mass-planted under trees or around shrubs. A moisture-lover, it grows well near ponds and streams and in damp and partially shady problem areas in the garden. Plant it in humus-enriched soil and provide constant moisture. It does not like hot, dry summers. *Astilbe* species, which need similar conditions, make ideal companion plants.
Other colors: White, red, purple, lavender.
Varieties/cultivars: 'Miller's Crimson', 'Postford's White'.

spring or autumn. 'Rubra Compacta' has deeper pink flowers and a more compact form.
Other colors: Red, white.
Varieties/cultivars: 'Alba', 'Rubra', 'Rubra Compacta', 'Splendens'.

Saponaria officinalis
BOUNCING BET, SOAPWORT
Family: CARYOPHYLLACEAE
Origin: Europe, Asia.
Flowering time: Summer.
Climatic zone: 3, 4, 5, 6, 7, 8, 9.
Dimensions: Up to 3 feet (1 meter) high.
Description: With its bright pink clusters of flowers often borne in profusion, soapwort is well suited to both wild and cottage gardens. Grow it in sandy, well-drained soil; in moist, fertile soil it tends to be invasive, so choose a position where its growth can be checked if necessary. Soapwort gets its name from the fact that if its leaves are bruised and swished in water, they form a lather. It was used in ancient times as a soap and also for its medicinal properties.
Other colors: Red, white.
Varieties/cultivars: 'Rubra Plena', 'Rosea Plena', 'Alba Plena'.

Prunella grandiflora 'Rosea'

Saponaria ocymoides
ROCK SOAPWORT
Family: CARYOPHYLLACEAE
Origin: Central and southern Europe.
Flowering time: Spring–summer.
Climatic zone: 3, 4, 5, 6, 7, 8.
Dimensions: Up to 8 inches (200 mm) high.
Description: With its masses of bright, showy flowers growing in loose clusters, this vigorous alpine rock plant looks graceful near steps or trailing over edges or rock walls. Rock soapwort thrives in a sunny position, in sandy soil with good drainage. It can be propagated from cuttings, from seed in early spring, or by division of rootstock in early

Prunella grandiflora 'Rosea'
SELF-HEAL, HEART-OF-THE-EARTH (U.S.A.), LARGE-FLOWERED SELF-HEAL (U.K.)
Family: LABIATAE
Origin: Cultivar.
Flowering time: Summer.
Climatic zone: 5, 6, 7, 8, 9.
Dimensions: Up to 12 inches (300 mm) high.
Description: A member of the mint family, self-heal is said to heal wounds, and cure headaches and sore throats. The parent species has been a common pasture plant in Europe and U.K. for centuries. The two-lipped tubular flowers appear in dense spikes on erect

Saponaria officinalis 'Rosea Plena'

Saponaria ocymoides

Saxifraga moschata 'Peter Pan'

Saxifraga moschata and hybrids

MOSSY SAXIFRAGE ○ ◐ ●

Family: SAXIFRAGACEAE
Origin: Southern Spain, Italy, Balkans.
Flowering time: Spring.
Climatic zone: 3, 4, 5, 6, 7, 8.
Dimensions: Up to 6 inches (150 mm) high.
Description: Mossy saxifrage is a quick-growing perennial which forms a low mound and is ideal in rock garden pockets, in courtyards, or under trees and shrubs. The leaves are fan-shaped and deeply lobed; the flowers are only ½–1 inch (12–24 mm) wide. There are several cultivars, some of which are hybrids with allied species. Many of these perennials prefer positions either shaded from midday sun or in complete shade. Moist, gritty soil with lime suits them best. Propagate them by seed, root division or cuttings.
Other colors: Scarlet, yellow, white.
Varieties/cultivars: 'Cloth of Gold', 'Triumph', 'Peter Pan'.

Scabiosa caucasica

PINCUSHION FLOWER, COMMON SCABIOUS, BORDER SCABIOUS ○

Family: DIPSACACEAE
Origin: Caucasus.
Flowering time: Summer, northern hemisphere; spring–summer, southern hemisphere.
Climatic zone: 4, 5, 6, 7, 8, 9.
Dimensions: Up to 2½ feet (750 mm) high.

Description: Introduced into Britain in 1591, pincushion flower blooms for a long time and the cut flowers are excellent in floral arrangements. The flowers are flat, 2–3 inches (50–70 mm) wide, and similar to the daisy in appearance. Grow it in a border in full sun, in well-drained, limy soil. It resents being moved; if this is necessary, move it in the spring. Propagate it by root division in winter. If the plants become sickly try another cultivar.
Other colors: Lavender, lavender-blue, white.
Varieties/cultivars: 'Moorheim Blue', 'Bressingham White', 'Loddon White', 'Clive Greaves', 'Miss Willmott'.

Sedum maximum 'Atropurpureum'

ICE PLANT, GREAT STONECROP ○ ◐

Family: CRASSULACEAE
Origin: Cultivar.
Flowering time: Summer–autumn.
Climatic zone: 4, 5, 6, 7, 8, 9, 10.
Dimensions: Up to 2 feet (600 mm) high.
Description: The spectacular flowers and foliage make this a good plant in a border or rock garden. The thick, fleshy leaves, green at first and turning a deep

claret color later, look dramatic with the pink flowers. Plant it where this effect will brighten a bare part of the garden in autumn. It is easy to grow if it has good drainage, particularly in winter. For best results, plant it in average soil, in sun or partial shade.

Scabiosa caucasica

Sedum maximum 'Atropurpureum'

growing, it is a good choice for wild or cottage gardens and in sunny, slightly unruly gardens is a good companion plant for delphiniums and gypsophila. Easily grown in average, well-drained soil with some moisture, it likes full sun in colder climates and partial shade in hot areas. Propagate it by seed or root division.

Other colors: Red.
Varieties/cultivars: 'Loveliness', 'Brilliant', 'Croftway Red', 'Sussex Beauty', 'William Smith', 'Rose Green', 'Elsie Heugh'.

Thalictrum aquilegifolium
KING-OF-THE-MEADOW, COLUMBINE MEADOWRUE

Family: RANUNCULACEAE
Origin: Eastern and central Europe–northern Asia.
Flowering time: Early summer, northern hemisphere; spring, southern hemisphere.
Climatic zone: 5, 6, 7, 8, 9, 10.
Dimensions: Up to 3 feet (1 meter) high.
Description: With its fluffy heads of tassel-like, pink flowers and decorative ferny foliage, king-of-the-meadow makes a handsome border plant. It is unusual in that the male and female flowers bloom on separate plants, the male being the more showy. King-of-the-meadow provides a good foil for larger-flowered plants. Easy to grow in moist, well-drained soil enriched with humus, it needs shade in hot summers. Water regularly, protect it from the wind, and apply complete fertilizer in late winter.
Other colors: White, purple, mauve.

Thalictrum aquilegifolium

Sidalcea malviflora

Sedum spectabile 'Autumn Joy'

Sedum spectabile

and butterflies love them. A compact perennial which is ideally suited to borders, it is easy to grow in average soil. Good drainage is essential, particularly in winter. Propagation is by division, cuttings, or leaves.

Sidalcea malviflora
CHECKERBLOOM, PRAIRIE MALLOW

Family: MALVACEAE
Origin: Oregon–California, Mexico.
Flowering time: Summer.
Climatic zone: 5, 6, 7, 8, 9, 10.
Dimensions: Up to 3 feet (1 meter) high.
Description: This graceful, long-flowering, herbaceous perennial has spikes of pink flowers resembling a small hollyhock. The spikes may need staking if the plant becomes too tall. Fast-

Sedum spectabile
LIVE-FOR-EVER, SHOWY STONECROP (U.S.A.), ICE PLANT (U.K.)

Family: CRASSULACEAE
Origin: Korea–central China.
Flowering time: Late summer–autumn.
Climatic zone: 4, 5, 6, 7, 8, 9, 10.
Dimensions: Up to 2 feet (600 mm) high.
Description: Much loved by butterflies and bees, ice plant is grown for its showy, plate-like heads of starry, pink flowers, borne in clusters on sturdy stems. The oval, succulent leaves help the plant withstand long dry periods. Good drainage is necessary, particularly in winter, for robust, freely blooming plants. An excellent plant in a border or rock garden, it is easy to grow in average soil, in either sun or partial shade. Apply complete fertilizer in spring and propagate by seed, division, cuttings, or from the leaves themselves.
Other colors: Red, rose-salmon, white.
Varieties/cultivars: 'Brilliant', 'Meteor', 'Autumn Joy', 'Iceberg', 'September Ruby', 'Stardust', 'Variegatum'.

Sedum spectabile 'Autumn Joy'
WILD THYME, MOTHER OF THYME

Family: CRASSULACEAE
Origin: Cultivar.
Flowering time: Summer.
Climatic zone: 4, 5, 6, 7, 8, 9, 10.
Dimensions: Up to 2 feet (600 mm) high.
Description: The salmon-pink aging to rusty-red flowers of this plant form in clusters resembling broccoli heads. Bees

Thalictrum delavayi

Thalictrum delavayi syn.
T. dipterocarpum

MEADOWRUE, LAVENDER SHOWER

Family: RANUNCULACEAE
Origin: Western China.
Flowering time: Summer, northern hemisphere; spring, southern hemisphere.
Climatic zone: 5, 6, 7, 8, 9.
Dimensions: Up to 5 feet (over 1 meter) high.
Description: The delicate branching stems of this meadowrue produce numerous gracefully hanging, mauve-pink blooms with yellow anthers. The ferny foliage resembles maidenhair, giving the plant a delicate, oriental look. It forms a good backdrop to annuals or among other perennials. For best results, mulch the plant annually with compost or well-rotted manure. Care is needed when cultivating the soil around the plant, as new growth, which emerges near the parent plant, may be easily severed. It is easy to grow in moist, well-drained soil and should be divided in early spring.
Other colors: White, rose-purple, mauve.
Varieties/cultivars: 'Album', 'Purple Cloud', 'Hewitt's Double'.

Thymus praecox arcticus

Thymus praecox arcticus syn. **T. drucei**

MOTHER OF THYME, WILD THYME

Family: LABIATAE
Origin: Europe.
Flowering time: Spring-summer.
Climatic zone: 4, 5, 6, 7, 8, 9.
Dimensions: Up to 4 inches (100 mm) high.
Description: Mother of thyme is a prostrate, evergreen groundcover. One of the carpet-forming thymes, it is very useful in the rock garden and needs little attention. It can also be placed among paving stones and around paths, emitting a pungent aroma when walked on. The flowers are two-lipped, small, and tubular, appearing in terminal spikes. Plant it in fertile, sandy soil and prune it if it becomes invasive. It is propagated by root division or cuttings. This herb can be used in cooking.
Other colors: White, red.
Varieties/cultivars: 'Albus', 'Coccineus', 'Annie Hall', 'Pink Chintz'.

Tradescantia x andersoniana 'Carmine Glow'

Tradescantia x andersoniana syn.
T. virginiana

WIDOW'S TEARS, COMMON SPIDERWORT

Family: COMMELINACEAE
Origin: Hybrid.
Flowering time: Spring-summer.
Climatic zone: 5, 6, 7, 8, 9.
Dimensions: Up to 2 feet (600 mm) high.
Description: Related to the American wandering Jew, this free-flowering perennial produces attractive clumps. The blooming period is long, though the flowers themselves are short-lived. The clumps may become untidy unless pruned in autumn. Plant it in well-drained soil, in partial shade in hotter areas, and in full sun in cooler climates. Divide it in spring.
Other colors: Many colors.
Varieties/cultivars: Great variety of cultivars available.

Valeriana officinalis

COMMON VALERIAN

Family: VALERIANACEAE
Origin: Europe, Asia.
Flowering time: Summer.
Climatic zone: 5, 6, 7, 8, 9.
Dimensions: Up to 4 feet (approx. 1 meter) high.
Description: Valerian is an ancient plant with medicinal uses. The aromatic roots have a great attraction for cats. A good border plant, it produces numerous pink flowers in fragrant dusters. It may be prey to aphids. Easy to grow, it prefers very moist, well-drained soil in full sun. Propagate it by seed or division.
Other colors: White, lavender.

Valeriana officinalis

Andromeda polifolia

carries its pink and white flowers over a long period; after these have fallen the reddish-brown calyxes remain attractive for months. The leaves are dark-green and glossy. The shrub will grow in any type of free-draining soil in a sheltered site. It can be pruned after flowering if required. Cut back into the old wood so that new arching branches can be formed.
Varieties/cultivars: 'Prostrata'.

Dimensions: 12 inches (300 mm) high.
Description: This is an extremely pretty shrub having clusters of delicate, urn-shaped, pale-pink flowers. As the common name suggests, it will only grow in moist and cool soil which must be acidic. Adding peat to the soil and using it as a mulch around the shrub provides perfect conditions. Summer heat and dry soil will kill the plant. It may become straggly with age, but this can be overcome by an occasional heavy pruning after flowering has finished.

Bauera rubioides
DOG ROSE, RIVER ○ ◖ ●
ROSE, WIRY BAUERA

Family: BAUERACEAE
Origin: Australia.
Flowering time: Spring–summer.
Climatic zone: 9.
Dimensions: 3 feet (900 mm) high.
Description: This semi-prostrate, heath-like shrub, with its small, dainty, pale-pink flowers, blooms for a long period. Dog rose will grow in full sun, but prefers a shaded position and damp, acidic, well-drained soil. A mulch of leaf

Abutilon 'Tunisia'

Abutilon 'Tunisia'
CHINESE LANTERN, ○ ◖
FLOWERING MAPLE (U.K.)

Family: MALVACEAE
Origin: Cultivar.
Flowering time: Summer.
Climatic zone: 9, 10.
Dimensions: 4–6 feet (1–2 meters) high.
Description: Chinese lantern is a spectacular shrub having large, fuchsia-pink flowers similar in appearance to the old-fashioned hollyhock. Prune it back to at least two-thirds of the current year's growth each winter to maintain bushy growth. Fertilize in spring with a complete plant food or mulch around the plant with manure or compost. Ample summer water is required. Chinese lantern makes an excellent background shrub for a perennial border or can be used as a feature plant. It can also be grown in a large tub.

Andromeda polifolia
BOG ROSEMARY ◖

Family: ERICACEAE
Origin: Europe, northern Asia, North America.
Flowering time: Spring–summer.
Climatic zone: 2, 3, 4, 5, 6, 7.

Bauera rubioides

Abelia schumannii

Abelia schumannii ○ ◖

Abelia schumannii
SCHUMANN'S
ABELIA

Family: CAPRIFOLIACEAE
Origin: Western China.
Flowering time: Summer–autumn.
Climatic zone: 7, 8, 9.
Dimensions: 4–6 feet (1–2 meters) high.
Description: In the northern hemisphere, Schumann's abelia is semi-deciduous but in the southern hemisphere it is evergreen. The new leaves are purplish at first, changing later to a mid-green. Attractive rosy-pink flowers cover the plant for a long period. Plant it in a shrub border or use as a screen plant. Mulch with manure or feed with a complete plant food in early spring. It is not fussy about soil type, but it needs a well-drained position.

Abelia x grandiflora
GLOSSY ABELIA ○ ◖

Family: CAPRIFOLIACEAE
Origin: Hybrid.
Flowering time: Summer–autumn.
Climatic zone: 6, 7, 8, 9.
Dimensions: 3–6 feet (1–2 meters) high.
Description: A fast-growing semi-evergreen shrub, glossy abelia is widely used as a hedge or screen plant. It

Abelia x grandiflora

mold around the plant will keep the soil moist and cool. This delicate shrub is suited to a cottage garden or rockery, but in cold climates, it needs to be grown under glass. Fertilize in spring with manure, compost or organic fertilizer. Dog rose does not appreciate artificial fertilizers.

Boronia floribunda
PINK BORONIA

Family: RUTACEAE
Origin: Australia (N.S.W.).
Flowering time: Spring.
Climatic zone: 9.
Dimensions: 3 feet (900 mm) high.
Description: Pink boronia is a very free-flowering, small shrub, bearing fragrant, pale-pink, star-like flowers. The small leaves are a soft, light-green. Plant it near a doorway or window so that the strong fragrance can be appreciated. In very cold areas, it needs to be grown under glass. The main requirements of pink boronia are good drainage and a sandy soil. Apply a heavy mulch of leaf litter under which the surface roots can remain cool. Feed in spring with well-rotted compost, cow manure, or an organic fertilizer.

Boronia floribunda

Callistemon citrinus 'Pink Clusters'
BOTTLEBRUSH

Family: MYRTACEAE
Origin: Cultivar.
Flowering time: Spring.
Climatic zone: 9, 10.
Dimensions: 10–11 feet (3–4 meters) high.
Description: This pretty cultivar has very light-green young leaves which turn darker as they age. The pink flower spikes are 3 inches (80 mm) long.

Callistemon citrinus 'Pink Clusters'

Although the main flowering period is spring, there are always one or two flowers on the shrub throughout the year. Use in the garden as a specimen shrub or at the back of a shrub border. A warm climate plant, crimson bottlebrush likes well-drained soil. Mulch with manure or compost in spring, or feed with blood and bone.

Calluna vulgaris and cultivars
HEATHER

Family: ERICACEAE
Origin: Europe, Asia Minor.
Flowering time: Depends on the cultivar but always summer–autumn.
Climatic zone: 5, 5, 7, 8, 9.
Dimensions: 18 inches (450 mm) high. Height of cultivars differs.
Description: Many varieties of heather are cultivated in gardens, and vary in their shades of pink, flowering time, and habit. The flowers are valued for indoor decoration. They are all easily-grown

Calluna vulgaris 'Anne Marie'

plants, tolerant of lime-free soils and even, moist positions. Although tolerant of some shade, they flower better in full sun. Pruning, if necessary, can be carried out after flowering finishes. Heather combines well with old-fashioned plants in a cottage garden scheme.
Other colors: Red, white, mauve, purple, crimson.
Varieties/cultivars: There are many different cultivars throughout the world.

Callistemon citrinus 'Pink Clusters'

Camellia japonica and cultivars
JAPANESE CAMELLIA, COMMON CAMELLIA

Family: THEACEAE
Origin: China, Korea, Japan.
Flowering time: Winter–spring.
Climatic zone: 7, 8, 9.
Dimensions: 20 feet (6.0 meters) high.
Description: There are hundreds of different cultivars of this plant in every shade of pink imaginable. Flower shape includes single, double, semi-double, and formal double. The leaves are a shiny dark-green. Camellias like moist, but free-draining, acid soil. The root systems are shallow, so mulch around the plant with peat or leaf mold to encourage acid conditions and to keep the soil damp. Lack of water, especially during summer, will cause the buds to drop.
Other colors: Many different shades of pink, red and white, and combinations of these.
Varieties/cultivars: There are many different cultivars throughout the world.

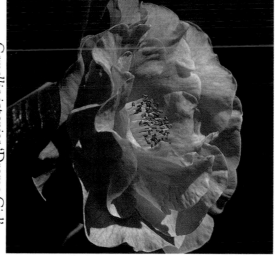

Camellia japonica 'Drama Girl'

Dais cotinifolia

Dais cotinifolia
POMPOM TREE ○

Family: THYMELAEACEAE
Origin: South Africa.
Flowering time: Spring.
Climatic zone: 9, 10.
Dimensions: 10–20 feet (3–6 meters) high.
Description: The bark of this shrub is the strongest fiber known to the Africans who use it as a thread. The whole bush is covered for at least a month in attractive pompom-like heads of pinkish-lilac flowers measuring about 2 inches (50 mm) across. The smooth leaves are a bluish-green. Plant in a well-drained soil that is enriched annually with cow manure or compost. Pruning, if necessary, can be carried out after flowering.

Daphne cneorum

Daphne cneorum
ROSE DAPHNE (U.S.A.), ○ ◑
GARLAND FLOWER (U.K.)

Family: THYMELIACEAE
Origin: Central and southern Europe.
Flowering time: Spring.
Climatic zone: 4, 5, 6, 7, 8.

---

well-drained and mulched every spring with manure or compost, or alternatively fed with a small amount of complete plant food. Pruning is not necessary.

Cercis chinensis

Cotinus coggyria
VENETIAN SUMACH ○ ◑
(U.S.A.), SMOKE TREE (U.K.),
SMOKEBUSH

Family: ANACARDIACEAE
Origin: Central and southern Europe.
Flowering time: Summer.
Climatic zone: 5, 6, 7, 8, 9.
Dimensions: 10–15 feet (3–5 meters) high.
Description: A pretty, deciduous shrub, smoke tree is grown for its lovely autumn color and profusion of fawny-pink feathery flower-stalks which eventually turn a smoky-gray. The flower stalks persist for months and actually do look like clouds of smoke. Smoke tree is easy to grow in any ordinary garden soil that is not too rich or moist.
Other colors: Purple. The leaves of some cultivars are also purple or red.
Varieties/cultivars: 'Purpureus', 'Royal Purple', 'Foliis Purpureis', 'Flame'.

Camellia sasanqua 'Plantation Pink'

Camellia sasanqua cultivars ○ ◑
SASANQUA
CAMELLIA

Family: THEACEAE
Origin: Japan.
Flowering time: Autumn–spring.
Climatic zone: 7, 8, 9.
Dimensions: 6–10 feet (2–3 meters) high.
Description: A similar-looking plant to *Camellia japonica*, *C. sasanqua* is hardier and has a more open habit. There are several cultivars of this plant in various shades of pink. In cold areas it requires protection near a wall, but as it ages it becomes more tolerant of cold. The soil should be acidic and moist but free-draining. A mulch is essential to protect the surface roots. Use pine leaves, peat, or leaf mold.
Other colors: Color range is from white through to red with combinations of these.
Varieties/cultivars: There are several different cultivars throughout the world.

Cercis chinensis
CHINESE REDBUD (U.S.A.), ○
CHINESE JUDAS TREE (U.K.)

Family: LEGUMINOSAE
Origin: China.
Flowering time: Spring.
Climatic zone: 7, 8, 9.
Dimensions: 15 feet (5 meters) high.
Description: Chinese redbud is a pretty, deciduous shrub with large round, but pointed, glossy green leaves. In spring it is clothed in clusters of bright pink flowers. Although it is a hardy shrub which is easily grown under average conditions, it does not transplant readily. The soil should be

Cotinus coggyria

Dimensions: 12 inches (300 mm) high.
Description: Garland flower is a popular plant on account of its fragrant, rose-pink flowers which are borne in clusters on prostrate branches. It is an ideal shrub for a rock garden or as a border to a large shrubbery. Garland flower requires a cool, lime-free soil which must be friable and well-drained. Before planting, dig in copious amounts of leaf mold or peat. Do not use chemical fertilizers. A mulch of leaf mold or cow manure annually will suffice and will not harm the plant.
Other colors: White.
Varieties/cultivars: 'Eximea', 'Alba', 'Variegata', 'Major'.

Deutzia scabra 'Flore Pleno'
SNOWFLOWER ◐

Family: SAXIFRAGACEAE
Origin: Cultivar.
Flowering time: Summer.
Climatic zone: 5, 6, 7, 8, 9.
Dimensions: Up to 6 feet (2 meters) high.
Description: This pretty, deciduous shrub has a compact shape with arching branches of dull green foliage, and abundant clusters of white flowers that are suffused with rose-purple on the outside. Adaptable to a wide range of soils and conditions, this shrub benefits from a light pruning after flowering to maintain its shape. It makes an excellent addition to a cottage garden.

Deutzia scabra 'Flore Pleno'

Erica canaliculata
TREE HEATH, PURPLE HEATH ◐

Family: ERICACEAE
Origin: South Africa.
Flowering time: Late winter–early summer.
Climatic zone: 8, 9, 10.
Dimensions: 4–6 feet (1–2 meters) high.
Description: A hardy shrub which, in flower, becomes entirely covered in pale pink or white bells. It forms a neat bush and looks most delightful when planted at the back of a perennial border. Since an acid soil is essential for success, dig in copious amounts of peat or leaf mold, and add a handful of sulfur before planting. Tree heath is easily propagated from self-rooted layers or late summer cuttings.

growth. Bush mold, decayed oak leaves, or peat worked into the soil will provide the desired conditions. Heath makes an ideal cut flower.
Other colors: A wide range through the white-pink-purple spectrum.
Varieties/cultivars: Numerous cultivars have been developed from this species.

Erica canaliculata

Erica carnea and cultivars
HEATH, SPRING HEATH, HEATH, WINTER HEATH ◯

Family: ERICACEAE
Origin: Central Europe.
Flowering time: Winter–spring. Different cultivars flower at different times during this period.
Climatic zone: 5, 6, 7, 8, 9.
Dimensions: 8–12 inches (200–300 mm) high and twice this wide.
Description: The delightful urn-shaped, rosy-red flowers are about 3 inches (75 mm) long, but there are innumerable cultivars available in a wide range of shades. Cultivars can be planted so that one of them is in flower from late autumn to late spring. *Erica carnea* and its cultivars prefer an acid soil, too much lime can actually retard

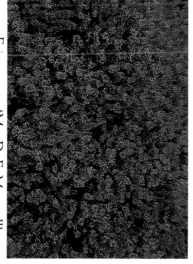

Erica carnea cultivars

Erica vagans
CORNISH HEATH ◐

Family: ERICACEAE
Origin: Southwestern Europe.
Flowering time: Summer–autumn.
Climatic zone: 6, 7, 8, 9.
Dimensions: 1–3 feet (300–900 mm) high.
Description: A small, hardy shrub which produces an abundance of purplish-pink flowers, Cornish heath can be used in a rockery or in the front of a shrub border. The main requirements for healthy growth are an acid, well-drained but moist soil. This can be provided by digging leaf mold or peat into the soil before planting and by sprinkling a handful of sulfur around the plant. Picking the flowers for indoor decoration helps to keep the bush more compact.
Other colors: White, shades of pink and red.
Varieties/cultivars: There are numerous cultivars of this shrub.

Erica vagans 'Mrs D. F. Maxwell'

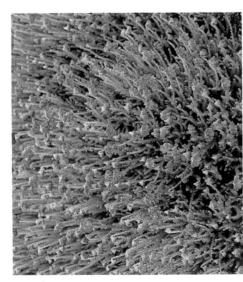

Erica tetralix 'Con Underwood'
CROSS-LEAVED HEATH

Family: ERICACEAE
Origin: Northern and western Europe.
Flowering time: Summer–autumn.
Climatic zone: 6, 7, 8, 9.
Dimensions: 12–18 inches (300–450 mm) high.
Description: *Erica tetralix* has dainty, urn-shaped, soft-pink flowers and grayish-green foliage. There are several different cultivars and many of them are in different shades of pink. An acid, moist soil is essential for success with this plant. Add peat or leaf mold to the soil when planting, or as a mulch to provide the necessary acidity. A handful of sulfur sprinkled around the plant is also beneficial. This is an ideal shrub for a rockery. It also makes a pretty groundcover.
Other colors: White, shades of pink and red.
Varieties/cultivars: There are numerous cultivars of this shrub.

Erica x darleyensis
DARLEY HEATH

Family: ERICACEAE
Origin: Hybrid.
Flowering time: Winter–spring.
Climatic zone: 6, 7, 8, 9.
Dimensions: 4 feet (approx. 1 meter) high.
Description: When in flower this hardy hybrid, with its compact, cushion-like habit, is smothered with numerous small, rosy-pink bells. It looks like a natural companion when planted with *Erica carnea*. It is as lime-tolerant as *E. carnea*, but thrives when mulched with leaf mold or peat. Plant it in a cottage garden or use at the front of a shrub border. The cut flowers last for a long time indoors.
Other colors: Magenta, red, white, shades of pink.
Varieties/cultivars: There are several cultivars of this species.

Erica x darleyensis 'Darley Dale'

Fuchsia x hybrida
FUCHSIA

Family: ONAGRACEAE
Origin: Hybrids.
Flowering time: Spring, summer, autumn.
Climatic zone: 7, 8, 9, 10.
Dimensions: 2 feet (600 mm) high.
Description: There are hundreds of different cultivars of fuchsias throughout the world, many of them in the pink color range. These delightful plants will flower freely for many months. When cut back severely in autumn in cooler areas, they will burst forth with new shoots the following spring. Fuchsias like a rich, well-drained soil. A mulch of manure or a handful of complete plant food in early spring will ensure a good flower display. They are very suited to pot culture.
Other colors: Red, purple, blue, white, violet, and combinations of these.
Varieties/cultivars: Numerous cultivars are available.

Fuchsia x hybrida

Grevillea rosmarinifolia

Grevillea rosmarinifolia
ROSEMARY GREVILLEA

Family: PROTEACEAE
Origin: Eastern Australia.
Flowering time: Throughout the year.
Climatic zone: 9, 10.
Dimensions: 4 feet (approx. 2 meters) high.
Description: This pretty shrub has thin green leaves and flowers which vary from red to creamy pink mainly in spring and summer. Some flowers remain throughout the year. Plant rosemary grevillea where it can be seen from a window, as it is very attractive to birds. It can be heavily pruned to make a formal hedge if required. It requires a greenhouse environment in cool climates. Its main requirements are a well-drained soil and applications of organic fertilizer. Propagation can be carried out from cuttings taken in early spring.
Other colors: Red and dark pink.
Varieties/cultivars: 'Jenkinsii', 'Olympic Flame'.

Hibiscus rosa-sinensis cultivars
ROSE-OF-CHINA, CHINESE HIBISCUS

Family: MALVACEAE
Origin: Southern China.
Flowering time: Spring–summer.

Hibiscus rosa-sinensis

Climatic zone: 9, 10.
Dimensions: 6–10 feet (2–3 meters) high.
Description: This is a beautiful flowering shrub with literally hundreds of different cultivars, many of which grow in various shades of pink. They make beautiful feature plants or can be grown in a shrub border. In cool climates, a greenhouse environment is essential. Bushes should be pruned back to near half height each winter to maintain a good shape and to produce a better display of flowers the following year. A well-drained soil and regular applications of plant food during spring and summer are their main requirements.
Other colors: White, orange, red.
Varieties/cultivars: There are numerous cultivars.

Justicia carnea
PINK JACOBINIA,
BRAZILIAN-PLUME FLOWER,
KING'S-CROWN ◑

Other common names: PINK ACANTHUS
Family: ACANTHACEAE
Origin: Brazil.
Flowering time: Summer–autumn.
Climatic zone: 9, 10.
Dimensions: 5 feet (approx. 2 meters) high.
Description: Pink jacobinia has large, deeply veined, dark-green leaves and big cone-shaped flower heads. Each flower head consists of many rosy-pink flowers. It is a fast-growing shrub which becomes straggly and unattractive unless it is drastically pruned every spring. It is often grown as an indoor plant. For best results, plant in a rich, well-drained soil and feed every spring with a complete plant food. It is easily propagated from early spring cuttings.

Justicia carnea

Kalmia latifolia

Kalmia latifolia
MOUNTAIN LAUREL,
CALICO BUSH ◑

Family: ERICACEAE
Origin: Eastern North America.
Flowering time: Summer.
Climatic zone: 4, 5, 5, 7, 8, 9.
Dimensions: 7–15 feet (2–5 meters) high.
Description: This is one of the most beautiful and valued evergreen shrubs for a cold-climate garden. The delightful shell-pink, saucer-shaped flowers are crinkled at the edges. An acid, lime-free soil is an essential requirement. It will not grow in heavy clay soils nor in areas which have hot, dry summers. Plant it in soil that has been heavily enriched with leaf mold or peat and apply a mulch of this around the shrub.

Kolkwitzia amabilis
BEAUTYBUSH ○

Family: CAPRIFOLIACEAE
Origin: Western China.
Flowering time: Spring–summer.
Climatic zone: 5, 6, 7, 8, 9.
Dimensions: 8–12 feet (2.4–4 meters) high.
Description: Beautybush is an extremely attractive, erect shrub. The

bell-like flowers are pink with a yellow throat. It is useful for a cottage garden. Although not fussy about soil type, it appreciates a handful of complete plant food sprinkled around its base in late winter. Do not prune unless absolutely necessary. Pruning will not only spoil the shape but will prevent flowering for a season as flowers are produced on the previous year's growth.

Kolkwitzia amabilis

Lantana camara
COMMON LANTANA,
RED SAGE, YELLOW SAGE (U.K.) ○

Family: VERBENACEAE
Origin: Tropical America.
Flowering time: Summer–autumn, but in warmer climates there are some flowers on the shrub throughout the year.
Climatic zone: 9, 10.
Dimensions: 3 feet (1 meter) high.
Description: A prickly-stemmed shrub, lantana has dull-green, strangely-scented leaves which are rough to the touch. It is valued for its yellow flowers ageing to red or white which stay on the plant for a long period. The flowers are followed by shining black, berry-like seeds that are relished near the coast or in areas that experience drought. Grow common lantana in a sandy, free-draining soil. It needs to be pruned in spring to prevent legginess.
Other colors: White, cream, lilac, orange yellow.
Varieties/cultivars: There are several cultivars throughout the world.

Lantana camara

SHRUBS

Leptospermum scoparium and cultivars
TEA TREE, MANUKA

Family: MYRTACEAE
Origin: Australia, New Zealand.
Flowering time: Spring–summer.
Climatic zone: 8, 9, 10.
Dimensions: 3–6 feet (1–2 meters) high, depending on the cultivar.
Description: Tea trees are attractive evergreen shrubs bearing white, red, or pink flowers. They are very suited to coastal planting as the majority of them often thrive where not much else will grow. All the cultivars of leptospermum like a slightly acid soil of a sandy nature, and an open sunny position, but they can become accustomed to dappled shade. Prune lightly after flowering if they become too straggly. The cut flowers are pretty indoors.
Other colors: Various shades of white, red, pink.
Varieties/cultivars: Numerous cultivars are available.

Lonicera tatarica

Tatarian honeysuckle is not fussy about soil type as long as the drainage is good.
Other colors: White, red.
Varieties/cultivars: 'Alba', 'Arnold Red', 'Hack's Red', 'Sibirica'.

Lonicera tatarica
TATARIAN HONEYSUCKLE

Family: CAPRIFOLIACEAE
Origin: Central Asia, Russia.
Flowering time: Spring.
Climatic zone: 4, 5, 6, 7, 8.
Dimensions: 8–10 feet (2–3 meters) high.
Description: An old-fashioned, bushy honeysuckle which has multitudes of fragrant, soft-pink flowers during spring, followed by red berries. This species is variable and the flowers are often rich pink. The leaves are oval. It makes an ideal background shrub in a cottage garden. If it becomes too leggy it can be pruned after flowering has finished.

Leptospermum scoparium 'Sunraysia'

Melaleuca decussata
TOTEM POLES, CROSS-LEAVED HONEY-MYRTLE

Family: MYRTACEAE
Origin: Australia (S.A., Vic.).
Flowering time: Spring–summer.
Climatic zone: 9, 10.
Dimensions: 6–11 feet (2–4 meters) high.
Description: This rounded shrub, with fine, stiff, narrow gray-green leaves, has mauve-pink bottlebrush-like flowers that quickly fade to white. They are very attractive to birds. It is an adaptable shrub which will survive wet or dry conditions. *Melaleuca* can be used as a specimen shrub or as a windbreak or hedge. Feed annually with cow manure or compost. Alternatively, apply a handful of blood and bone around the plant in spring.

Melaleuca decussata

Luculia gratissima
LUCULIA, PINK SIVA

Family: RUBIACEAE
Origin: Himalayas, India.
Flowering time: Late autumn–late winter.
Climatic zone: 9, 10.
Dimensions: 4–6 feet (1–2 meters) high.
Description: Luculia is one of the most beautiful winter-flowering shrubs. Fragrant clusters of soft-pink flowers cover the bush. The large leaves are light-green with a slightly downy underside. Plant near a window or door where the beautiful fragrance can be appreciated. Luculia flowers last well when picked and brought indoors. A well-drained soil and ample summer water are essential. Prune moderately after flowering — severe pruning can lead to the death of the plant.

Nerium oleander and cultivars
OLEANDER, ROSE-BAY (U.S.A.)

Family: APOCYNACEAE
Origin: Southern Europe, North Africa, Japan.
Flowering time: Summer–autumn.
Climatic zone: 9, 10.
Dimensions: 4–15 feet (1–5 meters) high.
Description: Oleander is an extremely hardy shrub which will tolerate heat, drought, and salt. However, in cool climates, it needs to be grown under glass. The large, open-faced pink or white flowers stay on the plant throughout summer. There are few shrubs which flower for so long a period. The dark-green leaves are in pairs or whorls of three around the stem. All parts of this plant are poisonous, so keep children and pets from eating it. Do not burn the leaves. The many cultivars of this plant have

Luculia gratissima

Nerium oleander

become much more popular than the species itself.
Other colors: White, yellow, buff, red.
Varieties/cultivars: Several cultivars have been developed throughout the world.

Paeonia suffruticosa

Paeonia suffruticosa and cultivars
TREE PEONY, ○ ◑
MOUNTAIN PEONY (U.S.A.)

Family: PAEONIACEAE
Origin: China.
Flowering time: Early summer.
Climatic zone: 6, 7, 8, 9.
Dimensions: Up to 6 feet (2 meters) high.
Description: The tree peony and its cultivars are among the finest of all spring-flowering shrubs. The large, shaggy-petalled flower heads are 6–8 inches (150–200 mm) wide. Flower color of the species is pink to white, each petal having a maroon splash at the base. Whilst tree peony and its cultivars are frost-hardy, the new growth is susceptible to late-spring frosts so it should be given protection. Tree peonies grow best in a neutral to acid,

95

humus-rich soil, with shelter from strong winds.
Other colors: White, red.
Varieties/cultivars: 'Godaishu', 'Hodai', 'Kumagai', 'Sakurajishi', 'Taiyo'.

Climatic zone: 9, 10.
Dimensions: 2–6 feet (1–2 meters) high.
Description: Giant protea is the most spectacular of all the proteas. The beautiful flower heads of soft silvery pink are 8–12 inches (200–300 mm) across. In the right position the shrub will flower for nine months of the year. In some cold areas, a greenhouse is required. All proteas strongly resent over-rich soils and will thrive in rather poor, slightly acid soil that contains a lot of rubble or sand. Add sulfur to the soil if it is too alkaline. Avoid using phosphates. Do not overwater.

Pimelea ferruginea

Pimelea ferruginea
PINK RICE FLOWER ○ ◑

Family: THYMELAEACEAE
Origin: Western Australia.
Flowering time: Late spring – summer.
Climatic zone: 9, 10.
Dimensions: 1–3 feet (100–900 mm) high.
Description: A neat, rounded shrub with small, glossy green leaves, pink rice flower has a profusion of pink flowers borne in terminal heads during spring. It is an ideal plant for use in a rockery. Salt-tolerant, it is a useful shrub for beachside planting. It likes a well-drained soil. Very little fertilizer or pruning is required to maintain this shrub.

Protea cynaroides

Protea cynaroides
GIANT PROTEA, KING ○
PROTEA (U.K.)

Family: PROTEACEAE
Origin: South Africa.
Flowering time: Winter–summer.

Protea neriifolia

Protea neriifolia
OLEANDER-LEAF PROTEA ○

Family: PROTEACEAE
Origin: South Africa.
Flowering time: Spring–winter.
Climatic zone: 9, 10.
Dimensions: 4–6 feet (1–2 meters) high.
Description: One of the most popular proteas, *P. neriifolia* has deep rose-pink flowers 5 inches (125 mm) long and 3 inches (75 mm) wide. The tips of the petals are black and furry. The long leaves are a soft green. Grow proteas in soil that is not too rich. A poor, slightly acid soil that contains a lot of rubble or sand is ideal. Add sulfur to the soil if it is too alkaline. Avoid using phosphates. Do not overwater, especially in winter. A greenhouse may be necessary in cold climates.
Other colors: Salmon-red.
Varieties/cultivars: 'Taylors Surprise', 'Snow Crest'.

SHRUBS

Rhaphiolepis x delacourii
PINK INDIAN HAWTHORN ○

Family: ROSACEAE
Origin: Hybrid.
Flowering time: Spring and autumn.
Climatic zone: 8, 9.
Dimensions: 6 feet (2 meters) high.
Description: This is a charming shrub which has a neat rounded habit and glossy-green leaves. The rose-pink flowers are borne in terminal branching clusters. Pink Indian hawthorn is a slow-growing shrub, but a worthwhile addition to the garden. It is used for hedges and in shrub borders. It is not fussy about soil type, but appreciates a handful of complete plant food around its base in late winter.
Other colors: Crimson.
Varieties/cultivars: 'Coates Crimson'.

Rhaphiolepis x delacourii

Rhododendron indicum
INDIAN AZALEA ○ ◑

Family: ERICACEAE
Origin: Southern Japan.
Flowering time: Winter–spring.
Climatic zone: 8, 9.
Dimensions: 3–8 feet (1–2 meters) high.
Description: This species is the origin of most of the garden forms developed by hybridizing with the allied species. It is a small, dense, evergreen bush. The funnel-shaped flowers are single or in pairs. There are hundreds of different cultivars, many of which are in the pink color range. Indian azaleas require an acid, well-drained soil enriched with leaf mold or compost. Mulching around the plant is also important as the roots are very shallow.
Other colors: White, red, orange, purple.
Varieties/cultivars: There are numerous cultivars of this species.

Rhododendron spp.
RHODODENDRON, AZALEA ◑ ○ ◑

Family: ERICACEAE
Origin: Japan, China, Himalayas, Burma.
Flowering time: Winter–spring.
Climatic zone: 5, 6, 7, 8, 9.
Dimensions: 1–10 feet (up to 3 meters) high.
Description: The genus rhododendron is one of the largest, numbering over 800 species, which range from tiny, prostrate plants to large shrubs. The flowers vary through the whole color spectrum. The majority of the species like a sheltered position and an acid, well-drained soil that has been enriched with leaf mold or compost. A mulch around the shallow, fibrous roots is essential to keep them cool and moist.
Other colors: White, red, yellow, purple, blue.
Varieties/cultivars: There are numerous cultivars.

Rhododendron indicum 'Alphonse Andersen'

Rhododendron Kurume Group
KURUME AZALEA ○ ◑

Family: ERICACEAE
Origin: Japan.
Flowering time: Spring.
Climatic zone: 6, 7, 8.
Dimensions: Can reach 4 feet (over 1 meter) high.
Description: Kurume azaleas originated from the Kurume province in Japan so they can withstand more cold than *R. indicum*. They are evergreen, with small, rounded leaves. Although the flowers are smaller than other azaleas, they are produced in such profusion that they completely cover the bush. Plant in an acid, well-drained soil which has been enriched with leaf mold or compost. Mulching around the base of the plant is important, as the roots are very shallow.
Other colors: Orange, red, purple, white.
Varieties/cultivars: There are numerous hybrids and varieties of this species.

Rhododendron indicum

Rhododendron spp.

Ribes sanguineum
FLOWERING CURRANT (U.K.), AMERICAN CURRANT ◑ ○

Family: GROSSULARIACEAE
Origin: Western North America.
Flowering time: Spring.
Climatic zone: 6, 7, 8.
Dimensions: 5–12 feet (2–4 meters) high.
Description: An ornamental and pretty, deciduous shrub, flowering currant can be used as a feature shrub or in a shrub border of a cottage garden. During spring it is covered in hanging flower heads, 3–4 inches (75–100 mm) long, of rosy-pink flowers which are followed by black berries with a waxy, white patina which makes them look gray from a distance. The leaves have a characteristically pungent smell. Flowering currant is an easily grown

Rhododendron Kurume Group 'Fairy Queen'

Ribes sanguineum

shrub, thriving in any soil. Prune after flowering. It can be propagated from layering, cuttings, or seeds.
Other colors: White, red, crimson.
Varieties/cultivars: 'King Edward VII', 'Splendens', 'Album', 'Albescens', 'Carneum'.

Rondeletia amoena
YELLOW-THROAT RONDELETIA ○ ◐

Family: RUBIACEAE
Origin: West Indies.
Flowering time: Summer.
Climatic zone: 9, 10.
Dimensions: 6-10 feet (2-3 meters) high.
Description: Yellow-throat rondeletia is a bushy evergreen shrub, with large, handsome, rather leathery leaves. The salmon-pink, fragrant, tubular flowers are borne in terminal clusters and have a golden beard at the throat. It is useful as a screen or feature shrub, and will grow in any well-drained garden soil. However, in cold climates it grows best in a greenhouse. Prune, if required, to just above the lower leaves on the branches as the flowers finish.

Rondeletia amoena

Spiraea japonica
JAPANESE SPIRAEA, PINK MAY ○ ◐

Family: ROSACEAE
Origin: Japan.
Flowering time: Summer.
Climatic zone: 5, 6, 7, 8, 9.

Dimensions: 4-6 feet (1-2 meters) high.
Description: This hardy deciduous shrub, valued for its flattened heads of pink flowers, is a popular landscape or feature plant. Japanese spiraea is easily grown in any type of garden soil as long as it is well-drained. Removing some of the older, less productive branches at the base each year after flowering will encourage the growth of new, vigorous wood. The cut flowers last well indoors.
Other colors: Red, white, crimson.
Varieties/cultivars: 'Alpina', 'Atrosanguinea', 'Bullata', 'Fastigiata', 'Little Princess', 'Ruberrima', var. *albiflora*.

SHRUBS

Robinia kelseyi
ALLEGHENY MOSS LOCUST (U.S.A.) ○ ◐

Family: LEGUMINOSAE (U.S.A.).
Origin: South Allegheny Mountains (U.S.A.).
Flowering time: Spring, southern hemisphere; summer, northern hemisphere.
Climatic zone: 6, 7, 8, 9.
Dimensions: 8-10 feet (2-3 meters) high.
Description: This graceful shrub or small tree with slender branches and elegant foliage has slightly fragrant rose-pink flowers hanging in clusters. Allegheny moss locust makes a perfect feature shrub. A sheltered position is essential as the branches are very brittle and easily broken by wind. It is excellent in dry, inland areas, as it will withstand near-drought conditions.

Robinia kelseyi

Spiraea japonica 'Ruberrima'

Spiraea japonica 'Ruberrima'

Weigela florida and cultivars
WEIGELA, APPLE BLOSSOM (U.S.A.) ○ ◐

Family: CAPRIFOLIACEAE
Origin: Japan, Korea, northern China.
Flowering time: Spring-summer.
Climatic zone: 5, 6, 7, 8, 9.
Dimensions: 7-10 feet (2-3 meters) high.
Description: This is a pretty, deciduous shrub with cane-like branches covered in funnel-shaped, rose-pink flowers which are pale-pink inside. There are many attractive hybrids of this plant. Weigela will grow in any garden soil and should be pruned only after flowering has finished as flowers are borne on the current season's growth. Grow in a shrub border or as a feature plant.
Other colors: White, red, crimson, rosy-crimson.
Varieties/cultivars: There are numerous varieties throughout the world.

Weigela florida cultivar

Aesculus x carnea 'Briottii' syn. *A. rubicunda*
RED HORSE CHESTNUT

Family: SAPINDACEAE
Origin: Hybrid.
Flowering time: Late spring–early summer.
Climatic zone: 4, 5, 6, 7, 8, 9.
Dimensions: Up to 40 feet (13 meters) high.
Description: This strikingly beautiful horse chestnut tree has an attractive rounded shape and a profusion of large heads of deep pink blooms during its flowering period. It can be grown from seed, and should be planted where there is plenty of space to allow its shape to develop. Like most horse chestnuts it is quite slow growing, and unless rich, moist soil is provided the foliage will burn and growth will be retarded.

Aesculus x carnea 'Briottii'

Albizia julibrissin
MIMOSA TREE (U.S.A.), PERSIAN SILK TREE

Family: LEGUMINOSAE
Origin: Western Asia–Japan.
Flowering time: Late spring–early summer.
Climatic zone: 9, 10.
Dimensions: 16–20 feet (5–6 meters) high x 25–27 feet (7–8 meters) wide.
Description: Soft, feathery green leaves combined with pretty, fluffy, pink-and-cream flowers belie the toughness of this small, deciduous tree. Once established, it thrives in hot, dry areas, in light sandy soils. Typical of the Leguminosae family, it closes its leaves at night to conserve moisture. A fast grower, it is particularly suitable to plant in a new garden as a screen or splendid shade

tree. Much smaller and bushier is *A. j.* 'Rosea'. Both are easily grown from seed.
Other colors: White.
Varieties/cultivars: 'Alba', 'Rosea'.

Albizia julibrissin

Bixa orellana
LIPSTICK TREE, ANNATTO TREE

Family: BIXACEAE
Origin: Tropical America.
Flowering time: Summer.
Climatic zone: 9, 10.
Dimensions: 10–30 feet (3–10 meters) high.
Description: An evergreen tree for very warm climates only, bixa is normally bushy in habit but can be trained by careful pruning into a single-stemmed, small tree. Quick-growing, it makes a handsome screen or hedging plant. The flowers form at the tips of branches, and are followed by red-brown spiny fruit. To enjoy summer-long fragrant flowering, trim after the fruits deteriorate, then allow new buds to form. Water well in dry weather. Bixa can be grown from seed.

Bixa orellana

Bauhinia x blakeana
HONG KONG ORCHID TREE, BUTTERFLY TREE

Family: LEGUMINOSAE
Origin: Hybrid.
Flowering time: Winter, northern hemisphere; late summer–late spring, southern hemisphere.
Climatic zone: 9, 10.
Dimensions: 15–25 feet (5–7 meters) high.
Description: Floral emblem of Hong Kong, this tree deserves that honor, for there are not many months when it is not actually producing flowers. An evergreen, growing almost as wide as it does high, it produces a dense, leafy canopy offering welcome shade in hot climates. The fragrant and exotic orchid-like flowers do not produce the bean pods common to its genus (which can look rather messy), for it is a sterile hybrid. Grow it from cuttings. Prune to shape it while young and prune after each flush of flowers. Hong Kong orchid tree grows well in California and Florida.

Bauhinia x blakeana

Brachychiton discolor
QUEENSLAND LACEBARK, PINK FLAME TREE (U.K.), HAT TREE

Other common names: WHITE KURRAJONG (Aust.)
Family: STERCULIACEAE
Origin: Australia (northern N.S.W., Queensland, and Northern Territory coastal regions).
Flowering time: Late spring–early autumn.

Climatic zone: 9, 10.
Dimensions: 20–65 feet (6–20 meters) high.
Description: The Queensland lacebark is widely grown as a shade tree in hot, dryish climates, including California, South Africa, and the Mediterranean. Although normally evergreen, it loses some leaves in cooler regions. The leaves are variable in shape, smooth above and woolly beneath. In a good year, the flowers are spectacular and when they fall, they create a carpet beneath the tree, forming a picture of mirrored beauty. Lacebark prefers deep soils and high rainfall. It is commonly planted as a street tree.

Brachychiton discolor

Calodendrum capense
CAPE CHESTNUT ○
Family: RUTACEAE
Origin: South Africa (coast to tropics).
Flowering time: Late spring–mid-summer in southern hemisphere.
Climatic zone: 8, 9, 10.
Dimensions: 30–45 feet (9–15 meters) high.
Description: An extremely beautiful and adaptable tree, Cape chestnut grows in a range of climates from warm temperate to tropical. Sprays of highly perfumed, mottled pink flowers that cover the canopy seem to be orchid look-alikes. Because it is slow to flower from seed, it is best grown as a grafted plant. Given a good start in fertile soil, it grows fairly quickly, but slows down later, seldom reaching more than 30 feet (10 meters) in the garden. It needs plenty of water in dry weather. Cape chestnut is evergreen in warm climates, but semideciduous in frost areas.

Camellia reticulata cultivar

Camellia reticulata and cultivars
NET VEIN CAMELLIA, NETTED CAMELLIA ○ ◐
Family: THEACEAE
Origin: Yunnan, western China.
Flowering time: Late autumn and early spring, southern hemisphere; spring, northern hemisphere.
Climatic zone: 8, 9.
Dimensions: 6–35 feet (2–10 meters) high.
Description: Really a large shrub, *Camellia reticulata* grows to tree proportions in the wild. Its flowers are larger than other camellias and very free-forming, and although its growth is not as compact as in *C. japonica*, the new cultivars are producing denser

Calodendrum capense

growth. Easily grown in tubs or for use as tall, background plants, reticulatas are long-lived, requiring only good drainage and a fairly acid soil. Like all camellias and azaleas, their roots are shallow-surfaced, so constant mulching is very beneficial. Reticulatas perform well in full sun, protected from winds.
Other colors: Red, coral, crimson, dark purple-red, white.
Varieties/cultivars: 'Pagoda', 'Letitia', 'Buddha', 'Franci L', 'Howard Asper', 'Purple Gown', 'Tali Queen'.

Cercis canadensis
EASTERN REDBUD, AMERICAN JUDAS TREE (U.K.) ○ ◐
Family: LEGUMINOSAE
Origin: Southeastern Canada, eastern United States, northeastern Mexico.
Flowering time: Spring.
Climatic zone: 4, 5, 6, 7, 8, 9.
Dimensions: 20–40 feet (6–12 meters) high.
Description: Related to the Judas tree, with similar, but heart-shaped leaves and narrower growth habit, the eastern redbud is a beautiful feature of the spring landscape in the eastern and central states of America. One of the first trees to bloom after winter, numerous clusters of stemless flowers are borne on mature branches, often coming straight out of the wood. It quickly grows into a small, round-headed tree in cultivation. Although not fussy as to soil, it must have good drainage and plenty of water in dry, hot summers. It is deciduous.
Other colors: White.
Varieties/cultivars: 'Alba', 'Plena'.

Cercis canadensis

Eucalyptus caesia

Cercis siliquastrum
JUDAS TREE,
LOVE TREE (U.S.A.)

Family: LEGUMINOSAE
Origin: Southern Europe, western Asia.
Flowering time: Early–late spring.
Climatic zone: 7, 8, 9.
Dimensions: 20–30 feet (6–9 meters) high.
Description: This was the tree from which Judas Iscariot supposedly hanged himself after betraying Christ. Like all *Cercis* species, it grows into a delightful small tree, smothering itself with rosy-colored blossom in spring. Typical of the genus, the pea-shaped flowers appear on all parts of the bare wood, even straight out of the trunk. The leaves are kidney-shaped. Most adaptable, it will flourish in heat and drought, is resistant to light frost and will grow in coastal gardens. It is deciduous.
Other colors: White.
Varieties/cultivars: 'Alba'.

Cornus florida 'Rubra'

small, wide-canopied tree. It needs excellent drainage in acid soil but must not be allowed to dry out. Mulch regularly.

Dombeya x cayeuxii
MEXICAN ROSE, PINK BALL DOMBEYA, CAPE WEDDING FLOWER

Family: BYTTNERIACEAE
Origin: Hybrid.
Flowering time: Late autumn–spring.
Climatic zone: 9, 10.
Dimensions: 15–30 feet (4–9 meters) high.
Description: The parents of this hybrid are *D. burgessiae* and *D. wallichii*. The hanging clusters of shell-pink flowers are somewhat like those of a viburnum and the leaves are poplar-shaped and large. A good fill-in plant for a warm corner position or background situatic ', it develops a shrubby growth habit. It is easily grown from cuttings in spring and is widespread in many climates including those of Florida, India, Africa, and Australia.

Cercis siliquastrum

Cornus florida 'Rubra'
PINK-FLOWERING DOGWOOD

Family: CORNACEAE
Origin: Cultivar.
Flowering time: Spring.
Climatic zone: 5, 6, 7, 8, 9.
Dimensions: 13–40 feet (4–12 meters) high.
Description: Pink-flowering dogwood is one of the most beautiful sights of spring when it flowers on bare wood from upturned twigs. The actual flowers are small and greenish in color, surrounded by four, showy, rosy-pink bracts. A second treat arrives with autumn as the scarlet-colored fruit ripens and the leaves become crimson. Happiest in cool, moist climates, it develops into a

Eucalyptus caesia
GUNGUNNA, GUNGURRU ○
(Aust.)

Family: MYRTACEAE
Origin: Southwestern Western Australia.
Flowering time: Winter–mid-spring in southern hemisphere.
Climatic zone: 9, 10.
Dimensions: Up to 27 feet (8 meters) high.
Description: One of the most delightful small eucalypts, it develops an open, somewhat sprawling, tree-like habit when cultivated. It is admired for the showy stamens of the flowers which appear on branches covered in a whitish waxy patina. Very decorative, mealy-covered, urn-shaped gumnuts form later which hang for months, and make interesting indoor dried arrangements. Gungunna will not tolerate bad drainage or a prolonged humid atmosphere. Grown from seed, it should be pruned lightly for more compact growth.
Varieties/cultivars: 'Silver Princess'.

Magnolia campbellii
CHINESE TULIP TREE, PINK
TULIP TREE, CAMPBELL MAGNOLIA

Family: MAGNOLIACEAE
Origin: Himalayas.
Flowering time: Spring.
Climatic zone: 7, 8, 9.
Dimensions: 40–160 feet (12–50 meters) high.
Description: Probably seen at its

Dombeya x cayeuxii

maximum height only in its native habitat, the Chinese tulip tree is very slow-maturing, and takes about 12–15 years to come into flower. Plant it for your children to enjoy! Its maximum height in the U.K. is 60 feet (18 meters). The flowers sit on bare wood and are large, pink, and waxy. Large velvety leaves follow, their color in autumn complementing the spikes of scarlet seeds. This tree grows best in frost-free areas.
Other colors: White, purple.
Varieties/cultivars: M. c. var. mollicomata.

Magnolia campbellii

Description: Although some crab apples are inclined to bloom only every two years, *M. floribunda* is renowned for its reliability in flowering every year. The backs of the petals are a rosy color and the insides white — which produces a delightful sight when rosy buds are opening among already-opened, white flowers. Beautiful fruits, yellow with a reddish flush, develop in autumn, although in the U.K. this species fruits poorly and the very small 'apples' are not usually brightly colored. The crab apple prefers a moist climate with long winters. Protect it from strong winds but allow it plenty of root space.
Other colors: Purplish-red.
Varieties/cultivars: 'Gibb's Golden Gage', 'Indian Magic', 'Indian Summer', 'Liset', 'Makamik', 'Mary Potter', 'Robinson'.

Malus ioensis 'Plena'
PRAIRIE CRAB (U.S.A.),
BECHTEL CRAB APPLE

Family: ROSACEAE
Origin: Cultivar.
Flowering time: Late spring–early summer.
Climatic zone: 2, 3, 4, 5, 6, 7, 8, 9.
Dimensions: 20–30 feet (6–9 meters) high.
Description: This is arguably the most beautiful of the flowering crab apples, but is not a strong grower. *M. ioensis* 'Plena' is a double-flowered bud-mutant (that is, produced by a mutation in one of the buds) of *M. ioensis*, discovered by Bechtel, an Illinois nurseryman.

Flowers are abundant and sweetly perfumed, opening later than those of most crab apples, which is useful if you want to prolong spring flowering. Fruit is seldom seen, but the leaves color in autumn to vivid shades of yellow, orange, and crimson. It can be susceptible to juniper rust.

Malus floribunda
JAPANESE CRAB APPLE

Family: ROSACEAE
Origin: Japan, China.
Flowering time: Spring.
Climatic zone: 5, 6, 7, 8, 9.
Dimensions: 16–25 feet (5–7 meters) high.

Malus floribunda

Malus ioensis 'Plena'

Malus spectabilis 'Plena'
CHINESE CRAB APPLE,
DOUBLE FLOWERED CHINESE
CRAB APPLE

Family: ROSACEAE
Origin: Cultivar.
Flowering time: Mid–late spring.
Climatic zone: 4, 5, 6, 7, 8, 9.
Dimensions: 16–30 feet (5–9 meters) high.
Description: This is possibly a natural hybrid of Chinese origin. It is unknown as a native tree growing in the wild. Flowers of *M. s.* 'Plena' are semidouble, rose-pink when in bud, opening to blush-pink, then fading to white. They are faintly perfumed. Its beauty when flowering, plus its vigorous growth habit, make this tree a valuable addition to any cool, moist, elevated garden in regions with longish winters. A row of crab apples lining a driveway or footpath, in blossom or in fruit, is a breathtaking sight.

Malus spectabilis 'Plena'

Malus x *purpurea* 'Eleyi'
PURPLE CRAB APPLE

Family: ROSACEAE
Origin: Hybrid.
Flowering time: Late spring.
Climatic zone: 4, 5, 6, 7, 8, 9.
Dimensions: 20–25 feet (6–7 meters) high.
Description: Flowers of *M.* x *p.* 'Eleyi' are a pretty rosy-magenta in bud, opening to a paler shade. Purplish-red fruits persist into late autumn. It is a deciduous tree. Trees and shrubs with reddish to purplish leaves are best used with discretion for they can easily dominate a garden landscape. *Malus* x *p.* 'Eleyi', can be beautifully integrated with plants that have silvery-gray foliage. Try planting it with willow-leaved pear (*Pyrus salicifolia*) as did Vita Sackville-West in her famous White Garden at Sissinghurst. For best results, plant in well-drained, rich soil and mulch annually with well-rotted compost or manure. Water well in summer.

Prunus persica

Varieties/cultivars: 'Alba Plena', 'Alba Plena Pendula', 'Foliis Rubis', 'Klara Mayer', 'Lilian Burrows', 'Magnifica', 'Rosea Plena', 'Versicolor'.

Description: The semidouble, rosy-red flowers of *P. m.* 'Geisha' appear in clusters on one- and two-year-old wood in winter or spring. Being on very short stalks, they appear as solid branches of color. The small, deciduous tree, which develops a broadly rounded crown, is ideal for planting bulbs beneath. Plant it against a warm wall in cold areas.

Prunus mume 'Geisha'

Prunus mume 'Geisha'
JAPANESE APRICOT

Family: ROSACEAE
Origin: Cultivar.
Flowering time: Early–late spring, northern hemisphere; winter, southern hemisphere.
Climatic zone: 7, 8, 9.
Dimensions: 20–27 feet (6–8 meters) high.

Malus x *purpurea* 'Eleyi'

Prunus 'Amanogawa' syn. *P. serrulata erecta*
JAPANESE FLOWERING CHERRY

Family: ROSACEAE
Origin: Hybrid.
Flowering time: Late spring, northern hemisphere; mid–late spring, southern hemisphere.
Climatic zone: 5, 6, 7, 8, 9.
Dimensions: 13–20 feet (4–6 meters) high.
Description: Unlike most Japanese flowering cherries, which either spread their branches wide to form a flattened crown or develop a broad vase shape, *P.* 'Amanogawa' develops into a narrow, upright form. Given its narrow habit, this cherry is best used as a background tree or in a narrow space. Semidouble, blush-pink, fragrant flowers appear in erect clusters on this deciduous tree. Do not prune it. Cherries, badly pruned, can die from producing excess gum.

Prunus 'Amanogawa'

Prunus persica
PEACH, WILD PEACH

Family: ROSACEAE
Origin: China.
Flowering time: Spring.
Climatic zone: 5, 6, 7, 8, 9.
Dimensions: 10–25 feet (3–7 meters) high.
Description: Many varieties have been bred from this species, first found growing in the wild in China. Rose-pink flowers appear, followed by round, edible fruits. Unfortunately the tree is subject to borer attack and peach leaf curl (a fungus disease). In parts of Australia the fruit is attacked by fruit fly, and must be treated as the fruit begin to ripen. Keep the tree vigorous by regular feeding and watering, and spray the leaves with a fungicide at bud-swell stage. If you only want flowers, it is advisable to grow one of the many cultivars.
Other colors: White, rosy-red, white-and-red stripes.

Prunus serrulata 'Shimidsu Sakura'

JAPANESE FLOWERING CHERRY

Family: ROSACEAE
Origin: Cultivar.
Flowering time: Mid-late spring.
Climatic zone: 5, 6, 7, 8, 9.
Dimensions: 10–13 feet (3–4 meters) high.
Description: Pink buds opening to pure white, hanging clusters of flowers adorn this small, deciduous tree from mid- to late spring. Considered one of the most beautiful of the flowering cherries, it develops wide-spreading, gracefully arching branches to form a broad, flattened crown. Green leaves color brilliantly in autumn. It prefers a cool, moist climate on elevated soils.

Prunus serrulata 'Shimidsu Sakura'

Prunus subhirtella

Prunus subhirtella and cultivars

HIGAN CHERRY, ROSEBUD CHERRY

Family: ROSACEAE
Origin: Hybrid.
Flowering time: Spring.
Climatic zone: 6, 7, 8, 9.
Dimensions: 20–30 feet (6–9 meters) high.
Description: The tiny, pink flowers of the natural hybrid P. *subhirtella* are not as beautiful as in the cultivated varieties. Slender branches carry small, green leaves which color well in autumn and then drop. As with all flowering cherries, avoid pruning, but if it becomes necessary prune in summer. For showier flowers and smaller growth, plant the cultivars.
Other colors: Deep to light pink, single and double.
Varieties/cultivars: 'Pendula', 'Pendula Rosea', 'Pendula Rubra', 'Autumnalis', 'Fukubara'.

Description: Other cherries may be much more showy, displaying beautiful, hanging clusters of flowers, but this cultivar has the advantage of flowering over an extended period. In a mild winter it can begin to flower in autumn and continue intermittently into spring. The modest clusters of flowers cling to small shoots that grow straight out of the trunk. As with all deciduous cherries, it performs best in a cool, moist climate.

Prunus subhirtella 'Autumnalis'

Prunus subhirtella 'Autumnalis'

WINTER SPRING, WINTER CHERRY (U.K.)

Family: ROSACEAE
Origin: Cultivar.
Flowering time: Autumn, winter, spring.
Climatic zone: 6, 7, 8, 9.
Dimensions: 20–30 feet (6–9 meters) high.

Prunus subhirtella 'Pendula Rosea'

WEEPING CHERRY, SPRING CHERRY

Family: ROSACEAE
Origin: Cultivar.
Flowering time: Spring, northern hemisphere; late spring, southern hemisphere.
Climatic zone: 6, 7, 8, 9.
Dimensions: 6–10 feet (2–3 meters) high.
Description: Fountains of delightful, dainty, pink, single flowers cascade from the canopy of this weeping small tree each spring. They are a rich pink when in bud, fading later to blush pink. Beautiful, slender, arching branches give the tree the appearance of a miniature weeping willow. It can provide an avenue of color, or be grown as an individual against a background of evergreen trees. Often grown as a small standard, this tree makes an ideal specimen in a small garden. Very little pruning is necessary.

Prunus subhirtella 'Pendula Rosea'

Prunus x *amygdalo-persica* 'Pollardii'
FLOWERING ALMOND

Family: ROSACEAE
Origin: Hybrid.
Flowering time: Spring, southern hemisphere.
Climatic zone: 6, 7, 8, 9.
Dimensions: 10–20 feet (3–6 meters) high.
Description: A cross between a peach and an almond, this Australian-raised hybrid quickly grows into a robust, small tree. Single, soft rose-pink flowers appear in profusion each spring, well before the leaves unfurl. If cut while still in bud, the flowers will open indoors, lasting a week in water. It is reasonably resistant to the peach leaf curl which attacks so many flowering peaches. Fruits are almond-shaped. The green leaves do not produce good autumn coloring.

Prunus x *blireana*

demand for use in floral art and as an indoor cut flower. The tree has coppery-purple leaves, and as with all trees and shrubs with reddish leaves, in a small garden it may overpower other plants. In a larger setting, plant as an avenue.
Other colors: Pale pink flowers, pale reddish-purple leaves.
Varieties/cultivars: 'Moseri'.

Prunus x *yedoensis*
JAPANESE FLOWERING CHERRY, YOSHINO CHERRY

Family: ROSACEAE
Origin: Hybrid.
Flowering time: Spring, northern hemisphere.
Climatic zone: 6, 7, 8, 9.

Prunus x *amygdalo-persica* 'Pollardii'

Prunus x *blireana*
DOUBLE ROSE CHERRY, FLOWERING CHERRY PLUM

Family: ROSACEAE
Origin: Hybrid.
Flowering time: Spring, northern hemisphere; early spring, southern hemisphere.
Climatic zone: 6, 7, 8, 9.
Dimensions: 8–17 feet (2–5 meters) high.
Description: Flowering cherry plum is a cross between *P. cerasifera* 'Atropurpurea' and *P. mume* 'Alphandii'. It is a small, compact, deciduous tree, bearing semidouble, rose-pink, fragrant flowers. These appear en masse and are much in

Dimensions: 27–40 feet (8–12 meters) high.
Description: This beautiful deciduous tree has long been cultivated in Japan and is the principal park and street cherry tree grown in that country. Thought to be a cross between *P. subhirtella* and *P. speciosa*, it has a short main trunk, and forms a flattish, broad-domed shape. Almond-scented, blush-pink flowers appear in profusion each spring. Ideal for cool and temperate climates, it thrives in well-drained, moderately rich soil that is well watered in summer. Incorporate plenty of well-rotted compost prior to planting.
Other colors: White, pale pink.
Varieties/cultivars: 'Ivensii', 'Shidare Yoshino', 'Akebono'.

Rhododendron arboreum

Rhododendron arboreum
TREE RHODODENDRON

Family: ERICACEAE
Origin: Himalayas.
Flowering time: Mid-winter–spring, northern hemisphere.
Climatic zone: 8, 9.
Dimensions: 20–50 feet (6–15 meters) high.
Description: Parent to many sturdy hybrids, this tall species rhododendron was first discovered in the Himalayas in 1820 and is the first known tree rhododendron. It injected a rich, red color into the breeding program. Regal-looking flower clusters open atop rosettes of handsome, evergreen leaves which droop down at flowering time to display the blooms. It prefers a cool, moist climate and acid soils, and needs regular mulching.
Other colors: White.
Varieties/cultivars: 'Blood Red', 'Roseum', 'Sir Charles Lemon', 'Cornubia', 'Gill's Triumph', 'Glory of Penjerrick'.

Prunus x *yedoensis*

Delphinium consolida syn. *Consolida regalis*

DELPHINIUM

Family: RANUNCULACEAE
Origin: Southern and central Europe–western Asia.
Flowering time: Summer–autumn.
Climatic zone: 5, 6, 7, 8, 9.
Dimensions: Up to 7 feet (2 meters) high.
Description: The majestic tall flower spikes of this Delphinium species make it the most-prized of these useful perennials. The flowers are soft and blue/purple in color, while the kidney-shaped foliage is mid green. Ideal for an old-fashioned flower garden, it should be positioned towards the back. Plant in deep, rich and slightly alkaline soil and provide some shelter from strong winds as the tall flower spikes are prone to collapse if not protected.
Other colors: Pink, mauve, lilac, white.

Delphinium consolida

Eustoma grandiflorum syn. *Lisianthus russellianus*

LISIANTHUS, PRAIRIE GENTIAN

Family: GENTIANACEAE
Origin: Central southern United States.
Flowering time: Summer.
Climatic zone: 6, 7, 8, 9.
Dimensions: Up to 3 feet (1 meter) high.
Description: This flower is shaped like an upturned bell, flaring at the edges and blotched at the base, being some 2 inches (50 mm) wide. It is long-lasting

109

Exacum affine

PERSIAN VIOLET

Family: GENTIANACEAE
Origin: South Yemen.
Flowering time: Spring–autumn.
Climatic zone: 9, 10.
Dimensions: Up to 10 inches (250 mm) high.
Description: This is a low-growing, compact plant, suitable for borders in sheltered areas in warm climates. It needs partial shade because the stems and leaves are tender and will not tolerate frost. The tiny flowers, lavender with yellow centers, are about ½ inch (13 mm) wide and cover the plant profusely. They have a sweet perfume. Its compact habit makes it an ideal plant for small containers. It will live and flower indoors or under shelter in good light for three to four months. It does not like to be overwatered. It is a short-lived perennial usually grown as an annual. It is well-suited to a greenhouse in cold climates.
Other colors: White, pink.

Eustoma grandiflorum

Limonium sinuatum

STATICE, SEA LAVENDER, SEA PINK

Family: PLUMBAGINACEAE
Origin: Mediterranean region–Portugal.
Flowering time: Spring–summer.
Climatic zone: 6, 7, 8, 9, 10.
Dimensions: Up to 18 inches (450 mm) high.
Description: Its strong, wiry stems and many-colored flowers, added to its lasting qualities when picked, make statice popular with florists and for indoor arrangements. The tiny flowers are only ⅜ inch (9 mm) wide, but are tightly clustered to give good color. They are dry and papery when in full bloom, and are borne on winged branches. The plant is biennial but is mostly grown as an annual. The foliage is in a rosette at the base of the plant and of minor importance. Valued for its tolerance to low rainfall and also to seaspray, it is excellent in both seaside and country gardens. Apply a general fertilizer when buds are forming, to encourage a good floral display.
Other colors: Dark-red, yellow, pink, white.

Limonium sinuatum

as a cut flower, and useful as an indoor flowering pot plant in a well-lit situation. The foliage is pale-green, dull, and not impressive. It is hardy, tolerating a wide range of conditions.
Other colors: White, pink, lavender, dark purple.
Varieties/cultivars: 'Yodel Pink', 'Yodel Blue', 'Yodel White' (all compact to 18 inches (450 mm) high).

Exacum affine

ANNUALS

Lobelia erinus
COMMON LOBELIA, EDGING LOBELIA

Family: LOBELIACEAE
Origin: South Africa.
Flowering time: All seasons, excluding frost.
Climatic zone: 5, 6, 7, 8, 9, 10.
Dimensions: Up to 6 inches (150 mm) high.
Description: This is a wiry-stemmed bushy plant but some types have a trailing habit. Although short in stature with small flowers, it gives a mass of color when in bloom. Individual flowers, which are barely ½ inch (13 mm) wide, are deep-blue and often have a white eye. When grown with multicolored annuals, their rich color forms a vivid contrast. The stems are slender but when the plants are grown closely together they form a continuous color border. The trailing varieties are used effectively in hanging baskets in cool but light situations. Best results are obtained if planted in rich, moist soil.
Other colors: Pale blue, white, purple, red, cream.
Varieties/cultivars: 'String of Pearls' (mixed variety), 'Basket Lobelia' (trailing).

Lobelia erinus

Lupinus hartwegii
LUPIN, ANNUAL LUPIN, HAIRY LUPIN

Family: LEGUMINOSAE
Origin: Mexico.
Flowering time: Summer–autumn.
Climatic zone: 7, 8, 9.
Dimensions: Up to 2½ feet (750 mm) high.
Description: This is a tall, upright, strong-growing annual, with a long flowering period. The foliage is compact and stiff and produces flower stems up to 18 inches (450 mm) high, making lupin an ideal cut flower. The long-lasting flowers are about 1 inch (25 mm) long and cover the stems densely in pastel shades of blue, pink, and white. All the foliage and the flowers are covered with soft, silky hairs. A fertile, moist soil ensures best results. Full sun and good drainage are essential.
Varieties/cultivars: 'Pixie' (dwarf form, growing 8 inches (200 mm) high).

Lupinus hartwegii

Nemophila menziesii
BABY-BLUE-EYES

Family: HYDROPHYLLACEAE
Origin: California.
Flowering time: Summer.
Climatic zone: 5, 6, 7, 8, 9.
Dimensions: Up to 8 inches (200 mm).
Description: While this plant grows only to a low height, it spreads well and has dainty fern-like foliage. On the tips of the stems are many bright blue flowers with white centers, saucer-like in shape, up to 1½ inches (40 mm) wide. The outstanding blue with white shows prominently in the garden when baby-blue-eyes is planted closely in groups. It is not suitable for picking, but is attractive in hanging baskets in a cool situation.
Other colors: White, blue-margined white, and brownish-purple margined white.
Varieties/cultivars: 'Alba', 'Peter Blue' (veined purple), 'Crambeoides', 'Atomaria', 'Disoidalis'.

Nemophila menziesii

Nierembergia hippomanica
CUPFLOWER

Family: SOLANACEAE
Origin: Argentina.
Flowering time: Summer–autumn.
Climatic zone: 6, 7, 8, 9, 10.
Dimensions: Up to 15 inches (380 mm) high.
Description: This plant is usually grown as an annual, but is a shrubby perennial in mild winters. It is hardy and withstands strong sunlight. The flowers though small, up to 1 inch (25 mm) wide, are numerous and tightly packed. They are shaped like a tiny cup, yellow in the center and violet on the rim. Cupflower is useful for hanging baskets, but has no picking value. Easy to cultivate in a wide range of soils and conditions, in full sun or semishade.
Varieties/cultivars: 'Violacea', 'Purple Robe'.

Nierembergia hippomanica

Nigella damascena
LOVE-IN-A-MIST, DEVIL-IN-THE-BUSH, WILD FENNEL

Family: RANUNCULACEAE
Origin: Southern Europe, North Africa.
Flowering time: Summer–autumn.
Climatic zone: 5, 6, 7, 8, 9.
Dimensions: Up to 18 inches (450 mm) high.
Description: Bright green, lace-like foliage gives an attractive background to the small flowers scattered on the surface. The flowers may be white, light blue, rose-pink, mauve, or purple, and are up to 1½ inches (40 mm) wide. Both the flowers and the globe-shaped dried seed pods keep well when cut. The plant is hardy and has a long flowering season. Choose a sunny position and ensure that soil is well-drained.

Nigella damascena

up to 3 inches (75 mm) long, and flower spikes are up to 12 inches (300 mm) long. Plant in a sunny but sheltered position and enrich the soil with plenty of well-rotted manure or compost prior to planting.
Other colors: White.
Varieties/cultivars: 'Alba'.

Salvia patens
GENTIAN SAGE

Family: LABIATAE
Origin: Mexico.
Flowering time: Summer.
Climatic zone: 5, 6, 7, 8, 9, 10.
Dimensions: Up to 3 feet (1 meter) high.
Description: This is a hardy plant usually grown as an annual, but may persist as a perennial especially if old flower heads are cut back. The flower spike is upright and protrudes from the foliage, which is dull green and hairy. When grown closely, 12 inches (300 mm) apart, the plant makes an attractive hedge or background for other annuals. Flowers are bright blue,

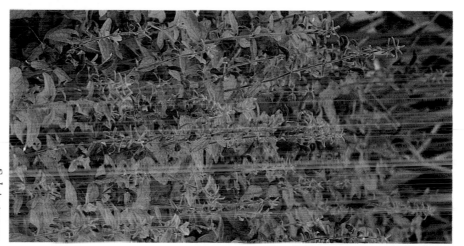

Salvia patens

Torenia fournieri
WISHBONE FLOWER, BLUEWINGS

Family: SCROPHULARIACEAE
Origin: Vietnam.
Flowering time: Summer.
Climatic zone: 6, 7, 8, 9.
Dimensions: Up to 12 inches (300 mm) high.
Description: These low-growing, rather tender plants need to be grown closely together to give a massed border effect. The flowers are 1½ inches (35 mm) long and 1 inch (25 mm) wide with four petals, three of them purple and the largest pale blue, all with yellow spots in the throat. They are attractive in hanging baskets but no use as a cut flower. Warm, humid conditions and a

Torenia fournieri

rich, moist soil are essential. In the right climate it can be grown in full sun or shade.
Other colors: White, also with yellow spots in the throat.
Varieties/cultivars: 'Alba'.

Viola tricolor
JOHNNY-JUMP-UP, PANSY, HEARTSEASE

Family: VIOLACEAE
Origin: Europe, Asia.
Flowering time: Spring–autumn.
Climatic zone: 6, 7, 8, 9.
Dimensions: Up to 12 inches (300 mm) high.
Description: Viola tricolor is the true wild species pansy which varies in size and color. One plant produces many tiny flowers in two tones of blue to purple, often bicolored. Flowers are usually borne singly and are from ¾ inch (19 mm) to 4 inches (100 mm) wide. It is useful for planting over naturalized bulbs and also in pots and baskets. Rich, moist soil and a sunny to semishaded position are ideal for pansies.

Viola tricolor

Allium aflatunense

ORNAMENTAL ONION

Family: LILIACEAE
Origin: Central Asia–China.
Flowering time: Spring.
Climatic zone: 6, 7, 8.
Dimensions: Up to 2½ feet (750 mm) high.
Description: This plant, which belongs to the leek, chive, garlic and shallot family, produces large, beautiful flowers. It is one of the larger varieties and can be featured in mixed borders naturalized in grass, woodland and rock gardens. This Asian variety produces large round heads of purple star-like flowers and has attractive strap-like leaves. Clumps can be lifted and divided in early autumn.

Anemone coronaria

WINDFLOWER, POPPY-FLOWERED ANEMONE

Family: RANUNCULACEAE
Origin: Mediterranean.
Flowering time: Spring.
Climatic zone: 8, 9.
Dimensions: Up to 18 inches (450 mm) high.
Description: During the Crusades, soil from the Holy Land was taken to Pisa as ship's ballast to bury dead soldiers. The following spring, the area was carpeted with anemones. The flowers were called "blood drops of Christ" and spread across Europe. These anemones will grow abundantly in full sun or partial shade. Provide well-drained sandy soil rich in humus. Both single and double blooms are available and look pretty in borders or massed under trees.
Other colors: Red, white, mauve, yellow.
Varieties/cultivars: 'St. Brigid'.

Anemone coronaria 'St. Brigid'

Chionodoxa luciliae

Babiana stricta

BABOON FLOWER (U.K.), BABOONROOT, WINE CUPS

Family: IRIDACEAE
Origin: South Africa.
Flowering time: Spring.

Climatic zone: 9, 10.
Dimensions: Up to 8 inches (200 mm) high.
Description: These plants were named by early settlers to South Africa when they discovered baboons eating the corms. The plants produce about six purple flowers, not unlike freesias, on each stem. They are well-suited to growing in pots, tubs, or window boxes. This species will adapt equally well to naturalizing in woodlands and lawns. Full sun is needed and successful growth depends on the bulbs being planted deeply in sandy soil. The same procedure applies if planting in pots. A greenhouse environment is necessary in cold climates.
Other colors: Mauve, cream, red, white, yellow.

Babiana stricta

Chionodoxa luciliae

GLORY-OF-THE-SNOW

Family: LILIACEAE
Origin: Turkey.
Flowering time: Spring.
Climatic zone: 4, 5, 6, 7, 8, 9.
Dimensions: Up to 6 inches (150 mm) high.
Description: This small, colorful bulb is at its best when clustered under deciduous trees and shrubs. It is one of the early flowers of spring, hence the common name, glory-of-the-snow. Naturalize it in wooded areas or rock gardens. This plant will tolerate shade and can be grown indoors in pots or window boxes. Plant in well-drained soil mixed with organic matter. Apply fertilizer when flowering has finished. This flower is a good choice for a blue garden.
Other colors: Pink and white.
Varieties/cultivars: 'Rosea', 'Zwanenburg', 'Pink giant'.

Crocus tommasinianus

Crocus speciosus
AUTUMN CROCUS

Family: IRIDACEAE
Origin: Turkey, Iran, Crimea, Caucasus.
Flowering time: Autumn.
Climatic zone: 5, 6, 7, 8, 9.
Dimensions: Up to 5 inches (150 mm) high.

Description: This is an easily grown corm producing via a corm. Naturalize in grassy areas or under trees. This plant is also adaptable to rock gardens and pot-planting. As with most corms, it looks best when massed generously, rather than used as a small feature. There are many other species available offering a good color selection. Plant in organic mulch in well-drained soil. Water regularly from when flowers first appear to when the leaves die back. Fertilize weekly during the growing period.

Other colors: White, lavender, blue, yellow.

Varieties/cultivars: 'Whitewell purple', 'Ruby giant'.

Colchicum cilicicum 'Byzantinum'
AUTUMN CROCUS

Family: LILIACEAE
Origin: Cultivar.
Flowering time: Autumn.
Climatic zone: 4, 5, 6, 7, 8, 9.
Dimensions: Up to 12 inches (300 mm) high.

Description: Autumn crocus are best planted in a nook by themselves with a groundcover. The funnel-shaped flowers of rose-pink and purple shoot out of the ground without any leaves. Their lush, coarse foliage appears in spring. Crocus prefer well-composted, well-drained soil. This perennial will flourish in an open sunny situation. To divide the plants, lift and move them while they are dormant before flowering. Replant immediately, as the root growth is active at that time. As it is a woodland species, it should not be allowed to dry out too much.

Other colors: White, pink, purple.

Colchicum cilicicum 'Byzantinum'
WINTER CROCUS

Family: IRIDACEAE
Origin: Yugoslavia–Hungary.
Flowering time: Winter–spring.
Climatic zone: 5, 6, 7, 8, 9.
Dimensions: Up to 5 inches (130 mm) high.

Description: Affectionately known as "Tommies" by many gardeners, these crocus pop up everywhere, even among pebbles. Landscape usage is very flexible. They can be planted in rock gardens, borders, and pots. Although easy to grow, these crocus do like definite cold in winter. Provide light to medium-rich soil in a sunny open position. If naturalizing in a lawn, do not mow once buds emerge from the soil.

Crocus speciosus

corms. Mainly used as a potted specimen it does well in a warm but not hot position. It must be grown under glass in colder climates. Fragrant strains are available and there is a wide choice of colors. Grow in pots of gritty compost with leaf mold and add pieces of chalk or limestone in the drainage area. Excessive temperatures will lead to failure. This species needs plenty of light (though not more than four hours of direct sunlight per day) and a slightly moist atmosphere and does not tolerate high temperatures. Wet soil will cause the buds and leaf base to rot.
Other colors: White, pink, purple, red.
Varieties/cultivars: Many cultivars are available.

Dierama pulcherrimum

Dierama pulcherrimum
WANDFLOWER, FAIRY FISHING ROD, FAIRY BELLS
Family: IRIDACEAE
Origin: South Africa.
Flowering time: Spring–summer.
Climatic zone: 8, 9.
Dimensions: Up to 5 feet (approx. 2 meters) high.
Description: A delightful plant, it has long fishing-rod stems which arch with the weight of hanging flowers. The graceful, arching growth merits a front row position in a border. The fairy quality of this flower enhances cottage gardens. A hardy grower, it requires sun in temperate climates but needs shade in the tropics. The soil should be moist, fertile, and well-drained.
Other colors: White, pink, purple, red.
Varieties/cultivars: 'Blackbird', 'Jay', 'Kingfisher'.

Crocus vernus 'Enchantress'

Crocus vernus and cultivars
DUTCH CROCUS, SPRING CROCUS
Family: IRIDACEAE
Origin: Mediterranean region.
Flowering time: Spring.
Climatic zone: 3, 4, 5, 6, 7, 8, 9.
Dimensions: Up to 8 inches (200 mm) high.
Description: Originally the purple or white crocus found growing wild on alpine slopes, it is now cultivated to produce free-flowering bulbs. It can be planted in clumps in lawns, under trees, and in beds or window boxes. It looks attractive indoors in blue delft pots to accentuate the "Dutch touch". For selective planting, grow it in rock walls, gravel pathways, or between paving stones. Crocus is not very particular about soil types, but needs good drainage. A sunny location is necessary in cold climates to open the flowers, but in hot areas, filtered sun is best.
Other colors: Pale lilac, mauve, white, deep purple, golden-yellow.
Varieties/cultivars: 'Yellow Giant', 'Dutch Yellow', 'Negro Boy', 'Striped Beauty', 'Haarlem Gem', 'Enchantress'.

Cyclamen persicum

Cyclamen persicum
FLORIST'S CYCLAMEN, COMMON CYCLAMEN
Family: PRIMULACEAE
Origin: Eastern Mediterranean.
Flowering time: Winter–spring.
Climatic zone: 9.
Dimensions: Up to 12 inches (300 mm) high.
Description: This plant needs special attention if grown from seed or tuber-

Endymion hispanicus hybrid

Endymion hispanicus and hybrids, syn. *Scilla hispanica, S. campanulata*

SPANISH BLUEBELL, GIANT BLUEBELL

Family: LILIACEAE
Origin: Spain and Portugal–central Italy.
Flowering time: Spring.
Climatic zone: 5, 6, 7, 8, 9.
Dimensions: Up to 18 inches (450 mm) high.
Description: Bluebells look pretty planted in borders, edges, rock gardens or under deciduous trees and shrubs. They blend well with lily-of-the-valley and a carpet of alyssum. They will naturalize rapidly if planted in woodland settings. Bluebells can also be grown in containers indoors. Plant the bulbs in autumn in deep, fertile soil in a lightly shaded or sunny position. Water regularly in winter and spring but keep them dry once foliage turns yellow.
Other colors: Pink, white.

Fritillaria meleagris

SNAKE'S-HEAD FRITILLARY (U.K.), BLOODY WARRIOR, LEOPARD LILY

Other common names: CHECKERED LILY, GUINEA FLOWER
Family: LILIACEAE
Origin: U.K., central Europe, Scandinavia.
Flowering time: Spring.
Climatic zone: 4, 5, 6, 7, 8, 9.
Dimensions: Up to 18 inches (450 mm) high.
Description: This is an old-fashioned favorite that lasts for years and is easy to grow. It looks well in rock gardens. The solitary and delicate bell-shaped flower belies its fierce common names. Leopard lily is a corruption of leper lily, so-named because the flower resembled the warning bell of lepers. The checkered bells add a distinctive contrast to a garden. Plant in deep humus-rich soil, in a sunny position. It is native to damp European meadows.
Other colors: Orange, white, green, purple, yellow.
Varieties/cultivars: 'Alba'.

Fritillaria meleagris

Hyacinthus orientalis

DUTCH HYACINTH, COMMON HYACINTH

Family: LILIACEAE
Origin: Mediterranean region.
Flowering time: Winter–spring.
Climatic zone: 5, 6, 7, 8, 9.
Dimensions: Up to 18 inches (450 mm) high.
Description: Hyacinths are best suited to formal settings because of their stiff stems and dense flower spikes. They have heavily perfumed, waxy, bell-shaped flowers and do well indoors. They can also be grown most effectively if planted in groups in the garden. They can be susceptible to fungal conditions in soil that is too wet; the bulbs becoming soft and rotten. All garden hyacinths are derived from *H. orientalis*. Some varieties have double blooms. For an exotic touch they can be grown indoors in water in special hyacinth glasses.
Other colors: White, yellow, pink, mauve, purple.
Varieties/cultivars: *H. o. albulus*.

Hyacinthus orientalis

Ipheion uniflorum

TRITELEIA, SPRING STARFLOWER

Family: LILIACEAE
Origin: Peru.
Flowering time: Spring-summer.
Climatic zone: 7, 8, 9.
Dimensions: Up to 8 inches (200 mm) high.
Description: *Ipheion* is well suited to massing at the front of borders or rock gardens. This prolific plant produces numerous solitary flowers. The perfumed blooms are funnel-shaped, with white, pale mauve, or lilac petals. The grassy leaves emit a faint onion-like odor when pressed. *Ipheion* multiplies rapidly in a sunny position in well-drained soil. Bulbs should be left undisturbed for several years until clumps form. They will flower for up to eight weeks and need little attention.

Ipheion uniflorum

Muscari armeniacum

Climatic zone: 6, 7, 8, 9.
Dimensions: Up to 18 inches (450 mm) high.
Description: Early botanists thought that this plant was an English native. Although it flourished for centuries near Bristol, it had been brought from Spain by merchant seamen. It blooms in various shades of blue, except for one white form. This blue and gold beauty makes a colorful addition to the rose garden and flowers for up to eight weeks. Iris, which was named after the goddess of the rainbow, is an excellent cut flower. It requires cool, moist soil in a sunny area protected from strong wind.

Iris reticulata
SPANISH IRIS

Family: IRIDACEAE
Origin: Central Turkey, Caucasus, Iran, Iraq.
Flowering time: Spring.
Climatic zone: 6, 7, 8, 9.
Dimensions: Up to 18 inches (450 mm) high.
Description: Spanish iris is a violet-scented beauty with grassy leaves and deep-blue or purple flowers. In some areas it is best grown in a cool greenhouse. It is suitable for rock gardens, the front of borders and will grow well in pots. Iris likes sandy light soil in a sunny position protected from wind. The best results are achieved if bulbs are lifted after flowering. They should be stored in dry sand. It is important to keep the bulbs as dry as possible during their dormant period.
Other colors: Yellow.
Varieties/cultivars: There are many cultivars available.

Iris xiphioides
ENGLISH IRIS

Family: IRIDACEAE
Origin: Spain, the Pyrenees.
Flowering time: Spring-summer.

Iris xiphium
SPANISH IRIS

Family: IRIDACEAE
Origin: Spain, Portugal, southern France.
Flowering time: Early summer.
Climatic zone: 6, 7, 8, 9.
Dimensions: Up to 2 feet (600 mm) high.
Description: *I. xiphium* is a parent of the dutch iris. The flowers have petals the standards and falls of which are often of different colors. Use it in borders or in a sunny corner against a fence or trellis. Their eye-catching beauty makes them ideal for indoor floral arrangements and ornamental pot plants. Plant in fertile soil using plenty of organic matter and protect from winds.
Other colors: White, yellow, orange, bronze.
Varieties/cultivars: Several cultivars are available.

Iris xiphium 'Franz Hals'

Iris xiphioides

Iris reticulata

Muscari armeniacum
GRAPE HYACINTH

Family: LILIACEAE
Origin: Asia Minor.
Flowering time: Spring.
Climatic zone: 4, 5, 6, 7, 8, 9.
Dimensions: Up to 8 inches (200 mm) high.
Description: The dense heads of rich blue fragrant flowers suit borders and edges. Several varieties of these grape-shaped flowers are available. They make good companions for yellow violas and white primula. They will readily naturalize when planted in grass or lightly wooded areas, and are good plants for potting indoors. Cultivate in well-rotted compost and water regularly.
Other colors: Mauve, white.
Varieties/cultivars: 'Blue spike', 'Cantab'.

Puschkinia scilloides
STRIPED SQUILL

Family: LILIACEAE
Origin: Eastern Turkey, Caucasus, Lebanon.
Flowering time: Spring.
Climatic zone: 4, 5, 6, 7, 8, 9.
Dimensions: Up to 6 inches (150 mm) high.

Puschkinia scilloides

Description: These dainty powder-blue flowers with deep-blue stripes blend well with violas and rock garden plants. They need to be placed where they complement other plants, as they are not very showy on their own. Easy to grow in sandy soil enriched with humus, they will take full sun or partial shade. The bulbs need not be disturbed for several years. If flowering diminishes, they will need to be relocated in new soil.

Plant in rich, sandy soil in sun or partial shade. They will benefit from an occasional top dressing of good soil or old manure. Divide small bulblets from older bulbs in autumn to accelerate their spread.

Scilla peruviana
CUBAN LILY, PERUVIAN SCILLA, PERUVIAN LILY (U.K.)
Family: LILIACEAE
Origin: Southern Europe.
Flowering time: Early summer.
Climatic zone: 8, 9

Scilla peruviana

Dimensions: Up to 18 inches (450 mm) high.
Description: Cuban lily is a showy bulb featuring clusters of fifty or more flowers. It can be massed in beds, planted as a backdrop to annuals, or used as a border along fences, and as an edge between garden beds. This species is easy to grow in rich, sandy soil in sun or partial shade. Divide the bulbs for extra plantings in autumn. At this time, they will also benefit from an occasional top dressing of old manure or good soil.

Scilla sibirica
SIBERIAN SCILLA, SPRING SQUILL (U.K.)
Family: LILIACEAE
Origin: Turkey, Iran, Caucasus.
Flowering time: Spring.
Climatic zone: 3, 4, 5, 6, 7, 8.
Dimensions: Up to 6 inches (150 mm) high.
Description: As its origins suggest, this dainty species is hardy. The deep-blue, drooping flowers produce three to five blooms to a stem. *Scilla* is ideal for rock gardens or planted under azaleas and camellias. Intersperse it with other bulbs where it can form a carpet. If rich, sandy soil is provided, it will rapidly increase. Top dress with good soil, compost, or old manure. Divide the plant when dormant to cover a large area quickly.
Varieties/cultivars: 'Spring Beauty', 'Atrocaerulea'.

Scilla bifolia

Scilla bifolia
BLUEBELL, TWIN-LEAF SQUILL
Family: LILIACEAE
Origin: Southern Europe–Turkey.
Flowering time: Spring.
Climatic zone: 5, 6, 7, 8, 9.
Dimensions: Up to 6 inches (150 mm) high.
Description: These hardy bulbs are adaptable to most cool soils and positions. *Scillas* are good carpet plants in beds of early-flowering tulips. They are easy to grow, will rapidly increase, and are suitable for borders, edges, pots, and in clumps under deciduous trees.

Scilla sibirica

117

Clematis x jackmanii
CLEMATIS, LARGE-
FLOWERED CLEMATIS

Family: RANUNCULACEAE
Origin: Hybrid.
Flowering time: Summer.
Climatic zone: 5, 6, 7, 8, 9.
Description: One of the early hybrids of this magnificent genus, this clematis has a profusion of 4–5 inch (100–125 mm), rich purple flowers. Later hybrids have larger, but not as many, flowers. Rich soil, full sun, and cool roots are the requirements for these vines. This one flowers on new season's growth, so severe pruning is necessary in the winter, or when leaves drop. Lime

Clematis x jackmanii

Clematis 'Barbara Jackman'

118

4–5 inches (100–125 mm) across. Clematis needs plenty of compost and protection from heat around the roots. It can be grown beside a sheltering shrub, and if grown in pots or large containers, needs a climbing support and a deep mulch as well as shade for the whole root system from becoming overheated.

Akebia quinata

Akebia quinata
AKEBIA, FIVE-LEAFED
AKEBIA

Family: LARDIZABALACEAE
Origin: China, Korea, Japan.
Flowering time: Spring.
Climatic zone: 4, 5, 6, 7, 8, 9.
Description: Akebia's unusual purplish-brown flowers are often the subject of much comment. They appear in spring on short stems, are often freely produced, and are quite fragrant. This is a fast-growing vine, but not invasive. The attractive leaves, in clusters of five, make a handsome cover for fences or pergolas, and it will tolerate a shady position. It is evergreen in warm zones. If it becomes too thick or unmanageable, cut it back to a few small, branching canes, and it will soon become green and dense again.

Clematis 'Barbara Jackman'
BARBARA JACKMAN
CLEMATIS, LARGE-FLOWERED
CLEMATIS

Family: RANUNCULACEAE
Origin: Cultivar.
Flowering time: Early summer.
Climatic zone: 5, 6, 7, 8, 9.
Description: A popular cultivar, this clematis has purple flowers, not as dark as those of *C. x jackmanii*, and about

may be needed in the soil, as it is not tolerant of very acid soil.
Varieties/cultivars: Many, including 'Rubra', 'Henry', 'Mrs Cholmondeley', 'The President'.

Clytostoma callistegioides
VIOLET TRUMPET VINE, ARGENTINE TRUMPET VINE

Family: BIGNONIACEAE
Origin: Brazil, Argentina.
Flowering time: Late spring-summer.
Climatic zone: 9, 10.
Description: Lavender streaked with violet is the color of the large funnel-shaped flowers, which appear in pairs at the ends of long, drooping stems. Although evergreen, this strong-growing climber may be semideciduous in cooler zones. Tendrils help it to climb a fence or a wall, but some support is required. A sunny position with rich soil and regular watering suits this very attractive and colorful vine, but it will also tolerate a semishaded site, as long as it is a warm one. A greenhouse is necessary for cold climates.

Clytostoma callistegioides

flowers. They are large and bell-shaped, up to 2 inches (50 mm) long, opening yellow-green and changing to purple. They have a slight resemblance to a cup sitting on a saucer. A branched tendril at the end of the group of leaflets is the means of support to hold this vine against a wall. Grow it in a warm semishady position and protect it from wind. It needs good soil, deep mulch, and regular watering. It can be grown as an annual.

Distictis laxiflora
VANILLA TRUMPET VINE

Family: BIGNONIACEAE
Origin: Mexico.
Flowering time: Most of the year.
Climatic zone: 9, 10.
Description: Less rampant than many of the trumpet vines, *Distictis laxiflora* has two or three leaflets, the leaves giving this evergreen climber an attractive appearance for the short time that the flowers are not present. The

Cobaea scandens

flowers are vanilla-scented and about 3½ inches (80 mm) long. They open as a violet color and fade to lavender and white. This is a hot climate plant and needs a greenhouse in colder areas.

Hardenbergia comptoniana
LILAC VINE (U.S.A.), WILD SARSAPARILLA, NATIVE WISTERIA (Aust.)

Family: LEGUMINOSAE
Origin: Western Australia.
Flowering time: Late winter-spring.
Climatic zone: 9.
Description: Violet-blue pea-flowers are massed in graceful sprays on this evergreen climber. Grow it over a low mesh fence, or trail it over the wall of a raised garden bed. It is an easily controlled vine, growing to about 10 feet (3 meters), or a groundcover, when it grows quite flat and spreading. Choose a sunny, well-drained position with minimum water. A wire frame in a container makes a good base for a pillar shape, but it can be trained into any shape. A warm climate plant, it needs to be grown under glass in other areas.

Distictis laxiflora

Clytostoma callistegioides

Cobaea scandens
CUP-AND-SAUCER VINE, CUP-AND-SAUCER CREEPER (U.K.), CATHEDRAL BELLS

Family: POLEMONIACEAE
Origin: Mexico-northern Chile.
Flowering time: Spring, summer, autumn.
Climatic zone: 5, 6, 7, 8, 9, 10.
Description: *Cobaea* is a fast-growing, vigorous climber with most unusual

Hardenbergia comptoniana

Ipomoea purpurea

Hardenbergia violacea

Hardenbergia violacea
PURPLE CORAL PEA, NATIVE SARSAPARILLA (Aust.), WILD SARSAPARILLA
Family: LEGUMINOSAE
Origin: Eastern and southern Australia.
Flowering time: Spring.
Climatic zone: 9.
Description: Masses of small purple-blue flowers on slender, wiry stems make a glorious display in spring. This twining vine has long, oval, and pointed leaves, and will endure harsh, dry conditions. Plant it in full sun in well-drained soil. It will be happy to creep over banks and trees, or it can be trained as a vine. The denser and coarser texture of this species makes it more tolerant of wind and very sunny positions than the lilac vine, and it is faster growing.
Other colors: White, pink.

or in pots on a terrace or patio. Kept restricted in root space, there is a tendency for earlier flowering. The flowers last only one day, fading to a lighter color in the afternoon.
Other colors: Scarlet, white.
Varieties/cultivars: 'Heavenly Blue', 'Alba', 'Rose Marie', 'Scarlet O'Hara'.

Kennedia nigricans
BLACK CORAL PEA
Family: LEGUMINOSAE
Origin: Western Australia.
Flowering time: Summer.
Climatic zone: 9, 10.
Description: A vigorous evergreen twiner, *Kennedia nigricans* has black-purple flowers with a yellow blotch on the top petal. They are most unusual and distinctive, and are followed by flat, hairy pods. The vine is tolerant of a shady position, but prefers a warm site with very good drainage. Being quite

chance of frost has passed. Young shoots can be trained to cover a trellis or column.
Other colors: Pink, blue.

Ipomoea tricolor
MORNING GLORY
Family: CONVOLVULACEAE
Origin: Tropical America.
Flowering time: Summer–autumn.
Climatic zone: 4, 5, 6, 7, 8, 9, 10.
Description: This is the popular morning glory cultivated as an annual in gardens all over the world. In warm zones it is a perennial climber. The flower buds are red and open to large, purplish-blue blooms 4 inches (100 mm) across. It is an excellent plant for climbing fences, or growing over arches,

Ipomoea purpurea
MORNING GLORY
Family: CONVOLVULACEAE
Origin: Tropical America.
Flowering time: Summer.
Climatic zone: 4, 5, 6, 7, 8, 9, 10.
Description: A vigorous, twining climber, morning glory has broadly ovate leaves and large open purple flowers that bloom in profusion during summer. Easy to cultivate in a wide range of soils and conditions, it can become a pest in warmer climates as it tends to take a stranglehold on the garden. In cooler climates treat as an annual planting in spring after the

Kennedia nigricans

Ipomoea tricolor

drought-tolerant when established, it is worth growing in an awkward spot to give a good fence cover or groundcover. A hot climate plant, it needs greenhouse protection in colder areas.

Lathyrus latifolius

Lathyrus latifolius
EVERLASTING PEA, PINK PERENNIAL PEA ○
Family: LEGUMINOSAE
Origin: Southern Europe.
Flowering time: Summer.
Climatic zone: 5, 6, 7, 8, 9.
Description: Many new shoots come from the base of this perennial climber each year. It is happy in most conditions, including windy sites near the sea, and will grow up to 10 feet (3 meters) high. The large attractive sprays of flowers are held on long, upright stems. The vine looks beautiful trained over a summerhouse, porch or trellis, but needs a sunny position. Although quick-growing, it is not featured as often as it deserves. Mulch well and prune off all old growth at the end of summer.

Lonicera japonica var. *repens* syn. *L. j.* var. *flexuosa*, *L. j.* 'Purpurea'
JAPANESE HONEYSUCKLE ◐ ◑
Family: CAPRIFOLIACEAE
Origin: Japan, China, Korea.
Flowering time: Summer.
Climatic zone: 6, 7, 8, 9.
Description: The white flowers of this well-known climber are tinged with purple on the outside. An evergreen or semideciduous, this Japanese honeysuckle has highly fragrant flowers which appear in summer, growing in pairs. A vigorous vine, it can quickly cover a fence, and should be planted in a warm, sheltered position. It will tolerate quite cool conditions if grown under trees or given some protection from frost. It does not seem to be fussy about soil, and will thrive almost anywhere.

Lonicera japonica var. *repens*

Passiflora caerulea
BLUE-CROWN PASSION FLOWER, BLUE PASSION FLOWER, COMMON PASSION FLOWER (U.K.) ○ ◑
Family: PASSIFLORACEAE
Origin: Western and central South America.
Flowering time: Summer.
Climatic zone: 8, 9.
Description: This is the best *Passiflora* for growing in frosty districts, although it is happy in warm areas. A slender, but strong-growing vine, which will quickly climb up a tree or over a fence, it needs either plenty of space, or regular pruning. The flowers are white with a central fringe of blue, white, and purple, and are followed by orange-colored fruit which is not edible. This species was often used as root stock on which the edible types of passionfruit were grafted.

Perrea volubilis
QUEEN'S WREATH, PURPLE WREATH ○
Family: VERBENACEAE
Origin: Mexico–Panama, West Indies.
Flowering time: Winter–spring.
Climatic zone: 9, 10.
Description: Rough, brittle leaves on this wiry-stemmed twiner contrast with the beauty of the rich-colored, five-lobed petals. The lilac calyx remains on the plant for a long time and finally falls, spinning like a tiny top. A hot climate is necessary for this evergreen vine. Rich soil and ample water will give best foliage. It is a delightful climber which is easy to control and will never be invasive. It can combine with another light climber with white flowers, to give a two-colored effect.

Perrea volubilis

Passiflora caerulea

Phaseolus caracalla

Phaseolus caracalla syn. *Vigna caracalla*
SNAIL FLOWER,
CORKSCREW FLOWER

Family: LEGUMINOSAE
Origin: Tropical South America.
Flowering time: Spring or summer.
Climatic zone: 5, 6, 7, 8, 9, 10.
Description: This relative of the scarlet runner bean is an equally vigorous grower and has masses of curious flowers with a delightful fragrance. The flowers are coiled like snails and fleshy, with creamy, purple colors. Quick-growing, this deciduous twiner can be pruned back to ground level in late autumn and will soon cover a fence in the following spring. It does best in rich soil and prefers a sheltered position. The dense, lush foliage needs a wire support to help it attain an upright growth. In cooler climates, it is best grown as an annual.

Sollya heterophylla
AUSTRALIAN
BLUEBELL CREEPER

Family: PITTOSPORACEAE
Origin: Western Australia.
Flowering time: Summer–autumn.
Climatic zone: 9.
Description: This vine's slender twining stems will gradually cover a fence without ever becoming a problem. Clusters of tiny, bell-shaped, bright-blue flowers hang in delicate little sprays in spring and summer, and are followed by purple berries. Tolerant of semishade, it is a good groundcover, or will twine around a post or pergola. Best foliage is obtained when it is given sheltered conditions, with ample water and good drainage. The narrow, glossy green leaves are attractive, and make this evergreen vine a good choice for container-growing. In cold climates, it will grow well in a greenhouse.
Other colors: Pink, white.

Sollya heterophylla

Thunbergia grandiflora
SKY FLOWER, CLOCK
VINE, BLUE TRUMPET VINE

Family: ACANTHACEAE
Origin: Northern India–southern China.
Flowering time: Summer, autumn.

Wisteria floribunda

Climatic zone: 9, 10.
Description: Rough, toothed leaves cover this woody twiner with vigorous growth. The bell-shaped flowers, 2 inches or more across (50–60 mm), are a clear periwinkle blue with a white throat. The flowers are single, appear in the leaf axils, and are slightly pendant. This is a showy, robust climber which needs good soil and adequate summer water to look its best. It is not tolerant of frost, although if grown in a sheltered position it will survive quite cool conditions. A greenhouse is ideal for cooler zones.

Wisteria floribunda syn. *W. multijuga*
JAPANESE WISTERIA

Family: LEGUMINOSAE
Origin: Japan.
Flowering time: Early summer.
Climatic zone: 4, 5, 6, 7, 8, 9.
Description: The fragrant pea-shaped flowers on this lovely vine appear at the same time as the new leaves. The flower sprays are in shades of violet-blue, and hang in clusters 18 inches (450 mm) long. The display lasts longer than in other species as the flowers at the base of the spray open first, followed gradually by those nearer the tip. The attractive, glossy leaves are made up of between thirteen and nineteen leaflets. It is a vigorous climber and needs a strong support for the dense canopy produced in the summer time.
Varieties/cultivars: 'Rosea', 'Violacea Plena', 'Macrobotrys', 'Alba'.

Thunbergia grandiflora

122

Wisteria floribunda 'Macrobotrys'

Wisteria floribunda 'Macrobotrys' syn. W. multijuga
JAPANESE WISTERIA, LONG JAPANESE WISTERIA

Family: LEGUMINOSAE
Origin: Cultivar.
Flowering time: Spring-early summer.
Climatic zone: 5, 6, 7, 8, 9.
Description: Honey-scented violet-purple flowers hang in enormous sprays, up to 3 feet (900 mm) long, on this tall-climbing woody vine. Each flower is about 1 inch (25 mm) long. They appear either before or with the glossy green leaves which have thirteen to nineteen leaflets. The flowering season is very short, and flowers are followed by long, soft-green, velvety pods. For an eye-catching display, grow this wisteria over a tall pergola, or arbor, which the blossoms can cascade down. Water well during flowering to hold the blossoms.

Wisteria floribunda 'Violacea Plena'
DOUBLE JAPANESE WISTERIA

Family: LEGUMINOSAE
Origin: Cultivar.
Flowering time: Spring.
Climatic zone: 5, 6, 7, 8, 9.
Description: Both the flowering and the growth habit distinguish this cultivar from its parent plant. The small, tight, flower clusters hang in sprays 6–8 inches (150–200 mm) long,

Wisteria sinensis

Wisteria floribunda 'Violacea Plena'

Wisteria sinensis

but they are double flowers and held in a fairly tightly packed group. The dense, bushy growth is more shrub-like, and can be trained into a shrub or small tree if pruned during summer. It will need support on which to climb when used as a vine. Loamy acid soil is best, with plenty of water at flowering time.

Wisteria sinensis
CHINESE WISTERIA

Family: LEGUMINOSAE
Origin: China.
Flowering time: Spring-early summer.
Climatic zone: 5, 6, 7, 8, 9.
Description: This wisteria is an early spring favorite. The slightly fragrant, lilac flowers are in drooping clusters from 8–12 inches (200–300 mm) in length, and tend to open nearly the full length of the cluster at one time. A very vigorous deciduous vine, it will develop a trunk like a tree, but with constant pruning in summer it can be trained as a weeping standard tree, or it can become a gnarled-trunked shrub. Velvety, bean-like pods are attractive decoration among the leaves when the flowers are finished.
Other colors: White.
Varieties/cultivars: *Wisteria sinensis* 'Alba.'

Wisteria sinensis

monkshood was regarded as a valuable ingredient in medieval potions.
Other colors: White, pink.
Varieties/cultivars: 'Album', 'Carneum'.

Aconitum napellus

Aconitum x bicolor
HYBRID MONKSHOOD, MONKSHOOD, WOLFBANE

Family: RANUNCULACEAE
Origin: Hybrid.
Flowering time: Summer.
Climatic zone: 3, 4, 5, 6, 7, 8, 9.
Dimensions: 3–4 feet (approx. 1 meter) high.
Description: This dramatic old-fashioned favorite gives a wonderful display of violet-blue and white, helmet-shaped flowers that are borne in a

Aconitum x bicolor

Aconitum carmichaelii syn. *A. fischeri*
AZURE MONKSHOOD

Family: RANUNCULACEAE
Origin: Eastern Asia.
Flowering time: Late summer–autumn.
Climatic zone: 3, 4, 5, 6, 7, 8, 9.
Dimensions: Up to 4 feet (approx. 1 meter) high.
Description: Azure monkshood is one of the most popular of the garden monkshoods. The dramatic blue hoods of the flowers extend into a spur-like visor and are borne on long stems. These may need staking. A showy border plant, it needs a position in partial shade and does not like to be disturbed. Plant it in rich, moist, well-drained soil. As the juice is highly poisonous, it is not wise to plant monkshood in a garden used by small children.

Aconitum carmichaelii

Aconitum napellus
COMMON MONKSHOOD

Family: RANUNCULACEAE
Origin: Europe, Asia.
Flowering time: Summer.
Climatic zone: 3, 4, 5, 6, 7, 8, 9.
Dimensions: Up to 5 feet (approx. 2 meters) high.
Description: Common monkshood has brilliant green foliage and tall spikes of helmet-like flowers in a rich violet-blue. It is a useful cottage garden plant, and suitable as a background border. It grows best in cool-climate gardens, in deep, rich, moist soil that has adequate drainage. The foliage dies back in winter. Despite the fact that all parts of the plant are poisonous, common

---

terminal raceme. The foliage is mid-green in color. Ideal for an herbaceous border, monkshood should be grown in semishade in rich, moist soil with good drainage. The plant may require staking when it reaches its full height.
Other colors: Deeper violet blue, blue and white.

Adenophora confusa
LADYBELLS

Family: CAMPANULACEAE
Origin: Eastern Asia.
Flowering time: Mid-late summer.
Climatic zone: 4, 5, 6, 7, 8, 9.
Dimensions: Up to 3 feet (1 meter) high.
Description: Ladybells is a charming plant with tall, slender stems and large, dark-purple, bell-shaped flowers, measuring up to ¾ inch (18 mm) in length. Plant it in either full sun or semishade in well-drained, moderately rich soil. It can even be grown in rather poor soils providing there is adequate moisture and good drainage. It makes a very pretty addition to a mixed bed of summer-flowering annuals and perennials.

Adenophora confusa

Agapanthus praecox syn. *A. umbellatus*
AGAPANTHUS, AFRICAN LILY, BLUE AFRICAN LILY

Family: AMARYLLIDACEAE
Origin: South Africa.
Flowering time: Summer.

Agapanthus praecox

Amsonia tabernaemontana

Amsonia tabernaemontana
BLUE STAR, WILLOW AMSONIA

○ ◐

Family: APOCYNACEAE
Origin: Central and eastern United States.
Flowering time: Summer.
Climatic zone: 4, 5, 6, 7, 8, 9.
Dimensions: Up to 2 feet (600 mm) high.
Description: The very pale, small, star-like flowers of this perennial form in clusters at the top of the tall, leaved stems. It is suited to partially shaded or sunny herbaceous borders and in the right position will become quite bushy. If growth is sparse and open, cut back the plant to half its size to encourage denser growth. It looks attractive planted with campanulas; C. lactiflora 'Alba' complements it well. Blue star is easy to grow in any moist, ordinary garden soil and can be propagated by division in spring or autumn. It is often sold as A. salicifolia.

Climatic zone: 8, 9.
Dimensions: 2–3 feet (600–900 mm) high.
Description: Agapanthus is a useful and hardy specimen, which looks most attractive as a border or background plant. It forms a large clump of strap-like leaves and produces tall stems in summer, topped by large, globular flower heads in various shades of blue to purple. Full sun or semishade suits it best, and it will grow in most soil conditions providing reasonable drainage is provided. The clumps can be divided during winter to produce new plants.
Other colors: White.
Varieties/cultivars: Many varieties and cultivars are available.

plant, it is attractive in rock gardens, under large trees, or between pavers. Plant it in a sunny or semishaded position and water regularly. It will tolerate poor and wet or heavy soils. Cut back the dead flower heads. Propagate it by its free-rooting stems or by seed in spring. An infusion of the plant was used for centuries to cure coughs, bruises and hemorrhages.
Other colors: White, pink.
Varieties/cultivars: 'Burgundy Glow', 'Alba', 'Atropurprea', 'Delight', 'Multicolor', 'Pink Elf', 'Variegata'.

Ajuga reptans
COMMON BLUE BUGLEWEED, BUGLE, COMMON BUGLE

○ ◐

Family: LABIATAE
Origin: Europe–Southwestern Asia.
Flowering time: Spring–summer.
Climatic zone: 4, 5, 6, 7, 8, 9.
Dimensions: 8–12 inches (200–300 mm) high.
Description: This is a spreading perennial groundcover with oval, dark-green leaves and spikes of blue flowers. Cultivars have variegated cream, pink, and burgundy foliage. A quick-growing

Ajuga reptans

Arisaema triphyllum

Arisaema triphyllum
JACK-IN-THE-PULPIT, INDIAN TURNIP

●　◐　●

Family: ARACEAE
Origin: North America.
Flowering time: Spring–summer.
Climatic zone: 4, 5, 6, 7, 8, 9.
Dimensions: Up to 2½ feet (750 mm) high.
Description: A cool fernery or rock garden is the ideal position for *Arisaema*, with its purplish-green hooded spathe. Plant it in rich, moist humus soil in a sheltered, partially shaded site, and give it plenty of water in summer. Propagate by offsets or by seed. The North American Indians used the turnip-shaped, acrid root to cure headaches, and also as a contraceptive.
Varieties/cultivars: *A. t. stewardsonii, A. t. zebrinum*.

Aster thomsonii
ASTER, THOMSON'S ASTER (U.K.)

○

Family: COMPOSITAE
Origin: Western Himalayas.
Flowering time: Summer–autumn.
Climatic zone: 7, 8, 9.
Dimensions: Up to 2 feet (600 mm) high.
Description: This is one of the lavender-blue group of asters which has produced many hybrids. The daisy-like flowers are profuse and the almost heart-shaped leaves are serrated. Plant it in sunny, open borders where the soil will not dry out during the growing season. Protect it from wind and stake it if necessary. This is a good plant for cut

lance-shaped, gray-green foliage and small, round, bright blue flowers. It likes an open, sunny position and can be grown in a wide range of soils, as long as drainage is good and water is provided during hot summer weather.
Varieties/cultivars: 'Loddon Royalist', 'Morning Glory'.

Aquilegia caerulea
ROCKY MOUNTAIN COLUMBINE

○　◐

Family: RANUNCULACEAE
Origin: Rocky Mountains, North America.
Flowering time: Late spring–early summer.
Climatic zone: 4, 5, 6, 7, 8, 9.
Dimensions: Up to 2 feet (600 mm) high.
Description: *A. caerulea*, with its soft lavender-blue and creamy white blooms, is the state flower of Colorado. Plant it in sun or partial shade and leave undisturbed so that the seeds drop and colonies form. Moist soils that neither dry out in summer nor become waterlogged in winter suit it best.

Anchusa azurea

Anchusa azurea syn. *A. italica*
ITALIAN BUGLOSS

○

Family: BORAGINACEAE
Origin: Caucasus–central Europe.
Flowering time: Late spring–early summer.
Climatic zone: 4, 5, 6, 7.
Dimensions: 3–5 feet (approx. 1–2 meters) high.
Description: This delightful wild plant is a relative of the herb borage, and has

Aquilegia caerulea

Aster thomsonii 'Nana'

arrangements. A fragrant perennial plant that is well suited to cottage gardens, it will grow quite quickly into an attractive clump. Plant it in full sun along pathways and low fences or beside a front gate. It likes fertile, well-drained soil, and may be prone to mildew in humid areas.

Astilbe chinensis 'Pumila'
ASTILBE, DWARF FALSE GOATSBEARD
Family: SAXIFRAGACEAE
Origin: Cultivar.
Flowering time: Summer.
Climatic zone: 4, 5, 6, 7, 8, 9.

Dimensions: Up to 12 inches (300 mm) high.
Description: This handsome perennial is a good choice for the front of borders. The densely clustered, mauve-pink flowers and attractive foliage contrast well with white daisies or silver-gray artemisia. 'Pumila' tolerates drier soils than other astilbes and, being a gross feeder, needs an extra application of fertilizer during summer. Easy to grow in any ordinary, moist garden soil, it reproduces quickly and should either be given plenty of space to spread or be divided every three years.

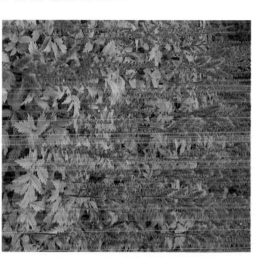

Astilbe chinensis 'Pumila'

floral arrangements. The dwarf form, 'Nana', grows to a height of about 15 inches (375 mm).
Varieties/cultivars: 'Nana'.

Aster x frikartii
ASTER
Family: COMPOSITAE
Origin: Hybrid.
Flowering time: Summer-autumn.
Climatic zone: 5, 6, 7, 8, 9.
Dimensions: Up to 3 feet (1 meter) high.
Description: These vibrant lavender-blue daisies with yellow centers provide a constant source of flowers for floral

Astilbe taquetii 'Superba'
ASTILBE, FALSE GOATSBEARD
Family: SAXIFRAGACEAE
Origin: Cultivar.
Flowering time: Late summer.
Climatic zone: 5, 6, 7, 8, 9.
Dimensions: Up to 4 feet (approx. 1 meter) high.
Description: Long, feathery spikes of magenta or reddish-purple flowers accompany bronze-green foliage. A single plume may have hundreds of florets and the overall effect is spectacular. 'Superba' suits borders and rock gardens and particularly the surrounds of rock pools. A deep, rich, moisture-retaining soil with a liberal application of humus is the ideal environment for it. This cultivar is more drought-tolerant than some strains.

Astilbe taquetii 'Superba'

Aster x frikartii

Baptisia australis

Baptisia australis syn. *B. exaltata*
WILD INDIGO, FALSE INDIGO

Family: LEGUMINOSAE
Origin: Eastern United States.
Flowering time: Spring–summer, northern hemisphere; summer, southern hemisphere.
Climatic zone: 4, 5, 6, 7, 8, 9.
Dimensions: Up to 5 feet (over 1 meter) high.
Description: Wild indigo has numerous deep purplish-blue, pea-like flowers borne in terminal racemes. These are followed by attractive seed pods. Resembling lupins, they are attractive in indoor floral arrangements. The plant likes an open, sunny position in sandy loam which has had compost added, and is useful for the drier parts of borders or in wild gardens. Cut it back after flowering. This plant was used in ancient times to cure infections.

Brunnera macrophylla syn. *Anchusa myosotidiflora*
SIBERIAN BUGLOSS
(U.S.A.), FORGET-ME-NOT (U.K.), ANCHUSA (U.K.)

Family: BORAGINACEAE
Origin: Western Caucasus.
Flowering time: Spring.
Climatic zone: 4, 5, 6, 7, 8, 9.
Dimensions: Up to 18 inches (450 mm) high.

Description: The branching, starry, blue flowers of Siberian bugloss resemble forget-me-nots. A member of the borage family, this woodland species has rough, heart-shaped leaves and hairy stems. Grow it in open woodland areas, under trees and shrubs, or in borders. Tolerant of soil types, it can survive in dry, shady positions, but prefers partial shade in moist soil.
Varieties/cultivars: 'Variegata'.

Brunnera macrophylla

Campanula carpatica
CARPATHIAN HAREBELL

Family: CAMPANULACEAE
Origin: Carpathian mountains.
Flowering time: Spring–summer.
Climatic zone: 4, 5, 6, 7, 8, 9.

Dimensions: Up to 12 inches (300 mm) high.
Description: Carpathian harebell grows in clumps. The large (2 inches (50 mm) wide), deep-blue flowers are bell-shaped and the leaves are oval. A quick-growing plant, it is useful for groundcover in rock gardens or on sloping sites. Plant it in fertile, moist soil protected from summer sun and water it liberally. Propagate it by division or from cuttings.
Other colors: Many shades from white to sky-blue.
Varieties/cultivars: 'Loddon Fairy', 'Riverslea', 'White Star'.

Campanula cochleariifolia syn. *C. pusilla*
BELLFLOWER

Family: CAMPANULACEAE
Origin: European mountains.
Flowering time: Summer.

Campanula cochleariifolia

Campanula carpatica

128

Climatic zone: 6, 7, 8, 9.
Dimensions: Up to 6 inches (150 mm) high.
Description: This is another easy-to-grow campanula which is useful for edging beds or planting in rock garden pockets. The solitary, drooping bells appear in great profusion during summer. In larger areas such as sloping sites, plant several different varieties and colors of campanula together to form an effective display. It likes moist, fertile soil protected from summer sun. It is propagated by division or seed.
Other colors: White.
Varieties/cultivars: 'Alba', 'Oakington Blue', 'Miranda'.

Campanula garganica

Campanula garganica
BELLFLOWER
Family: CAMPANULACEAE
Origin: Italy, Greece.
Flowering time: Summer–autumn, northern hemisphere; spring–autumn, southern hemisphere.
Climatic zone: 5, 6, 7, 8, 9.
Dimensions: Up to 4 inches (100 mm) high.
Description: This sprawling, low-growing evergreen is often grown in rock gardens or as a groundcover. Wheel-shaped flowers are borne on long, slender stems, and the leaves are kidney-shaped and coarsely toothed. Flowering begins early in the season and may continue in a sporadic fashion until autumn. Plant it in partial shade in warmer climates, and in full sun in cooler zones. Ordinary garden soil is suitable, but this plant benefits from the addition of compost. Do not allow the soil to dry out.

Campanula glomerata

Campanula glomerata
CLUSTERED BELLFLOWER, DANESBLOOD BELLFLOWER
Family: CAMPANULACEAE
Origin: Europe–western Asia.
Flowering time: Summer.
Climatic zone: 3, 4, 5, 6, 7, 8, 9.
Dimensions: Up to 3 feet (1 meter) high.
Description: This is one of the taller types of *Campanula*. The individual funnel-shaped blooms are rich violet, large, and showy. They form in clusters at the top of stems that are about 1–2 feet (300–600 mm) high and are suitable for floral arrangements. *C. glomerata* is useful in shaded rockeries and is also popular in a border. It grows well in ordinary garden soil. A double-flowered form is available and a variety with deep-violet flowers growing in large clusters.
Other colors: White, violet.
Varieties/cultivars: Several varieties and cultivars are available including *C. g. dahurica*.

Campanula latifolia
GIANT BELLFLOWER
Family: CAMPANULACEAE
Origin: Europe–western Asia, Siberia.
Flowering time: Summer.
Climatic zone: 4, 5, 6, 7, 8.
Dimensions: Up to 4 feet (approx. 1 meter) high.
Description: Now growing widely across Europe to the mountains of Kashmir, giant bellflower, with its numerous, showy, violet-colored, bell-shaped flowers, makes a fine border plant once established. Self-seeding, it will create a good summer display if

allowed to colonize. Although tall, giant bellflower seldom requires staking. It is at home in shady, moist areas but, depending on the climate, will grow in a sunny or semishaded position, in ordinary garden soil. The cultivar 'Macrantha' has purple flowers that are wider than those of giant bellflower.
Other colors: White.
Varieties/cultivars: 'Alba', 'Brantwood', 'Macrantha'.

Campanula latifolia

Campanula medium

Campanula medium
CANTERBURY-BELLS
Family: CAMPANULACEAE
Origin: Southern Europe.
Flowering time: Summer.
Climatic zone: 7, 8, 9.
Dimensions: Up to 3 feet (1 meter) high.
Description: These flowers are said to have been named in honor of St. Thomas à Becket because they resemble the horse bells used by pilgrims visiting his shrine at Canterbury Cathedral. A hardy, quick-growing biennial with blue bell-shaped flowers, they make an excellent border plant that will flower from six to nine weeks. Plant the seeds in soil mixed with fertilizer and compost. An application of lime will benefit growth. It likes a sunny position sheltered from wind.
Other colors: White, pink, mauve.
Varieties/cultivars: *C. m. calycanthema*.

Campanula rotundifolia

Campanula rotundifolia
HAREBELL OF ENGLAND, BLUEBELL OF SCOTLAND

Family: CAMPANULACEAE
Origin: Northern temperate and arctic regions.
Flowering time: Summer.
Climatic zone: 3, 4, 5, 6, 7, 8, 9.
Dimensions: Up to 12 inches (300 mm) high.
Description: One of the more easily grown alpine campanulas, harebell is not unlike *C. cochleariifolia* in form. The nodding bells of bright blue flowers grow in a loose cluster on thread-like stems. It is best planted in open areas, and in wild gardens, or shrubberies, where it will quickly establish itself and self-seed. This little sun-lover is at home in the Scottish Highlands, where it grows wild.
Other colors: White.
Varieties/cultivars: 'Alba'.

Campanula poscharskyana

where it can ramble unhindered. One of the easier campanulas to grow, it is drought-resistant. Plant it in ordinary garden soil in sun or partial shade.
Varieties/cultivars: 'E. K. Toogood'.

Campanula portenschlagiana syn. *C. muralis*
DALMATIAN BELLFLOWER

Family: CAMPANULACEAE
Origin: Yugoslavia.
Flowering time: Spring–summer.
Climatic zone: 5, 6, 7, 8, 9.
Dimensions: Up to 6 inches (150 mm) high.
Description: This little alpine is easier to grow than many other campanulas. The deep bluish-purple, bell-shaped flowers look attractive in rock garden pockets, in rock walls, or edging garden beds. Woodland drifts are also suitable sites for this plant. Its masses of dark-green, heart-shaped leaves make it a good groundcover, but the foliage may be susceptible to slugs. Plant in well-drained, gritty soil in sun or partial shade.
Other colors: White.

Campanula persicifolia

Campanula persicifolia
PEACH-LEAVED BELLFLOWER

Family: CAMPANULACEAE
Origin: Europe, Asia.
Flowering time: Summer.
Climatic zone: 4, 5, 6, 7, 8, 9.
Dimensions: Up to 3 feet (1 meter) high.
Description: Once used medicinally, this evergreen, perennial border plant produces excellent blue, bell-shaped flowers suitable for cutting. Remove spent blooms to encourage a second flowering. It likes moist, ordinary garden soil and a position in partial shade or full sun, depending upon the climate.
Other colors: White.
Varieties/cultivars: 'Alba'.

Campanula poscharskyana
SERBIAN BELLFLOWER

Family: CAMPANULACEAE
Origin: Western Yugoslavia.
Flowering time: Summer–autumn.
Climatic zone: 4, 5, 6, 7, 8, 9.
Dimensions: Up to 6 inches (150 mm) high.
Description: Serbian bellflower produces masses of lilac flowers which create a dense carpet of color. Its sprawling habit makes it a good choice for a sloping site or a well-drained rock garden; it is also suited to wild gardens,

Catananche caerulea
CUPID'S-DART, BLUE SUCCORY

Family: COMPOSITAE
Origin: Portugal–Italy.
Flowering time: Summer.
Climatic zone: 6, 7, 8, 9, 10.
Dimensions: Up to 2 feet (600 mm) high.
Description: A romantic flower, as its common name implies, cupid's dart was once used as an ingredient in love potions. A cornflower-like plant, the mauve heads are protected by silver, papery bracts. The leaves are hairy. Apart from its garden value, the flowers, which rustle when touched, are

Campanula portenschlagiana

Catananche caerulea

excellent for dried floral arrangements. A drought-tolerant plant, it is easy to grow in a sunny position in ordinary garden soil, but good drainage is essential, and wet soil in winter may kill it.

Centaurea montana
MOUNTAIN BLUET, PERENNIAL CORNFLOWER, MOUNTAIN CORNFLOWER (U.K.)

Other common names: KNAPWEED (U.K.)
Family: COMPOSITAE
Origin: European mountains.
Flowering time: Mid-spring–early summer.
Climatic zone: 3, 4, 5, 6, 7, 8, 9.
Dimensions: 1½–2 feet (450–600 mm) high.
Description: Mountain bluet is one of the most popular of the perennial *Centaurea* species. Its flowers are thistle-like, with large, deeply fringed, marginal florets. It has a long blooming period,

Centaurea montana

and needs only average, well-drained soil. It looks attractive at the front of a cottage garden border. Propagate it by root division in spring. It is a good cut flower for mixed spring arrangements.
Other colors: White, pink, red.
Varieties/cultivars: 'Alba', 'Rosea', 'Rubra'.

Cheiranthus mutabilis
WALLFLOWER, CHANGEABLE WALLFLOWER

Family: CRUCIFERAE
Origin: Canary Islands, Madeira.
Flowering time: Late spring–early summer.
Climatic zone: 8, 9.
Dimensions: Up to 12 inches (300 mm) high.
Description: A perennial cousin of the commonly grown wallflower, this species has attractive gray-green foliage and masses of slightly fragrant flowers which open yellow but age lilac-purple. It likes full sun, and soil that is either neutral or slightly alkaline, with excellent drainage. Take care not to overwater. Feed it well during summer to extend the flowering season.
Varieties/cultivars: C. m. var. *variegatus*.

Cheiranthus mutabilis

Clematis heracleifolia

Clematis heracleifolia
TUBE CLEMATIS

Family: RANUNCULACEAE
Origin: China.
Flowering time: Summer.
Climatic zone: 4, 5, 6, 7, 8, 9.
Dimensions: Up to 4 feet (approx. 1 meter) high.
Description: This is a woody-based clematis suited to the herbaceous border. The blue, narrowly bell-shaped flowers resemble the hyacinth and are fragrant. It likes full sun to partial shade and moist, fertile soil, which should not be allowed to become either too wet or too dry. If the soil is light and sandy, apply peat moss, compost, or leaf mold generously before planting. It is advisable to mulch in spring.
Varieties/cultivars: 'Wyevale', 'Davidiana'.

Convolvulus sabatius syn.
C. mauritanicus
GROUND MORNING GLORY (U.S.A.), BINDWEED

Family: CONVOLVULACEAE
Origin: North Africa.
Flowering time: Summer.
Climatic zone: 8, 9, 10.
Dimensions: Up to 12 inches (300 mm) high.
Description: This perennial, evergreen, trailing plant has widely funnel-shaped, satiny, violet or blue flowers with white throats. It is an attractive basket plant for a greenhouse or a rambler in sheltered rock gardens, and looks particularly effective spilling over rock

Convolvulus sabatius

walls. Plant it as rooted cuttings in ordinary garden soil mixed with compost and a complete fertilizer and water it well.
Other colors: Pink.

Cynoglossum nervosum

Cynoglossum nervosum
GREAT HOUND'S TONGUE BLUE HOUND'S TONGUE

Family: BORAGINACEAE
Origin: Himalayas.
Flowering time: Summer.
Climatic zone: 5, 6, 7, 8, 9.
Dimensions: Up to 2 feet (600 mm) high.
Description: The small, intensely blue flowers of this hound's tongue are borne on tall, branching stems and resemble forget-me-nots. The long, thin, hairy leaves easily identify it as a member of the borage family. Use it in borders or rock gardens where the soil is not very rich, as very fertile soil may cause the stems to fall over. This is a plant which will thrive in full sun and average, well-drained soil. Propagate it by division or seed in spring.

Delphinium elatum hybrids
DELPHINIUM, CANDLE LARKSPUR

Family: RANUNCULACEAE
Origin: Hybrids.
Flowering time: Summer, northern hemisphere; spring–summer, southern hemisphere.
Climatic zone: 4, 5, 6, 7, 8, 9.
Dimensions: Up to 6 feet (2 meters) high.
Description: The name *Delphinium* comes from the Greek word for "dolphin" which the flower buds were thought to resemble. The stately, candle-like flowers on their tall stems make these hybrids most striking in a border. Grow them in moist soil in full sun, and fertilize them regularly. Protect them from the wind, staking if necessary. They are susceptible to pests and mildew and the juice of the plants is poisonous.
Other colors: Red, pink, white, cream.
Varieties/cultivars: Many hybrid cultivars are available.

Delphinium elatum

Dianella caerulea
FLAX LILY

Family: LILIACEAE
Origin: Eastern and southern Australia.
Flowering time: Early spring and summer.
Climatic zone: 9, 10.
Dimensions: Up to 4 feet (approx. 1 meter) high.
Description: This is an attractive,

132

Dianella caerulea

fibrous-rooted perennial which spreads by means of underground rhizomes. The foliage appears at various intervals and is tough and flax-like. The flowers are up to ½ inch (12 mm) wide, starry, six-petaled and blue or whitish with a central cone of yellow stamens, carried in large, airy panicles. They are followed by pretty, deep-blue berries. Flax lily can be grown in most soils and conditions, but must be watered well in summer. The rhizomes can be easily divided to create new plants.

Digitalis purpurea
COMMON FOXGLOVE ◑

Family: SCROPHULARIACEAE
Origin: Western Europe and U.K.
Flowering time: Spring–summer.
Climatic zone: 5, 6, 7, 8, 9.
Dimensions: Up to 4 feet (approx. 2 meters) high.
Description: Foxglove is a good choice for a high backdrop to a border. It likes shade and blends well with ferns and campanulas. Although loved by cottage gardeners, it is considered a noxious weed in some countries. This plant possesses an important medicinal compound, digitalin, which is extracted from the leaves and used for certain

Digitalis purpurea

heart conditions. In the past, herbalists prescribed foxglove for fevers and liver complaints. With its masses of bell-shaped flowers, this biennial will bloom for six to ten weeks. Plant it in a shady position in humus-rich soil.
Other colors: Yellow, white, pink, red, purple.
Varieties/cultivars: 'Alba', 'Excelsior', 'Shirley'.

Echinops ritro 'Veitch's Blue'

Echinops ritro
GLOBE THISTLE ○

Family: COMPOSITAE
Origin: Eastern Europe–western Asia
Flowering time: Summer.
Climatic zone: 3, 4, 5, 6, 7, 8, 9, 10.
Dimensions: Up to 4 feet (approx. 1 meter) high.
Description: This is a handsome, old-world, thistle-like plant which is useful in hardy borders. The blue flowers and the white, woolly foliage can be cut and used in dried floral arrangements. A bold and showy plant, it associates well with phlox in the garden, but needs plenty of space and a moderately sunny position. It prefers ordinary garden soil and may need to be staked if the soil is too moist or fertile. Propagate by division or seed.
Varieties/cultivars: 'Taplow Blue', 'Veitch's Blue'.

Erinus alpinus
SUMMER STARWORT, ○ ◑ FAIRY FOXGLOVE (U.K.) ◐

Family: SCROPHULARIACEAE
Origin: European Alps, Pyrenees.
Flowering time: Spring–summer.
Climatic zone: 3, 4, 5, 6, 7, 8, 9.
Dimensions: Up to 6 inches (150 mm) high.
Description: Rock crevices or confined spaces in a wall are ideal environments for this little alpine. When planted in

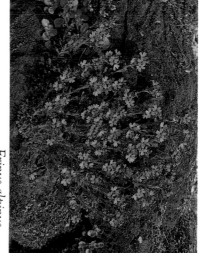

Erinus alpinus

rock garden pockets it will form a close-tufted, evergreen mound. Starry, rosy-purple flowers are borne in profusion on terminal sprays. Mix the seed with moist loam or peat and place it in cracks of walls or rocks to germinate. Well-drained soil in full sun or half-shade will ensure good results.
Other colors: White, pink.
Varieties/cultivars: *E. a.* var. *albus*, 'Dr. Hanaele', 'Mrs. Boyle'.

Eryngium x zabelii
ZABEL ERYNGO, SEA ○ HOLLY (U.K.)

Family: UMBELLIFERAE
Origin: Hybrids.
Flowering time: Summer.
Climatic zone: 6, 7, 8, 9.
Dimensions: Up to 2½ feet (750 mm) high.
Description: These hybrids are thistle-like plants with blue flowers. The flowers can be dried for use in floral arrangements. Plant them in well-drained, sandy soil that is moderately fertile, and provide plenty of space for growth. They are difficult to transplant. In ancient times they had many medicinal uses.

Eryngium x zabelii

Hosta fortunei

Hesperis matronalis

Gentiana asclepiadea

Gentiana acaulis

Gentiana acaulis syn. *G. excisa*
STEMLESS GENTIAN,
TRUMPET GENTIAN (U.K.)

Family: GENTIANACEAE
Origin: European mountains.
Flowering time: Spring.
Climatic zone: 5, 6, 7, 8, 9.
Dimensions: Up to 4 inches (100 mm) high.
Description: This is one of the best known of the gentians that grow in the alpine meadows in Europe, and needs similar conditions if it is to thrive in the garden. If the environment is right and not too warm, stemless gentian produces a glorious carpet of vivid blue flowers that enhance garden edges and rock garden pockets, or it can be planted in drifts. It needs cool, moist, light, well-drained soil. If it produces leaves but no flowers, it needs to be moved to a warmer position.

habitat. As a rule, gentians do not appreciate root disturbance so a thriving colony should be left alone.
Other colors: White.
Varieties/cultivars: *G. a.* var. *alba*.

Gentiana asclepiadea
WILLOW GENTIAN

Family: GENTIANACEAE
Origin: European Alps, Apennines.
Flowering time: Late summer–autumn.
Climatic zone: 5, 6, 7, 8, 9.
Dimensions: Up to 2 feet (600 mm) high.
Description: One of the more reliable and easy-to-grow perennial gentians, it produces flowers of a deep purple-blue, which bloom year after year on long arching stems. Planted in shaded borders or in rock gardens, willow gentian will freely reproduce from seed. It is best grown in acid, humus-rich soil that is kept moist and cool, emulating the mountain conditions of its native

purple flowers resemble phlox, and have a lovely fragrance which is given out only at night. In modern gardens, it is a short-lived perennial and needs to be replaced with seedlings. It likes moist, well-drained soil and is longer lived in poorer soils.
Other colors: White.
Varieties/cultivars: 'Alba'.

Hosta fortunei
FORTUNE'S PLANTAIN
LILY, PLANTAIN LILY

Family: LILIACEAE
Origin: Japan.
Flowering time: Summer.
Climatic zone: 3, 4, 5, 6, 7, 8, 9.
Dimensions: Up to 2 feet (600 mm) high.
Description: This spectacular plant has striking foliage and handsome spikes of mauve or violet flowers. This lily is ideal for special positions where fine foliage effects are desired — stone planter boxes, by a garden seat, in shady borders, or reflected in a water feature. The clumps will improve with age and should be left undisturbed. Plant it in rich humus soil that does not dry out. Avoid full sun as it may burn the leaves. Divide in spring to propagate it. Cultivars differ in the markings and color of foliage.
Other colors: White.
Varieties/cultivars: 'Aurea-marginata', 'Albopicta'.

Hesperis matronalis
DAME'S ROCKET,
DAME'S VIOLET

Family: CRUCIFERAE
Origin: Europe–central Asia.
Flowering time: Summer.
Climatic zone: 5, 6, 7, 8, 9.
Dimensions: Up to 3 feet (1 meter) high.
Description: Known to cooks as "garden rocket", the acrid leaves are eaten like cress in salads in some countries. The purple, mauve or lilac-

Hosta sieboldiana

Hosta sieboldiana
SIEBOLD PLANTAIN LILY, PLANTAIN LILY

Family: LILIACEAE
Origin: Japan.
Flowering time: Summer.
Climatic zone: 3, 4, 5, 6, 7, 8, 9.
Dimensions: Up to 18 inches (750 mm) high.
Description: The large, striking leaves which seem almost to be stitched or quilted are an outstanding feature of this lily. The lilac flowers with deeper stripes rise on a slender stem that is generally shorter than the foliage. Place this plant in a key position near a water feature, flanking shady steps, or beside a garden seat. In summer it prefers cool, moist soil, but wet soil in winter may damage the leaves. It is susceptible to slugs and snails.

Hosta ventricosa
BLUE PLANTAIN LILY, PLANTAIN LILY

Family: LILIACEAE
Origin: Eastern Asia.
Flowering time: Late summer.
Climatic zone: 3, 4, 5, 6, 7, 8, 9.
Dimensions: Up to 3 feet (1 meter) high.
Description: One of the plantain lily family, it is usually grown for its spectacular foliage. Common in old-fashioned gardens and easy to grow, *H. ventricosa* has long, heart-shaped leaves, and deep-violet, funnel-shaped flowers occurring in loose, terminal

Hosta ventricosa

clusters. This is a drought- and frost-tender perennial suited to borders. It prefers shade, and soil that is moist in summer. Increase it by division in spring or autumn.

Iris germanica
TALL BEARDED IRIS

Family: IRIDACEAE
Origin: Southern Europe.
Flowering time: Summer, northern hemisphere; spring, southern hemisphere.
Climatic zone: 4, 5, 6, 7, 8, 9.
Dimensions: Up to 2½ feet (750 mm) high.
Description: This is one of the species from which most bearded irises have

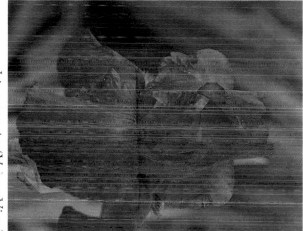

Iris germanica 'Velvet Vista'

been bred. Tall, it is best suited to growing in separate beds or in groups among shrubs. The flowers are deep purple with a yellow beard and a pretty effect can be achieved by planting it in a circular bed or as a backdrop along a sunny wall. It likes very well-drained, fertile soil mixed with plenty of organic matter, and protection from wind. Water it freely during its growing period.
Other colors: Orange with yellow, cream.
Varieties/cultivars: 'Ola Kala', 'Rippling Waters', 'Starshine', 'Velvet Vista'.

Iris kaempferi syn. I. ensata
JAPANESE WATER IRIS, JAPANESE IRIS

Family: IRIDACEAE
Origin: Japan, China.
Flowering time: Spring.
Climatic zone: 5, 6, 7, 8, 9.
Dimensions: Up to 3 feet (1 meter) high.
Description: This moisture-loving iris is well suited to waterside planting. Some of the cultivars are very colorful, some double-flowered, blotched, stippled, or striped. It makes a good companion plant with primula in a damp border that is free of lime. Plant it at the water's edge, but not below the water surface. Japanese iris will also grow well in ordinary garden soil, providing it has plenty of moisture throughout the growing season. It will die back completely during winter, when dead leaves should be removed.
Other colors: White, pink, red.
Varieties/cultivars: Several cultivars are available.

Iris kaempferi 'Garry Gallant'

PERENNIALS

Iris pumila

grows best in slightly moist soil but will still do well in conditions that are less than ideal.
Other colors: White, pearly-gray.
Varieties/cultivars: 'Caesar', 'Caesar's Brother', 'White Swirl', 'Snow Queen', 'Mrs Rowe', 'Perry's Blue', 'Cambridge Blue'.

Climatic zone: 6, 7, 8.
Dimensions: Up to 12 inches (300 mm) high.
Description: This low-growing perennial is ideally suited to sunny rock garden pockets. It has a dense rosette of leaves and lilac-blue flower heads composed of many tiny florets which resemble pincushions. The heads are borne on erect stems. Plant it in winter in light, open soil in a sunny or semishaded position. Apply complete fertilizer in early spring and propagate it by root division in winter.

Limonium latifolium
BORDER SEA LAVENDER ○

Family: PLUMBAGINACEAE
Origin: Southeastern Europe–U.S.S.R.
Flowering time: Summer-autumn.
Climatic zone: 4, 5, 6, 7, 8, 9, 10.
Dimensions: Up to 2 feet (600 mm) high.

Limonium latifolium

Iris sibirica 'Cambridge Blue'

Jasione perennis
SHEPHERD'S SCABIOUS (U.S.A.), SHEEP'S-BIT (U.K.) ○ ◐

Family: CAMPANULACEAE
Origin: Europe.
Flowering time: Spring–summer.

Jasione perennis

136

Iris pumila
DWARF BEARDED IRIS ○

Family: IRIDACEAE
Origin: Central Europe–Turkey, southern U.S.S.R.
Flowering time: Spring.
Climatic zone: 4, 5, 6, 7, 8, 9.
Dimensions: Up to 8 inches (200 mm) high.
Description: This broad-leafed dwarf iris flowers earlier than the taller flag irises, and looks most effective planted in rock garden pockets or massed at the front of borders. It is short-stemmed and the leaves grow longer after the plant has flowered. Most of the dwarf bearded irises are cultivars and a good selection of colors is available. Irises rarely need mulching. Propagate by division. They are prone to iris borer.
Other colors: White, yellow.
Varieties/cultivars: 'Blue Denim', 'Pogo'.

Iris sibirica
SIBERIAN IRIS ◐ ○

Family: IRIDACEAE
Origin: Central Europe–Lake Baikal, U.S.S.R.
Flowering time: Summer.
Climatic zone: 4, 5, 6, 7, 8, 9.
Dimensions: Up to 4 feet (approx. 1 meter) high.
Description: The parent species of several cultivars and hybrids, *I. sibirica* is a moisture-lover which will form large clumps at the edge of ponds. The flowers are lilac-blue to blue-purple with a purple-veined, white basal patch. It

Description: This member of the plumbago family is resistant to salt spray. It has rosettes of large leaves topped by long stems packed with masses of deep lavender-blue flowers. Bunches may be gathered and dried for semipermanent floral arrangements. It is easy to grow in sunny positions in light, sandy, moist soil, and is a good choice for the gardens of holiday houses which cannot be constantly maintained.
Varieties/cultivars: 'Violetta', 'Chilwell Beauty'.

Linum perenne syn. *L. sibiricum*
PERENNIAL FLAX

Linum perenne

Family: LINACEAE
Origin: Europe.
Flowering time: Summer.
Climatic zone: 6, 7, 8, 9.
Dimensions: Up to 2 feet (600 mm) high.
Description: Perennial flax is a hardy border plant with gray-green leaves and clusters of pale blue, saucer-shaped flowers. The roots generally throw up numerous stems. It likes ordinary, well-drained soil, a sunny position, and regular watering. Apply a complete fertilizer in spring. Propagate it by seed in spring.

Lobelia x *gerardii*
LOBELIA

Lobelia x *gerardii*

Family: CAMPANULACEAE
Origin: Hybrid.
Flowering time: Summer.
Climatic zone: 5, 6, 7, 8, 9, 10.
Dimensions: Up to 3 feet (1 meter) high.
Description: This is a less commonly grown hybrid Lobelia, whose ancestry is uncertain due to back-breeding. In general it is a robust plant with leafy stems and a striking display of violet-purple flowers appearing in terminal racemes. The flowering period is spread over many weeks as the axillary branches are later to bloom. It prefers moderately rich and well-drained soil, with a good mulch of organic matter to protect the roots in winter. Makes a beautiful cut flower.
Other colors: Pink.
Varieties/cultivars: 'Surprise'.

Mazus reptans
TEAT FLOWER

Mazus reptans

Family: SCROPHULARIACEAE
Origin: Himalayas.
Flowering time: Spring.
Climatic zone: 6, 7, 8, 9.
Dimensions: Up to 9 inches (225 mm) high.
Description: This low-growing perennial forms a dense carpet and is well suited to sloping sites and rock gardens. Plant several close together near large rocks where the prostrate stems can form mats. The flowers are light purplish-blue with white, yellow and purple markings on the lower lips. It adapts to most soil types, but likes a moist soil and an open, sunny position. It is frost-resistant but susceptible to drought.

Mecomopsis betonicifolia syn. *M. baileyi*
HIMALAYAN BLUE POPPY, TIBETAN POPPY

Mecomopsis betonicifolia

Family: PAPAVERACEAE
Origin: Himalayas.
Flowering time: Early summer.
Climatic zone: 6, 7, 8, 9.
Dimensions: Up to 4 feet (approx. 1 meter) high.
Description: The satiny, rich-blue, poppy-like flowers of Tibetan poppy are borne in groups of three or four at the tops of strong, slim stems. A cold-climate species, this herbaceous perennial from the Himalayan mountains needs deep, cool, fertile, moist soil in semishade or full sun. Protect it from the wind, water it regularly, and apply a complete fertilizer in the spring. Propagation is by seed in autumn.

Mertensia virginica

Mertensia virginica
VIRGINIA BLUEBELLS

Family: BORAGINACEAE
Origin: Central eastern and southeastern United States.
Flowering time: Late spring.
Climatic zone: 4, 5, 6, 7, 8, 9.
Dimensions: Up to 18 inches (450 mm) high.
Description: This pretty perennial has pale blue-green foliage and long, tubular, purple-blue flowers in drooping clusters. It needs cool soil that is kept moist, especially in the warm weather when organic matter and that is kept moist, especially in the warm weather when the foliage dies back after flowering. Mulch the soil well with rotted compost.
Other colors: White, pink.
Varieties/cultivars: 'Alba', 'Rubra'.

Myosotis sylvatica
FORGET-ME-NOT

Family: BORAGINACEAE
Origin: Europe.
Flowering time: Spring.
Climatic zone: 5, 6, 7, 8, 9.
Dimensions: Up to 12 inches (300 mm) high.
Description: This bushy biennial makes a good indoor winter pot plant. If using in borders it will spread rapidly and needs to be checked. It is best used with spring bulbs in pots, and under deciduous trees and shrubs where it will self-sow many seedlings each season. Cottage gardens are an ideal environment for it. Forget-me-not will grow in ordinary garden soil and thrives in rich, limed, sandy loam.
Varieties/cultivars: 'Royal Blue'.

Nepeta x faassenii
CATMINT

Family: LABIATAE
Origin: Hybrid.
Flowering time: Summer.
Climatic zone: 4, 5, 6, 7, 8, 9, 10.
Dimensions: Up to 18 inches (450 mm) high.
Description: When the leaves of catmint are bruised, the aroma has a curious fascination for some cats, who chew the plant, roll on it, and eventually become quite intoxicated. This useful edging plant has aromatic spikes of small, mauve flowers and silver-gray leaves. It likes warm, sandy, well-drained soil and is easily grown and propagated from seeds in spring or by root division.

Nepeta x faassenii

Omphalodes verna
CREEPING FORGET-ME-NOT, BLUE-EYED MARY

Family: BORAGINACEAE
Origin: Central southern Europe.
Flowering time: Spring.
Climatic zone: 5, 6, 7, 8, 9.
Dimensions: Up to 8 inches (200 mm) high.
Description: Creeping forget-me-not forms a clearblue groundcover when planted in woodland or under large trees and shrubs. The erect stems bear clusters of forget-me-not-like flowers in loose sprays. The plant thrives in neutral or slightly alkaline soil, provided it is cool, moist, and well-drained, and enriched with organic matter. It likes full shade and in the right position will flower for several months. Propagation is by seed in spring or by root division in spring or autumn.
Other colors: White.
Varieties/cultivars: 'Alba'.

Omphalodes verna

Myosotis sylvatica 'Royal Blue'

Perovskia atriplicifolia

Perovskia atriplicifolia
AZURE SAGE ○

Family: LABIATAE
Origin: Western Himalayas, Afghanistan.
Flowering time: Summer.
Climatic zone: 6, 7, 8, 9, 10.
Dimensions: Up to 5 feet (approx. 2 meters) high.
Description: Although this plant is a member of the mint family, it has a strong, sage-like aroma when bruised. With its attractive blue flowers it makes a good companion plant with globe thistle in an open border. In full sun it forms a very attractive, upright plant, but in shaded situations it is inclined to sprawl. Cut it back to ground level each spring to promote strong new growth and good flowering. Azure sage is easy to grow in well-drained soil and is propagated by cuttings in late summer.

Platycodon grandiflorus
BALLOON FLOWER,
CHINESE BELLFLOWER (U.S.A.) ○

Family: CAMPANULACEAE
Origin: Eastern Asia.
Flowering time: Late summer.
Climatic zone: 4, 5, 6, 7, 8, 9.
Dimensions: Up to 3 feet (1 meter) high.
Description: This compact, clump-forming, herbaceous plant sends up numerous leafy flower stems. The balloon-like buds open to form wide, cup-shaped flowers. It is an easy plant to grow provided it has a sunny position in an enriched, loamy soil. It makes an

attractive picture when planted in combination with fuchsias. Propagation is either by division or from seed in spring.
Other colors: White, pink.
Varieties/cultivars: 'Mariesii', 'Mother of Pearl', 'Capri'.

Platycodon grandiflorus

Platycodon grandiflorus 'Mariesii'
DWARF BALLOON
FLOWER ○

Family: CAMPANULACEAE
Origin: Cultivar.
Flowering time: Summer.
Climatic zone: 4, 5, 6, 7, 8, 9.
Dimensions: Up to 18 inches (450 mm) high.
Description: This smaller growing cultivar of *Platycodon grandiflorus* was introduced into England from Japan and is now the form of balloon flower most widely grown in gardens. It is a vigorous perennial, forming quite large clumps after two or three years. The flowers last well both on the plant and when picked. It is easily propagated by

Platycodon grandiflorus 'Mariesii'

lifting the clumps after a few years and carefully dividing them, replanting the separated pieces immediately.
Other colors: White.

139

Polemonium caeruleum
JACOB'S-LADDER ○ ◑

Family: POLEMONIACEAE
Origin: Northern hemisphere.
Flowering time: Summer.
Climatic zone: 4, 5, 6, 7, 8, 9.
Dimensions: 2–3 feet (600–900 mm) high.
Description: The neatly divided leaflets, arranged in opposite pairs resembling the rungs of a ladder, give this plant its common name. The blooms are arranged in loose clusters of small, silky, bell-shaped flowers, with prominent orange stamens. It is an easily grown plant, though often short-lived unless divided in spring and replanted. Alternatively, it can be easily increased by seed.
Other colors: White.
Varieties/cultivars: 'Richardsonii', 'Dawn Flight', 'Sapphire'.

Polemonium reptans

Description: The tubular flowers of this species are purple-pink at first but become shades of purple and then violet-blue as they mature. The large, bristly, heart-shaped leaves are irregularly spotted with white and were thought by ancient herbalists to cure spots on the lung. This plant is not particular about soil type, but prefers moist conditions. It is usually propagated by division in late winter.
Other colors: White.

Pulsatilla vulgaris syn. *Anemone pulsatilla*
PASQUE FLOWER ○ ◑

Family: RANUNCULACEAE
Origin: Europe and western U.S.S.R.
Flowering time: Spring.

Pulsatilla vulgaris

plant has a spreading rather than creeping habit, and prefers rich and moist well-drained soils and a protected position. It is frost-resistant but sensitive to drought. It can be propagated by seed or division.

Pulmonaria officinalis
LUNGWORT, SPOTTED ◑ ●
DOG, SOLDIERS AND SAILORS
(U.K.)

Family: BORAGINACEAE
Origin: Central Europe.
Flowering time: Spring.
Climatic zone: 4, 5, 6, 7, 8, 9.
Dimensions: Up to 12 inches (300 mm) high.

Pulmonaria officinalis

140

Polemonium reptans
DWARF JACOB'S- ○ ◑
LADDER, CREEPING
POLEMONIUM

Family: POLEMONIACEAE
Origin: Eastern United States.
Flowering time: Spring–summer.
Climatic zone: 4, 5, 6, 7, 8, 9.
Dimensions: 8–12 inches (200–300 mm) high.
Description: This is an early flowering species which has branching stems and leaves divided into six or seven pairs. The pendant, cup-shaped flowers are carried in loose terminal clusters. This

Polemonium caeruleum

Climatic zone: 3, 4, 5, 6, 7, 8, 9.
Dimensions: 8-12 inches (200-300 mm) high.
Description: Pasque flower is an attractive rock garden plant with ferny leaves and nodding flowers on erect, hairy stems. Its common name was given because it comes into bloom round about Easter in the northern hemisphere. Well-drained garden soil suits it best and it is propagated by seed.
Other colors: Pink, mauve.

Salvia officinalis and cultivars
COMMON SAGE

Family: LABIATAE
Origin: Southern Europe.
Flowering time: Summer.
Climatic zone: 6, 7, 8, 9.
Dimensions: Up to 3 feet (1 meter) high.
Description: Common sage has strongly aromatic, gray-green leaves and blush-purple flowers. It has been cultivated for centuries as a culinary herb. The cultivar 'Purpurascens' is commonly called purple-leafed sage because both new stems and foliage are suffused with purple. 'Tricolor' is very distinctive with its gray-green leaves splashed with creamy white and suffused with purple and pink. Sage will grow in any free-draining garden soil. The leaves can be used fresh for cooking and in salads, or picked and dried for later use.
Other colors: White.
Varieties/cultivars: 'Alba', 'Icterina', 'Purpurascens', 'Tricolor'.

Salvia officinalis

Salvia farinacea
MEALY-CUP SAGE

Family: LABIATAE
Origin: Texas, New Mexico.
Flowering time: Summer-early autumn.
Climatic zone: 7, 8, 9.
Dimensions: 3-4 feet (approx. 1 meter) high.
Description: A slightly frost-tender member of the salvia genus, this species makes an excellent display in the summer border. The flowers are borne on long, graceful spikes, somewhat resembling lavender but much larger, and the aromatic leaves are long and narrow. Propagate the plant by division, or sow the seeds in spring. It is advisable to plant out in the garden after the risk of frost has passed.
Other colors: White.
Varieties/cultivars: 'Blue Bedder', 'Alba'.

Salvia farinacea 'Blue Bedder'

Salvia pratensis
MEADOW CLARY

Family: LABIATAE
Origin: Europe and North Africa.
Flowering time: Summer.
Climatic zone: 5, 6, 7, 8, 9.
Dimensions: 2-3 feet (approx. 1 meter) high.
Description: This sturdy plant forms a good basal clump of leaves below long spikes of violet-blue flowers. The leaves, slightly spotted with red, are rather coarse and the flower stems are square in shape. Like most members of the salvia genus, it prefers warm and dryish conditions and does not tolerate heavy frosts. It should be cut back after flowering and can be propagated from cuttings.
Other colors: White, pink.
Varieties/cultivars: 'Baumgartenii', S. p. tenorii.

Salvia pratensis

Salvia x superba

Salvia x superba
VIOLET SAGE

Family: LABIATAE
Origin: Hybrid.
Flowering time: Summer-early autumn.
Climatic zone: 5, 6, 7, 8, 9.
Dimensions: 2-3 feet (up to 1 meter) high.
Description: The violet-red bracts which surround the crimson-purple flowers of this species persist after the flowers themselves have finished, providing a long and colorful display. The small, green leaves on the upright stems are aromatic. It is a useful plant for a mixed border and the flowers are excellent for cutting and drying. It grows well in ordinary garden soil and can be propagated by seed.
Varieties/cultivars: 'Lubeca', 'East Friesland'.

Stachys byzantina syn. *S. lanata*, *S. olympica*
LAMB'S EARS, LAMBS' TONGUES, DONKEY'S EARS (U.S.A.)

Family: LABIATAE
Origin: Southwestern Asia–Turkey.
Flowering time: Summer.
Climatic zone: 5, 6, 7, 8, 9.
Dimensions: Up to 18 inches (450 mm) high.
Description: This is an excellent groundcover with its dense mats of woolly, gray leaves. It thrives in full sun or part shade and often succeeds in poor soil. The spikes of small purple flowers are half-hidden by silver bracts. Propagation is by division.
Varieties/cultivars: 'Silver Carpet' (non-flowering), 'Cotton Boll'.

Stachys macrantha

inches (100 mm) across with paler centers. They last well on the plant and are also good for picking. The plants thrive in any good, well-drained soil, and are usually propagated by division in late winter.
Other colors: Pink, white.
Varieties/cultivars: 'Blue Star', 'Alba', 'Rosea'.

Teucrium fruticans
MINT GERMANDER, SHRUBBY GERMANDER

Family: LABIATAE
Origin: Western Mediterranean region and Portugal.
Flowering time: Summer–autumn.
Climatic zone: 8, 9, 10.
Dimensions: 4 to 7 feet (1–2 meters) high.

Teucrium fruticans

division in early spring. Plant in well-drained soil.
Other colors: Pink, white
Varieties/cultivars: 'Superba', 'Robusta'.

Stokesia laevis
STOKES' ASTER

Family: COMPOSITAE
Origin: Southeastern United States.
Flowering time: Summer–autumn.
Climatic zone: 5, 6, 7, 8, 9.
Dimensions: 18 inches (450 mm) high.
Description: From a basal rosette of plain, green leaves, the flower stems emerge with a cornflower-like bloom set off by a collar of green leaves (or bracts). The blue flowers can often be up to 4

Stachys byzantina

Stachys macrantha syn. *S. grandiflora*, *Betonica macrantha*
BIG BETONY (U.S.A.), GRAND WOUNDWORT (U.K.)

Family: LABIATAE
Origin: The Caucasus.
Flowering time: Summer.
Climatic zone: 4, 5, 6, 7, 8, 9.
Dimensions: Up to 2 feet (600 mm) high.
Description: The dark-green, downy leaves of this plant have an unusual wrinkled or corrugated appearance. From the dense clumps of leaves, erect flower stems emerge with three or four whorls of hooded blooms of a purplish-mauve color. Garden forms exist which have deeper and richer violet flowers and there are also those with pink and white blooms. It is easily propagated by

Stokesia laevis

142

Description: Mint germander is an easily cultivated, evergreen shrub with attractive gray-green oval leaves, slightly curled at the edges. It flowers over a long period. It is a dense shrub and can be clipped to shape, making it ideal for hedges. A quick grower in any good garden soil, even the slightly alkaline, it is also useful for seaside planting, tolerating warm, dry conditions. In cooler areas, it grows well against a sunny wall, or in a container on a patio. It can be propagated from cuttings taken in late summer, or from seed.

Teucrium marum

Teucrium marum syn. *Micromeria corsica*
CATNIP, CAT THYME ○

Family: LABIATAE
Origin: Yugoslavia and Mediterranean islands.
Flowering time: Summer.
Climatic zone: 7, 8, 9, 10.
Dimensions: 6–12 inches (150–300 mm) high.
Description: This is an adaptable plant, growing well in most types of soil providing it is well-drained. It is frost-resistant and will tolerate drought. The gray-green, oval leaves on wiry stems have an aromatic odor. It can sometimes be an unfortunate addition to a garden as cats are said to be inordinately fond of it, tearing it to pieces and rolling on its neighbors! It can be grown in a rockery and propagated by seed or cuttings.

Tricyrtis formosana
TOAD LILY ◐ ●

Family: LILIACEAE
Origin: Taiwan.
Flowering time: Early autumn.
Climatic zone: 5, 6, 7, 8, 9.
Dimensions: 2–3 feet (600–900 mm) high.
Description: Toad lilies, so called because of their spotted flowers, have shiny, dark leaves and upright flower stems that branch into heads of mauve-white flowers having yellow, purple-spotted throats. Grow them in a soil that does not dry out and that contains plenty of organic matter. They do well in a shady position, although a little dappled sunshine will hasten the development of flowers. Propagation is by seeds or offsets.
Other colors: Reddish-purple.
Varieties/cultivars: *T. f. stolonifera*.

Tricyrtis formosana

Veronica austriaca teucrium
SPEEDWELL, BLUE SPEEDWELL, HUNGARIAN SPEEDWELL (U.S.A.) ◐

Family: SCROPHULARIACEAE
Origin: Europe.
Flowering time: Summer.
Climatic zone: 4, 5, 6, 7, 8, 9.
Dimensions: 1–2 feet (300–600 mm) high.
Description: This charming perennial has slender spikes of lavender-blue flowers and narrow, deep-green leaves on slender stems. A useful plant for borders or rockeries, it likes a sunny or semishaded position and a fertile, well-drained soil. Cut it back in autumn to encourage strong growth the following spring, and divide clumps every four years to produce new, healthy plants.

Feed it with a liquid fertilizer in spring to encourage good flower production.
Other colors: Various shades of blue.
Varieties/cultivars: 'Blue Fountain', 'Crater Lake Blue', 'Trehane', 'Pavane', 'Shirley Blue', 'Knallblau'.

Veronica austriaca teucrium 'Knallblau'

Veronica spicata
SPIKE SPEEDWELL, CAT'S TAIL SPEEDWELL (U.K.) ○ ◐

Family: SCROPHULARIACEAE
Origin: Europe and Asia.
Flowering time: Summer–early autumn.
Climatic zone: 4, 5, 6, 7, 8, 9.
Dimensions: 18 inches (450 mm) high.
Description: This is a valuable plant for the front of a border as it makes a fine display. It forms a compact tussock of leaves from which arise the numerous dense spikes of flowers. It is easy to grow in most soil types, provided they are well-drained. Over the years it has been successfully crossed with other species to produce many attractive garden varieties. The best method of propagation is by division.
Other colors: Pink, white.
Varieties/cultivars: 'Sarabande', 'Icicle', 'Blue Fox', 'Red Fox', 'Blue Peter', 'Snow White'.

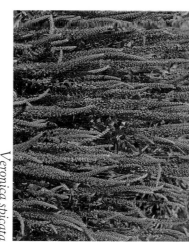

Veronica spicata

good show in the garden and has a long flowering period. The best method of propagation is by division, either in autumn or in spring.
Other colors: Pink.
Varieties/cultivars: 'Barcarolle', 'Minuet'.

Vinca minor
LESSER PERIWINKLE (U.K.), RUNNING MYRTLE

Family: APOCYNACEAE
Origin: Europe and western Asia.
Flowering time: Spring–summer.
Climatic zone: 5, 6, 7, 8, 9.
Dimensions: Prostrate to 4 inches (100 mm) high.
Description: A hardy, trailing plant with small, dark-green, shiny leaves, dwarf periwinkle spreads rapidly over the soil surface, rooting at every node to form new plants. This is a most useful plant for covering the ground in shaded areas under trees. The flower color is somewhat variable, but always in shades of blue, purple, and white. There are several cultivars, including two with variegated foliage. It is easily propagated by simply cutting the rooted stems and planting them elsewhere. Vinca grows well in most well-drained soils.
Other colors: Pink, white.
Varieties/cultivars: 'Alba', 'Bowles Variety', 'Rosea'.

Veronica spicata var. incana

Veronica spicata var. incana syn. *V. incana*
GRAY SPIKE SPEEDWELL (U.K.), WOOLLY SPEEDWELL (U.S.A.)

Family: SCROPHULARIACEAE
Origin: Northern Asia and U.S.S.R.
Flowering time: Summer.
Climatic zone: 4, 5, 6, 7, 8, 9.
Dimensions: 12–18 inches (300–450 mm) high.
Description: Gray speedwell is a more-or-less evergreen plant that is easy to grow in average garden soil provided it receives ample sunshine. The deep blue flowers are carried in terminal spikes, and the leaves are silvery-gray and slightly toothed. This plant makes a

Viola cornuta

Viola cornuta
HORNED VIOLET

Family: VIOLACEAE
Origin: Pyrenees.
Flowering time: Late spring–autumn.
Climatic zone: 5, 6, 7, 8, 9.
Dimensions: Up to 8 inches (200 mm) high.
Description: This dainty little edging or rock garden plant is a short-lived perennial which prefers a semishaded position in ordinary garden soil. The evergreen leaves form a compact tuft and violet-colored flowers are held on long stalks. The flowering period can be prolonged if the dead flowers are removed regularly. Once established, this viola will spread well to form an attractive groundcover. It is closely related to pansies and violets.
Other colors: White.

Viola hederacea
WILD VIOLET, AUSTRALIAN NATIVE VIOLET, IVY-LEAVED VIOLET

Family: VIOLACEAE
Origin: Southeastern Australia.
Flowering time: Spring–autumn.
Climatic zone: 8, 9, 10.
Dimensions: Prostrate to 4 inches (100 mm) high.
Description: This dense mat-forming plant with kidney-shaped leaves spreads on long runners that bind the soil or cascade over banks. A good groundcover plant for either sandy or clay soils, it prefers a moist and semisheltered position. One plant will cover up to 1 square yard

Vinca minor

Viola hederacea

(approximately 1 square meter) of soil. It is tolerant of some frost and snow provided that winters are not too severe. It is also moderately tolerant of limy soil.
Other colors: White.
Varieties/cultivars: 'Baby Blue'.

Viola labradorica 'Purpurea'
LABRADOR VIOLET

Family: VIOLACEAE
Origin: Cultivar.
Flowering time: Spring–summer.
Climatic zone: 3, 4, 5, 6, 7, 8, 9.
Dimensions: 4 inches (100 mm) high.
Description: This little violet is an attractive groundcover all year round due to the deep purple-green of its leaves. It makes a useful color contrast in the garden, especially if near plants with lime-yellow foliage. The flowers are a pretty lavender-blue, but without any perfume. It spreads easily in most soils, rooting at the nodes, and is usually propagated by division during autumn or winter.

Viola labradorica 'Purpurea'

Viola odorata

Viola odorata
COMMON VIOLET,
SWEET VIOLET (U.K.)

Family: VIOLACEAE
Origin: Europe North Africa, Asia
Climatic zone: 6, 7, 8, 9.
Dimensions: 6 inches (150 mm) high.
Description: For the size of this little perennial, the flowers are relatively large, being up to 1 inch (25 mm) across. The perfume is sweet and quite strong. The plant spreads by runners and it can be divided in autumn and spring. It often self-sows. It is an easily grown groundcover, which likes moist, moderately rich soil. There are now many garden forms.
Other colors: White, pink, apricot.
Varieties/cultivars: 'Marie Louise', 'Princess of Wales', 'Czar', 'Royal Robe'.

Dimensions: Prostrate, spreading up to 3 sq. feet (1 sq. meter).
Description: This is a very showy creeper which spreads quite rapidly by suckering. It is a hardy, frost-resistant plant although it does not withstand severe winters. It grows best in a loamy soil with plenty of moisture. It looks spectacular when mass-planted, but it can also be grown successfully and looks attractive in a tub or large pot. Its flower is the floral emblem of the Australian Capital Territory.

Wahlenbergia gloriosa
ROYAL BLUEBELL

Family: CAMPANULACEAE
Origin: Southeastern Australia.
Flowering time: Late spring–summer.
Climatic zone: 8, 9.

Wahlenbergia gloriosa

145

Brunfelsia australis

Brunfelsia calycina

Buddleia davidii

Buddleia alternifolia

Description: A large shrub with gracefully arching branches bearing long, narrow leaves, fountain buddleia produces an abundance of fragrant, lilac-purple flowers that weigh the branches down. Pruning, if required, should be carried out after flowering has finished, as flowers appear on the previous year's growth. Fountain buddleia is popular in cottage gardens and makes a good screen plant. It will grow in any well-drained garden soil. Apply a handful of complete plant food in early spring.

Other colors: Mauve-pink.
Varieties/cultivars: 'Argentea', 'Hever Castle'.

Brunfelsia australis syn. *B. latifolia*
YESTERDAY-TODAY-AND-TOMORROW
○ ◑

Family: SOLANACEAE
Origin: Central America.
Flowering time: Spring-summer.
Climatic zone: 9, 10.
Dimensions: 3–6 feet (1–2 meters) high.
Description: The common name is derived from the flowers which, over a period of three days, change from violet-blue, fading to lavender and eventually to white. The phlox-like flowers are very fragrant and the leaves are grayish-green. In cold climates, yesterday-today-and-tomorrow is grown in greenhouses or indoors. It likes a warm, sheltered position and benefits from a light pruning after flowering. Feed in early spring with a complete plant food.

Brunfelsia calycina
DWARF BRUNFELSIA, YESTERDAY-TODAY-AND-TOMORROW
○ ◑

Family: SOLANACEAE
Origin: South America.
Flowering time: Spring-summer.
Climatic zone: 9, 10.
Dimensions: 3–4 feet (approx. 1 meter) high.
Description: Compact, with slender, semi-glossy green foliage, dwarf brunfelsia makes a pretty feature shrub. The fragrant violet flowers virtually cover the plant and fade to white as they age. The shrub requires a warm, sheltered position and well-drained soil. A mulch of manure or compost in

spring will feed it and keep the roots moist. A light pruning after flowering encourages more compact growth.
Varieties/cultivars: 'Eximea', *B. c.* var. *floribunda*.

Buddleia alternifolia
FOUNTAIN BUDDLEIA, ALTERNATE-LEAFED BUDDLEIA
○ ◑

Family: LOGANIACEAE
Origin: China.
Flowering time: Early summer.
Climatic zone: 5, 6, 7, 8, 9.
Dimensions: 10–20 feet (3–6 meters).

Buddleia davidii
BUTTERFLY BUSH, BUDDLEIA
○ ◑

Family: LOGANIACEAE
Origin: China.
Flowering time: Summer.
Climatic zone: 5, 6, 7, 8, 9.
Dimensions: 10 feet (3 meters) high.
Description: Butterfly bush is a very worthy addition to gardens because of its hardiness, attractiveness to butterflies, and its tolerance of a wide range of soils, temperatures, and environments. Its rapid growth makes it useful for screen plantings. The gray-green foliage is attractive and complements the mauve spikes of the flower heads. Pruning in winter is essential to control the shape of the bush.

Other colors: Rich red-purple, white.
Varieties/cultivars: 'Royal Red', 'White Bouquet', 'Ile de France'.

146

Callicarpa bodinieri var. giraldii

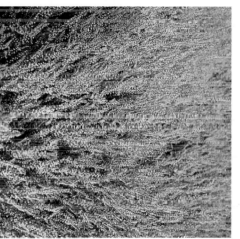

Calluna vulgaris

Caryopteris incana

Caryopteris x clandonensis

Callicarpa bodinieri var. giraldii
CHINESE BEAUTYBERRY,
BEAUTY BERRY (U.K.) ○

Family: VERBENACEAE
Origin: Western China.
Flowering time: Summer.
Climatic zone: 6, 7, 8, 9.
Dimensions: 6 feet (2 meters) high.
Description: This is a handsome shrub valued for its downy foliage and rosy-lilac flowers, which are followed by clusters of shining bluish-lilac fruits. Use it as a background plant for a shrub border. Easily grown, Chinese beautyberry will thrive in any well-drained soil that does not dry out. A sunny aspect is essential. Pruning is not necessary unless the plant becomes straggly, when it can be cut back heavily in late winter. Chinese beautyberry can be propagated from cuttings or seed.

Calluna vulgaris
LING, HEATHER,
SCOTCH HEATHER ○ ◑

Family: ERICACEAE
Origin: Europe, western Asia, Morocco, the Azores.
Flowering time: Spring and summer.
Climatic zone: 5, 6, 7, 8, 9.
Dimensions: 12 inches (450 mm) high.
Description: Heather is loved for its evergreen foliage and profusion of small, bell-like, purplish-pink, nodding flowers and is a good shrub to use in front of borders or as a groundcover in a small garden. It will grow in poor soil as long as it is well-drained and acidic. Cultivate around the plant with care as the roots are very close to the surface. A mulch of leaf mold or peat is beneficial. Pruning can be carried out after flowering to keep the plants compact.
Other colors: White, mauve, crimson, pink.
Varieties/cultivars: There are numerous cultivars of heather throughout the world.

Caryopteris incana
BLUEBEARD, BLUE
SPIRAEA (U.K.) ○

Family: VERBENACEAE
Origin: Japan, Korea, China.
Flowering time: Late summer–autumn.
Climatic zone: 5, 6, 7, 8, 9.
Dimensions: 3 feet (1 meter) high.
Description: This small shrub has an abundance of grayish-green, aromatic leaves. The axillary clusters of violet-blue flowers appear at the tips of the shoots. A valued shrub because it flowers when few other blue-flowering shrubs are in bloom, bluebeard will thrive in a moisture-retentive but well-drained loamy soil. Because flowers are produced on the new wood, prune during winter.

Caryopteris x clandonensis
BLUEBEARD, BLUE
SPIRAEA (U.K.) ○

Family: VERBENACEAE
Origin: Hybrid.
Flowering time: Summer–autumn.
Climatic zone: 5, 6, 7, 8, 9.
Dimensions: 2 feet (600 mm) high.
Description: This pretty plant is also known as *Caryopteris x clandonensis* 'Arthur Simmonds' after the man who first raised it. The bright blue flowers appear among the aromatic, dull green, downy foliage. A hardy shrub, it will grow in almost any soil and is an ideal subject for mass-planting. Pruning during winter will encourage more flowers the next season. Apply mulch, manure, compost, or a handful of complete plant food in early spring.
Other colors: Lilac-blue.
Varieties/cultivars: 'Ferndown', 'Heavenly Blue', 'Blue Mist', 'Kew Blue'.

Ceanothus thyrsiflorus var. *repens*

Ceanothus x *veitchianus*

blue flowers. The impressed vein pattern of the foliage is distinctive, dark green marked with pale green. Use ceanothus in a shrub border or as a feature plant. It is semideciduous in colder climates, but tends to remain evergreen in temperate climates. Plant it in well-drained soil and feed with a complete plant food during spring. It can be pruned when it has finished flowering.

handful of complete plant food. Pruning, if necessary, should be done just after flowering. The plant is easily propagated from cuttings taken in early spring or late summer.

○

Ceanothus x *veitchianus*
CALIFORNIA LILAC,
WILD LILAC (U.S.A.),
BUCKBRUSH (U.S.A.)

Family: RHAMNACEAE
Origin: Hybrid.
Flowering time: Early summer.
Climatic zone: 7, 8, 9.
Dimensions: 10 feet (3 meters) high.
Description: An evergreen hybrid,

Ceanothus impressus

◑ ○

Ceanothus thyrsiflorus var. *repens*
CREEPING BLUE
BLOSSOM, CALIFORNIAN
LILAC, SANTA BARBARA
CEANOTHUS

Other common names: WILD LILAC (U.S.A.), BUCKBRUSH (U.S.A.)
Family: RHAMNACEAE
Origin: California.
Flowering time: Summer.
Climatic zone: 8, 9.
Dimensions: 3 feet (900 mm) high.
Description: This shrub, prostrate when young and then gradually building up into a mound-shaped bush, produces generous quantities of sky-blue flowers. Use creeping blue blossom in the front of a shrub border or in a rockery. Plant it in well-drained soil that is enriched annually with manure or compost or, alternatively, apply a

Ceanothus 'Pacific Beauty'

○

Ceanothus cultivars
CALIFORNIA LILAC,
WILD LILAC (U.S.A.),
BUCKBRUSH (U.S.A.)

Family: RHAMNACEAE
Origin: Cultivars.
Flowering time: Spring–summer.
Climatic zone: 7, 8, 9.
Dimensions: 3–12 feet (1–4 meters) high, depending on the cultivar.
Description: There are many different cultivars of *Ceanothus* in a wide variety of shades of blue. Varying in size from small, prostrate plants to vigorous, tall shrubs, when in bloom, they are almost entirely covered with flowers. These showy plants will thrive in any well-drained soil, and are excellent shrubs for seaside plantings. Prune after flowering has finished.
Other colors: Lavender, violet and various shades of blue.
Varieties/cultivars: There are numerous cultivars of *Ceanothus*.

○

Ceanothus impressus
CEANOTHUS,
CALIFORNIAN LILAC, SANTA
BARBARA CEANOTHUS

Other common names: WILD LILAC (U.S.A.), BUCKBRUSH (U.S.A.)
Family: RHAMNACEAE
Origin: California.
Flowering time: Spring.
Climatic zone: 8, 9.
Dimensions: 6–10 feet (2–3 meters) high.
Description: *Ceanothus impressus* is a dense, compact shrub, which, during spring, is completely covered in deep-

148

California lilac forms a bushy, many-branched shrub with small oval leaves and clusters of deep-blue flowers. The flowers appear at the tips of the flowers and towards the end of the previous year's growth. Plant California lilac in a sheltered position, as it has a tendency to produce growth quickly during the first couple of years and then die off equally quickly if it is damaged by prolonged frost.

Ceratostigma griffithii

Ceratostigma griffithii
CERATOSTIGMA,
BURMESE PLUMBAGO,
HARDY PLUMBAGO (U.K.)

Family: PLUMBAGINACEAE
Origin: Himalayas, Burma.
Flowering time: Summer.
Climatic zone: 8, 9.
Dimensions: 2 feet (600 mm) high.
Description: A beautiful shrub, ceratostigma makes a delightful, hardy feature shrub, producing an abundance of deep-blue flowers over a long period. The leaves often turn conspicuously red in autumn. It likes full sun, a sheltered site, and a well-drained soil, and during spring should be mulched with manure or compost. Alternatively, apply a handful of complete plant food. Regular feeding will ensure a good flower display. Propagation can be carried out easily from cuttings or by root division.

Ceratostigma willmottianum
CERATOSTIGMA,
CHINESE PLUMBAGO,
HARDY PLUMBAGO (U.K.)

Family: PLUMBAGINACEAE
Origin: Western China.
Flowering time: Late summer.

Cistus x purpureus

Ceratostigma willmottianum

Climatic zone: 8, 9.
Dimensions: 2–3 feet (600–900 mm) high, 3–4 feet (approx. 1 meter) wide.
Description: Ceratostigma is a loose, open bush with distinctive sharp-angled stems. Red autumn foliage and bright

Cistus x purpureus
PURPLE ROCK ROSE,
ORCHID ROCK ROSE,
SUNROSE (U.K.)

Family: CISTACEAE
Origin: Hybrid.
Flowering time: Summer.
Climatic zone: 8, 9, 10.
Dimensions: 3–4 feet (over 1 meter) high.
Description: The showy purple flowers of purple rock rose have a darker blotch on each petal and a yellow "eye". The gray-green leaves are nearly stalkless. It is an ideal plant for the seaside and hot, dry areas, but will grow in cool areas if given a warm position and well-drained soil. It will not tolerate overwet soil or severe frost. During spring, feed it with a complete plant food.

blue tubular flowers make a colorful show for a large part of the year. It can be used at the front of a border or as an informal low hedge. It is hardy and tolerates a wide range of soils. Annual pruning is required.

Daphne odora

Disanthus cercidifolius
DISANTHUS

Family: HAMAMELIDACEAE
Origin: Japan, South-east China.
Flowering time: Autumn.
Climatic zone: 5, 6, 7, 8, 9.
Dimensions: 6–10 feet (2–3 meters) high.
Description: This large and beautiful deciduous shrub has slender branches and heart-shaped, thick leaves which turn from green to glorious shades of red and orange in autumn. The dark purple flowers have thin, spidery petals and are borne in pairs on short stalks. Best grown in cool, moist, and slightly acid soil, it should be located in a sheltered position and pruned lightly to keep the growth habit dense.

Disanthus cercidifolius

previous year's shoots and are followed by scarlet fruits, which are poisonous. Daphne's survival seems to depend on a cold winter. It likes a well-drained, alkaline soil. Daphne does not like chemical fertilizers — a mulch of cow manure or leaf mold annually will suffice.
Other colors: White, rose-pink.
Varieties/cultivars: 'Alba', 'Grandiflora', 'Rosea'.

Daphne mezereum

Daphne odora
DAPHNE

Family: THYMELAEACEAE
Origin: China.
Flowering time: Late winter-spring.
Climatic zone: 7, 8, 9.
Dimensions: 3 feet (900 mm) high x 4 feet (approx. 1 meter) wide.
Description: Daphne, though often difficult to grow, is worthy of a place in the garden because of its wonderful perfume. These small, evergreen, compact bushes require special conditions of good drainage and rich, crumbly, slightly acidic soils. At their flowering peak, the bushes are covered with dense heads of up to thirty star-shaped flowers which are rose-purple in bud and paler within. They are happy growing in association with rhododendrons or in containers as a focal point.
Other colors: Pink, white.
Varieties/cultivars: 'Alba', 'Aureo-marginata', 'Rubra'.

150

Daboecia cantabrica

Daboecia cantabrica and cultivars
IRISH HEATH, ST. DABEOC'S HEATH, CONNEMARA HEATH

Family: ERICACEAE
Origin: Western Europe.
Flowering time: Early summer–early autumn.
Climatic zone: 5, 6, 7, 8.
Dimensions: 12–18 inches (300–450 mm) high.
Description: These low-growing shrubs are popular for their long flowering period. There are several cultivars in various shades of purple, which can be used in rockeries or mass-planted. They thrive in cold climates in a free-draining, acidic soil. To ensure that the soil is acid, mulch around the plants with peat to a depth of about 1 foot (300 mm). Irish heath are easily propagated from seed or autumn cuttings.
Other colors: White, rich pink.
Varieties/cultivars: There are several cultivars of this shrub.

Daphne mezereum
DAPHNE, FEBRUARY DAPHNE, MEZEREON (U.K.)

Family: THYMELAEACEAE
Origin: Central and southern Europe, Asia Minor, Siberia.
Flowering time: Spring.
Climatic zone: 5, 6, 7, 8.
Dimensions: 3 feet (1 meter) high.
Description: A deciduous shrub, daphne is loved for its sweet-smelling, purple-red flowers. These cover the

Echium fastuosum

Echium fastuosum
VIPER'S BUGLOSS, PRIDE OF MADEIRA (U.K.) ○

Family: BORAGINACEAE
Origin: Canary Islands.
Flowering time: Spring–summer.
Climatic zone: 9, 10.
Dimensions: 4 feet (approx. 1 meter) high.
Description: Viper's bugloss is a soft-wooded shrub which is sometimes classed as a woody perennial. The dense branches bear a great profusion of lance-shaped, gray-green, hairy leaves. These develop central spikes up to 12 inches (300 mm) long, tightly packed with long-stamened, blue or purple flowers. Viper's bugloss will thrive near the seaside in a hot, sunny position. It needs a well-drained soil and tends to flower more profusely in poor and fairly dry soils. Cut off the older rosettes after flowering.

Eupatorium megalophyllum
SHRUB AGERATUM, MIST FLOWER, EUPATORIUM (U.K.) ◐

Family: COMPOSITAE
Origin: Southern Mexico.
Flowering time: Late spring.

Eupatorium megalophyllum

Climatic zone: 9, 10.
Dimensions: 6 feet (2 meters) high.
Description: Eupatorium requires temperatures above 32°F (0°C) and consequently is not commonly seen in northern hemisphere gardens. The plant looks like an overgrown ageratum, but is distinguished from it by its furry foliage with dense clusters of mauve flowers in late spring. The size of eupatoriums gives scale to a shrub border. They are an attractive companion plant to rondeletias.

Felicia amelloides
BLUE MARGUERITE, BLUE DAISY, AGATHAEA, FELICIA ○

Family: COMPOSITAE
Origin: South Africa.
Flowering time: Early summer and intermittently through into autumn.
Climatic zone: 9, 10.
Dimensions: 20 inches (500 mm) high.
Description: This is a hardy, evergreen shrub with a compact form which becomes covered with a profusion of bright blue, daisy-like flowers with yellow centers. It is a very useful fill-in plant, and will complement a perennial border. It likes full sun and good drainage, and a moderate pruning after flowering helps maintain its shape. It differs from *F. angustifolia*, its near relative, in its leaf arrangement.

Felicia amelloides

Hebe speciosa 'La Seduisante'

Hebe x andersonii

Hebe speciosa 'La Seduisante'
SPEEDWELL HEBE, ○ ◑
SHRUBBY VERONICA (U.K.)

Family: SCROPHULARIACEAE
Origin: Cultivar.
Flowering time: Summer.
Climatic zone: 8, 9.
Dimensions: 3 feet (1 meter) high.
Description: This French cultivar has bright rosy-purple flowers, and interesting, dark-green leaves that are purple underneath. It makes a lovely feature plant as it looks attractive even when not in flower. Mulch around the plant with manure or compost to prevent the shallow roots from drying out during summer. It can be pruned after flowering if it loses its shape.

Hebe x andersonii
SPEEDWELL HEBE, ○ ◑
SHRUBBY VERONICA (U.K.)

Family: SCROPHULARIACEAE
Origin: Hybrid.
Flowering time: Summer-autumn.

Felicia angustifolia

Hebe hulkeana

growth and glossy green leaves. It bears large clusters of delicate, lilac-blue flowers. It is easily grown in any type of soil, but dislikes drying out during summer. A mulch of manure or compost will keep the soil moist, as well as providing food. New Zealand lilac may need pruning every second winter to maintain a good shape.

Felicia angustifolia
FELICIA (U.K.), ○ ◑
KINGFISHER DAISY

Family: COMPOSITAE
Origin: South Africa.
Flowering time: Spring.
Climatic zone: 9, 10.
Dimensions: 3 feet (1 meter) high.
Description: A very free-flowering small shrub, felicia has daisy-like, light-purple flowers which cover the bright green foliage for a few weeks during spring. Because of its spreading and trailing habit, it makes a good groundcover or rockery plant. It is a hardy plant which will thrive in any well-drained garden soil. A light pruning after flowering encourages more flowers the following season. Feed in early spring with a handful of complete plant food.

Hebe hulkeana
NEW ZEALAND LILAC, ○ ◑
VERONICA

Family: SCROPHULARIACEAE
Origin: New Zealand.
Flowering time: Spring-summer.
Climatic zone: 8, 9.
Dimensions: 3 feet (1 meter) high.
Description: This is one of the most beautiful species of *Hebe* in cultivation. It is a small shrub, with a loose, open

Hebe x andersonii 'Anne Pimm'

Climatic zone: 8, 9.
Dimensions: 4–6 feet (1–2 meters) high.
Description: This vigorous shrub has leaves 4–6 inches (100–150 mm) and 5-inch (125-mm) long spikes of soft lavender-blue flowers which fade to white. There is also a variegated form which has creamy-white margins along the leaves. It is a fast-growing shrub which makes an excellent screen plant. Before planting, enrich the soil with manure or compost and mulch around it to protect the shallow roots. Speedwell hebe can be lightly pruned after flowering to encourage a denser habit.
Varieties/cultivars: Cultivars include 'Variegata', 'Anne Pimm'.

Hebe x andersonii 'Anne Pimm'
SPEEDWELL HEBE,
SHRUBBY VERONICA (U.K.) ◐

Family: SCROPHULARIACEAE
Origin: Hybrid.
Flowering time: Summer–autumn.
Climatic zone: 8, 9.
Dimensions: 4–6 feet (1–2 meters) high.
Description: This vigorous shrub has leaves 4–6 inches (100–150 cm) long, mid-green and flushed with reddish-purple underneath when young. The soft lavender-purple flowers are borne on long spikes, making a most attractive display over many weeks. It is a fast-growing shrub, which makes an excellent screen plant. Incorporate plenty of compost into the soil prior to planting, and mulch well to protect the shallow roots. Lightly prune after flowering to encourage a denser habit.

Hebe x franciscana 'Blue Gem'
SPEEDWELL HEBE,
SHRUBBY VERONICA (U.K.) ◐

Family: SCROPHULARIACEAE
Origin: Cultivar.
Flowering time: Summer.
Climatic zone: 8, 9.
Dimensions: 3 feet (1 meter) high.
Description: This compact shrub produces dense racemes of bright blue flowers. It is one of the hardiest hebes, and its resistance to salt-laden winds makes it a popular shrub for seaside plantings. It is often used for low hedges. Plant it in soil that has been enriched with manure or compost. This will provide food as well as keep the soil moist. It can be pruned to shape during winter.

Heliotropium arborescens
CHERRY-PIE,
HELIOTROPE ○ ◐

Family: BORAGINACEAE
Origin: Peru.
Flowering time: Spring–summer.

Heliotropium arborescens

Hebe x franciscana 'Blue Gem'

Climatic zone: 9, 10.
Dimensions: 6 feet (2 meters) high.
Description: Cherry-pie is a pretty shrub with wrinkled, hairy leaves and branched spikes crowded with fragrant, violet or lilac flowers. Powerfully scented, these flowers are used in the manufacture of perfume. It will adapt to any well-drained soil and should be fed in spring with a handful of complete plant food. Water it well during the summer months.

and some overhead shade to grow successfully. The roots must be kept cool with a mulch of leaf litter or well-rotted compost. It can be easily propagated from seed.

Hibiscus syriacus

Hibiscus syriacus
ROSE-OF-SHARON, SYRIAN HIBISCUS, MALLOW

Other common names: BLUE HIBISCUS
Family: MALVACEAE
Origin: Eastern Asia.
Flowering time: Late summer–autumn.
Climatic zone: 5, 6, 7, 8, 9.
Dimensions: 8 feet (over 2 meters) high.
Description: A hardy, deciduous shrub, rose-of-Sharon is valued for its late summer and autumn flowers, which vary greatly in color. Although predominantly blue and purple, there are often two or more shades in the same flower. One of its common names is Syrian hibiscus, but it has never been found growing wild in that country.
Other colors: Red, white, rose, carmine, pink.
Varieties/cultivars: There are numerous varieties throughout the world.

Hovea chorizemifolia
HOLLY-LEAF HOVEA

Family: LEGUMINOSAE
Origin: Western Australia.
Flowering time: Spring.
Climatic zone: 9.
Dimensions: 22 inches (600 mm) high.
Description: An erect, sparsely branched, small shrub with holly-like leaves and deep-purple pea flowers, this very pretty shrub is not often found in cultivation. It needs excellent drainage

Flowering time: Spring–summer.
Climatic zone: 7, 8, 9, 10.
Dimensions: 3–6 feet (1–2 meters) high.
Description: Hydrangeas are popular plants because of their hardy nature and beautiful flower colors; the various shades of blue available depend on the cultivar. The color of the flower generally depends on the soil. An alkaline soil produces pink flowers while an acid soil produces blue flowers. To maintain the blue color of the flowers add aluminum sulfate annually to the soil (1 tablespoon per square meter), or keep the soil mulched with peat moss or oak leaves.
Other colors: Pink, red, mauve.
Varieties/cultivars: There are numerous cultivars throughout the world.

Indigofera australis
AUSTRALIAN INDIGO

Family: LEGUMINOSAE
Origin: Australia.
Flowering time: Spring.
Climatic zone: 9, 10.
Dimensions: 6 feet (2 meters) high.
Description: This open, spreading plant, which grows to 6 feet (2 meters) wide, is covered in sprays of purple, pea-like flowers in spring. Australian indigo

Hovea chorizemifolia

Hydrangea macrophylla and cultivars
COMMON HYDRANGEA, BIGLEAF HYDRANGEA (U.S.A.), FLORIST'S HYDRANGEA (U.K.)

Other common names: HORTENSIA (U.S.A.)
Family: HYDRANGEACEAE
Origin: Japan.

Hydrangea macrophylla

154

Indigofera australis

Dimensions: 3 feet (1 meter) high.
Description: What garden is complete without the fragrance of lavender? The beautiful lavender-blue spikes of flowers attract bees to the garden and the leaves have a similar scent to the flowers. Plant it along the side of a path where the perfume can be appreciated. English lavender will thrive in a sandy soil and is a handy shrub for seaside gardens. Prune it after flowering to maintain a compact shape. It is easily propagated from cuttings taken in late summer.
Other colors: Pink, white, violet.
Varieties/cultivars: There are several varieties of this shrub.

flowers just as well in full sun as in the shade, and will grow in most soils except those which are very wet. Prune it after the flowers have finished, to maintain a good shape. It is easily propagated from seed or cuttings.
Varieties/cultivars: 'Signata'.

Lavandula angustifolia syn. *L. officinalis, L. spica, L. vera*
ENGLISH LAVENDER, COMMON LAVENDER (U.K.)
Family: LABIATAE
Origin: Mediterranean region.
Flowering time: Summer.
Climatic zone: 6, 7, 8, 9.

Lavandula angustifolia

155

Lavandula dentata
FRENCH LAVENDER, SPANISH LAVENDER, TOOTHED LAVENDER
Family: LABIATAE
Origin: Spain and Balearic Islands.
Flowering time: Summer.
Climatic zone: 8, 9.
Dimensions: 3 feet (1 meter) high.
Description: *Lavandula dentata* is a popular, hardy, garden plant, grown for its silvery leaves and its wonderful perfume. It is distinguished by a gray, toothed leaf and a mauve spike of aromatic flowers, both of which are used for potpourri. It is tolerant of a wide range of soils, providing drainage is good, and grows well near the sea. Pruning is essential to maintain its shape and prevent it from becoming woody. Lavender requires full sun.

Lavandula stoechas
FRENCH LAVENDER, TOPPED LAVENDER
Family: LABIATAE
Origin: Mediterranean region, Portugal.
Flowering time: Summer.
Climatic zone: 7, 8, 9.
Dimensions: Up to 2 feet (600 mm) high.
Description: This is a small, intensely aromatic shrub with narrow, grayish-green leaves. The dark-purple flowers are borne in dense, terminal heads. It can be used as a low, fragrant hedge along the side of a path or as a border around a cottage garden. The main requirements of French lavender are a warm, sunny position and a sandy, well-drained soil. Cutting off the flower heads when the flowers have finished will keep it more compact in shape.

Lavandula dentata

Lavandula stoechas

Lithospermum diffusum

Lavatera maritima

Lechenaultia biloba

Lavatera maritima
SHRUBBY MALLOW, FRENCH MALLOW, SEA MALLOW (U.K.)

Family: MALVACEAE
Origin: Southern France.
Flowering time: Summer–autumn.
Climatic zone: 8, 9.
Dimensions: 4–6 feet (up to 2 meters) high.
Description: This elegant shrub has unusual grayish, downy stems and leaves. The large saucer-shaped flowers are pale lilac with purple veins and eye, and remain on the plant for a long period. It makes an ideal feature shrub, but to be grown successfully it must be given a warm, sheltered position, preferably against a wall. Mulch it annually with well-rotted manure or compost or apply a handful of complete plant food.

Lechenaultia biloba
BLUE LECHENAULTIA

Family: GOODENIACEAE
Origin: Western Australia.
Flowering time: Spring.
Climatic zone: 9, 10.
Dimensions: 16 inches (400 mm) high.
Description: This straggly plant, though short-lived in cultivation, is most desirable because of its intense

blue flowers. It needs excellent drainage to survive, and is best used in the garden trailing over rocks or walls, or as an informal groundcover.
Varieties/cultivars: 'White Flash'.

covered in lovely blue flowers. It is valued for its long flowering period, and for its usefulness as a rockery plant and a groundcover. Old plants tend to die out in bad winters, especially in poorly drained soils, but if they are cut back a little after flowering they seem to be more durable. Add peat or leaf mold to the soil to keep it acidic, as lithospermum dislikes lime.
Other colors: White.
Varieties/cultivars: 'Album', 'Grace Ward', 'Heavenly Blue'.

Lithospermum diffusum
LITHOSPERMUM, HEAVENLY BLUE

Family: BORAGINACEAE
Origin: Southern Europe.
Flowering time: Spring–summer.
Climatic zone: 8, 9.
Dimensions: 3–4 inches (75–100 mm) high.
Description: This prostrate shrub forms a large mat which becomes

Mackaya bella
MACKAYA

Family: ACANTHACEAE
Origin: South Africa.
Flowering time: Summer.
Climatic zone: 9, 10.
Dimensions: 4–6 feet (approx. 1–2 meters) high.
Description: An extremely pretty shrub, mackaya is valued for its 5-inch-long (125 mm), oblong leaves and large, spotted, lilac flowers. It makes an elegant feature shrub in warm climates. It is not fussy about soil type, but likes a sheltered position. Feed it in early spring by mulching with manure or compost, or, alternatively, apply a handful of complete plant food. Propagation is carried out from cuttings taken in early spring.

156

Mackaya bella

Michelia figo

Michelia figo
PORT WINE MAGNOLIA, ◑
BANANA SHRUB (U.K.),
FRUIT SALAD MAGNOLIA

Family: MAGNOLIACEAE
Origin: China.
Flowering time: Spring-summer.
Climatic zone: 9, 10.
Dimensions: 10–15 feet (3–5 meters) high.
Description: An attractive, evergreen shrub, port wine magnolia has a neat, rounded appearance. The young shoots are brown and hairy, and the elliptic, dark-green leaves are smooth and shiny. The purplish-colored flowers, initially enclosed in brown bracts, are strongly scented, emitting their perfume throughout the garden. This is a perfect shrub to plant near a doorway or window so that the perfume can be appreciated. It is easy to grow and its main requirement is a neutral to acid soil that does not dry out.

Oxypetalum caeruleum
TWEEDIA ○

Family: ASCLEPIADACEAE
Origin: South America, West Indies.
Flowering time: Summer-autumn.
Climatic zone: 9, 10.
Dimensions: 3 feet (1 meter) or more high.
Description: This is a weak-stemmed, small, spreading sub-shrub with grayish-green leaves which are covered in a soft down. The terminal clusters of starry, sky-blue flowers cover the plant from summer to autumn. In warm climates there are generally flowers on the plant throughout the year. It is pretty planted in the sunny foreground of shrubberies, or included in an annual or perennial garden. Tweedia is a short-lived plant, but it is easily raised from seed or cuttings.

Plumbago auriculata

Plumbago auriculata syn. *P. capensis*
CAPE LEADWORT, ○
PLUMBAGO (U.K.)

Family: PLUMBAGINACEAE
Origin: South Africa.
Flowering time: Early summer-autumn.
Climatic zone: 9, 10.
Dimensions: 4–8 feet (approx. 1–2 meters) high.
Description: A slender-stemmed, rambling shrub with neat, evergreen leaves and large trusses of sky-blue, phlox-like flowers, plumbago is a favorite in warm climate gardens. It clambers over other shrubs, makes attractive hedges, sprawls down banks, or becomes a good wall shrub. Given a sunny position with no frost, plumbago will flower off and on throughout the year. Plant it in a well-drained soil, enriched with manure or compost.

Oxypetalum caeruleum

157

SHRUBS

becomes thickly studded with clusters of blue, fragrant flowers. The green leaves have a pale downy underside and are very fragrant. Prostrate rosemary should be planted along the tops of walls or banks where it can cascade down the side. It needs a mild winter climate and does not tolerate frosts. It is a useful plant for seaside gardens.

Rosmarinus lavandulaceus

Rosmarinus officinalis
COMMON ROSEMARY ○

Family: LABIATAE
Origin: Mediterranean coastal regions.
Flowering time: Late spring–early summer.
Climatic zone: 7, 8, 9, 10.
Dimensions: 3–6 feet (1–2 meters) tall.
Description: Rosemary, though more commonly known for its culinary and medicinal uses, is a worthwhile addition

Rosmarinus officinalis

Polygala myrtifolia var. grandiflora

Polygala myrtifolia var. grandiflora ◐
BLUE CAPS,
MILKWORT (U.K.)

Family: POLYGALACEAE
Origin: South Africa.
Flowering time: Winter–autumn.
Climatic zone: 9, 10.
Dimensions: 4–8 feet (approx. 1–2 meters) high.
Description: The prolonged flowering period of this shrub is its greatest asset. The rich-purple, "sweet pea" like flowers are produced in clusters near the end of the shoots. It will tolerate dappled shade, but under these conditions flowers only for short periods. Blue caps will thrive in any soil type. It should be fed during early spring with a complete plant food. Pruning during this season will encourage more compact growth.

Prostanthera rotundifolia

Prostanthera rotundifolia
ROUND-LEAF MINTBUSH,
MINTBUSH (U.K.) ○

Family: LABIATAE
Origin: Eastern Australia.
Flowering time: Spring.
Climatic zone: 9.
Dimensions: 6 feet (2 meters) high.
Description: This outstanding but fairly short-lived shrub is covered in heavy masses of purple flowers during spring. The leaves are small and round.

Use it as a specimen shrub, or as a background shrub in herbaceous borders. The main requirement of the round-leaf mintbush is perfect drainage. Light pruning after flowering will keep it more compact.

Rosmarinus lavandulaceus
PROSTRATE ROSEMARY ○

Family: LABIATAE
Origin: Southern Spain, North Africa.
Flowering time: Spring–summer.
Climatic zone: 9, 10.
Dimensions: 1 foot (300 mm) high.
Description: This evergreen shrub forms a large, dense, mat which

158

to a garden because of its dark-green foliage and delicate lavender flowers. This plant requires heavy pruning to prevent bare woody growth. It makes a very suitable hedging plant.
Varieties/cultivars: 'Blue Lagoon'.

Strobilanthes anisophyllus

Strobilanthes anisophyllus
GOLDFUSSIA

Family: ACANTHACEAE
Origin: South East Asia.
Flowering time: Summer–autumn.
Climatic zone: 8, 9, 10.
Dimensions: 2–3 feet (up to 1 meter) high.
Description: A bushy shrub, goldfussia produces an abundance of purple, narrow, lance-shaped leaves. The small groups of long, tubular, lavender flowers with bell-shaped mouths appear between the leaves and stems. In colder climates it is often grown as an indoor plant. Best results are achieved if this shrub is given well-drained soil and regular spring applications of plant food.

Syringa vulgaris 'Charles Joly'
COMMON LILAC, EUROPEAN LILAC, ENGLISH LILAC

Family: OLEACEAE
Origin: Cultivar.
Flowering time: Late spring–early summer.

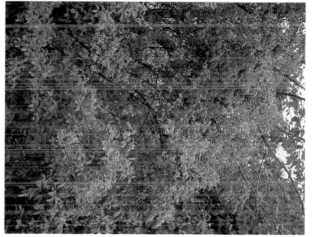

Syringa vulgaris 'Charles Joly'

Climatic zone: 4, 5, 6, 7, 8.
Dimensions: 4–10 feet (1–3 meters) high.
Description: Lilac is loved for its highly perfumed flowers. There is probably no other shrub or tree that has given rise to so many cultivars as *Syringa vulgaris*, the parent of 'Charles Joly'. 'Charles Joly' has dark purplish-red flowers which appear later in spring than most other

lilac varieties. During winter, cut the tops of the more vigorous stems to produce side shoots, as this new growth carries next season's flowers. Lilac likes a slightly limy, well-drained soil.

Tibouchina urvilleana
LASIANDRA, GLORY BUSH (U.K.), SPIDER FLOWER

Other common names: PRINCESS FLOWER (U.S.A.)
Family: MELASTOMATACEAE
Origin: Tropical America.
Flowering time: Summer–autumn.
Climatic zone: 9, 10.
Dimensions: 4–15 feet (approx. 1–5 meters) high.
Description: A handsome but straggly shrub, glory bush has very showy, large, vivid purple flowers and large velvety leaves. Its shape can be improved by pruning after flowering. Pinching the new shoots will also promote a denser bush. Even though glory bush needs full sun, its roots must be kept cool. This can be achieved by placing a mulch of leaf litter, compost, or manure around the base in late winter and again in early summer. Neutral to acid soil is essential for rich-green leaves and free-flowering.

Tibouchina urvilleana

TREES

Jacaranda mimosifolia
JACARANDA, FERN TREE

Family: BIGNONIACEAE
Origin: Northwestern Argentina.
Flowering time: Late spring.
Climatic zone: 9, 10.
Dimensions: 40–50 feet (12–15 meters) high.
Description: One of the loveliest trees of all time, jacarandas in flower, in a good year, are a breathtaking sight. A whole street planted in jacarandas appears misty blue. The drier the winter, the better they flower. Jacarandas develop a broad dome of lacy, soft green-colored leaves which, although deciduous, can remain on the tree until late winter. Given full sun and good drainage, jacarandas add immense charm to any garden in warm areas. They are excellent shade trees.

Lagerstroemia indica 'Heliotrope Beauty'

Lagerstroemia indica
CREPE MYRTLE

Family: LYTHRACEAE
Origin: India, South East Asia, China.
Flowering time: Late summer–early autumn.
Climatic zone: 9, 10.
Dimensions: 20–30 feet (6–9 meters) high.
Description: Many cultivars have been bred from the species, often much

Bauhinia variegata

Bauhinia variegata
BUTTERFLY TREE, ORCHID TREE, MOUNTAIN EBONY

Family: CAESALPINACEAE
Origin: Pakistan–Burma, China.
Flowering time: Spring, northern hemisphere; mid-spring–early summer and intermittently autumn, southern hemisphere.
Climatic zone: 9, 10.
Dimensions: 16–27 feet (5–8 meters) high.
Description: Bauhinias are easily identified by their showy, orchid-like flowers and bilobed leaves. *Variegata* in this case refers to the mixed streaks of color in the flowers which are about 2 inches (50 mm) across and usually rosy-purple, but the colors vary somewhat when the plant is grown from seed. The tree grows in warm districts. If cultivated in cooler climates, it develops a rather straggly canopy and becomes semideciduous. It enjoys rich, well-drained soils and a position in full sun, protected from cold or salty winds.
Other colors: White.
Varieties/cultivars: *B. v. var. candida.*

Jacaranda mimosifolia

smaller in habit. *L. indica* is a charming, deciduous tree, happiest in warm-climate gardens. Clusters of crinkly flowers are liberally borne in summer, lingering into autumn. When the leaves have dropped, the beautiful mottled bark is revealed. Many people spoil the tree's natural, graceful, spreading shape by severe pruning in the winter. In humid areas some pruning is necessary, though, for powdery mildew attacks the leaves if the tree is not pruned or treated each year.

Other colors: White, pink, lavender, red, bicolors.

Varieties/cultivars: 'Eavsii', 'Heliotrope Beauty', 'Matthewsii', 'Newmanii', 'Petites' (Californian series).

Paulownia tomentosa

Melia azedarach var. *australasica*

WHITE CEDAR, CHINABERRY

○

Family: MELIACEAE
Origin: Orient, South East Asia, Australia.
Flowering time: Mid-late spring, southern hemisphere.
Climatic zone: 9, 10.
Dimensions: 30–50 feet (10–15 meters) high.
Description: Rapid adaptability to a wide range of soils and climates has made this species a very popular garden tree. The woolly sprays of flowers are lilac in color, followed by oval, orange-yellow berries during winter. This variety has naturalized on much of the east coast of Australia, from N.S.W. to Queensland, and is in cultivation in many other parts of the country. The main species has adapted to many areas of the United States and is relatively pest-free. In coastal parts of Australia, however, this particular variety, which is deciduous, is attacked by white cedar caterpillars in autumn, which can be controlled by trapping them at night in a hessian bag wrapped around the tree trunk.

Paulownia tomentosa syn. *P. imperialis*

EMPRESS OR PRINCESS TREE, ROYAL PAULOWNIA, FORTUNE'S PAULOWNIA

○

Other common names: MOUNTAIN JACARANDA
Family: BIGNONIACEAE
Origin: Central China, Korea.

Flowering time: Spring, southern and northern hemispheres.
Climatic zone: 7, 8, 9.
Dimensions: 50 feet (15 meters) high.
Description: This beautiful, deciduous tree, named after a Russian princess, has a single trunk with a broad, spreading crown. Large, heart-shaped leaves are covered in downy hairs. The trumpet-like flowers, borne in upright clusters, are violet-blue, paling to white at the base which is marked with violet and yellowish streaks and spots. Severe winters may damage dormant flower buds. Easily grown from seed, paulownia likes a well-drained soil with ample water in summer. This tree is often mistaken for catalpa, a close relative.

Melia azedarach

WHITE
FLOWERS

Gypsophila elegans

Chrysanthemum parthenium

Euphorbia marginata

Asperula odorata

Asperula odorata syn. *Galium odoratum*
WOODRUFF ○ ◐ ●

Family: RUBIACEAE
Origin: Caucasus.
Flowering time: Spring–summer.
Climatic zone: 6, 7, 8, 9, 10.
Dimensions: Up to 12 inches (300 mm) high.
Description: This leafy plant sprawls and is useful for filling gaps among shrubs and perennials. As an annual it also has its own place in summer beds and borders. The masses of tiny, tubular, white flowers are ⅜ inch (9 mm) long and borne in tight, terminal clusters. Beneath each flower is a leafy bract which persists after the flower has died. In hot climates, woodruff prefers shade and ample moisture, but in general it is hardy. The flowers are not suitable for floral work.

prior to planting. Best results when planted in full sun.
Varieties/cultivars: 'Golden Feather', 'White Stars', 'Selaginoides', 'Aureum'.

Euphorbia marginata
SNOW-ON-THE-
MOUNTAIN, GHOSTWEED ○ ◐

Family: EUPHORBIACEAE
Origin: Central United States.
Flowering time: Summer.
Climatic zone: 6, 7, 8, 9.
Dimensions: Up to 3 feet (1 meter) high.
Description: This plant forms a good background hedge for lower annuals, or a tall border for a shrubbery. The flowers are tiny, up to ¼ inch (7 mm) and greenish white. They are almost concealed by clusters of showy, white and green bracts. The lower leaves are bright green; those nearing the top are white-margined. Snow-on-the-mountain is a very decorative plant and in much demand for floral work. Valued for its ease of cultivation in a wide range of soils and conditions, in either full sun or partial shade.

Chrysanthemum parthenium syn.
Matricaria eximia
FEVERFEW, ○ ◐
MAYWEED

Family: COMPOSITAE
Origin: Southeastern Europe–Caucasus.
Flowering time: Summer–autumn.
Climatic zone: 4, 5, 6, 7, 8, 9.
Dimensions: Up to 3 feet (1 meter) high.
Description: Small, white daisy-like flowers cover this plant in profusion. It is useful for floral work and flowers for many weeks in cooler climates. *Chrysanthemum parthenium* is a herb which can be used as an insect repellant and medicinally for headaches. It is excellent as a border for a vegetable garden. Good soil preparation is vital. Add some dolomite, well-rotted cow manure, and an all-purpose fertilizer

Gypsophila elegans
ANNUAL BABY'S BREATH ○

Family: CARYOPHYLLACEAE
Origin: Caucasus, Iran, Turkey.
Flowering time: Summer–autumn.
Climatic zone: 4, 5, 6, 7, 8, 9.
Dimensions: Up to 18 inches (450 mm) high.
Description: Although this rather slim annual has a delicate appearance, it is

164

Iberis umbellata

tough. Its stems are stiff and upright and the leaves are small and sparse. The tiny flowers (¼ inch (6 mm) wide) which appear on many-branched stems are usually white and move with the lightest wind. Baby's breath is very popular with florists for use in bunches of mixed flowers and table decorations. It lasts well and is grown as a hardy annual. Well-drained, slightly alkaline soil is preferred. After the first flush of flowers fade, trim back to allow new blooms to be produced.

Other colors: Rose, purple, pink.
Varieties/cultivars: 'Carminea', 'Grandiflora Alba', 'Purpurea', 'Rosea'.

Iberis umbellata

GLOBE CANDYTUFT, ANNUAL CANDYTUFT

Family: CRUCIFERAE
Origin: Mediterranean region.
Flowering time: Summer–autumn.
Climatic zone: 5, 6, 7, 8, 9.
Dimensions: Up to 16 inches (400 mm) high.
Description: This is an erect, many-branched annual which prefers cool but sunny climates. The flower clusters, which are up to 2 inches (50 mm) wide, are carried just above the foliage, often in abundance. They are shaped like a pincushion and may be cut for decoration. Plant in full sun in any moderately rich, well-drained soil.
Other colors: Pink, mauve, violet, purple-red.
Varieties/cultivars: 'Atropurpurea', 'Cardinal', 'Lavender', 'Lilac', 'Rosea'.

Lobularia maritima syn. *Alyssum maritimum*

SWEET ALYSSUM

Family: CRUCIFERAE
Origin: Mediterranean region.
Flowering time: Spring–autumn.
Climatic zone: 5, 6, 7, 8, 9.
Dimensions: Up to 6 inches (150 mm) high.
Description: This low-growing annual is very popular with gardeners because it grows easily, readily produces viable seeds, and thus may persist for many years. The small plants grow closely together to form a continuous edging of color. The flowers, though tiny, form tight clusters, and have a honeyed perfume that attracts bees. It is excellent for window boxes or hanging baskets. This adaptable annual can be grown in virtually any well-drained soil, thriving in full sun or partial shade.
Other colors: Pink, purple.
Varieties/cultivars: 'Rosie O'Day', 'Royal carpet'.

Lobularia maritima

Moluccella laevis

BELLS-OF-IRELAND, MOLUCCA BALM, SHELL-FLOWER

Family: LABIATAE
Origin: Turkey-Syria.
Flowering time: Summer–autumn.
Climatic zone: 6, 7, 8, 9, 10.
Dimensions: Up to 2 feet (600 mm) high.
Description: The tiny flowers of this plant are ½ inch (6 mm) wide and are enclosed in cup or shell-shaped, bright green calyces which form conspicuous spikes. The profusion of the flower spikes is a feature of the plant, which is prized by florists and home decorators. Plant in spring in moderately rich soil, and water and feed sparingly during the main growing period.

Moluccella laevis

Nicotiana alata

FLOWERING TOBACCO

Family: SOLANACEAE
Origin: South America.
Flowering time: Spring, summer, autumn.
Climatic zone: 6, 7, 8, 9, 10.
Dimensions: Up to 3 feet (1 meter) high.
Description: This soft-foliaged short-lived perennial grown as an annual forms an ideal background in cottage gardens and perennial borders. It produces many stems about 12 inches (300 mm) long, terminating in fragrant, outward-pointing flowers. These are tubular, up to 4 inches (100 mm) long, and about 2 inches (50 mm) wide at the mouth. Flowering tobacco seeds readily. This fragrant annual likes average garden soil with good drainage.
Other colors: Cream-yellow, rose-red, green, pink, maroon, purple.
Varieties/cultivars: 'Nana' (dwarf form to 18 inches (450 mm) high), 'Rubelle' (dwarf red).

Nicotiana alata

Convallaria majalis

Allium triquestrum

Allium triquestrum
TRIQUESTROUS ○ ◐ ●
GARLIC

Family: ALLIACEAE
Origin: Mediterranean region.
Flowering time: Spring.
Climatic zone: 8, 9, 10.
Dimensions: Up to 18 inches (450 mm) high.
Description: Numerous small, white flowers which occur in terminal umbels create a pretty spring display. The stem is erect, while the slender mid-green foliage is linear. Adaptable to most soils, it prefers a protected, sunny position and requires regular watering in summer if the conditions are hot and dry. Pretty in a cottage garden landscape, or as a potted specimen on a sunny verandah or balcony.

Cardiocrinum giganteum
GIANT LILY ○ ◐

Family: LILIACEAE
Origin: Himalayas, southeastern Tibet.
Flowering time: Summer.
Climatic zone: 7, 8, 9.
Dimensions: Up to 10 feet (3 meters) high.
Description: Giant lily is a magnificent plant for a damp position in an open

woodland area. The tall, robust stem produces many drooping, long, white flowers, like those of a trumpet lily. Because of its heart-shaped leaves, and the size of the plant, it merits a special place in the garden. The bulbs usually take more than a year to settle down before they flower; it takes five to seven years from seeding to flowering. After flowering, the main bulb dies, but produces small offset bulbs which can be lifted.

Convallaria majalis
LILY-OF-THE-VALLEY ◐ ● ●

Family: LILIACEAE
Origin: Northern temperate zone.
Flowering time: Spring.
Climatic zone: 4, 5, 6, 7, 8.
Dimensions: 6–8 inches (150–200 mm) high.
Description: Lily-of-the-valley is a favorite with many gardeners because of its sweet perfume. The delicate, waxy, bell-shaped flowers appear with the broad leaves, and the foliage persists through the summer. It likes a rich soil full of humus and, once established, should not be disturbed for a number of years until the clump becomes overcrowded. In good conditions, the flowers are followed by scarlet berries. The rhizomes should be planted in early winter.

Other colors: Pink, beige.
Varieties/cultivars: 'Everest', 'Fortune's Giant', 'Variegata'.

Crinum x powellii 'Album' ◑
CRINUM

Family: AMARYLLIDACEAE
Origin: Hybrid.
Flowering time: Summer.
Climatic zone: 8, 9.
Dimensions: Up to 4 feet (1.2 meters) high.

Cardiocrinum giganteum

166

Description: A tender hybrid, crinum produces six to eight large white flowers on each long stem. This handsome plant is a rich feeder and needs plenty of water. Suited to water landscapes near ponds, among ferns and trees, it can be temperamental if moved and may not flower for a season after being lifted. If left alone it will produce a clump of striking-looking flowers. Propagate from the offset bulbs which will take two to three years to flower. Crinum also does well grown in pots in a greenhouse.
Other colors: Pink.

Crinum x powellii 'Album'

Crocus biflorus weldonii

Description: Autumn crocus provides delicate color in a bare season. Emerging from light groundcovers, its delicacy is accentuated. It is a useful addition to herb gardens which often die back in autumn. Plant in a sunny spot with warm, well-drained soil where it can self-sow, naturalize it in lawns, but do not mow the grass until the foliage dies back. Definite cold is required in winter.
Other colors: Pale lilac.

Crocus niveus
AUTUMN CROCUS, CROCUS (U.K.) ○
Family: IRIDACEAE
Origin: Southern Greece.
Flowering time: Autumn.
Climatic zone: 6, 7, 8, 9.
Dimensions: Up to 6 inches (150 mm) high.

Crocus niveus

Crocus biflorus
SCOTCH CROCUS ○
Family: IRIDACEAE
Origin: Italy–Caucasus and Iran.
Flowering time: Spring.
Climatic zone: 5, 6, 7, 8, 9.
Dimensions: Up to 4 inches (100 mm) high.
Description: Scotch crocus is a pretty addition to the rock garden. The closed, white petals of the flower are striped in purple and open to reveal the delicate, yellow-throated center. When flowering in small clumps it resembles a bouquet. Plant it near gates and pathways where visitors can admire its beauty. It may be naturalized in lawns, which should not be mown until the foliage dies down. This species needs a cold winter.
Other colors: Violet, blue.
Varieties/cultivars: C. b. adamii, C. b. weldonii.

167

Erythronium dens-canis 'White Splendour'

Erythronium dens-canis 'White Splendour'
DOG-TOOTH VIOLET ◑
Family: LILIACEAE
Origin: Cultivar.
Flowering time: Spring.
Climatic zone: 5, 6, 7, 8.
Dimensions: Up to 6 inches (150 mm) high.
Description: Called "dog-tooth" because of its small, tooth-shaped bulb, this violet will flower for up to three weeks. Plant in rock garden pockets and at the front of shady borders. A beautiful and graceful specimen, it is quite hardy and adapts to woodlands and wet areas. If planted in open positions, it will multiply rapidly. Clumps need to be divided every three to four years. It can be grown successfully indoors in containers and should be watered well.

Erythronium revolutum 'White Beauty'
COAST FAWN LILY,
AMERICAN TROUT-LILY,
DOG-TOOTH VIOLET (U.K.)

Family: LILIACEAE
Origin: California.
Flowering time: Spring.
Climatic zone: 6, 7, 8, 9.
Dimensions: Up to 6 inches (150 mm) high.
Description: This is one of the finest trout-lilies from America, with its cream flowers accompanying faintly mottled foliage. It establishes itself well in a damp position. Plant it in rock gardens or at the front of shaded borders. When planted in open places it may increase very quickly. Avoid transplanting it as Erythronium does not like being moved. Indoor cultivation in pots is possible if it is given rich, moist soil and is well maintained.
Other colors: Pink.

hybridized, but the older cultivars seem to have a stronger scent. Many colors are available.
Other colors: Yellow, orange, pink, blue.
Varieties/cultivars: 'Snow Queen', 'Orange Favourite', 'Pink Giant', 'Sapphire'.

Galanthus elwesii
GIANT SNOWDROP

Family: AMARYLLIDACEAE
Origin: Western Turkey.
Flowering time: Winter–spring.
Climatic zone: 4, 5, 6, 7, 8.
Dimensions: Up to 8 inches (200 mm) high.

Galanthus elwesii

Freesia x hybrida

Freesia x hybrida
FREESIA

Family: IRIDACEAE
Origin: Hybrid.
Flowering time: Spring–late summer, northern hemisphere; spring, southern hemisphere.
Climatic zone: 9, 10.
Dimensions: Up to 2 feet (600 mm) high.
Description: Freesias are highly popular flowers especially for the cut-flower market. Most of the present-day hybrids have been derived from *F. refracta* and *F. armstrongii*. The highly perfumed, trumpet-shaped flowers open successively in branched spikes. Greenhouse cultivation is preferable in very cold climates. Outdoors they can be naturalized in grass and wooded areas or planted in pots and window boxes. Freesias have been heavily

Eucharis grandiflora

168

Erythronium revolutum 'White Beauty'

Eucharis grandiflora
AMAZON LILY

Family: AMARYLLIDACEAE
Origin: South America.
Flowering time: Spring–summer.
Climatic zone: 9, 10.
Dimensions: Up to 2 feet (600 mm) high.
Description: "Eucharis" is Greek for pleasing or graceful, a word which describes the beauty of these fragrant white flowers. Four to six snow-white blooms, up to 5 inches (120 mm) across, droop from a long stem. Amazon lily is a glasshouse plant in temperate areas, but can be grown outdoors in semishade in warmer zones. The easiest and most effective way to grow this plant is by planting several bulbs together in a large pot. The bulbs need a constant mild temperature and frequent watering.

Description: *G. elwesii* is one of the largest flowers in the genus. The white drops have green patches at the base and tip and two wing-like petals on either side. Naturalize them in wooded areas, under trees, in rock gardens, and in pots. They prefer partial shade and cool, slightly moist soil with a mulch of well-rotted manure or compost in autumn.

Galanthus nivalis
SNOWDROP
Family: AMARYLLIDACEAE
Origin: Europe and western Asia.
Flowering time: Winter.
Climatic zone: 4, 5, 6, 7, 8.
Dimensions: 4–8 inches (100–200 mm) tall.
Description: The common snowdrop is one of the earliest bulbs to bloom, its delicate, bell-shaped flowers appearing in mid-winter. The pure white petals are tipped with bright green. Snowdrop prefers cool, moist soil, and should be planted in shade, except in the coldest districts where partial sun is of some benefit to open the flowers. It looks best when grown in clumps scattered through beds and borders, or when allowed to naturalize at the base of trees or in the lawn.
Varieties/cultivars: 'Atkinsii', 'S. Arnott'.

Galanthus nivalis

Galtonia candicans
SUMMER HYACINTH (U.K.), CAPE HYACINTH
Family: LILIACEAE
Origin: South Africa.
Flowering time: Summer.
Climatic zone: 7, 8, 9.
Dimensions: Up to 4 feet (approx. 1 meter) high.

Description: Summer hyacinth has numerous showy, fragrant, bell-shaped, white flowers on a single stem. It is well-suited to herbaceous borders and seaside gardens, especially with red-hot-pokers or agapanthus as companions. Plant the bulbs in well-rotted compost about 6 inches (150 mm) deep, in a sunny, open position protected from wind, and water regularly during spring and summer. The plants can be propagated by offsets from the bulbs in late winter, and should not be lifted until they become crowded.

Galtonia candicans

Leucojum aestivum
GIANT SNOWFLAKE, SUMMER SNOWFLAKE (U.K.)
Family: AMARYLLIDACEAE
Origin: Europe.
Flowering time: Spring.
Climatic zone: 4, 5, 6, 7, 8.
Dimensions: Up to 2 feet (600 mm) high.
Description: *Leucojum*, from the Greek for "white violet", probably alludes to the perfume of the giant snowflake. The nodding, bell-like, white blooms, with a green spot near the apex, appear in clusters of between two and five to a stem. Plant between shrubs, in borders among ferns, in rock gardens, or under deciduous trees. A sunny, moist position is best. The bulbs should be planted in very moist soil with plenty of compost and leaf mold. Giant snowflake can be grown indoors in containers.
Varieties/cultivars: 'Gravetye'.

Leucojum vernum
SPRING SNOWFLAKE (U.K.), SNOWFLAKE
Family: AMARYLLIDACEAE
Origin: Southern Europe.
Flowering time: Late winter–early spring.
Climatic zone: 4, 5, 6, 7, 8.
Dimensions: 6–10 inches (150–250 mm) high.
Description: The dainty quality of this plant belies its hardiness. Similar to its sister *L. aestivum*, it is suitable for growing in rock gardens, under deciduous trees, or in containers indoors. The large, usually solitary, fragrant blooms bear a yellow or green spot at the apex of each petal. Like *L. aestivum*, it too has a preference for a damp location. Plant it in humus-rich, sandy, well-drained soil. Once planted, the bulbs need not be disturbed for several years. Propagate by separating offset bulbs when the plant is dormant.

Leucojum aestivum 'Gravetye'

Leucojum vernum

Dimensions: Up to 4 feet (approx. 1 meter) high.
Description: This elegant lily is sweetly perfumed. Grown by the Cretans and Egyptians, it was portrayed on vases and other artifacts around 1750 BC. It was popular in monasteries in the Middle Ages, and in Renaissance art was associated with the Virgin, as the name Madonna lily suggests. The immaculate white flowers are carried on long stems, and it prefers to be undisturbed once it is established. This lovely lily merits a special place of its own in the garden. It can also be planted among herbaceous perennials. It requires plenty of moisture.

Lilium candidum

Description: This is a tender species susceptible to virus disease. Cultivated in the Orient, it is best grown in a greenhouse environment or among ferns in a sheltered position. If planted close to a house, the fragrance from the trumpet-shaped flowers will waft in through open windows. The long, white blooms are stained purplish-red on the outside and grow horizontally from the top of leafy stems. Most lilies benefit from a light groundcover to shade their roots. This also protects new shoots as they emerge from the soil.

Lilium longiflorum

Lilium auratum

Lilium auratum
GOLDEN-RAYED LILY

Family: LILIACEAE
Origin: Japan.
Flowering time: Summer.
Climatic zone: 7, 8, 9.
Dimensions: Up to 5 feet (approx. 2 meters) high.
Description: This lily created a sensation when introduced into Europe from Japan in the mid-19th century. The spectacular flowers can measure up to 12 inches (300 mm) across, and sometimes individual stems will bear 20–30 buds. The large, white, fragrant flowers have golden bands from throat to petal edge and have purplish-red flecks. Give this lily a special place of its own. It likes acid to neutral, not alkaline soil, but is not easy to keep growing for more than a few years.
Other colors: Yellow, orange, red, pink, purple.

Lilium candidum
MADONNA LILY (U.K.), ANNUNCIATION LILY

Family: LILIACEAE
Origin: Mediterranean region.
Flowering time: Summer.
Climatic zone: 7, 8, 9.

Lilium formosanum

Lilium longiflorum
TRUMPET LILY, EASTER LILY

Family: LILIACEAE
Origin: Japan.
Flowering time: Summer.
Climatic zone: 8, 9.
Dimensions: Up to 3 feet (1 meter) high.
Description: These traditional white, trumpet-shaped lilies are used extensively in garden landscapes. They are popular with the cut-flower trade and for church floral decorations. Providing they are not overcrowded, they associate well with other herbaceous perennials. At no time should the bulbs be allowed to dry out. Sun and shade are required in equal amounts, so plant them against a garden wall which receives early morning sun and afternoon shade. Trumpet lilies can also be cultivated in well-drained pots which are kept well watered.
Varieties/cultivars: *L. l.* var. *eximium.*

Lilium formosanum
FORMOSAN LILY

Family: LILIACEAE
Origin: Taiwan.
Flowering time: Summer–autumn.
Climatic zone: 7, 8, 9.
Dimensions: Up to 7 feet (approx. 2 meters) high.

170

Lilium regale 'Album'

Lilium regale
REGAL LILY

Family: LILIACEAE
Origin: Western China.
Flowering time: Summer.
Climatic zone: 5, 6, 7, 8, 9.
Dimensions: 3–6 feet (1–2 meters) high.
Description: A popular lily discovered in China by E. H. Wilson in 1904, these fragrant funnel-shaped flowers have rose-purple markings on the outside, with a white throat blending to yellow. The large flower clusters are extremely useful for garden display. Use as a majestic backdrop to a lower front bed and border, but do not overcrowd them. *L. regale* is quite hardy and should be grown in full sun in moist but well-drained soil. It becomes soft if overfed.
Varieties/cultivars: 'Album'.

Lilium speciosum var. album

Lilium speciosum var. album
JAPANESE LILY, PINK TIGER LILY

Family: LILIACEAE
Origin: Japan.
Flowering time: Summer-autumn.
Climatic zone: 7, 8, 9.
Dimensions: 3–5 feet (1–1.5 meters) high.
Description: The long stems of this lily carry 6–10 white flowers with strongly-reflexed petals with crimson spots. The large, drooping flowers are 4–6 inches (100–150 mm) across, and are perfumed. Plant Japanese lily in clumps in full sun or partial shade in leafy glades near trees. It may also be cultivated in large, movable tubs. If the position is too hot, move the tub to a cooler area in summer. This exotic, fragrant lily enhances any garden setting. Keep the soil it is in moist and well-drained.

Narcissus poeticus
POET'S NARCISSUS

Family: AMARYLLIDACEAE
Origin: Spain-Greece.
Flowering time: Spring.
Climatic zone: 5, 6, 7, 8, 9.
Dimensions: Up to 18 inches (450 mm) high.
Description: *Narcissus poeticus* is named after the mythological youth who fell in love with his own reflection in a pool and became a flower. Fragrant, starry white blooms blend well with early-flowering perennials. Grow the bulbs at random under trees and in wild gardens. The cut flowers are excellent for use indoors where their perfume lingers. Bulbs will grow in full sun or part shade. Plant in light, crumbly, well-drained soil to which has been added some compost. Water regularly during the growing period and fertilize when buds appear.
Other colors: Yellow.
Varieties/cultivars: 'Actaea', 'Queen of Narcissi'.

Narcissus poeticus 'Actaea'

Narcissus tazetta 'Paper White'
WHITE NARCISSUS

Family: AMARYLLIDACEAE
Origin: Cultivar.
Flowering time: Later winter-early spring.
Climatic zone: 7, 8, 9.
Dimensions: 18 inches (450 mm) high.
Description: An exquisite member of the polyanthus narcissus group, white narcissus has star-like flowers with pure white petals. It flowers quite early, bringing life to the garden before the main flush of spring. The best results are achieved by planting the bulbs in autumn in deep, rich, well-drained soil, and by making sure that the ground is lightly damp — never wet — during the cool winter. Choose a sunny position, except in warmer climates where the shade of a deciduous tree is beneficial. Never cut back the greenery after flowering, and remember to divide the clumps every four years. Often grown indoors in cool climates.
Varieties/cultivars: 'Paper White Grandiflora'.

Ornithogalum thyrsoides

Ornithogalum thyrsoides
WONDER FLOWER, CHINCHERINCHEE (U.K.)

Family: LILIACEAE
Origin: South Africa.
Flowering time: Summer.
Climatic zone: 9, 10.
Dimensions: Up to 18 inches (450 mm) high.
Description: Wonder flower is a splendid bloomer, producing masses of cream or yellow buds opening from the base of the conical head. When cut it will last for several weeks even without water. Cultivate it as a border plant, in a cool greenhouse, or in pots on sunny window ledges. This species is tender and needs good drainage to prevent rot. Use a compost of sandy loam and leaf mold, and water well once the plant is established. Give it fertilizer when the buds appear.

A pretty effect can be achieved by planting it under trees or shrubs or in a wild garden. Considered in parts of North America as an invasive garden pest, it is used by some herbalists as a remedy for sadness or depression. Allow it free range in an open, sunny area.

Ornithogalum umbellatum

Ornithogalum umbellatum
STAR-OF-BETHLEHEM

Family: LILIACEAE
Origin: Europe, U.K., North Africa.
Flowering time: Late spring–early summer.
Climatic zone: 5, 6, 7, 8.
Dimensions: Up to 8 inches (200 mm) high.
Description: A seemingly delicate, but quite hardy, little perennial, star-of-Bethlehem will spread rapidly when naturalized. The flowers, twelve to twenty in a cluster, open late in the morning and close late in the afternoon.

Polianthes tuberosa 'The Pearl'

Offsets can be planted when frosts have finished. This is a good pot plant for greenhouses in colder climates.
Varieties/cultivars: 'The Pearl' (double).

Polianthes tuberosa
TUBEROSE

Family: AGAVACEAE
Origin: Central America.
Flowering time: Summer–autumn.
Climatic zone: 9, 10.
Dimensions: Up to 3 feet (1 meter) high.
Description: Tuberose is easy to grow where the summers are long and warm. A favorite with brides for bouquets and headdresses, it is also cultivated widely in France for the perfume industry. The exquisite fragrance is produced from white, single or double flowers. Plant tuberose in the garden in rich soil near open windows and doors. The tubers will not flower in the second year and are usually discarded after flowering.

172

Watsonia hybrids
BUGLE LILY
Family: IRIDACEAE
Origin: South Africa.
Flowering time: Summer–autumn, northern hemisphere; spring-summer, southern hemisphere.
Climatic zone: 9, 10.
Dimensions: Up to 6 feet (2 meters) high.
Description: A colorful and showy plant for high borders and wild gardens, *Watsonia* thrives in warmer areas, but dislikes the cold. Like its relative the *Gladiolus*, it will form clumps and is easy to grow in the right environment. It appreciates plenty of water and sun, and rich, but well-drained soil. Popular as cut flowers, *Watsonia* hybrids offer a profusion of colors. Deciduous and evergreen hybrids are available, the former being the hardier as they can be lifted and rested. *Watsonia* is a good greenhouse plant in cold climates.
Other colors: Red, orange, pink, purple.

Watsonia hybrids

Zantedeschia aethiopica
ARUM LILY (U.K.), LILY OF THE NILE
Family: ARACEAE
Origin: South Africa.
Flowering time: Spring–late summer, northern hemisphere; summer, southern hemisphere.
Climatic zone: 9, 10.
Dimensions: Up to 4 feet (approx. 1 meter) high.
Description: This perennial water-plant is suited to ponds, marshy areas, and damp sites in the garden. It was called "pig lily" by the early settlers in South Africa when they found porcupines (which they called pigs) eating the fleshy roots. The flower, because of its interesting bracts, is widely cultivated for the cut flower market, and is often seen in church floral arrangements. Plant arum lily tubers in permanently damp soil or in very shallow water. It needs generous feeding and will flower profusely.

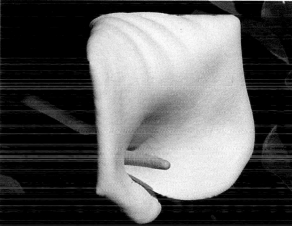

Zantedeschia aethiopica

Zephyranthes candida
WIND FLOWER (U.K.), RAIN LILY, ZEPHYR LILY
Family: AMARYLLIDACEAE
Origin: Argentina, Uruguay.
Flowering time: Autumn.
Climatic zone: 8, 9, 10.
Dimensions: Up to 12 inches (300 mm) high.
Description: This dainty perennial looks like a crocus. When massed in rock gardens and edges the white, star-like flowers provide a showy display, and planted in a warm, sheltered border against a wall the plant will multiply rapidly. Suited to pot-planting in temperate climates, it needs well-drained soil enriched with organic matter. Water well during the flowering period and apply a complete fertilizer when buds first appear.

Zephyranthes candida

Aristolochia elegans

CALICO DUTCHMAN'S PIPE

Family: ARISTOLOCHIACEAE
Origin: Brazil.
Flowering time: Summer.
Climatic zone: 7, 8, 9, 10.
Description: A most attractive evergreen vine that can grow to 10 feet (3 meters) in the right conditions. The woody, twining stems are covered with large, heart-shaped leaves while the reddish-purple flowers are marked with white and yellow. The vine also carries interesting fruit, in basket-like pods. Plant in a sheltered, semi-shaded position in rich, moist soil with plenty of organic matter added. Will not withstand frost, or drought conditions.

Aristolochia elegans

Beaumontia grandiflora

HERALD'S-TRUMPET, EASTER-LILY VINE

Family: APOCYNACEAE
Origin: India.
Flowering time: Spring.
Climatic zone: 9, 10.
Description: An arching, semi-twining, evergreen vine, *Beaumontia* will spread to 30 feet (10 meters). Its large, dark-green leaves are smooth and shiny, and its white, fragrant, trumpet-shaped

Beaumontia grandiflora

flowers, 5 inches (125 mm) long, somewhat resemble Easter lilies. Prune after flowering to promote new shoots. The flowering shoots grow on old wood, so avoid removing all old wood. It appreciates deep, rich soil and plenty of fertilizer. A warm wall with strong support for climbing is the most suitable position.

Clematis armandii

EVERGREEN CLEMATIS, ARMAND CLEMATIS

Family: RANUNCULACEAE
Origin: Central and western China.
Flowering time: Spring.
Climatic zone: 7, 8, 9.
Description: One of the most beautiful, evergreen, flowering climbers, this clematis has the same requirements as other woodland plants. It needs deep, rich soil, shaded from the sun, but is able to take hot sunny conditions on the upper canopy. Severe winters will kill it. The pure white flowers, 2 inches (50 mm) across, are clustered three to a stalk. They are perfumed with a fragrance like honey and almonds, and gradually change color from white to rose-pink. As the blooms are on old wood, prune lightly after flowering, and when the vine becomes too dense, prune out old and dead wood.
Varieties/cultivars: 'Apple Blossom' (rose pink), 'Snowdrift' (white).

Clematis armandii 'Snowdrift'

174

Clematis montana
ANEMONE CLEMATIS

○ ◑

Family: RANUNCULACEAE
Origin: Himalayas, China.
Flowering time: Spring.
Climatic zone: 5, 6, 7, 8, 9.
Description: Vigorous, hardy, and easy to grow, anemone clematis blooms magnificently in early spring. The flowers are white when they open and change to delicate pink. Prune the vine after flowering, as flowers appear on old wood. For heavy pruning, selectively remove some branches to thin out the vine and reduce its overall size. This lovely deciduous climber tolerates warmer conditions than most clematis, but prefers cool or mountain climates. Plant it where the roots will remain in shade, but where it can reach up to the sun.
Varieties/cultivars: 'Rubens' (rose pink), 'Tetrarose' (rose pink, more vigorous than 'Rubens').

Clematis montana

Clerodendrum thomsonae
BLEEDING-HEART VINE

○

Family: VERBENACEAE
Origin: Tropical West Africa.
Flowering time: Summer.
Climatic zone: 9, 10.
Description: This eye-catching flower is a crimson tube encased in a large, white calyx with very long white stamens. The blooms hang in forking clusters from this delicate, evergreen vine, which requires frost-free conditions and a warm, sheltered, humid position. Suitable for container growing, it can be grown successfully as an indoor plant. Prune regularly to obtain a compact plant. Feed and water it well until it is established, then reduce the feeding and watering to mature the wood and induce flowering.

Hoya australis
AUSTRALIAN WAX PLANT, PORCELAIN FLOWER (U.S.A.)

◑

Family: ASCLEPIADACEAE
Origin: Northern and eastern Australia.
Flowering time: Summer.
Climatic zone: 9, 10.
Description: The very fragrant, long-stalked, waxy-white flowers of *H. australis* form a dome-shaped cluster about 4 inches (100 mm) across. The leaves are thick, textured, and look attractive all year round. This strong-growing vine climbs by twining stems and can be trained onto a frame. It makes a good pot plant, but needs support and requires a warm, moist, shaded position.

Hoya australis

Hoya carnosa
COMMON WAX PLANT, WAXFLOWER

○ ◑

Family: ASCLEPIADACEAE
Origin: Southern China-northern Australia.
Flowering time: Early summer-autumn.
Climatic zone: 9, 10.
Description: Common wax plant is one of the most highly prized of small climbing plants. It twines by using aerial roots. Its fleshy, waxy leaves hang sparsely from the firm stems of this lovely vine which has fragrant star-shaped waxy, white flowers with deep-pink centers. As the flowers emerge from the same stalk each year, cutting or pruning will reduce the blooms for the following year. It thrives in a pot in a sunny or shady position, but must have well-drained soil, and does not seem to mind being in a too-small container.
Varieties/cultivars: Variegated form.

Hoya carnosa

Clerodendrum thomsonae

Hydrangea petiolaris syn. *H. anomala* var. *petiolaris*
CLIMBING HYDRANGEA

Family: SAXIFRAGACEAE
Origin: Japan, Taiwan.
Flowering time: Summer.
Climatic zone: 5, 6, 7, 8, 9.
Description: Climbing hydrangea is a vigorous, deciduous vine which grows well only in cooler climates. Its flat, white flowers are borne on long stems and form clusters about 6–10 inches (150–250 mm) across. The attractive, heart-shaped leaves are 2–4 inches (50–100 mm) wide. A sturdy climber, the vine attaches itself to upright surfaces by aerial rootlets, but grown without support, it can be trained as a shrub if pruned annually to remove the long stems.

Jasminum grandiflorum

Jasminum nitidum syn. *J. ilicifolium*
ANGEL-WING JASMINE, STAR JASMINE (U.K.)

Family: OLEACEAE
Origin: South Pacific.
Flowering time: Spring, summer.
Climatic zone: 9, 10.
Description: Angel-wing jasmine's windmill-like, fragrant white flowers are 1 to 1½ inches (25–40 mm) long, and are grouped in small sprays. The buds have a purplish color, and open out to bright-white, flat-topped flowers. With its attractive, glossy leaves this evergreen vine makes a good specimen for a container plant. It can be grown as a shrub or a climber, but it will need to be trained if it is to climb up a post or over a wall. Suited to warm conditions only, it is attractive all year round.

Hydrangea petiolaris

Jasminum grandiflorum
SPANISH JASMINE

Family: OLEACEAE
Origin: South East Asia.
Flowering time: Spring, summer, autumn.
Climatic zone: 7, 8, 9.
Description: Spanish jasmine grows very rapidly. The leaves are made up of five to seven leaflets, and the large, single flowers, which are intensely fragrant, are pink in the bud and open to white. Although each flower lasts only a short time, the vine bears flowers for several months. The long, arching branches can be cut to maintain a shrubby growth, or can be retained and trained onto walls or pergolas. Spanish jasmine always has a light, open, lacy appearance.

Jasminum polyanthum
PINK JASMINE, CHINESE JASMINE, SWEET-SCENTED JASMINE

Family: OLEACEAE
Origin: Western China.
Flowering time: Early spring–late summer.
Climatic zone: 8, 9, 10.
Description: Grown in sun or shade this jasmine can become invasive if not kept under control. The pink buds open to white flowers in a great burst in the springtime, giving out an exceptionally pervasive perfume. This magnificent display lasts for about a month. A vigorous climber, pink jasmine will build up a thick layer of dense, twiggy growth, with new foliage appearing on the surface. A strong support is necessary and, occasionally, very hard pruning. Branches will take root where they make contact with the soil. It will not survive severe winters.

Jasminum polyanthum

Jasminum nitidum

176

Jasminum samvac

Jasmimum samvac
ARABIAN JASMINE, PIKAKE
○ ◑

Family: OLEACEAE
Origin: India.
Flowering time: Spring, summer, autumn.
Climatic zone: 9, 10.
Description: An evergreen, shrubby vine up to 8 feet (2.4 meters) high, this is a very versatile plant. With support and training it can grow as a climber or it can be pruned to form a compact shrub, and is also excellent as a container plant. The white, intensely-perfumed flowers appear in tight clusters at the ends of branchlets, and are used for the flavoring in jasmine tea. The leaves are shiny, pointed and very decorative. Jasmine has a long flowering period, but can only be grown in warm conditions.
Varieties/cultivars: 'Grand Duke of Tuscany'.

Description: This honeysuckle has white flowers which turn yellow as they age. They are very fragrant and their nectar is enjoyed by both birds and children! It is a very quick-growing vine, and will cover a fence or a shed in one good growing season. It needs to be controlled, or it will find its way to the top of adjoining trees. Its evergreen habit makes it useful for the quick disguising of old sheds.

Mandevilla laxa syn. *M. suaveolens*
CHILEAN JASMINE, HUG ME TIGHT, MANDEVILLA
○ ◑

Family: APOCYNACEAE
Origin: Bolivia, Argentina, Peru.
Flowering time: Summer.
Climatic zone: 8, 9.
Description: A vigorous grower in warm climates, Chilean jasmine prefers the shelter of surrounding foliage in cooler climates, and will happily use shrubs or trees to climb through or up to get to the sun. It also grows well on a sheltered wall. The white, intensely fragrant flowers are funnel-shaped and appear in sprays during summer. They tend to be at the tops of the long, arching, slender branches. The vine is widely grown in mild climates, but needs to have its size or spread reduced if it is to be kept under control. Rich, sandy loam and regular water are essential. It cannot withstand severe winters.

Mandevilla laxa

Lonicera japonica 'Halliana'
HALL'S HONEYSUCKLE, JAPANESE HONEYSUCKLE
○ ◑

Family: CAPRIFOLIACEAE
Origin: Cultivar.
Flowering time: Spring and summer.
Climatic zone: 4, 5, 6, 7, 8, 9.

Lonicera japonica 'Halliana'

Pandorea jasminoides
BOWER PLANT,
BOWER-OF-BEAUTY

○ ◖

Family: BIGNONIACEAE
Origin: Australia (Queensland, N.S.W.).
Flowering time: Summer–autumn.
Climatic zone: 9, 10.
Description: An attractive, fast-growing, evergreen climber, this *Pandorea* will tolerate coastal conditions or cooler inland conditions. It is a very useful, versatile climber, and produces a mass of trumpet-shaped white flowers with pink throats, standing out from the shiny, dark-green leaves. Protection from strong wind and frost will be needed, but in a sheltered position it will withstand occasional cold nights. Good soil and summer water give best results.
Varieties/cultivars: 'Rosea' (pink), 'Alba' (pure white).

Pandorea pandorana

Without support the vine can become a sprawling shrub, but needs pruning if a rounded shape is required. A warm climate plant, it cannot tolerate frost.

Polygonum aubertii syn. *Fallopia aubertii*
SILVER FLEECE VINE,
SILVER LACE VINE, RUSSIAN
VINE (U.K.)

○

Family: POLYGONACEAE
Origin: Western China–Tibet.
Flowering time: Late summer.
Climatic zone: 4, 5, 6, 7, 8, 9.
Description: A rapid grower, silver lace vine can quickly cover an area of 100 square feet (9 square meters), with its heart-shaped, glossy leaves. It is covered with masses of small, creamy-white flowers in long sprays in summer. Grow it to provide quick cover for fences or arbors, or as groundcover. It is not fussy about soil, and is tolerant of coastal conditions. Although it is evergreen in mild climates, it may be deciduous in cooler areas. Prune it hard to control its size; it can become invasive.

Polygonum aubertii

Passiflora edulus
PASSION FRUIT, PURPLE
GRANADILLA, PASSION
FLOWER

○

Family: PASSIFLORACEAE
Origin: Brazil–northern Argentina.
Flowering time: Summer.
Climatic zone: 9, 10.
Description: Passion fruit's attractive white and green flowers with a purple zoned center are partially hidden by the dense foliage. The flowers are followed by thick-skinned, purple fruit which is edible, and which falls to the ground when ripe. Tolerant of occasional very light frost only, this very quick-growing vine can be used for covering fences, pergolas, or be trained through lattice or wire frames. Excellent drainage and regular summer watering will produce good fruit. Passion fruit is often a relatively short-lived vine.
Varieties/cultivars: *P. e.* var. *flavicarpa* (yellowish fruits).

Pandorea jasminoides

Pandorea pandorana
WONGA-WONGA
VINE

○ ◖ ●

Family: BIGNONIACEAE
Origin: Southern and eastern Australia–New Guinea.
Flowering time: Throughout the year.
Climatic zone: 9, 10.
Description: Small, cream flowers with purple or maroon-striped throats are produced in abundance on this shiny, evergreen vine. The foliage is attractive all year, and the vine is fast-growing. Rich soil will help it become established, and it is happy in either a sunny or shady position. Pruning is advisable after flowering to tidy up the branchlets, and to induce further compact growth.

Rosa banksiae 'Alba Plena'
BANKS' ROSE, LADY
BANKS' ROSE, BANKSIA ROSE
(Aust.)

○

Family: ROSACEAE
Origin: Cultivar.
Flowering time: Summer.
Climatic zone: 8, 9.
Description: Double, white flowers cover this popular, thornless rose in summer. It is a vigorous plant, resistant to many of the diseases that plague most

Passiflora edulus

178

roses. In a sheltered position on a sunny wall this old favorite will grow in quite cool climates. Prune old growth regularly to help reduce the many stems rising from the base, and make the vine easier to control. If space permits, allow it to flow, sprawl, and climb to fill a wide space.

Rosa banksiae 'Alba Plena'

Rosa laevigata
CHEROKEE ROSE ○

Family: ROSACEAE
Origin: China.
Flowering time: Summer.
Climatic zone: 7, 8, 9.
Description: The single, fragrant, white flowers of this beautiful old rose grow up to 5 inches (125 mm) wide, have prominent yellow stamens, and are followed by bright red hips. Although this rose was common in the temperate zones of China, surprisingly, it was found in the southern states of the United States, where it is now the state flower of Georgia. Trained up a pillar, or over a pergola, this delightful rose will be evergreen in mild climates. It is not tolerant of cold zones.

Rosa laevigata

Rosa wichuraiana
MEMORIAL ROSE ○

Family: ROSACEAE
Origin: Japan, China, Korea, Taiwan.
Flowering time: Summer.
Climatic zone: 6, 7, 8, 9.
Description: This nearly prostrate, semi-evergreen, rambler has long, horizontal branches and can be trained as an upright vine. Individual fragrant flowers are 2 inches (50 mm) across and are held in clusters above the foliage.

Rosa wichuraiana

Solanum jasminoides, 'Album'
POTATO CREEPER, POTATO VINE, JASMINE NIGHTSHADE (U.K.) ○

Family: SOLANACEAE
Origin: Cultivar.
Flowering time: Summer-autumn.
Climatic zone: 8, 9.
Description: The potato creeper is a quick-growing, evergreen climber, popular in warm climates. It is not fussy about soil, but requires a warm, sunny position. Severe winters will kill it. The dainty foliage and clusters of white flowers make a delightful contrast with the stems which become strong and woody over the years. Some support is needed to help the vine climb a wall or fence, or it can be trailed over a low wall or fence. Try it as a container plant, either spilling over the edges, or trained up a slender frame. Train it over old trees, or stumps, or use it to cover sloping banks. Because the branches root if left in contact with soil, the vine makes a good groundcover.
Varieties/cultivars: Many hybrid cultivars have been developed from this hardy plant.

Solanum jasminoides, 'Album'

Flowering time: Summer–autumn.
Climatic zone: 9, 10.
Description: This white variety of the skyflower is perhaps not quite so vigorous a grower as *Thunbergia grandiflora*, but it will cover a fence or pergola and give good shade. The flowers are slightly drooping, and hang singly or in small clusters. An attractive, evergreen vine, it needs a sheltered position protected from wind and frost if grown in cooler climates. In hot, inland districts, a semishaded position is tolerated. Prune gently to reduce the size; heavy pruning will result in few flowers the following year.

Trachelospermum asiaticum ○ ◐
JAPANESE STAR
JASMINE ● ●

Family: APOCYNACEAE
Origin: Japan, Korea.
Flowering time: Summer.
Climatic zone: 8, 9.
Description: Creamy-yellow flowers and smaller, darker leaves distinguish this vine from the Chinese star jasmine. Generally it is a tidier vine, more easily held to a flat surface. The sweetly-scented flowers appear for several months, but not in such profusion as on the Chinese jasmine. Although it is a vigorous climber, it is slow to start, and needs well-drained, rich soil, with regular watering in summer. Tolerant of cool conditions, it will withstand quite heavy shade. However, it cannot withstand severe winters.

Trachelospermum asiaticum

Stephanotis floribunda

Thunbergia grandiflora 'Alba'

Thunbergia grandiflora 'Alba' ○
BENGAL CLOCK ◐
VINE, SKYFLOWER, TRUMPET
VINE (U.K.)

Family: ACANTHACEAE
Origin: Cultivar.

Stephanotis floribunda ◐
MADAGASCAR ○
JASMINE, CHAPLET FLOWER,
CLUSTERED WAXFLOWER

Family: ASCLEPIADACEAE
Origin: Madagascar.
Flowering time: Late spring–early autumn.
Climatic zone: 9, 10.
Description: The delightful fragrance of this beautiful trumpet-shaped flower has made it a highly prized bloom for floral arrangements, especially wedding bouquets. The flowers hang in clusters of eight to ten from late spring to early autumn. Rich, free-draining soil is required and although the roots should be in a shady, cool position, the vine needs to be able to climb up in the sunlight. This is a light climber which will enhance an archway or patio, or can be grown in a container. In cool climates, this makes a good house or greenhouse plant.

Family: APOCYNACEAE
Origin: Southern China, Japan.
Flowering time: Spring, early summer.
Climatic zone: 9.
Description: Wiry stems with their milky sap will develop into a sturdy trunk after many years. The very fragrant, star-shaped flowers are borne in profusion during spring and early summer. Glossy dark-green foliage makes an excellent background for the bright white blossoms. Support is necessary to grow this vine as a climber, but it will enhance a wall or fence, and is also excellent as a groundcover, a spill-over, or pruned to a small shrub. It can also be trained up a slender pole as a container plant. In cool climates, a greenhouse is preferred.
Varieties/cultivars: 'Variegatum' (variegated leaf color).

Trachelospermum jasminoides

base of the cluster and gradually continue opening towards the tip, thus prolonging the blooming period, but not making quite such a spectacular display as those of *W. floribunda*. Developing a dense canopy, it will quickly cover a pergola, fence, or wall, or it can be trained up the face of a building. Regular pruning is required during the summer to remove long arching branches, and to restrict the overall size.

Wisteria floribunda 'Alba'

Wisteria sinensis 'Alba'
CHINESE WISTERIA

Family: LEGUMINOSAE
Origin: Cultivar.
Flowering time: Late spring.
Climatic zone: 5, 6, 7, 8, 9.
Description: The white flowers of Chinese wisteria appear before the leaves, and the 12 inch (300 mm) long clusters open from base to tip at the same time. The flowering period is short, but the masses of flowers with their slight fragrance make a wonderful display. Annual pruning in winter to reduce size, as well as regular summer pruning, is necessary to control this vigorous vine. Cold winters may damage flower buds. Grow only grafted or layered plants or cuttings, as seedlings may not bloom for many years.

Wisteria venusta syn. *W. brachybotrys* 'Alba'
SILKY WISTERIA,
JAPANESE WISTERIA

Family: LEGUMINOSAE
Origin: Japan.
Flowering time: Spring.
Climatic zone: 5, 6, 7, 8, 9.
Description: Large, white, long-stalked flowers are carried on 6-inch-long (150 mm) sprays. Such a spectacular display of massed blossoms makes this one of the best of the white wisterias. Silky hairs on the surface of the white blossoms give the species its name. The leaves have nine to thirteen broad leaflets. Trained to a tree shape, this plant will bloom profusely, and is a magnificent specimen, especially when it becomes old. It needs constant pruning if it is to develop tree proportions, but looks beautiful, even when bare-branched in the winter.

Wisteria sinensis 'Alba'

Wisteria floribunda 'Alba' syn.
W. f. 'Longissima Alba'
JAPANESE WISTERIA

Family: LEGUMINOSAE
Origin: Cultivar.
Flowering time: Early summer.
Climatic zone: 4, 5, 6, 7, 8, 9.
Description: The clusters of white flowers on this vigorous, deciduous vine appear at the same time as the early leaves. The flowers begin opening at the

Wisteria venusta

Anaphalis cinnamomea
PEARLY EVERLASTING

Family: COMPOSITAE
Origin: India, Burma.
Flowering time: Late summer.
Climatic zone: 5, 6, 7, 8, 9, 10.
Dimensions: Up to 2½ feet (750 mm) high.
Description: This attractive herbaceous perennial forms a wide clump of downy grey-green leaves and in summer is covered with globular clusters of white flowers. An adaptable plant which can be grown with success in a wide range of soils and conditions, it prefers a semishaded, protected position and good soil drainage. It can be propagated either by seed or by division.

Anaphalis cinnamomea

Anaphalis nubigena

Anaphalis nubigena
PEARLY EVERLASTING

Family: COMPOSITAE
Origin: Himalayas.
Flowering time: Summer.

Achillea millefolium

Actaea rubra
RED BANEBERRY, RED COHOSH (U.S.A.)

Family: RANUNCULACEAE
Origin: North America.
Flowering time: Spring.
Climatic zone: 3, 4, 5, 6, 7, 8.
Dimensions: 18 inches to 2 feet (450–600 mm) high.
Description: The two main features of this plant are its stems of small, white flowers in spring and its clusters of glistening scarlet berries in autumn. The berries are poisonous, hence the name baneberry. Although adaptable and very hardy, it grows best in cool, shaded positions in moist and fertile soils. The clumps of green, coarse, ferny leaves contrast well with other foliage. Propagation is by division, or from seeds which take many months to germinate.
Varieties/cultivars: *A. r.* var. *album*, *A. r.* var. *neglecta*.

Actaea rubra var. *album*

Achillea ageratifolia

Achillea ageratifolia
YARROW

Family: COMPOSITAE
Origin: Greece.
Flowering time: Summer.
Climatic zone: 5, 6, 7, 8, 9, 10.
Dimensions: Up to 6 inches (150 mm) high.
Description: A handsome, low-growing, spreading shrub, it has a covering of grey-green foliage, and masses of small, white, daisy-like flowers with yellow centers. Plant it in an open, sunny position in light, well-drained soil that has been enriched with plenty of organic matter. It is easily propagated either by division during autumn or spring, or by cuttings.

Achillea millefolium
COMMON YARROW, MILFOIL

Family: COMPOSITAE
Origin: Europe, Caucasus, Himalayas, Siberia.
Flowering time: Summer.
Climatic zone: 3, 4, 5, 6, 7, 8, 9, 10.
Dimensions: 2 feet (600 mm) high.
Description: This plant, with its invasive roots, spreads quickly and can be a troublesome weed if it infests a lawn. Each root produces a clump of feathery, dark-green leaves and the strong, wiry stems produce a white flower head. It is strongly resistant to both cold and drought and will grow in all types of soil, particularly sandy soils near the sea. Propagation is easy by division in spring or autumn.
Other colors: Pink, red.
Varieties/cultivars: 'Cerise Queen', 'Red Beauty', 'Fire King'.

Climatic zone: 4, 5, 6, 7, 8, 9.

Dimensions: 8–12 inches (200–300 mm) high.

Description: This tufted plant has silvery-gray, woolly leaves with inrolled margins. The little starry, daisy-like flowers are on wide branching stems above the foliage. They are excellent for cutting and can be successfully dried. The plant quickly makes a large clump if grown in any good garden soil in an open position, but will droop if the roots are allowed to dry out. It can be propagated from seed but is usually divided in spring.

Anaphalis triplinervis

Androsace lanuginosa

Androsace lanuginosa

ROCK JASMINE

Family: PRIMULACEAE

Origin: Himalayas.

Flowering time: Summer.

Climatic zone: 4, 5, 6, 7, 8.

Dimensions: Up to 4 inches (100 mm) high.

Description: This low-growing, tussock-forming alpine perennial has trailing stems of silvery foliage in rosettes. The white to pale pink flowers occur in dense terminal clusters. It is an excellent rock garden plant in the right conditions, due to showy flowering and cascading habit. It prefers well-composted, well-drained soils and an open, sunny position. Cuttings can be taken in spring.

Anemone sylvestris

SNOWDROP ANEMONE, SNOWDROP WINDFLOWER

Family: RANUNCULACEAE

Origin: Europe–Siberia.

Flowering time: Late spring–summer.

Climatic zone: 3, 4, 5, 6, 7, 8.

Dimensions: 18 inches (450 mm) high.

Description: In light soil, this anemone spreads freely and quickly but is more restrained in heavier clay soils. The erect to somewhat nodding white flowers are pleasantly fragrant and set

off by a group of yellow stamens in the center. The blooms are followed by clusters of woolly seed heads. It is best propagated by seed, although the clumps formed in light soil can be easily divided.

Varieties/cultivars: 'Grandiflora'.

Anemone sylvestris

Anaphalis triplinervis

PEARLY EVERLASTING

Family: COMPOSITAE

Origin: Himalayas.

Flowering time: Late summer–autumn.

Climatic zone: 3, 4, 5, 6, 7, 8, 9.

Dimensions: Up to 18 inches (450 mm) high.

Description: This is a tufted plant which forms a clump of silver-gray foliage. This later becomes buried beneath the wide sprays of crisp, white daisies which are excellent for cutting and drying. To dry them, hang the cut flower heads upside down. An ideal plant for the edge of a border, pearly everlasting makes a pleasing combination with pink flowers. It is an easy plant to grow, but will not tolerate drought.

Varieties/cultivars: 'Summer Snow'

Anemone vitifolia 'Robustissima'

Anemone vitifolia 'Robustissima'
JAPANESE ANEMONE ○ ◐

Family: RANUNCULACEAE
Origin: Himalayas—China.
Flowering time: Late summer–autumn.
Climatic zone: 5.
Dimensions: 2–3 feet (approx. 1 meter) high.
Description: The Japanese anemone, a delight in the autumn garden when the summer blooms are fading, has showy flowers borne on longish stem clusters. The plant grows in clumps which are slow to develop in their first year, but then spread rapidly and prefer to remain undisturbed. It prefers rich, well-drained soil, with ample water in dry conditions, especially if it is grown in full sun. It makes an attractive show planted with Michaelmas daisies and old-fashioned autumn climbing roses. Japanese anemone is a good cut flower.

Anemone x hybrida
JAPANESE ANEMONE, JAPANESE WINDFLOWER ◐ ●

Family: RANUNCULACEAE
Origin: U.K.
Flowering time: Late summer–autumn.
Climatic zone: 5, 6, 7, 8, 9.
Dimensions: Up to 4 feet (over 1 meter) high.
Description: This is one of the most elegant and beautiful of the autumn perennials, with its rounded blooms produced on ascending branching stems over a period of many weeks. Once established, the plant can spread quite rapidly, making fine clumps of trifoliate dark-green leaves. Derived from the

Anemone x hybrida

species A. hupehensis, which is pink-flowered, there are now many shades of color in this garden hybrid, the single white being one of the most popular. This anemone prefers good soil and moist conditions.
Other colors: Deep pink, rosy pink, red.
Varieties/cultivars: 'Honorine Jobert', 'Queen Charlotte', 'Whirlwind', 'Margarete', 'Lorelei'.

Arabis caucasica
ROCK CRESS ○

Family: CRUCIFERAE
Origin: Caucasus.
Flowering time: Late spring–summer.
Climatic zone: 4, 5, 6, 7, 8, 9.
Dimensions: 6–10 inches (150–250 mm) high.
Description: The most widely grown rock cress, this vigorous trailing plant is suited to a spacious walled garden which will allow it plenty of room. It will also grow on a sunny bank and does best in poor soil and an open position. Cut it back after flowering. The cuttings will easily take root in a pot or in the ground, or the plant can also be divided. The leaves are grayish-green and the flowers slightly scented.
Varieties/cultivars: 'Flore Pleno', and a variegated leaf form.

Arabis caucasica

Arabis procurrens
ROCK CRESS ○ ◐

Family: CRUCIFERAE
Origin: Southeastern Europe.
Flowering time: Spring.
Climatic zone: 4, 5, 6, 7, 8, 9.
Dimensions: Up to 12 inches (300 mm) high.
Description: Rock cress is one of the more showy species in this group of low-

Arabis procurrens

Climatic zone: 9, 10.
Dimensions: Up to 2 feet (600 mm) high.
Description: These exquisite, soft white poppy flowers have bright yellow stamens that exude a sticky sap. The prickly stems are unpleasant to touch except with gloves. The plant is ideal for borders or mixed beds of annuals and likes full sun and warm weather. The soil should be light and well-drained. The seeds can be sown in summer and the seedlings transplanted in autumn for flowering the following year.

Armeria lactiflora
CHINESE MUGWORT, ○ ◑
WHITE MUGWORT,
GHOSTPLANT (U.S.A.)

Family: COMPOSITAE
Origin: China, India.
Flowering time: Late summer–autumn.
Climatic zone: 4, 5, 6, 7, 8.
Dimensions: 4–5 feet (1.5 meters) high.
Description: This strong-growing plant is useful in the background of a garden bed as a foil for more brightly colored subjects. It has jagged, green leaves and conspicuous sheaves of tiny, creamy-white flowers which are long-lasting and suitable for cutting. Because of their color, the flowers tend to look "dirty" when placed near white flowers or silver foliage and are better when grouped with yellow or blue flowers. It prefers a moist and fertile soil.

Artemisia lactiflora

Armeria maritima
THRIFT, COMMON THRIFT ○
(U.K.), SEA PINK

Family: PLUMBAGINACEAE
Origin: Northern hemisphere (mainly coastal and mountainous areas).
Flowering time: Summer.
Climatic zone: 3, 4, 5, 6, 7, 8.
Dimensions: 6–12 inches (150–300 mm) high.
Description: This is a useful edging or front-of-the-border plant with rich green, grass-like foliage. Erect and rigid stems bear individual flower heads in the shape of a globe, each made up of many small flowers. It prefers a light, open soil and grows particularly well near the sea as indicated by its name, sea pink. Propagation can be by seed or, better still, by division or cuttings taken in early autumn.
Other colors: Pink, red, purple.
Varieties/cultivars: 'Alba', 'Grandiflora', 'Purpurea', 'Rubra', 'Splendens'.

Armeria maritima 'Alba'

Argemone glauca

Argemone glauca
PRICKLY POPPY ○

Family: PAPAVERACEAE
Origin: North America.
Flowering time: Summer.

growing members of the mustard family. The flowers are quite large for the size of the plant, and are borne on slender heads. The foliage spreads at ground level by a series of short runners. Ideal for rock gardens, the plant thrives in poor soils and dry conditions, but needs a well-drained position. Plant it in either full sun or partial shade.

PERENNIALS

185

Aruncus dioicus

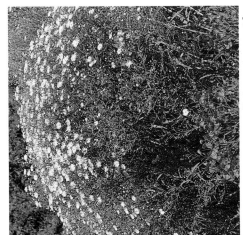

Boltonia asteroides

Cerastium tomentosum
SNOW-IN-SUMMER ○ ◑

Family: CARYOPHYLLACEAE
Origin: Italy and Sicily.
Flowering time: Summer.
Climatic zone: 5, 6, 7, 8, 9.
Dimensions: 4–6 inches (100–150 mm) high.
Description: A delightful groundcover plant, snow-in-summer spreads quickly in a sunny or lightly shaded spot. Its silvery-white foliage and white flowers give it its common name. It will grow in most soils, even sand, and is useful for retaining soil on steep banks as it puts down roots from each stem. Because it is invasive, it is not recommended for small gardens or choice spots. It is easily divided at any time except mid-winter.

Aruncus dioicus
GOATSBEARD ○ ◑

Family: ROSACEAE
Origin: Northern hemisphere.
Flowering time: Summer.
Climatic zone: 3, 4, 5, 6, 7, 8, 9.
Dimensions: 4–7 feet (1.2–2 meters) high.
Description: Goatsbeard is a handsome plant which forms a massive clump of fernlike foliage from which arise large plumes of minute creamy-white flowers. It can be used successfully as an isolated specimen, but is also good for general use, especially as a companion to shrub roses. It is easy to grow in most soils, but prefers moist conditions. Propagate by division or seed.
Varieties/cultivars: 'Kneiffii'.

Campanula persicifolia 'Alba'
PEACH-LEAVED ○ ◑
BELLFLOWER, PAPER
BELLFLOWER (U.K.)

Family: CAMPANULACEAE
Origin: Cultivar.
Flowering time: Summer.
Climatic zone: 4, 5, 6, 7, 8, 9.
Dimensions: 2–3 feet (1 meter) high.
Description: This is a popular perennial which forms wide clumps of dense, narrow leaves and strong but slender stems bearing large, cup-shaped flowers. Being evergreen, it makes a useful groundcover throughout the year. It flowers over a long period and is good for cutting. It can be grown from seed, or propagated by root division in autumn or spring.

Boltonia asteroides
WHITE BOLTONIA, ○ ◑
FALSE CHAMOMILE, FALSE
STARWORT (U.S.A.)

Family: COMPOSITAE
Origin: North America.
Flowering time: Autumn.
Climatic zone: 4, 5, 6, 7, 8, 9.
Dimensions: 5–6 feet (2 meters) high.
Description: This is an easily grown plant in most types of soil and ideal as a background plant. Massed heads of tiny, daisy-like flowers are produced in such vast quantities that the plants may need staking for support when in bloom. The pale-green leaves are quite small and insignificant. It is propagated by division in winter and is somewhat susceptible to mildew in warm, moist conditions.
Other colors: Pink, purple.
Varieties/cultivars: 'Snowbank'.

Cerastium tomentosum

Chrysanthemum frutescens
PARIS DAISY, ○
MARGUERITE DAISY

Family: COMPOSITAE
Origin: Canary Islands.
Flowering time: Spring–autumn and winter.
Climatic zone: 9, 10.
Dimensions: 3 feet (1 meter) high.
Description: This shrub-like evergreen perennial is of great value in the garden as it is covered in a mass of flowers for a long period if the spent blooms are removed. It has neatly divided, light-green foliage and does well in most garden soils, provided it gets plenty of water in summer. It makes a good specimen for planting in large

---

Campanula persicifolia 'Alba'

Chrysanthemum frutescens

Climatic zone: 5, 6, 7, 8, 9.
Dimensions: 3 feet (1 meter) high.
Description: A robust plant, shasta daisy is coarser in all its parts than most other chrysanthemums. The daisy flowers are large, up to 5 or 6 inches (130–150 mm) across, and last well when cut. It is one of the easiest plants to cultivate in almost any position, although it does best in full sun. It is available in single and double forms and there are now several cultivars. Plant it out in autumn, and lift and divide the clumps every two years.
Varieties/cultivars: 'Wirral Supreme', 'Aglaia', 'Fiona Coghill', 'September Snow', Mayfield Giant'.

---

containers and can be easily propagated from cuttings taken in spring or autumn.
Other colors: Pink, yellow.
Varieties/cultivars: 'Coronation', 'Mary Wootton'.

Chrysanthemum leucanthemum
OX-EYE DAISY,
COMMON DAISY

Family: COMPOSITAE
Origin: Europe, Asia.
Flowering time: Early to late summer.
Climatic zone: 3, 4, 5, 6, 7, 8, 9, 10.

Chrysanthemum leucanthemum

Dimensions: 2 feet (600 mm) high.
Description: This is the common, white field daisy which can be quite attractive when mass-planted, although it often becomes a nuisance in gardens. The flower heads, usually solitary, are on a long, sturdy stalk which rarely needs staking for wind protection. The cut flowers last quite well indoors. This hardy perennial reseeds easily and so spreads rapidly.
Varieties/cultivars: 'Maistern'.

Chrysanthemum x *superbum* syn.
C. maximum
SHASTA DAISY

Family: COMPOSITAE
Origin: Hybrid.
Flowering time: Summer.

Chrysanthemum x *superbum*

Crambe cordifolia
HEARTLEAF CRAMBE,
SEA KALE

Family: CRUCIFERAE
Origin: Caucasus.
Flowering time: Early summer.
Climatic zone: 5, 6, 7, 8, 9.
Dimensions: 6 feet (2 meters) high.
Description: This is a massive plant with bold basal leaves, gray-green in color and often deeply lobed or cut. The intricately branched flowering stems carry clouds of tiny, white flowers, rather strongly scented. It is a most effective plant for a large garden, given well-drained, slightly alkaline soil and a position preferably in full sunshine. It is sometimes attacked by the caterpillars of the cabbage white butterfly. Propagate it from root cuttings in late winter or early spring.
Varieties/cultivars: 'Grandiflora'.

Crambe cordifolia

Dianthus arenarius

Dictamnus albus

Dicentra cucullaria

Dietes vegeta

Dicentra cucullaria
DUTCHMAN'S-BREECHES, WHITE EARDROPS

Family: FUMARIACEAE
Origin: Eastern United States.
Flowering time: Late spring.
Climatic zone: 4, 5, 6, 7, 8, 9.
Dimensions: 8 inches (200 mm) high.
Description: This is a graceful, stemless plant with numerous feathery basal leaves. The pendant flowers, on their slender, arching stalks, are divided into two spurs, giving the bloom a forked appearance similar to the trousers worn by Dutch peasants, hence the common name. It prefers a rich, well-drained soil and is frost-resistant, but drought-tender. It can be propagated by seed or division.

Dictamnus albus
GAS PLANT, BURNING BUSH, DITTANY (U.K.)

Family: RUTACEAE
Origin: Eastern Europe.
Flowering time: Summer.
Climatic zone: 3, 4, 5, 6, 7, 8, 9.
Dimensions: 2–3 feet (up to 1 meter) high.
Description: A bushy perennial with simple upright stems, this plant is not extensively cultivated but is worth growing for the tangy lemon perfume of its leaves and its elegant flowers. It grows best in a fertile soil in a sunny position. The volatile oil from this plant will ignite if a lighted match is held near the developing seed pods on a windless day. The ripe seed pods explode violently in warm, dry weather and the seeds can take up to a year to germinate.
Other colors: Red, purple.
Varieties/cultivars: 'Purpureus', 'Rubrus'.

Dianthus arenarius
PRUSSIAN PINK, GRASS PINK (U.K.)

Family: CARYOPHYLLACEAE
Origin: Eastern Europe.
Flowering time: Summer.
Climatic zone: 4, 5, 6, 7, 8, 9.
Dimensions: 8-12 inches (200–300 mm) high.
Description: A useful mat-forming plant with masses of single, heavily fringed, white flowers with a greenish eye. This species prefers a semishaded position and a slightly gritty soil that has been enriched with a potassium-rich fertilizer. Make sure that plenty of water is supplied, especially during the warm summer months. Prussian pink is easily grown from either seed or cuttings.

Dietes vegeta syn. *Moraea iridioides*
AFRICAN IRIS

Family: IRIDACEAE
Origin: South Africa.
Flowering time: Summer.

Climatic zone: 9, 10.
Dimensions: Up to 2 feet (600 mm) high.
Description: The glorious lily-like flowers of this species appear in profusion on long, slender stems during the warm weather. Even when the plant is not in flower, the evergreen, sword-like foliage, in large clumps, is most attractive and makes an excellent feature. In its native environment, African iris is found growing in semishade under spreading trees. It can withstand extremely dry conditions, prefers light and well-drained soils, and is often grown as a low hedge. Once established it will readily self-seed.

Dimorphotheca ecklonis syn.
Osteospermum ecklonis
WHITE VELDT DAISY, SAILOR BOY DAISY

Family: COMPOSITAE
Origin: South Africa.
Flowering time: Summer-autumn.
Climatic zone: 9.
Dimensions: Up to 3 feet (1 meter) high.
Description: In a frost-free climate, this plant grows into a vigorous, upright, shrubby bush. It prefers a light, well-drained soil and is able to withstand periods of dryness. The petals of the daisy-like flower, white on top and purple underneath, close at night time. The long, narrow, light-green leaves are lightly toothed around the margin. It is easily propagated from cuttings and can also be grown from seed.
Varieties/cultivars: var. *prostrata*, 'Whirligig', 'Pink whirls'.

Dimorphotheca ecklonis

Epilobium glabellum
FIREWEED, WILLOW HERB

Family: ONAGRACEAE
Origin: New Zealand.
Flowering time: Summer.
Climatic zone: 8, 9, 10.
Dimensions: Up to 15 inches (375 mm) high.
Description: The shining, light-green leaves of this little alpine perennial form attractive clumps which gradually expand, but are never a nuisance. The tumbled masses of funnel-shaped flowers are followed by fluffy seed heads. As it comes from the rocky subalpine and alpine slopes, it needs an open, well-drained soil that is reasonably fertile. It can be propagated by division during spring.
Other colors: Yellow, pink.
Varieties/cultivars: 'Sulphureum'.

Epimedium x youngianum 'Niveum'
SNOWY BARRENWORT

Family: BERBERIDACEAE
Origin: Hybrid cultivar.
Flowering time: Spring.
Climatic zone: 5, 6, 7, 8, 9.
Dimensions: 6-12 inches (150-300 mm) high.

Description: This perennial is valued for its delicate-looking, but leathery-textured, leaves made up of heart-shaped leaflets on wiry stems. They are light green with pink veins in spring, turning to reddish-bronze in autumn. The flowers, borne in pendulous white clusters, composed of eight sepals and four petals, are excellent for cutting. It grows well in cool and temperate areas in light shade and moist soil that is well-nourished. The clumps may be divided in autumn or spring.

Epimedium x youngianum 'Niveum'

Epilobium glabellum

reasonably dry conditions and will grow well in either full sun or partial shade. It makes an excellent border subject when mixed with other plants of a different texture. It is usually propagated by division in autumn or spring.

Fragaria chiloensis
CHILOE STRAWBERRY, ○ ◑
BEACH STRAWBERRY

Family: ROSACEAE
Origin: Western North and South America from Alaska to Chile.
Flowering time: Spring.
Climatic zone: 5, 6, 7, 8, 9.
Dimensions: Up to 6 inches (150 mm) high.
Description: This is a low, spreading, groundcover plant which sends out stems, or runners, after it has finished flowering and fruiting. The attractive leaves are green and glossy above and pale bluish-white beneath. The fruit is large, firm and dark-red, this plant being one of the parents of our dessert strawberries. It prefers a position in cool, moist, fertile soil open to sunshine.

Fragaria chiloensis

that is moderately fertile. The flower heads are most useful for dried floral arrangements. Seed in spring or root cuttings in late winter are the best means of propagation.

Erigeron mucronatus

Erigeron mucronatus syn.
E. karvinskianus
BONYTIP FLEABANE, ○ ◑
MEXICAN FLEABANE (U.K.),
BABY'S TEARS (Aust.)

Family: COMPOSITAE
Origin: Mexico–Venezuela.
Flowering time: Spring-summer and autumn.
Climatic zone: 8, 9, 10.
Dimensions: 8 inches (200 mm) high.
Description: This attractive little plant self-seeds vigorously and will fill up many a bare space with endless clouds of little white and pink daisies. It is excellent around steps or in gaps in brick or stone paving. It also spreads by means of underground runners. It dies down in winter but will reappear in spring. It seems to do best in light, well-drained, sandy soil of low fertility, especially in areas near the sea.

Eryngium bourgatii

Eryngium bourgatii
MEDITERRANEAN ○
ERYNGO (U.S.A.), SEA HOLLY

Family: UMBELLIFERAE
Origin: Pyrenees.
Flowering time: Summer.
Climatic zone: 6, 7, 8, 9, 10.
Dimensions: 2 feet (600 mm) high.
Description: This is an eye-catching plant because of its unusual foliage. The leaves are crisp and curly, gray-green in color with white veins, and form a basal rosette. The blue-green, thistle-like flowers are protected by silvery-white bracts tipped with spines. It thrives in full sun and well-drained, sandy soil

Filipendula vulgaris 'Flore Pleno'

Filipendula vulgaris 'Flore Pleno' syn.
F. hexapetala 'Flore Pleno'
DOUBLE-FLOWERED ○ ◑
DROPWORT, MEADOWSWEET

Family: ROSACEAE
Origin: Eastern Europe, Siberia.
Flowering time: Summer.
Climatic zone: 4, 5, 6, 7, 8, 9.
Dimensions: Up to 2 feet (600 mm) high.
Description: This plant has finely divided foliage like that of the carrot and produces double, creamy-white flowers in a loose raceme. It will tolerate

Gypsophila paniculata

Helleborus corsicus

Gillenia trifoliata

INDIAN-PHYSIC, BOWMAN'S-ROOT (U.S.A.) ◑

Family: ROSACEAE
Origin: Eastern North America.
Flowering time: Summer.
Climatic zone: 4, 5, 6, 7, 8, 9.
Dimensions: 3 feet (1 meter) high.
Description: Indian-physic is a dainty and refined perennial with wiry, reddish stems and leaves divided into three parts. It forms a clump from which it sends up stems of small white flowers in airy clusters. After the petals fall, the red calyces persist and remain decorative until the seeds ripen. It can be grown in full sun except in very hot regions, and any type of soil that is not too dry seems to suit it. Propagate it by division of the clumps in spring.

Gypsophila paniculata

BABY'S-BREATH, CHALK PLANT ○ ◑

Family: CARYOPHYLLACEAE
Origin: Central Europe – central Siberia.
Flowering time: Summer.
Climatic zone: 3, 4, 5, 6, 7, 8, 9.
Dimensions: Up to 3 feet (1 meter) high.

Description: A wide-spreading plant up to 3 feet (1 meter) in diameter, baby's-breath produces dense tufts of intricately branched, erect stems covered in a froth of tiny star-like flowers. It prefers a neutral or slightly alkaline soil and resents disturbance of the roots once established. The plant's cloud-like appearance makes a dramatic contrast with other more striking subjects in the garden. It can be grown from seed.
Other colors: Pink.
Varieties/cultivars: 'Bristol Fairy', 'Flamingo', 'Rosy Veil'.

Helleborus corsicus syn. *H. lividus corsicus*, *H. argutifolius*

CORSICAN HELLEBORE ◑ ●

Family: RANUNCULACEAE
Origin: Corsica, Sardinia.
Flowering time: Winter-spring.
Climatic zone: 6, 7, 8, 9.
Dimensions: 2–3 feet (up to 1 meter) high.
Description: This handsome, evergreen perennial produces large, three-part leaves, serrated at the edges, during its first year. From the top of a short leafy stem the flower stalk develops in the second year. The single, upright spike bears a cluster of fifteen to twenty cup-shaped flowers of an unusual pale green, which last for many months. It is ideal for growing under deciduous trees in a moist, fertile soil. Propagate it from seed or by division, but exercise care with division; the roots are brittle.

Gillenia trifoliata

Helleborus foetidus

STINKING HELLEBORE, SETTERWORT, BEAR'S FOOT

Family: RANUNCULACEAE
Origin: Western Europe.
Flowering time: Winter–spring.
Climatic zone: 6, 7, 8, 9.
Dimensions: Up to 3 feet (1 meter) high.
Description: This plant has handsome, deeply divided, dark-green leaves which form a compact clump. The flowers are airy clusters at the end of the stems, thimble-shaped and of a pale green color edged with maroon. The plant has tough roots that penetrate the soil for a considerable depth. The shiny foliage makes an excellent foil for silver-leaved plants, and the masses of blooms stay fresh for some time. The plant self-seeds readily.

Helleborus lividus

Helleborus lividus

Helleborus lividus

MAJORCA HELLEBORE

Family: RANUNCULACEAE
Origin: Majorca.
Flowering time: Early spring.
Climatic zone: 9.
Dimensions: 12 inches (300 mm) high.
Description: This perennial has leathery leaves divided into three parts and overlaced with gray-white markings and purple beneath. The clusters of flowers appear on leafy stems in the second year and are yellowish-green flushed purplish-pink and delicately scented. The fragrance is most noted when the plant is grown under cover. Best grown under glass in cold climates.

Iberis sempervirens

Iberis sempervirens

Iberis sempervirens

PERENNIAL CANDYTUFT

Family: CRUCIFERAE
Origin: Mediterranean region.
Flowering time: Spring.
Climatic zone: 7, 8, 9.
Dimensions: Up to 12 inches (300 mm) high.
Description: This makes a fine edging plant or can be planted among rocks. Usually evergreen, it becomes covered in a mass of flattish white flower clusters. To avoid the formation of a noticeable space in the center of the plant after flowering, the stems should be lightly cut back. It prefers a sunny position but will stop flowering if allowed to dry out. It is easily propagated by division or from seed.
Varieties/cultivars: 'Little Gem', 'Plena'.

Helleborus niger

CHRISTMAS ROSE, BLACK HELLEBORE

Family: RANUNCULACEAE
Origin: Central Europe – Yugoslavia.
Flowering time: Winter.
Climatic zone: 4, 5, 6, 7, 8, 9.
Dimensions: 8–12 inches (200–300 mm) high.
Description: The leathery leaves are evergreen and the single flowers, up to 3 inches (75 mm) across, are pure white, becoming pinkish as they age. The name black hellebore refers to the color of the roots. It thrives best in heavy, moist soils in either full or partial shade. This plant has been in cultivation since the Middle Ages and is a welcome sight after Christmas in the northern hemisphere.
Other colors: Pink.
Varieties/cultivars: 'Louis Cobbett', 'Altifolius', 'Praecox'.

Helleborus niger

Lamium maculatum

SPOTTED DEAD NETTLE

Family: LABIATAE
Origin: Most of Europe – Russia and Turkey.
Flowering time: Early summer.
Climatic zone: 5, 6, 7, 8, 9.
Dimensions: 6–8 inches (150–200 mm) high.
Description: This useful groundcover plant has white flowers and attractively marked foliage. The midgreen leaves with their silver stripe will form a carpet under trees and in shaded areas. The semi-prostrate stems send out runners which will put down roots and these can be easily cut off and replanted elsewhere. It will thrive in poor soils and

Lamium maculatum 'White Nancy'

is useful for planting under hedges and for covering steep banks.
Other colors: Mauve-pink.
Varieties/cultivars: 'Beacon Silver', 'White Nancy', 'Roseum'.

Leontopodium alpinum
EDELWEISS

Family: COMPOSITAE
Origin: Central Europe.
Flowering time: Summer.
Climatic zone: 4, 5, 6, 7, 8.
Dimensions: 6 inches (150 mm) high.
Description: This well-known alpine plant from the European mountains produces small, low tufts of gray, furry leaves. It has clustered heads of small flowers, each surrounded by a collar of grayish-white, felted bracts. It is grown more for its romantic associations than its beauty. It needs well-drained soil in a sunny spot and resents the winter wet, which may cause it to rot. It can be grown readily from seed.

Leontopodium alpinum

Leontopodium alpinum

Macleaya cordata

Macleaya cordata syn. *Bocconia cordata*
PLUME POPPY

Family: PAPAVERACEAE
Origin: China, Japan.
Flowering time: Summer.
Climatic zone: 4, 5, 6, 7, 8, 9.
Dimensions: 7 feet (2 meters) high.

Description: This tall perennial combines handsome foliage with delightful, small white flowers that appear in masses of feathery plumes. The gray-green leaves, not unlike those of the culinary fig, are gray-white and downy underneath. At its best in reasonably moist soils, it is deciduous, self-supporting in spite of its height, and spreads by suckering roots. In hot areas, some shade is necessary. It should be planted in autumn or spring, divided in spring, or grown from root cuttings in late winter.

Minuartia verna syn. *Arenaria verna* var. *caespitosa*
IRISH MOSS, SPRING SANDWORT (U.K.)

Family: CARYOPHYLLACEAE
Origin: European and Rocky Mountains.
Flowering time: Late spring.
Climatic zone: 4, 5, 6, 7, 8.
Dimensions: 2 inches (50 mm) high.
Description: This alpine perennial produces dense, mosslike clumps and, in sufficient sunshine, small starry flowers. It grows well in ordinary soil but with the addition of leaf mold it will thrive. It tolerates full shade and partial sun.
Varieties/cultivars: 'Aurea'.

Minuartia verna

Paeonia lactiflora 'Lady Alexander Duff'

Paeonia lactiflora and hybrids
CHINESE PEONY

Family: RANUNCULACEAE
Origin: China, Siberia, Mongolia.
Flowering time: Early summer.
Climatic zone: 3, 4, 5, 6, 7, 8, 9.
Dimensions: 2–3 feet (up to 1 meter) high.
Description: This species, which has large, white, fragrant flowers, is the parent of many garden peony hybrids. These cultivars offer great variety in shape and color and are easy to grow given the right conditions. They need deep, fertile, neutral to slightly alkaline soil, well-drained, but moisture-retentive. A sunny position suits best, with an annual mulch over the crowns to keep them cool and moist during hot weather. They resent disturbance. Propagate by root division in autumn, but only when essential.
Other colors: Pink, crimson, scarlet.
Varieties/cultivars: 'Whitleyi Major', 'The Bride', 'Solange', 'Sarah Bernhardt', 'The Moor', 'Victoria', 'Duchesse de Nemours', 'Bunker Hill', 'Pink Delight', 'Lady Alexander Duff'.

Pachysandra terminalis
JAPANESE SPURGE

Family: BUXACEAE
Origin: China, Japan.
Flowering time: Spring.
Climatic zone: 4, 5, 6, 7, 8, 9.
Dimensions: Up to 12 inches (300 mm) high.
Description: This is a widely grown, evergreen groundcover with handsome, spoon-shaped leaves of a glossy dark green, and spikes of small, scented flowers. It does well in moist, well-drained soil in shaded areas. Too much exposure to the sun tends to turn the foliage yellow. It spreads quickly by underground stems and is vigorous and tough enough for planting in public places. Propagate by division in spring.
Varieties/cultivars: 'Variegata'.

Pachysandra terminalis

fertilizer during the growing period. The dense flower heads are fragrant and useful for cutting. The plants are prone to the fungal disease powdery mildew and to spider mites. Propagate it from root cuttings in winter or by division in spring.
Other colors: Pink, red, pale-blue, violet, salmon.
Varieties/cultivars: 'Mars', 'Purple King', 'Leo Schlageter', 'Mount Fuji', 'September Schnee', and others.

Phlox paniculata

Phlox paniculata and cultivars
PERENNIAL PHLOX, GARDEN PHLOX, BORDER PHLOX (U.K.)

Family: POLEMONIACEAE
Origin: Eastern North America.
Flowering time: Late summer.
Climatic zone: 4, 5, 6, 7, 8, 9.
Dimensions: 2–3 feet (up to 1 meter) high.
Description: The many cultivars of this species are easy to grow and provide masses of long-lasting color in border gardens. A sunny position is best, in a fairly rich soil with applications of liquid

Physostegia virginiana 'Summer Snow'

Physostegia virginiana 'Summer Snow'
FALSE DRAGONHEAD, OBEDIENT PLANT

Family: LABIATAE
Origin: Cultivar.
Flowering time: Late summer–early autumn.
Climatic zone: 4, 5, 6, 7, 8, 9.
Dimensions: Up to 4 feet (over 1 meter) high.
Description: This is an easy-to-grow, herbaceous perennial with leafy, upright stems, and spikes of tubular white flowers. The individual flowers have hinged stalks and will remain in any position they are moved to, hence the name obedient plant. The leaves are long and tapered, and toothed around the margins. It thrives in any fertile soil, but the soil must not be allowed to dry out. Propagation is best by the division of established plants in spring.

Polygonatum x hybridum

Polygonatum x hybridum
SOLOMON'S-SEAL, DAVID'S HARP

Family: LILIACEAE
Origin: Hybrid.
Flowering time: Late spring.
Climatic zone: 5, 6, 7, 8, 9.
Dimensions: 2 feet (600 mm) high.
Description: This plant likes being left undisturbed to allow the rhizomes to spread. A woodland plant, it looks particularly attractive when associated with ferns and hostas. The broad, green leaves are attractive and the dainty tubular flowers, carried one or two at a time, are fragrant. The leaves turn a buttery yellow in autumn. Any good garden soil will suit, provided it contains organic matter and is cool and moisture-retentive.
Varieties/cultivars: 'Flore Pleno'.

Potentilla tridentata
CINQUEFOIL, THREE-TOOTHED CINQUEFOIL

Family: ROSACEAE
Origin: North America.
Flowering time: Summer.
Climatic zone: 5, 6, 7, 8.
Dimensions: 6–10 inches (150–200 mm) high.
Description: This plant has trifoliate, evergreen, leathery leaflets, quite shiny on the upper surface. It is easy to grow in most types of soils provided they are well-drained, but it will not tolerate extra-dry conditions. Although not a particularly showy plant, it flowers for a prolonged period. It looks its best at the front of a border or in a rockery, and the stems can be cut back after flowering. Propagate it by seed or division in spring.

Rheum alexandrae

Rheum alexandrae
RHUBARB (not culinary)

Family: POLYGONACEAE
Origin: Himalayas.
Flowering time: Summer.
Climatic zone: 5, 6, 7, 8, 9.
Dimensions: 3 feet (1 meter) high.
Description: This is a curious species that scarcely resembles a rhubarb as growing all the way down the stems are straw-colored bracts which sheath the flowers and look like tiles on a house. The bracts protect the flowers and ripening seeds. The leaves are oval, dark shining green, and prominently ribbed. A fine plant, it is difficult to cultivate unless the climate is moist and cool. Propagation is by division, or by sowing seeds in spring.

Rodgersia podophylla
BRONZE LEAF, RODGERS' FLOWER

Family: SAXIFRAGACEAE
Origin: China, Japan.
Flowering time: Summer.
Climatic zone: 5, 6, 7, 8, 9.
Dimensions: 3–4 feet (approx. 1 meter) high.
Description: This plant, with its superb ornamental foliage, is very suitable for moist garden situations or beside water. The large, divided leaves are bronze when young, then turn green, and finally take on dark coppery tones as they mature in summer. The fluffy flowers are carried on arching stems well above the foliage. Strong winds can damage the foliage, so the plant should be given a sheltered position where it will form large colonies in time.

Rodgersia podophylla

Potentilla tridentata

Rheum alexandrae

Romneya coulteri

Romneya coulteri
CALIFORNIA TREE POPPY, MATILIJA POPPY
Family: PAPAVERACEAE
Origin: California.
Flowering time: Summer–autumn.
Climatic zone: 8, 9, 10.
Dimensions: Up to 8 feet (over 2 meters) high.
Description: Although a somewhat difficult plant to establish as it resents any root disturbance, the flowers make it well worth the effort. These are silky and crinkled, up to 6 inches (150 mm) wide, and sweetly fragrant. They contrast well with the green-gray, deeply divided foliage. The plant prefers a warm and well-drained position in normal garden soil, even slightly alkaline. It can be propagated by root cuttings, but disturbing the roots in this way can unfortunately result in the death of the parent plant.

Saxifraga stolonifera syn. *S. sarmentosa*
STRAWBERRY GERANIUM (U.K.), MOTHER OF THOUSANDS, CREEPING SAILOR
Family: SAXIFRAGACEAE
Origin: Eastern Asia.
Flowering time: Summer.
Climatic zone: 8, 9, 10.
Dimensions: Up to 18 inches (450 mm) high.
Description: This plant has long, prostrate stems which send out roots and then develop rosettes of round and toothed, glossy leaves. These are veined,

Saxifraga stolonifera

marbled, and colored a strawberry pink underneath. Delicate, small, white flowers are borne on loose panicles, standing above the foliage. It makes a useful and most decorative basket or pot plant, as well as a good groundcover provided it is given room to spread in a warm, sheltered spot. It can be propagated from seed in spring or by division in summer.
Varieties/cultivars: 'Tricolor'.

Shortia galacifolia
OCONEE-BELLS
Family: DIAPENSIACEAE
Origin: Eastern North America.
Flowering time: Summer.

Climatic zone: 4, 5, 6, 7, 8, 9.
Dimensions: Up to 6 inches (150 mm) high.
Description: The small, delicate, white blooms of oconee-bells resemble frilled bells. They emerge from their low foliage on slender, leafless stalks and have a nodding habit. The plant is not an easy one to grow, and once established should not be moved. It is an excellent choice for a rock garden. Grow it in cool, moist, well-drained, acid soil enriched with humus. Use peat moss as humus in clay-loam soils to make them acid. Propagate by division in early spring.

Smilacina racemosa
FALSE SPIKENARD, FALSE SOLOMON'S SEAL

Family: LILIACEAE
Origin: North America.
Flowering time: Late spring.
Climatic zone: 3, 4, 5, 6, 7, 8, 9.

Smilacina racemosa

Shortia galacifolia

196

Dimensions: Up to 3 feet (1 meter) high.
Description: This plant has erect to ascending stems of fresh green leaves and spikes of fluffy, creamy-white flowers, deliciously lemon-scented. As the flowers age they become tinged with pink and can be followed by red berries. The plant makes a good combination with ferns and primulas. It prefers shaded conditions in a lime-free soil and, with consistent moisture, is not difficult to grow. Propagate it by division in spring.

Symphytum grandiflorum

Symphytum grandiflorum
GROUND-COVER
COMFREY, CREEPING
COMFREY (U.K.)

Family: BORAGINACEAE
Origin: Caucasus.
Flowering time: Spring.
Climatic zone: 5, 6, 7, 8, 9.
Dimensions: Up to 12 inches (300 mm) high.
Description: This perennial herb makes an excellent groundcover, spreading by means of underground stems. The dark-green leaves are broad and hairy, and make a close carpet on the soil. The buds arise on hooked stems and open to tubular, cream flowers. The plant prefers moist, but not boggy, soil, and is easy to grow. Propagation is usually by division in spring or autumn.
Varieties/cultivars: 'Variegatum'.

Verbascum chaixii 'Album'
CHAIX'S MULLEIN,
NETTLE-LEAVED MULLEIN

Family: SCROPHULARIACEAE
Origin: Southern and central Europe.
Flowering time: Summer.
Climatic zone: 5, 6, 7, 8, 9.
Dimensions: 3 feet (1 meter) high.
Description: This variety has delightful, pure white flowers with rose-colored stamens, borne on showy spikes which rise from large basal leaves which are gray and hairy and often up to 12 inches (300 mm) long. An easy plant to grow, it likes a light, sandy, well-drained soil. It looks well combined with other plants in a border or wild garden, and is attractive with campanulas and as a contrast to rounded gray shrubs. It can be propagated by seed in spring.
Varieties/cultivars: 'Roseum'.

Trillium grandiflorum
WAKE ROBIN, SNOW
TRILLIUM, TRINITY FLOWER

Other common names: WOOD LILY (U.K.)
Family: LILIACEAE
Origin: Eastern North America.
Flowering time: Spring-early summer.
Climatic zone: 5, 6, 7, 8, 9.
Dimensions: 12-18 inches (300-450 mm) high.
Description: This woodland plant has undeniable appeal, but is often difficult to grow among other plants in a border. Each erect stem bears three leaves, three calyx lobes, and three petals — hence the names "trillium" and "trinity". The foliage dies down in summer and the plant can be lifted and divided then. It likes moist but well-drained soil, enriched with plenty of leaf mold, which must never be allowed to dry out.
Other colors: Pink.
Varieties/cultivars: 'Roseum'.

Trillium grandiflorum

Yucca filamentosa
ADAM'S-NEEDLE

Family: AGAVACEAE
Origin: Southeastern United States.
Flowering time: Late summer.
Climatic zone: 5, 6, 7, 8, 9.
Dimensions: 5 feet (over 1 meter) high.
Description: The grayish-green leaves of this semidesert plant are almost bayonet-like and have thread-like hairs along their margin — representing the needle and thread. The tall, beautiful flower spikes rising from these basal leaves are deliciously fragrant in the evening. The sharp outlines of this plant make it a useful specimen when landscaping. It does best in well-drained, sandy loam and can be propagated by seeds or offsets.
Varieties/cultivars: 'Variegata', 'Golden Sword'.

Yucca filamentosa

Verbascum chaixii 'Album'

Description: Bottlebrush buckeye is a spreading, suckering, free-flowering, deciduous shrub. The white flowers have very showy, dark-pink anthers and the leaves color attractively during autumn. Plant it as a specimen plant or in a shrub border, giving it plenty of room so that its spreading shape can be appreciated. It is not suitable for a small garden as suckers can spread widely creating thickets up to 20 feet (6 meters) across. It will thrive in almost any garden soil. A mulch of manure or compost around the roots in spring will provide food and keep the roots moist.

Arctostaphylos uva-ursi

Adenandra uniflora

compact shape, does not require pruning. It will tolerate most garden soils. In spring apply a handful of complete plant food around the base of the plant.

Aesculus parviflora
DWARF HORSE ○ ●
CHESTNUT (U.S.A.),
BOTTLEBRUSH BUCKEYE (U.K.)

Family: HIPPOCASTANACEAE
Origin: Southeastern United States.
Flowering time: Summer.
Climatic zone: 4, 5, 6, 7, 8, 9.
Dimensions: 8–12 feet (2–4 meters) high.

Arctostaphylos uva-ursi
BEARBERRY, RED ○
BEARBERRY, KINNIKINNICK
(U.S.A.)

Family: ERICACEAE
Origin: North America, Europe, Asia, circumpolar.
Flowering time: Spring.
Climatic zone: 2, 3, 4, 5, 6, 7, 8, 9.
Dimensions: Up to 6 inches (150 mm) high.

Description: Bearberry is an interesting, creeping, mountain or cold climate shrub. Its white, bell-shaped flowers are tinged with pink, and are followed by red berries. The prostrate stems are often up to 7 feet (2 meters) long. Because of its dense foliage it makes a good groundcover for large banks. Bearberry needs a well-drained, acid soil and, because it is salt-tolerant, will grow in sandy soils near the sea.

Adeliophyllum distichum

Abeliophyllum distichum

Abeliophyllum distichum
KOREAN ABELIALEAF, ○
WHITE FORSYTHIA

Family: OLEACEAE
Origin: Korea.
Flowering time: Spring.
Climatic zone: 5, 6, 7, 8, 9.
Dimensions: 3–5 feet (approx. 1–2 meters) high.

Description: Korean abelialeaf is a very pretty, slow-growing, deciduous shrub with arching stems. The white, bell-like flowers appear in early spring, covering leafless stems. Plant it in a shrub border or use it at the back of a perennial garden. It is easy to grow in most garden soils. Pruning should be carried out as soon as the flowers have finished, as flowers appear on wood from the previous year. New growth can be stimulated by removing old wood to the ground.

Adenandra uniflora
ADENANDRA, ○ ●
ENAMEL FLOWER

Family: RUTACEAE
Origin: South Africa.
Flowering time: Spring–summer.
Climatic zone: 8, 9, 10.
Dimensions: 3 feet (1 meter) high.

Description: This is a bushy, evergreen shrub with small, tapering leaves and numerous white flowers which have a rose-pink rib down the center of each petal and purplish-brown anthers. Adenandra looks pretty when grown in the front of a shrub border. It is a hardy shrub which, because of its naturally

Aesculus parviflora

198

Ardisia crispa

Ardisia crispa syn. *A. crenulata,*
A. crenata
CORALBERRY, ◑
SPICEBERRY, CORAL ARDISIA ● ●

Family: MYRSINIACEAE
Origin: Southeastern Asia.
Flowering time: Summer.
Climatic zone: 9, 10.
Dimensions: 3 feet (1 meter) high.
Description: This is a popular small shrub for shady situations and for use as an indoor plant. The fragrant, star-shaped, white flowers appear in terminal clusters and are followed by a heavy crop of scarlet berries, which remain on the plant throughout autumn and winter. The glossy, dark-green leaves have wavy margins. Coralberry requires a hot climate and a well-drained soil. In colder climates, it thrives as an indoor pot plant.

Aronia arbutifolia
RED CHOKEBERRY ○

Family: ROSACEAE
Origin: Eastern North America.
Flowering time: Spring-summer.
Climatic zone: 5, 6, 7, 8.
Dimensions: 6–8 feet (2–3 meters) high.
Description: This deciduous shrub has white flowers, tinted with pink, which are followed in autumn by masses of small, round berries that remain on the plant for a long period. The long, glossy green leaves with their gray undersides turn red in autumn. The plant will thrive in normal to acid soil. It increases freely by suckers which can easily be divided.
Varieties/cultivars: 'Erecta.'

199

Aronia melanocarpa
BLACK CHOKEBERRY ○

Family: ROSACEAE
Origin: Eastern North America.
Flowering time: Spring.
Climatic zone: 5, 6, 7, 8, 9.
Dimensions: 2–3 feet (up to 1 meter) high.

Description: Black chokeberry is a low-growing shrub which is covered in white flowers during spring. These are followed by lustrous, deep purple-black berries. It looks most striking at the back of a herbaceous border or planted with low-growing asters. Black chokeberry requires a free-draining soil.

Aronia arbutifolia

Aronia melanocarpa

Buddleia davidii 'White Bouquet'

Climatic zone: 9, 10.
Dimensions: 3–5 feet (approx. 1–2 meters) high.
Description: This pretty shrub has terminal heads of long, fragrant, white, jasmine-like flowers, and glossy green leaves. Plant white bouvardia near a doorway, window, or garden seat where the perfume can be appreciated. It will grow in any well-drained soil and should be pruned lightly after flowering has finished. Apply a handful of complete plant food in early spring.
Varieties/cultivars: There are numerous varieties throughout the world.

Buddleia davidii 'White Bouquet'
BUTTERFLY BUSH ○ ◗

Family: LOGANIACEAE
Origin: Cultivar.
Flowering time: Summer–autumn.
Climatic zone: 5, 6, 7, 8, 9.
Dimensions: 6–10 feet (2–3 meters) high.
Description: The fragrant, white flowers of this shrub have yellow eyes and are borne in large clusters which attract butterflies, hence the common name. Butterfly bush is a strong shrub with long, slender, dark-green leaves which are felted underneath. It grows well near the sea. A rapid grower, especially in sheltered sites, it likes good drainage. A yearly prune during winter produces a nicely shaped bush.

Azalea indica 'Alba Magna'

Azalea indica 'Alba Magna'
INDIAN AZALEA, ○ ◐
EVERGREEN AZALEA

Family: ERICACEAE
Origin: Cultivar.
Flowering time: Spring.
Climatic zone: 6, 7, 8, 9.
Dimensions: 6 feet (2 meters) high.
Description: A beautiful evergreen shrub, Indian azalea is covered in a profusion of large, white flowers during spring. It requires a well-drained, acid soil which should be enriched with leaf mold, compost, or peat before planting. Azaleas have a very shallow root system, which should not be allowed to dry out during summer. Drying out can be prevented by mulching the root area.

Calliandra portoricensis
WHITE TASSEL ○
FLOWER, SNOWFLAKE
ACACIA, WHITE POWDER PUFF

Family: LEGUMINOSAE
Origin: Southern Mexico–Panama, West Indes.
Flowering time: Spring–autumn.
Climatic zone: 9, 10.
Dimensions: 8–12 feet (approx. 2–4 meters) high.
Description: Admired for its fern-like foliage and long flowering period, this handsome shrub produces fragrant, fluffy white flowers that resemble flakes of snow. Unless grown where there are

Calliandra portoricensis

200

Bouvardia longiflora

Bouvardia longiflora
WHITE BOUVARDIA ○

Family: RUBIACEAE
Origin: Mexico.
Flowering time: Summer–autumn.

hot, dry summers, it tends to produce an abundance of foliage and odd-shaped flowers. Plant it in well-drained soil that has been enriched with leaf mold or compost. An occasional spring pruning will keep the shrub in good shape.

Calocephalus brownii

Calocephalus brownii
CUSHION BUSH, SKELETON PLANT

Family: COMPOSITAE
Origin: Australia.
Flowering time: Summer.
Climatic zone: 9, 10.
Dimensions: Up to 3 feet (1 meter) high.
Description: Cushion bush is a round, silvery, mound-like shrub with silvery-white, multi-branched stems and minute leaves which clasp the stem. The small, greenish-yellow flowers are insignificant compared with the foliage. Cushion bush grows in any soil and suits rockeries where its silvery appearance contrasts with other green shrubs. Alternatively, it is an ideal plant for a gray or white garden scheme. It is often found growing naturally on sandy and rocky seashores. Prune it after flowering has finished to maintain its bushy habit.

Carissa grandiflora
NATAL PLUM, AMATUNGULA (U.S.A.)

Family: APOCYNACEAE
Origin: South Africa.
Flowering time: Throughout the year.
Climatic zone: 9, 10.
Dimensions: Up to 15 feet (5 meters) high.
Description: A bushy shrub covered in long spines, natal plum is often used for

Carissa grandiflora

hedging. It has oval leaves and pretty, fragrant, white flowers which are 2 inches (50 mm) wide. The flowers are followed by egg-shaped berries, tasting similar to cranberries, which can be eaten fresh or made into a sauce. Natal plum is easy to grow and will thrive if given ample amounts of summer water. Mulching around its roots will help to keep the soil moist.

Carpenteria californica
CALIFORNIAN MOCK ORANGE

Family: PHILADELPHACEAE
Origin: California.
Flowering time: Summer.
Climatic zone: 8, 9, 10.
Dimensions: 6–8 feet (2–3 meters) high.
Description: A beautiful, bushy

evergreen, this shrub has long, smooth, narrow leaves which are bright green above and rather downy underneath. The fragrant flowers with their creamy-white central stamens are about 2½ inches (62 mm) across and borne in terminal clusters. Californian mock orange requires a moist but well-drained soil, otherwise the foliage will burn during summer. Add plenty of compost or manure to the soil and keep it mulched with this.
Varieties/cultivars: 'Ladham's Variety'.

Carpenteria californica

Chaenomeles speciosa 'Nivalis'

Chaenomeles speciosa 'Nivalis'
FLOWERING QUINCE, JAPONICA, JAPANESE QUINCE (U.K.)

Family: ROSACEAE
Origin: China.
Flowering time: Spring.
Climatic zone: 5, 6, 7, 8, 9.
Dimensions: 6–10 feet (2–3 meters) high.
Description: This deciduous shrub has spiny, smooth branches and oval leaves which may turn shades of red, orange, or yellow during autumn. 'Nivalis' is valued for its large, pure-white flowers which appear before the leaves in early spring. It makes a delightful feature plant or can be used with evergreen shrubs in a border. Flowering quince is easy to grow in any garden soil. Apply a handful of complete plant food in late winter to ensure a good flower display.

Chamelaucium uncinatum
GERALDTON WAXFLOWER
Family: MYRTACEAE
Origin: Western Australia.
Flowering time: Late spring–summer.
Climatic zone: 9, 10.
Dimensions: 9 feet (3 meters) high.
Description: Geraldton waxflower is a spreading, open shrub with fine foliage. The terminal sprays of dainty, waxy-textured flowers are white but can vary in color to pink or purple. The flowers are ideal for indoor decoration as they will last for a long time when picked. The shrub requires a sandy soil that contains some lime. It resents root disturbance so care should be taken not to cultivate in close proximity to it.
Other colors: Dark plum.
Varieties/cultivars: 'University'.

Choisya ternata

Choisya ternata
MEXICAN ORANGE BLOSSOM
Family: RUTACEAE
Origin: Mexico.
Flowering time: Spring.
Climatic zone: 7, 8, 9, 10.
Dimensions: 6–8 feet (2–3 meters) high.
Description: A compact, evergreen shrub, the dark-green, glossy leaves of Mexican orange blossom make a striking contrast with the abundant clusters of crisp, white, fragrant flowers. The leaves have an interesting aroma when crushed. Plant it near a door or window so that the delightful perfume can be appreciated. It is an adaptable shrub, growing just as well in full sun as in partial shade. It likes a well-drained, humus-rich soil, but can be damaged by prolonged frosty winters.

Chamelaucium uncinatum

Cistus ladanifer
CRIMSON SPOT ROCK ROSE, GUM CISTUS, CRIMSON SPOT SUNROSE (U.K.)
Other common names: GUM SUNROSE (U.K.)
Family: CISTACEAE
Origin: Southwestern Europe.
Flowering time: Summer.
Climatic zone: 7, 8, 9.
Dimensions: Up to 6 feet (2 meters) high.
Description: This erect species has lance-shaped leaves, and interesting, fragrant, white flowers with a yellow center and a purple blotch on each petal. The flowers are at least 3½ inches (85 mm) across. Crimson spot rock rose is a very hardy plant that will withstand salt winds and drought, although it may be killed by severe winters. It will thrive if given a well-drained, shady soil and a very hot, sunny position in the garden. Plant it alone, as a feature plant, or in a herbaceous garden.
Other colors: Pure white.
Varieties/cultivars: 'Albiflorus', 'Maculatus'.

Cistus salviifolius
ROCK ROSE, SAGE-LEAVED SUNROSE (U.K.)
Family: CISTACEAE
Origin: Southern Europe.
Flowering time: Summer.
Climatic zone: 7, 8, 9.
Dimensions: 3 feet (1 meter) high.
Description: This pretty, low-growing shrub, with its sage-like, grayish-green leaves, has white flowers with a yellow center. Plant it in a large rockery or at the front of a shrub border. It looks

Cistus salviifolius

Cistus ladanifer

interesting when planted either with dark-green shrubs or as part of a white and gray garden theme. Rock rose will thrive if given a well-drained, sandy soil and full sun in the hottest part of the garden. It can be killed by severe winters.

Varieties/cultivars: 'Prostratus'.

Clerodendrum trichotomum

Clerodendrum trichotomum
HARLEQUIN GLORY BOWER ○ ◑

Family: VERBENACEAE
Origin: China, Japan.
Flowering time: Summer-autumn.
Climatic zone: 5, 6, 7, 8, 9.
Dimensions: 8-12 feet (3-4 meters) high.
Description: Throughout summer, this attractive shrub is covered in fragrant, white flowers which are enclosed in maroon calyces. The flowers are followed by bright-blue berries still surrounded by the colorful calyces, hanging among the large leaves in their autumn tonings. It makes an interesting feature shrub, looking as wonderful when in flower as when covered with berries. Plant it in well-drained soil that has been previously enriched with manure or compost.

should be planted close to a door or window so that the delicious perfume can be appreciated. It is very easy to grow and will thrive in a moist, neutral to acid soil. Keep the soil around the base of the plant mulched with manure or compost. This will not only feed the shrub, but keep the soil moist.

Other colors: Pink.
Varieties/cultivars: 'Pink Spires', 'Rosea', 'Paniculata'.

Cleyera japonica

Cleyera japonica
SASAKI ○

Family: THEACEAE
Origin: Japan, China, Korea, Taiwan.
Flowering time: Spring.
Climatic zone: 8, 9.
Dimensions: 6-10 feet (2-3 meters) high.
Description: This slow-growing shrub has a distinctive growth habit. The branches spread rigidly and are very densely covered in dark-green, shining leaves. In spring, it can be covered in a profusion of small, white flowers.

Some of the leaves may turn red in winter, even though it is an evergreen. It likes sandy loam and responds to regular fertilizing in spring.

Clethra alnifolia

Convolvulus cneorum
SILVERBUSH ○

Family: CONVOLVULACEAE
Origin: Southeastern Europe.
Flowering time: Spring-summer.
Climatic zone: 7, 8, 9, 10.
Dimensions: Up to 3 feet (1 meter) high.
Description: The white flowers of this compact, little evergreen shrub look at first like partly opened umbrellas, but when fully open are about 2 inches (50 mm) across. The slender, silvery-gray foliage is covered in silky hairs. Silverbush makes a good non-invasive shrub in large rock gardens or can be included in a herbaceous border. It will thrive in a sunny position in sandy, well-drained soil, but may be killed by severe winters. Fertilize it with a handful of complete plant food in early spring.

Clethra alnifolia
SWEET PEPPERBUSH, SUMMER SWEET CLETHRA, SPIKED ALDER (U.S.A.) ○ ◐

Family: CLETHRACEAE
Origin: Eastern United States.
Flowering time: Summer.
Climatic zone: 4, 5, 6, 7, 8, 9.
Dimensions: 6-9 feet (2-3 meters) high.
Description: This hardy, deciduous shrub has long leaves and is covered in a profusion of very fragrant, terminal spikes of white flowers in summer. It

Convolvulus cneorum

Cornus alba
RED-BARKED
DOGWOOD, TARTARIAN
DOGWOOD

Family: CORNACEAE
Origin: Eastern Asia.
Flowering time: Early summer.
Climatic zone: 3, 4, 5, 6, 7, 8, 9.
Dimensions: 6–10 feet (2–3 meters) high.
Description: The white flowers of tartarian dogwood appear in profusion during early summer. An added feature is the deep-red, twiggy branches which add some color to the garden during the winter months. The oval leaves may color well in autumn. There are many different varieties of this plant, the majority of them having variegated leaves. Tartarian dogwood will grow well in either wet or dry soil.
Varieties/cultivars: There are numerous cultivars throughout the world. Flower color is generally white, but the color of the branches ranges from black-purple to bronze.

Cornus alba

Cornus sanguinea
COMMON
DOGWOOD, BLOOD-TWIG
DOGWOOD

Family: CORNACEAE
Origin: Europe, southwestern Asia.
Flowering time: Summer.
Climatic zone: 4, 5, 6, 7, 8, 9.
Dimensions: 4–6 feet (1–2 meters) high.
Description: Grown throughout England as a hedgerow plant, this attractive, hardy shrub has dark-reddish stems and oval leaves that turn a rich purple in autumn. The off-white, scented flowers are followed in autumn

Cornus sanguinea

by large clusters of black fruits. Plant it in a shrub border or with evergreen plants in an informal hedge. Prune it every second spring to encourage new shoots.

Cornus stolonifera syn. *C. sericea*
RED OSIER,
DOGWOOD

Family: CORNACEAE
Origin: North America.
Flowering time: Spring.
Climatic zone: 3, 4, 5, 6, 7, 8, 9.
Dimensions: 6 feet (2 meters) high.
Description: This is a rampant, suckering, hardy shrub which forms a dense thicket of purplish-red, upright

branches. The off-white flowers are followed by white berries. It thrives in wet soil and is often used for hedges, especially on large estates. It can be pruned heavily in late winter if required. Mulch around the base of the plant with manure, compost, or grass clippings to keep the soil moist.
Varieties/cultivars: 'Flaviramea'.

Cornus stolonifera 'Flaviramea'

Cornus stolonifera 'Flaviramea' syn.
C. sericea 'Flaviramea'
YELLOWTWIG,
DOGWOOD

Family: CORNACEAE
Origin: Cultivar.
Flowering time: Spring.
Climatic zone: 3, 4, 5, 6, 7, 8, 9.
Dimensions: 4–6 feet (1–2 meters) high.
Description: The white flowers of this low, spreading, deciduous shrub are produced in clusters and are followed by small, round, black berries. It has shining, bright greenish-yellow bark and looks particularly attractive when planted with the red-stemmed species, *C. sanguinea*. This hardy shrub will thrive in moist or wet conditions. If planted in ordinary garden soil, make sure the area around the base of the plant is continually mulched to keep the moisture in the soil, and supply ample water in the summer.

Cornus stolonifera

Correa alba
WHITE CORREA,
AUSTRALIAN FUCHSIA

Family: RUTACEAE
Origin: Eastern Australia, Tasmania.
Flowering time: Winter.

Correa alba

Cyrilla racemiflora

Family: LEGUMINOSAE
Origin: Hybrid.
Flowering time: Early summer.
Climatic zone: 6, 7, 8, 9.
Dimensions: 12 inches (300 mm) high.
Description: This is a deciduous, semiprostrate, mat-forming hybrid which was raised at Kew Gardens in England. The small trifoliate leaves are slightly hairy on the edges and underneath. The creamy-white flowers are produced in abundance, making a most magnificent display. Plant it in large rockeries, on banks, or at the front of shrub borders. Kew broom likes a free-draining soil.

Cytisus x kewensis
KEW BROOM ○

current year's shoots. The lance-shaped leaves may turn crimson in autumn. The shrub looks most attractive in a woodland garden. It requires an acid soil. Mulching around the base with oak leaves or peat will keep the soil acidic. It is easily propagated from cuttings taken in summer, or by seed.

Climatic zone: 9, 10.
Dimensions: 5 feet (approx. 2 meters) high.
Description: This rounded shrub has circular leaves with a waxy bloom. The white flowers are valued for providing winter color when, in most places, other flowers are scarce. Although this is the main flowering period there are usually some flowers on the plant throughout the year. They attract nectar-feeding birds. It is very salt-resistant and therefore suitable for seaside planting. The soil should be well drained and fed with an organic fertilizer in early spring.

Cyrilla racemiflora
LEATHERWOOD, SWAMP
CYRILLA ○

Family: CYRILLACEAE
Origin: Southeastern United States, West Indies, eastern South America.
Flowering time: Summer.
Climatic zone: 6, 7, 8, 9, 10.
Dimensions: 10–15 feet (3–5 meters) high.
Description: The white flowers of this pretty shrub are borne in whorls of slender racemes at the base of the

Cytisus x kewensis

Cytisus 'Snow Queen'

Cytisus 'Snow Queen'
BROOM, WHITE BROOM ○

Family: LEGUMINOSAE
Origin: Cultivar.
Flowering time: Spring.
Climatic zone: 6, 7, 8, 9.
Dimensions: 3–4 feet (approx. 1 meter) high.
Description: White broom looks magnificent when covered in its masses of white flowers in spring. These look impressive especially if near plants with dark-green foliage. Plant it at the front of a shrub border, or at the back of a herbaceous border. The main requirement of white broom is well-drained soil.

Cytisus x *praecox*
WARMINSTER BROOM ○

Family: LEGUMINOSAE
Origin: Hybrid.
Flowering time: Early summer.
Climatic zone: 6, 7, 8, 9.
Dimensions: 3–4 feet (approx. 1 meter) high.
Description: This extremely pretty plant has a dainty, loose habit. When in bloom it becomes a tumbling mass of creamy white as the long, thin stems hang down with the sheer weight of the flowers. It makes a delightful feature plant and fits in well with herbaceous plants in a border. Plant it in well-drained soil and fertilize it in spring with a handful of complete plant food.
Other colors: Golden yellow.
Varieties/cultivars: 'Alba', 'Allgold', 'Gold Spear', 'Hollandia'.

Cytisus x *praecox*

Daphne odora 'Alba'
FRAGRANT DAPHNE, ○ ◑
WINTER DAPHNE

Family: THYMELAEACEAE
Origin: Cultivar.
Flowering time: Winter–spring.
Climatic zone: 7, 8, 9.
Dimensions: 3 feet (1 meter) high.
Description: An attractive shrub, fragrant daphne has a spreading habit and smooth, showy, deep-green leaves. The extremely fragrant flowers are in tight clusters, each composed of thirty to forty flowers. The shrub requires a cool soil which must be crumbly and well-drained. Before planting, dig in leaf mold or peat. Do not use chemical fertilizers. A mulch of leaf mold annually will suffice to feed the plant and will not harm it.

Daphne x *burkwoodii* 'Albert Burkwood'
BURKWOOD DAPHNE ○ ◑

Family: THYMELAEACEAE
Origin: Hybrid.
Flowering time: Summer.
Climatic zone: 5, 6, 7, 8, 9.
Dimensions: Up to 3 feet (1 meter) high.
Description: This is a useful, low-growing, semi-evergreen shrub for the front border. In summer the stem tips are crowned with clusters of fragrant white flowers which age to pink. Burkwood daphne thrives in a neutral to limy soil. Do not use chemical fertilizer as, like other daphnes, it is easily killed with such kindness. A mulch of leaf mold or manure applied around the plant in spring is all that is required.

Daphne x *burkwoodii* 'Albert Burkwood'

Daphne odora 'Alba'

Datura suaveolens syn. Brugmansia suaveolens

ANGEL'S-TRUMPET

Family: SOLANACEAE
Origin: Mexico.
Flowering time: Summer.
Climatic zone: 9, 10.
Dimensions: 6–10 feet (2–3 meters) high.
Description: This large shrub has flannel-like leaves and bears large, hanging, trumpet-shaped, fragrant flowers during summer. It makes an eye-catching specimen shrub. Quick-growing, it flourishes in warm temperate to tropical climates, but withstands cold if it is cut back to near ground level during winter. In spring, new shoots will burst forth and flower during the first season. Angel's-trumpet is often grown in conservatories in cold climates.

Datura suaveolens

Deutzia gracilis

SLENDER DEUTZIA

Family: PHILADELPHACEAE
Origin: Japan.
Flowering time: Early summer.
Climatic zone: 4, 5, 6, 7, 8, 9.
Dimensions: Up to 4 feet (approx. 1 meter) high.
Description: This elegant, deciduous shrub maintains a bushy form and has yellow-gray bark on its hollow stems. It is excellent in cool-climate gardens, where its many-flowered heads of pure-white flowers are a delight in the summer. Prune it immediately after it has finished flowering.

shrub should be pruned immediately after flowering by removing the oldest canes at the base.
Varieties/cultivars: 'Candidissima', 'Pride of Rochester'.

Deutzia gracilis

Deutzia scabra

FUZZY DEUTZIA

Family: PHILADELPHACEAE
Origin: Japan, China.
Flowering time: Early summer.
Climatic zone: 5, 6, 7, 8, 9.
Dimensions: Up to 8 feet (approx. 3 meters) high.
Description: This widely cultivated deciduous shrub has produced some well-known cultivars including those with double flowers. The species produces abundant spikes, up to 5 inches (125 mm) long, of star-shaped flowers, which may show a faint flush of pink on the outside of the petals. Arising from the base, the branches are erect, arching canes, with the upper twigs coppery-green and furry and the older wood peeling in small shreds. The

Deutzia scabra

Deutzia x lemoinei

LEMOINE DEUTZIA

Family: PHILADELPHACEAE
Origin: Hybrid.
Flowering time: Early summer.
Climatic zone: 4, 5, 6, 7, 8, 9.
Dimensions: Up to 7 feet (2 meters) high.
Description: This hybrid from *D. gracilis* and *D. parviflora* was produced by Victor Lemoine of Nancy in France. A many-branched, deciduous shrub, it grows erect and has narrow leaves, up to 4 inches (100 mm) long, which are sharply toothed. The pure-white flowers are very numerous and, though individually only 3/4 inch (18 mm) wide, they appear in spikes up to 4 inches (100 mm) long. Annual pruning after flowering is advisable to encourage strong growth.

Deutzia x lemoinei

Erica carnea 'Springwood White'

Erica carnea 'Springwood White'
WINTER HEATH ○

Family: ERICACEAE
Origin: Cultivar.
Flowering time: Midwinter–early spring.
Climatic zone: 5, 6, 7.
Dimensions: Up to 1 foot (300 mm) high.
Description: Considered the finest white cultivar of Erica, this is a low, spreading shrub with masses of showy, urn-shaped flowers. Hardy and easy to cultivate, plant it in an open, sunny position in moderately rich, well-drained soil that is slightly acidic. It is ideal for grouping with dwarf rhododendrons and conifers which like the same growing conditions. Prune back immediately after flowering to maintain a neat shape.

Escallonia bifida syn. *E. montevidensis*
ESCALLONIA ○

Family: ESCALLONIACEAE
Origin: Uruguay, southern Brazil.
Flowering time: Summer–mid-autumn.
Climatic zone: 8, 9.
Dimensions: 13 feet (4 meters) high.
Description: The most beautiful of the white-flowered escallonias is this handsome evergreen shrub with a loose, open habit. It sometimes attains a tree-like form. The sweetly honey-scented flowers are star-shaped, ½ inch (12 mm) wide, and attached to the stem by a bell-shaped receptacle. Its shoots are hairless but sometimes slightly sticky, and its elliptic or spatula-shaped leaves, up to 3 inches (75 mm) long, are sprinkled on their undersides with small resinous

Escallonia bifida

Escallonia bifida

dots. Easy to cultivate, this shrub flowers generously over a long period and is suitable for seaside conditions. In colder climates, the protection of a wall is necessary as the shrub may be killed by severe winters.

Exochorda racemosa
PEARLBUSH ○

Family: ROSACEAE
Origin: China.
Flowering time: Spring.
Climatic zone: 5, 6, 7, 8, 9.
Dimensions: Up to 15 feet (5 meters) high.
Description: This is a deciduous shrub of considerable beauty, much prized for its showy display of paper-white flowers, which coincides with lilac flowering

time. Its buds in racemes are said to look like a string of pearls. The five petals of the open flowers spread to 1½ inches (35 mm) wide with many stamens arranged around the rim of the green center. Grown in slightly acid soil, the shrub needs to have the oldest branches pruned back to the base in late winter.

Fothergilla gardenii

Fothergilla gardenii
DWARF FOTHERGILLA ○

Family: HAMAMELIDACEAE
Origin: Southeastern United States.
Flowering time: Spring.
Climatic zone: 5, 6, 7, 8, 9.
Dimensions: 3 feet (1 meter) high.
Description: An attractive and unusual spring-bloomer, this small, deciduous shrub deserves greater popularity. The masses of flower spikes are without petals and appear as erect dish-mop heads of fragrant, white stamens measuring 1 inch (25 mm) long. These

Exochorda racemosa

208

bloom before the leaves unfold. In autumn, the leaves are a brilliant display of orange-crimson color. Plant the bush among other favorites in the shrub garden, preferably with an evergreen as a background so that the fluffy flower heads can be seen at their best.

Fothergilla major

WITCH ELDER, FOTHERGILLA, MOUNTAIN SNOW

Fothergilla major syn. *F. monticola*

Family: HAMAMELIDACEAE
Origin: Southeastern United States.
Flowering time: Spring.
Climatic zone: 5, 6, 7, 8, 9.
Dimensions: 6 feet (2 meters) high.
Description: The genus name honors John Fothergill, an eighteenth-century English physician and friend of Benjamin Franklin, who introduced many American plants into cultivation in England. Witch elder is a shrub with either an open, spreading habit or a rounded habit. Its roundish or heart-shaped leaves, becoming brilliant scarlet or crimson in autumn, make it one of the finest of the autumn coloring plants. In spring, it also offers a conspicuous show of terminal heads, up to 2 inches (50 mm) long, the petalless flowers relying on the spikes of stamens for their display. A lime-free soil will ensure continuous good growth.

FLORIST'S GARDENIA

Gardenia jasminoides 'Florida'

Family: RUBIACEAE
Origin: Cultivar.
Flowering time: Spring-summer.
Dimensions: Up to 5 feet (approx. 2 meters) high.
Description: Growing in warm climates, gardenias are cherished for their perfume, their white perfection, and their long flowering period. The glossy green leaves, up to 4 inches (100 mm) long, are also attractive all year. The solitary flowers stand clear of the top-most leaves and open from bright green buds in a spiral of overlapping petals to a width of 2½ inches (50 mm). The plants thrive in a slightly acid soil and should be planted near a doorway, window, or outdoor sitting area, where their perfume can be appreciated. Florists use the flowers because of their perfume and longevity.

Gardenia jasminoides 'Florida'

LARGE FLOWERED GARDENIA, FLORIST'S GARDENIA

Gardenia jasminoides 'Magnifica'

Family: RUBIACEAE
Origin: Cultivar.
Flowering time: Spring-summer.
Climatic zone: 9, 10.
Dimensions: Up to 6 feet (approx. 2 meters) high.
Description: This cultivar is a larger shrub than *G. jasminoides* 'Florida', being both taller and wider. Its leaves are also larger, 4½ inches (112 mm) long, more lustrous, and a brighter green. Most of the twenty large, unfurling petals of the flowers spread out to measure 4½ inches (112 mm) wide, but some remain unopened and stand erect in the center. Their perfume is heady. Among the choicest of evergreen flowering shrubs, this gardenia adds distinction to shrub beds and borders. A not-climate plant, plenty of water and an acid fertilizer are essential.

DWARF GARDENIA, FLORIST'S GARDENIA

Gardenia jasminoides 'Radicans' syn.

Family: RUBIACEAE
Origin: Cultivar.
Flowering time: Spring-summer.
Climatic zone: 9, 10.
Dimensions: 12 inches (300 mm) high.
Description: This low, broad-spreading cultivar is an excellent small-scale groundcover. The lower branches often self-layer. The leaves are narrow and small, about 1½ inches (35 mm) long, and a bright, glossy green. The fragrant flowers are semidouble, about 1½ inches (35 mm) wide, with somewhat twisted petals. The miniature flower makes a perfect buttonhole. As well as being an excellent border shrub, this evergreen makes a very effective, low, informal hedge if enough shrubs are planted close together. A hot, humid summer is its main requirement, but plenty of water and regular feeding with an acid plant food is necessary for good flowering. It is also a good container plant, so a greenhouse environment will enable it to cope with cold climates.

Gardenia jasminoides 'Prostrata' syn. 'Radicans'

Gardenia jasminoides 'Prostrata'

Gardenia jasminoides 'Magnifica'

Gaultheria procumbens

Gaultheria procumbens

Gaultheria procumbens
WINTERGREEN, CHECKERBERRY

Family: ERICACEAE
Origin: Eastern United States.
Flowering time: Spring.
Climatic zone: 3, 4, 5, 6, 7, 8, 9.
Dimensions: 6 inches (150 mm) high.
Description: Wintergreen is found growing naturally in acid soils in dry and moist woodlands over areas that are vastly different climatically. Spreading by means of rhizomes, the stems of this prostrate, creeping shrub stand erect with the foliage crowded near the top. The evergreen leaves are up to 2 inches (50 mm) long. About ⅓ inch (8 mm) long, the waxy, white, bell-shaped flowers are solitary and hang from the leaf axils. The highly decorative, bright scarlet fruits are spicy and aromatic and much sought after as winter food by deer, grouse, and partridges.

Gaultheria shallon
SALAL, SHALLON

Family: ERICACEAE
Origin: Western United States.
Flowering time: Early summer.
Climatic zone: 6, 7, 8, 9.
Dimensions: Up to 5 feet (approx. 2 meters) high.
Description: This plant forms a pleasing ornamental, open shrub. It has many hairy stems with broad, ovate leaves which measure up to 5 inches (125 mm) long and are hairless when mature. The felted blooms, which can be tinged with pink, are about ½ inch (12 mm) long and are suspended like bells in terminal clusters of slender racemes. They are followed by edible,

purple fruits which turn black when mature. Esteemed for its attractive leaves, flowers, and fruit, this shrub is a good choice in a lightly shaded shrub border or woodland garden, although it can be very invasive when grown in moist, acid soil.

Genista monosperma
WHITE BROOM, WHITE WEEPING BROOM, BRIDAL VEIL BROOM

Family: LEGUMINOSAE
Origin: Spain, Portugal, North Africa.
Flowering time: Spring.
Climatic zone: 9, 10.
Dimensions: Up to 10 feet (3 meters) high.
Description: Somewhat straggly, this

Gaultheria shallon

deciduous shrub has rush-like, wide-spreading, pendant branches that are silky-haired when young. When they appear, the leaves are sparse, up to ¾ inch (18 mm) long, narrow, and also covered with silky hairs. The very fragrant flowers, each about ½ inch (12 mm) wide, are scattered abundantly along the branches in short racemes. They, too, have a silky-haired covering. Dry, well-drained, alkaline soils with poor fertility best simulate the conditions of their native habitat. Annual pruning and thinning out of the oldest branches is recommended.

Grevillea banksii 'Alba'
BANKS' WHITE GREVILLEA

Family: PROTEACEAE
Origin: Cultivar.
Flowering time: Spring–early summer.
Climatic zone: 9, 10.
Dimensions: Up to 13 feet (4 meters) high.
Description: This upright, many-branched shrub has leaves of dark green with silky hairs giving a white appearance to their undersides. The leaves can measure up to 12 inches (300 mm) long. The flowers are produced in profusion, with forty to eighty crowded on an erect, terminal, cylindrical head up to 4 inches (100 mm) long. This white form of the red-flowering species has the same

Genista monosperma

210

Grevillea banksii 'Alba'

reputation as the red for blooming intermittently after the main flowering period is over. Thriving in a sunny position, it is a very hardy and rewarding plant. It attracts birds.

Hakea acicularis

Hakea acicularis syn. *H. sericea*
BUSHY NEEDLEWOOD,
SILKY HAKEA

Family: PROTEACEAE
Origin: Southeastern Australia.
Flowering time: Winter-spring.
Climatic zone: 9, 10.
Dimensions: 9 feet (3 meters) high.
Description: Care should be taken when positioning this shrub in the garden as its stiff, needle-like leaves, which spread in all directions, have sharp points which can prick the unwary. However, planted as an impenetrable hedge, this species would have few equals. The perfumed flowers, which sometimes show a tinge of pink, appear mostly as small clusters in the upper leaf axils and are a dainty foil to

the leaves. The prominent, woody fruits, measuring up to 1½ inches (35 mm) long, persist on the plant, unopened, for several years unless disturbed by fire or injury. It is easy to grow in well-drained soil.

Hebe albicans

Hebe albicans
NEW ZEALAND LILAC,
SHRUBBY VERONICA
(U.K.)

Family: SCROPHULARIACEAE
Origin: New Zealand.
Flowering time: Summer-autumn.
Climatic zone: 7, 8, 9.
Dimensions: Up to 3 feet (1 meter) high.
Description: This is a splendid dwarf, evergreen shrub with a dense, rounded shape. The gray-green leaves arranged opposite one another on the stem give way at the top to the flower heads. Here, numerous 1 inch (25 mm) long spikes of flowers cover the plant throughout its long flowering period. Hardy in most soils which are well drained, this is another species that can tolerate difficult locations near the sea. Pruning is not needed.

Hebe diosmifolia

Hebe diosmifolia
VERONICA

Family: SCROPHULARIACEAE
Origin: New Zealand.
Flowering time: Summer.
Climatic zone: 6, 7, 8, 9.
Dimensions: Up to 3 feet (1 meter) high.
Description: A small, neat shrub, this species has glossy green foliage and flat clusters of small white flowers, tinged with palest lilac. Like most veronicas it thrives in rich, well-drained soil if planted in an open, sunny position. It can withstand both frosts and drought conditions and can be easily propagated by cuttings taken at any time of the year.

SHRUBS

Hebe odora

Hebe odora syn. *H. buxifolia*
WHITE SPEEDWELL,
SHRUBBY VERONICA

Family: SCROPHULARIACEAE
Origin: New Zealand mountains.
Flowering time: Spring-summer.
Climatic zone: 8, 9.
Dimensions: Up to 6 feet (2 meters) high.
Description: Of the one hundred species of *Hebe*, all but a few are natives of New Zealand. This plant is a small, erect, evergreen shrub with polished green leaves less than 1 inch (25 mm) long. The flowers grow on 1-2-inch (25-50 mm) terminal spikes. When *H. odora* is in full bloom, the profusion of flowers almost hides the leaves. Very ornamental, this species is also invaluable for seaside and industrial estate planting.

Hebe salicifolia

Hebe salicifolia
KOROMIKO, SHRUBBY VERONICA

Family: SCROPHULARIACEAE
Origin: New Zealand, southern Chile.
Flowering time: Summer.
Climatic zone: 7, 8, 9.
Dimensions: Up to 15 feet (5 meters) high.
Description: With the specific name meaning "leaves like a *Salix* (or willow)" it is no surprise to find this evergreen species has narrow leaves up to 6 inches (150 mm) long, tapering to a point at the tips. They usually have toothed margins. The flower spikes are slender and cylindrical and are sometimes more than 6 inches (150 mm) long. The small, white, individual blooms can be tinged with pale to darker lilac. This is a shrub which is ideally suited to seaside areas and, as with the other *Hebe* species, is one of the easiest plants to maintain in the garden. It is a parent of many hardy hybrids. It does not, however, tolerate prolonged winter cold.

Hibiscus mutabilis
COTTON ROSE, CONFEDERATE ROSE, ROSE COTTON

Other common names: ROSE OF SHARON
Family: MALVACEAE
Origin: Southeastern China.
Flowering time: Autumn.
Climatic zone: 9, 10.
Dimensions: Up to 13 feet (4 meters) high.
Description: *Mutabilis*, meaning "to change", indicates the change in flower color, from white when they emerge to deep-red as they age. This transition means that the shrub is liberally clothed in flowers of white and red, as well as all

Hibiscus mutabilis

the intervening shades of pink. The long-stalked leaves are also distinctive. They are wider than they are long, about 7 inches (175 mm) across, with three to seven coarsely toothed, shallow triangular lobes, and both they and the young stems are thickly covered with yellowish hairs. It needs protection from frost and wind, and enjoys full sun and a well-drained soil.

Hydrangea arborescens 'Grandiflora'

Hydrangea arborescens
TREE HYDRANGEA, SMOOTH HYDRANGEA

Family: HYDRANGEACEAE
Origin: Southeastern United States.
Flowering time: Summer.
Climatic zone: 4, 5, 6, 7, 8, 9.
Dimensions: Up to 5 feet (approx. 2 meters) high.
Description: This ornamental, deciduous shrub has a somewhat loose and straggling growth. Its leaves are large and egg-shaped. Its flattish flower clusters are up to 6 inches (150 mm)

Hydrangea quercifolia

across, consisting of masses of small, fertile flowers and a dappling of a few large, showy, sterile ones on the outer edges. *H. arborescens* 'Grandiflora', known as Hills of Snow, is very popular and the more commonly cultivated form. An annual prune after flowering will keep this shrub compact. The cut blooms are very decorative in vases.
Varieties/cultivars: 'Grandiflora'.

Hydrangea quercifolia
OAK-LEAVED HYDRANGEA

Family: HYDRANGEACEAE
Origin: Southeastern United States.
Flowering time: Summer.
Climatic zone: 5, 6, 7, 8, 9.
Dimensions: Up to 6 feet (2 meters) high.
Description: This beautiful deciduous shrub is an elegant inclusion in an open woodland garden or positioned in light shade. Many cultivate it for its bold, handsome foliage. The leaves are 8 inches (200 mm) long, with three to five deep lobes, whitish on their undersides when newly opened, and changing in autumn to produce a spectacular display of bronzy-purple. The flower clusters are in 12-inch-long (300 mm) pyramids of long-stalked, showy, sterile blooms, as well as smaller, fertile ones. They age to a rosy-purple. It requires a humus-rich soil and may be damaged by severe winters.

Itea virginica

VIRGINIA WILLOW, SWEETSPIRE ○ ◐

Family: ITEACEAE
Origin: Southeastern United States.
Flowering time: Summer.
Climatic zone: 5, 6, 7, 8, 9.
Dimensions: Up to 10 feet (3 meters) high.
Description: A native of wet woods and swamps of the coastal region, this deciduous shrub branches into many slender stems which support its handsome leaves. Up to 4 inches (100 mm) long, with finely toothed margins, they turn beautiful shades of red in autumn. The small, fluffy, creamy-white flowers, which are tinged with green, are sweetly fragrant and produced in great profusion in semi-erect racemes measuring up to 6 inches (150 mm) long. Humus-rich soil is preferred and the protection of a wall or sheltered corner is desirable.

Itea virginica

Leucothoe axillaris syn. *L. catesbaei*

COAST LEUCOTHOE ◐

Family: ERICACEAE
Origin: Southeastern United States.
Flowering time: Summer.
Climatic zone: 5, 6, 7, 8, 9.
Dimensions: Up to 6 feet (2 meters) high.
Description: Named after Leucothoë, a legendary princess of Babylon who was believed to have been changed into a shrub by the god Apollo, this excellent evergreen shrub is generally similar to *L. fontanesiana*. It is, however, a native of moist woodlands of the coastal plain. The flower heads, which are about 3 inches (75 mm) long, are crowded with broad, urn-shaped flowers. The leaves are bluntly pointed and only sparsely toothed. This shrub likes moist, acid soil.

Leucothoe fontanesiana

DROOPING LEUCOTHOE ○ ◐

Family: ERICACEAE
Origin: Eastern United States.
Flowering time: Early summer.
Climatic zone: 5, 6, 7, 8, 9.
Dimensions: Up to 6 feet (2 meters) high.
Description: This is an attractive and useful evergreen shrub for lightly shaded garden areas, and open woodlands where naturalistic effects are sought. Its native habitat is along banks of mountain streams. The flowers, which are small, urn-shaped, and drooping, appear in clusters up to 4 inches (100 mm) long, all along the graceful, arching stems. The stems, reddish when young, support lance-like, leathery leaves which, in the cold months and

Leucothoe axillaris

especially in exposed positions, become tinged with deep reds and bronzy-purples. An acid, peaty soil is necessary which is moist but well-drained.

Leucothoe fontanesiana

be grown successfully in poor soils and remains semi-evergreen, except in very severe winters when it becomes deciduous. The short-stalked flowers appear in profuse clusters, up to 4 inches (100 mm) long. Many people dislike their smell. The leaves, which are glossy green and pointed, are up to 2½ inches (62 mm) long.

Varieties/cultivars: 'Aureum', 'Argenteum'.

Lonicera nitida 'Aurea'

Lonicera nitida
BOX-LEAF HONEYSUCKLE

Family: CAPRIFOLIACEAE
Origin: Western China.
Flowering time: Spring.
Climatic zone: 7, 8, 9.
Dimensions: Up to 6 feet (2 meters) high.
Description: This twiggy, evergreen shrub is a vigorous grower, stands clipping well, and makes a dense, compact hedge. The tiny, sweetly fragrant flowers appear in pairs from the leaf axils, and are followed by bluish-purple berries, ¼ inch (6 mm) wide. The leaves are small, thick, glossy, oval to rounded in shape, and up to ½ inch (12 mm) long. When training it as a hedge, establish a good basic framework when the plant is young by regular pruning. Grow in well-drained but moist soil.
Varieties/cultivars: Several cultivars are available.

Loropetalum chinense
FRINGE FLOWER, LOROPETALUM

Family: HAMAMELIDACEAE
Origin: China.
Flowering time: Spring.
Climatic zone: 8, 9, 10.

---

them. All privets have some unwelcome characteristics. The scent of the flowers is offensive to some people, and the roots are "hungry" and impoverish nearby soil.

Varieties/cultivars: 'Excelsum Superbum', 'Tricolor'.

Ligustrum lucidum

Ligustrum ovalifolium

Ligustrum ovalifolium
CALIFORNIA PRIVET (U.S.A.), OVAL LEAF PRIVET (U.K.), HEDGING PRIVET (U.K.)

Family: OLEACEAE
Origin: Japan.
Flowering time: Summer.
Climatic zone: 5, 6, 7, 8, 9.
Dimensions: Up to 13 feet (4 meters) high.
Description: This favorite hedge plant grows erect and stiff, but possesses the fine twiggy growth so essential for the formation of a good, dense hedge. It can

---

Ligustrum japonicum 'Rotundifolium'

Ligustrum japonicum
JAPANESE PRIVET, JAPANESE TREE PRIVET

Family: OLEACEAE
Origin: Japan, Korea.
Flowering time: Late summer–autumn.
Climatic zone: 7, 8, 9.
Dimensions: Up to 10 feet (3 meters) high.
Description: Sometimes assuming a tree-like form, this dense, evergreen shrub has shiny olive-green leaves over 4 inches (100 mm) long. The flowers are small and are borne in large clusters up to 6 inches (150 mm) long, on the terminal shoots. Many people find their scent unpleasant. These plants make an effective hedge, screen, or background. They can be clipped into formal shapes or left as a natural wall of greenery, and thrive even when neglected or grown in poor soils.
Varieties/cultivars: 'Rotundifolium'.

Ligustrum lucidum
CHINESE PRIVET

Family: OLEACEAE
Origin: Japan, Korea, China.
Flowering time: Late summer–autumn.
Climatic zone: 7, 8, 9.
Dimensions: Up to 30 feet (9 meters) high.
Description: Occasionally seen as a beautiful, symmetrical tree with an attractive, fluted trunk, this evergreen can also be clipped as a hedge. It has large, glossy green, pointed leaves, up to 6 inches (150 mm) in length, and large, handsome clusters of flowers with petals as long as the corolla tubes that support

Loropetalum chinense

Dimensions: Up to 12 feet (4 meters) high.
Description: This neat-foliaged, evergreen shrub grows well among azaleas and other shrubs which have the same well-drained, acid soil requirements. The showy flowers consist of four soft, strap-shaped petals about 1 inch (25 mm) long, freely produced in clusters of six to nine to give a fringed appearance to the shrub. The leaves are rough to the touch, egg-shaped, and up to 2 inches (50 mm) long. A warm, sheltered position is necessary for this shrub. It does not tolerate severe winter weather. It appreciates an application of lime-free compost.

Magnolia stellata
STAR MAGNOLIA

Family: MAGNOLIACEAE
Origin: Japan.
Flowering time: Spring.
Climatic zone: 5, 6, 7, 8, 9.
Dimensions: Up to 15 feet (5 meters) high.
Description: Slow-growing and deciduous, this shrub is distinctive and charming. With its many spreading branches, it grows wider than it does high and is prized for its brilliant spring floral display. The fragrant, star-like flowers burst open on bare branches. They comprise up to twenty-one petals and sepals, which look alike and are narrow, strap-shaped, 1½ inches (35 mm) long, and bend backwards with age. The leaves are broadly oval to oblong and up to 5 inches (125 mm) long. Plant in fertile, well-drained soil with plenty of humus.
Other colors: Pink, purplish-pink.
Varieties/cultivars: 'Rosea', 'Rubra'.

Magnolia stellata

Melaleuca armillaris
HONEY MYRTLE,
BRACELET HONEY MYRTLE

Family: MYRTACEAE
Origin: Eastern Australia.
Flowering time: Spring-summer.
Climatic zone: 9, 10.
Dimensions: Up to 17 feet (approx. 5 meters) high.
Description: This is a hardy, fast-growing, evergreen, bushy shrub, or small tree, which often grows wider than it does tall. Narrow, 1-inch-long (25 mm) leaves, thickly covering the many fine stems, form a dense, impenetrable barrier, making this an excellent choice for a windbreak or screen. The flowers are arranged in a spike up to 2½ inches (60 mm) long. Their conspicuous stamens give the whole flower the appearance of a "bottlebrush". The woody, capsular fruit with their seeds remain on the plant for several years. It grows well in most soils and will tolerate lime.

Melaleuca armillaris

Melaleuca incana
GRAY HONEY MYRTLE

Family: MYRTACEAE
Origin: Western Australia.
Flowering time: Late spring-early summer.
Climatic zone: 9, 10.
Dimensions: Up to 10 feet (3 meters) high.
Description: The Latin word *incana* meaning "quite gray", refers to the color of the foliage of this attractive and useful evergreen shrub. The twenty to forty tiny flowers are densely crowded onto spikes up to 1 inch (25 mm) long. The leaves are small, up to ½ inch (12 mm) long, and their soft, white, hairy covering extends also to the twigs supporting them. These leaves assume a grayish-purple tinge in winter. This species requires an extremely well-drained situation in open, light soil.

Melaleuca incana

Myrtus communis

Murraya paniculata

Myoporum parvifolium

Melaleuca linariifolia 'Snowstorm'

like flowers are borne all along the stems. The rich green of the foliage of this hardy plant is also a feature. The leaves are narrow, fleshy, and thickly produced. Fine, medium-, and broad-leaved as well as purple-stemmed forms are available. Well-drained soil in a sunny position gives the best results.

Myrtus communis
COMMON MYRTLE ○

Family: MYRTACEAE
Origin: Western Asia.
Flowering time: Summer.
Climatic zone: 8, 9, 10.
Dimensions: Up to 15 feet (5 meters) high.
Description: Esteemed since classical times as a symbol of love and peace, myrtle is often traditionally included in the bride's bouquet, from which cuttings are grown, to be kept as carefully tended plants throughout life. This dense, leafy, evergreen shrub has leaves that are glossy, spicily aromatic, elliptic to lance-shaped, and nearly 2 inches (50 mm) long. The four petals of the solitary flowers spread wide to ¾ inch (18 mm) across, to display a profusion of long stamens. The fruit is ½ inch (12 mm) long and ripens to bluish-black. Although fairly hardy, it grows best against a sunny, sheltered wall. In cooler climates, myrtle should be kept in a greenhouse in winter.
Varieties/cultivars: 'Flore Pleno', 'Microphylla', 'Tarentina', 'Variegata'.

flowers several times a year. The leaves are a bright, shining green, with three to nine leaflets, each up to 2 inches (50 mm) long, and, because this species belongs to the same family as *Citrus*, they emit a sweet smell when handled. This shrub requires lots of water and a humus-rich soil.

Myoporum parvifolium
CREEPING MYOPORUM ○

Family: MYOPORACEAE
Origin: Eastern Australia.
Flowering time: Spring.
Climatic zone: 9, 10.
Dimensions: Up to 10 inches (250 mm) high.
Description: This prostrate, evergreen shrub makes an excellent mat-forming plant, spreading readily to 3 feet (1 meter) and sending down roots as its trailing stems proceed. Tiny, white, star-

Melaleuca linariifolia 'Snowstorm'
SNOW-IN-SUMMER ○

Family: MYRTACEAE
Origin: Cultivar.
Flowering time: Late spring–summer.
Climatic zone: 9, 10.
Dimensions: Up to 5 feet (approx. 2 meters) high.
Description: This is a registered dwarf form of the well-known evergreen tree species. As its cultivated name indicates, at flowering time the display of flowers covers the plant so profusely that the fine, narrow leaves are not visible. The flower head is a slender spike containing thirty to forty-five flowers massed along its 2½-inch (60-mm) length. The light perfume is reminiscent of honey. The bark is thick, spongy, white, and papery, and the 1 inch (25 mm) long, leaves contain sweet-smelling oil glands. This shrub will thrive even in exposed positions in seaside gardens.

Murraya paniculata syn. *M. exotica*
MOCK ORANGE, ORANGE JESSAMINE ◑

Family: RUTACEAE
Origin: South East Asia.
Flowering time: Spring and intermittently.
Climatic zone: 9, 10.
Dimensions: Up to 10 feet (3 meters) high.
Description: This evergreen, ornamental shrub is highly esteemed in gardens or containers in the tropics and subtropics. The blooms, deliciously scented, open to a trumpet shape, about 1 inch (25 mm) across, in clusters of ten to twenty. The decorative oval fruit ripens to a bright red. The plant often

216

Nandina domestica

Olearia x haastii

Nandina domestica
SACRED BAMBOO, HEAVENLY BAMBOO

Family: BERBERIDACEAE
Origin: India-eastern Asia.
Flowering time: Spring.
Climatic zone: 7, 8, 9.
Dimensions: Up to 8 feet (approx. 2 meters) high.
Description: Somewhat like a bamboo in appearance, this evergreen shrub is grown in gardens and tubs for its ornamental qualities. Much of its beauty lies in the delicate tracery of the fine leaflets on leaves which can be up to 1½ feet (450 mm) long and which may assume brilliant shades of red to purple in autumn. The flowers, while not showy, are produced in terminal, pyramidal clusters, 12 inches (300 mm) long. The fruits, considered by some to be the most attractive feature of the plant, ripen to a handsome, rich red. It prefers a sheltered position away from cold winds and may be damaged by severe winters. Plant in humus-rich, neutral to acid soil.
Varieties/cultivars: 'Nana Compacta'.

Olearia x haastii
NEW ZEALAND DAISYBUSH

Family: COMPOSITAE
Origin: Hybrid.
Flowering time: Late summer.
Climatic zone: 7, 8, 9.
Dimensions: Up to 10 feet (3 meters) high.
Description: A wild hybrid between two New Zealand species, this shrub is one of the hardiest and, at the same time, the most floriferous and popular of the daisybushes. It is a many-branching, rounded shrub with small, crowded, oblong to egg-shaped leaves which are glossy green with white-felted undersides. The individual flower heads, about ⅓ inch (8 mm) across with yellow centers, are in flattish, long-stalked clusters up to 3½ inches (85 mm) in diameter. Ideally suited for hedges and thriving in seaside gardens, this shrub will withstand some frost. Well-drained but moist soil in a reasonably sunny position is required.

Osmanthus delavayi
DELAVAY OSMANTHUS

Family: OLEACEAE
Origin: Western China.
Flowering time: Spring.
Climatic zone: 7, 8, 9.
Dimensions: Up to 8 feet (approx. 2 meters) high.
Description: Introduced into Europe by Abbé Delavay as recently as 1890, this shrub is one of China's gems. It is a beautiful, fairly slow-growing, evergreen shrub densely covered with small, lustrous green, ovate leaves about 1 inch (25 mm) long. The freely produced tubular flowers are fragrant and jasmine-like, arising in small clusters from the leaf axils. The berry-like fruits, about ½ inch (12 mm) long, ripen in summer to a bluish-black. Although reasonably hardy, the shrub likes protection from the fiercest sun, and does not survive severe winters. Humus-rich, well-drained soil in a sheltered site is preferred.

Osmanthus delavayi

Osmanthus fragrans

Osmanthus fragrans
SWEET OSMANTHUS, FRAGRANT TEA OLIVE, SWEET OLIVE

Family: OLEACEAE
Origin: Himalayas-China.
Flowering time: Summer.
Climatic zone: 8, 9.
Dimensions: Up to 25 feet (8 meters) high.
Description: This evergreen shrub is grown for the beautiful, rich fragrance of its bell-shaped flowers. In its native lands, it has been cultivated for many centuries as an ornamental. Its dried flowers make a scented tea and, it is said, are used to keep clothes insect-free. It can be found in the garden in mild climates and in greenhouses in colder regions. The leaves are oval or oblong, up to 4 inches (100 mm) long, and finely toothed on the margins. A dense shrub, it can be trained as an espalier or small tree, or clipped as a hedge. Semishade and rich, acid soil suit it best.

Philadelphus x virginalis

Philadelphus mexicanus

wide (25 mm) flowers, with their many golden-yellow anthers standing out against the white of the petals, and with their sweet fragrance, are this deciduous shrub's main attraction. They are produced on short stalks in terminal clusters of from three to five flowers. The leaves are up to 3 inches (75 mm) long. Any well-drained garden soil in a sunny position will ensure a rewarding display of flowers.
Varieties/cultivars: 'Avalanche', 'Boule d'Argent', 'Innocence', 'Manteau d'Hermine'.

Philadelphus x virginalis
VIRGINAL MOCK
ORANGE

Family: SAXIFRAGACEAE
Origin: Hybrid.
Flowering time: Spring.
Climatic zone: 5, 6, 7, 8, 9.
Dimensions: Up to 10 feet (3 meters) high.
Description: This deciduous hybrid shrub is understandably popular, producing displays of double or semidouble blooms of superb quality. The flowers are generally large, up to 2 inches (50 mm) in diameter, and occur in abundance in clusters of five to seven on the many erect shoots. The rich fragrance of the flowers, which is likened to orange blossom, makes them an excellent inclusion in bridal bouquets. The leaves are up to 3 inches (75 mm) long with a coarsely toothed margin. Well-drained soil and a sunny position are preferred.
Varieties/cultivars: 'Virginal'.

---

spring floral display. The sweetly perfumed flowers measure about 1½ inches (35 mm) across and occur singly or in clusters of three on small shoots from the upper branches. The softly textured leaves are up to 2½ inches (60 mm) across and somewhat furry, as are the new stems. Requiring little in the way of cultivation, these shrubs respond to pruning immediately after flowering.

Philadelphus coronarius
COMMON MOCK
ORANGE, SWEET MOCK
ORANGE

Family: SAXIFRAGACEAE
Origin: Europe, southwestern Asia.
Flowering time: Early summer.
Climatic zone: 4, 5, 6, 7, 8, 9.
Dimensions: Up to 10 feet (3 meters) high.
Description: A deciduous shrub, sweet mock orange gives a splendid display of spring blossom. These very fragrant flowers, each about 1½ inches (35 mm) across, open wide to display four distinct, rounded petals and appear in five-to-seven-flowered heads at the ends of the many erect stems. The narrow leaves measure up to 3 inches (75 mm) long, have toothed margins, and change from a dark green to dull yellow in autumn. This very commonly cultivated species is particularly suited to dry soils.
Varieties/cultivars: 'Aureus', 'Variegatus'.

Philadelphus mexicanus
MEXICAN MOCK
ORANGE

Family: SAXIFRAGACEAE
Origin: Southern Mexico, Guatemala.
Flowering time: Late spring.
Climatic zone: 9, 10.
Dimensions: Up to 6 feet (2 meters) high.
Description: Mexican mock orange is an evergreen shrub whose numerous slender branches arise from the base and arch outwards to form a loose, rounded shape. It is included in gardens for its

Philadelphus coronarius

Philadelphus x lemoinei
LEMOINE MOCK
ORANGE

Family: SAXIFRAGACEAE
Origin: Hybrid.
Flowering time: Late spring.
Climatic zone: 5, 6, 7, 8, 9.
Dimensions: Up to 6 feet (2 meters) high.
Description: This is one of an array of hybrids bred during the nineteenth century by Victor Lemoine in France. Its parents are *P. coronarius* and *P. microphyllus*. The profusion of 1-inch-

Philadelphus x lemoinei

Pieris formosa

HIMALAYAN ANDROMEDA, LILY-OF-THE-VALLEY SHRUB

Family: ERICACEAE
Origin: Himalayas.
Flowering time: Spring–early summer.
Climatic zone: 7, 8, 9.
Dimensions: Up to 10 feet (3 meters) high.
Description: Attractive throughout the year, this is a magnificent evergreen shrub whose large leaves are leathery and a lustrous green, with a fine-toothed margin. When new, they are attractive, copper-tinted. The flowers, resembling lily-of-the-valley flowers, are clustered together into large panicles which hang from the terminal shoots. The presentation of attractive flowers and foliage in a compact form makes this a highly decorative shrub. However, some consider it is surpassed by the cultivar 'Forrestii', whose young growth is brilliant red. A rich, lime-free soil and a cool, moist, sheltered position are essential for best results. This shrub may be damaged by prolonged, frosty winters.
Varieties/cultivars: 'Forrestii'.

Pieris japonica 'Bert Chandler'

Physocarpus opulifolius

COMMON NINEBARK

Family: ROSACEAE
Origin: Eastern North America.
Flowering time: Spring.
Climatic zone: 3, 4, 5, 6, 7, 8, 9.
Dimensions: Up to 10 feet (3 meters) high.
Description: The name common ninebark refers to the shedding and peeling bark seen on all species of *Physocarpus*. These deciduous shrubs are closely related to spiraeas although they are less showy in bloom. They thrive in almost any open position, are hardy, vigorous, and remarkably free from pests and diseases. The small flowers, which are sometimes tinged with pink, form profuse clusters, nearly 2 inches (50 mm) wide, along the many arching stems. The leaves are three-lobed and about 3 inches (75 mm) long. Moderately fertile, well-drained soil in a sunny or partially shaded position will ensure best results.
Varieties/cultivars: 'Intermedius', 'Luteus'.

Physocarpus opulifolius

Pieris japonica

JAPANESE PIERIS, JAPANESE PEARL FLOWER, JAPANESE ANDROMEDA

Family: ERICACEAE
Origin: Japan.
Flowering time: Spring.
Climatic zone: 5, 6, 7, 8, 9.
Dimensions: Up to 10 feet (3 meters) high.
Description: Somewhat hardier than *P. formosa*, this is another very attractive evergreen shrub which, under favorable conditions, can reach a height of 30 feet (9 meters) but mostly does not exceed shrub dimensions. Its narrow leaves, up to 4 inches (100 mm) long, with a coppery tinge when young, mature to a dark, lustrous green. The pitcher-shaped flowers, individually up to ¼ inch (6 mm) long, are displayed in drooping racemes which measure about 6 inches (150 mm) long. The buds for these sprays appear in autumn. Plant in neutral to acid, peaty soil and provide shelter from cold winds.
Other colors: Pink.
Varieties/cultivars: 'Bert Chandler', 'Pygmaea', 'Variegata', 'Daisen', 'Christmas Cheer'.

Pieris formosa

Prunus glandulosa 'Alba Plena'

DOUBLE WHITE DWARF FLOWERING ALMOND, CHINESE BUSH CHERRY

Family: ROSACEAE
Origin: Cultivar.
Flowering time: Spring.
Climatic zone: 4, 5, 6, 7, 8, 9.
Dimensions: Up to 4 feet (over 1 meter) tall.
Description: Double white dwarf flowering almond, with its many slender, erect shoots, forms a neat, bushy shrub. It is grown for its spring display of large double flowers which are produced in such profusion that they bend the stems with their weight. Sprays of blossom are often cut for house decoration. The leaves, opening after the flowers, are up to 4 inches (100 mm) long and provide good autumn color. This shrub requires a warm sheltered position and can be pruned hard after flowering.

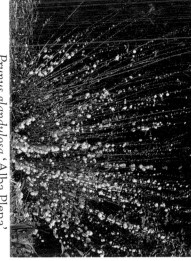

Prunus glandulosa 'Alba Plena'

Plumbago auriculata 'Alba'

Plumbago auriculata 'Alba' syn.
P. capensis 'Alba'
**PLUMBAGO, CAPE
PLUMBAGO LEADWORT**

Family: PLUMBAGINACEAE
Origin: Cultivar.
Flowering time: Summer, autumn.
Climatic zone: 9, 10.
Dimensions: Up to 10 feet (3 meters) tall.
Description: This is the white-flowering cultivar of the blue-flowering species. It is an upright, straggling, and partly climbing, evergreen shrub which responds well to pruning and is most effective against a wall or as a hedge. The flowers appear almost continually in warm, sunny conditions. They are in rounded clusters with five spreading petals at the top of a slender tube. Viscous glands at the base of the flowers make them very sticky to the touch. The 4-inch-long (100 mm) leaves are dull green. Well-drained soil and a partially shady or sunny site suit this warm-climate plant. It spreads rapidly from suckers.

Pyracantha coccinea
**SCARLET FIRETHORN,
COMMON FIRETHORN (U.K.)**

Family: ROSACEAE
Origin: Southern Europe–western Himalayas.
Flowering time: Spring–early summer.
Climatic zone: 6, 7, 8, 9.
Dimensions: Up to 15 feet (5 meters) high.
Description: The rich red fruits, formed in dense clusters in autumn and winter, and the thorny branches, have given

Pyracantha coccinea

the name "scarlet firethorn" to this shrub. The creamy-white flowers, looking like those of a hawthorn but smaller, appear in profusion, and are followed by the fruits, each about ⅓ inch (8 mm) wide. The evergreen leaves, which are about 1½ inches (37 mm) long, are narrow and oval with finely-toothed margins. This is an excellent shrub to grow in fertile, moist, well-drained soil.
Varieties/cultivars: 'Lalandei'.

Sambucus nigra

Sambucus nigra
ELDER, EUROPEAN ELDER

Family: CAPRIFOLIACEAE
Origin: Europe, western Asia, North Africa.
Flowering time: Summer.
Climatic zone: 5, 6, 7, 8, 9.
Dimensions: 10–30 feet (3–9 meters) high.

Description: European elder has been cultivated over a long period in history. It is a familiar large, deciduous shrub and is sometimes seen as a smallish tree with a rugged, fissured bark. It has attractive leaves with from five to seven leaflets, each up to 4 inches (100 mm) long. In autumn the leaves may change from their summer mid-green to bright yellow or dull purple. The flowers appear as flattened heads, up to 7 inches (175 mm) across, of masses of sweetly fragrant blooms. The fruits are glossy black and, with the flowers, are used in country wine-making. Moisture-retentive but well-drained soil creates ideal growing conditions.
Varieties/cultivars: 'Albovariegata', 'Aurea', 'Lanciniata', 'Purpurea'.

Serissa foetida
SERISSA

Family: RUBIACEAE
Origin: South East Asia.
Flowering time: Autumn.
Climatic zone: 9, 10.
Dimensions: Up to 3 feet (1 meter) high.
Description: Outdoors, in frost-free regions, this useful shrub is seen in shrubberies, rock gardens, and borders, commonly growing broader than it does tall. The attractive, small flowers, pink in bud, solitary or in small clusters, open to ½ inch (12 mm) across with petals that are hairy on the insides. In warm situations, serissa flowers for most of the year. The leaves are elliptic, up to 1 inch (25 mm) long, and dark green, with an unpleasant odor when crushed. In cooler climates they make good container plants in greenhouses where they grow well with minimum care.
Varieties/cultivars: 'Variegata'.

Serissa foetida

Skimmia japonica 'Fragrans'

Skimmia japonica
JAPANESE SKIMMIA ○ ◐

Family: RUTACEAE
Origin: Japan.
Flowering time: Spring.
Climatic zone: 7, 8, 9.
Dimensions: Up to 5 feet (approx. 2 meters) high.
Description: Among the most satisfactory broadleaf evergreens for shady areas, this shrub is also excellent for industrial or city areas and seaside gardens. Skimmias are slow-growing and compact, spreading wider than they are tall. The four-petaled, fragrant, white flowers appear in large panicles above the foliage. They are also grown for their decorative red fruits, about ¼ inch (6 mm) in diameter, which follow the flowers and last on the plants throughout winter. There are male and female flowers on different plants. Fruits are only produced if both sexes are planted together, one male to three females. Humus-rich soil is preferred.
Varieties/cultivars: 'Foremanii', 'Fragrans', 'Rubella', 'Rogersii'.

Skimmia reevesiana
SKIMMIA ●

Family: RUTACEAE
Origin: China, Taiwan, Philippines.
Flowering time: Late spring.
Climatic zone: 7, 8, 9.
Dimensions: Up to 2 feet (600 mm) high.
Description: This dwarf shrub forms a low, compact mound. It is slow-growing and because it withstands polluted air better than most evergreens, it is excellent for city gardens. It is also good planted beneath trees as it thrives in shade. The leaves are elliptic, up to 4 inches (130 mm) long, and dark green. The fragrant flowers are bisexual (unlike those of Japanese skimmia), small, about ½ inch (12 mm) wide, and are borne in a dense head up to 3 inches (75 mm) long. They are followed by oval, matte, crimson-red fruits which remain on the plant all winter.
Varieties/cultivars: 'Variegata'.

Skimmia reevesiana

Spiraea cantoniensis 'Flore Fleno'
MAY, REEVES SPIRAEA ○

Family: ROSACEAE
Origin: Southeastern China
Flowering time: Spring.
Climatic zone: 7, 8, 9.
Dimensions: Up to 5 feet (approx. 2 meters) high.
Description: The generic name comes from the Greek *speira* meaning a wreath, which appropriately describes this shrub when it is in full flower with its branches garlanded with clusters of blooms. These clusters, up to 2 inches (50 mm) wide, are rounded and contain twenty to twenty-five diminutive flowers. They grow in such profusion along the length of the arching stems that the stems can be bent to the ground. The narrow leaves, up to 2½ inches (60 mm) long, are dark green with irregularly toothed margins. Pruning, immediately after flowering, is essential.
Varieties/cultivars: 'Lanceata'.

Spiraea cantoniensis 'Flore Pleno'

Spiraea prunifolia syn. S. p. 'Plena'
BRIDAL-WREATH ○

Family: ROSACEAE
Origin: Japan.
Flowering time: Spring.
Climatic zone: 4, 5, 6, 7, 8, 9.
Dimensions: Up to 6 feet (2 meters) high.
Description: This popular plant is only known in cultivation and was first introduced into Europe from Japan in about 1845. It is a dense shrub with many slender, arching branches and grows almost as broad as it does high. The flowers are double and almost ½ inch (12 mm) across. They are borne in tight, button-like, stalkless clusters along the branches. The young shoots are slightly hairy, and the elliptic leaves, which open after the flowers, are up to 2 inches (50 mm) long. Autumn interest is provided by the orange and red foliage. Prune after flowering.

Spiraea prunifolia

Spiraea thunbergii

Spiraea thunbergii
THUNBERG SPIRAEA

Family: ROSACEAE
Origin: China.
Flowering time: Spring–summer.
Climatic zone: 5, 6, 7, 8, 9.
Dimensions: Up to 6 feet (2 meters) high.
Description: Generally the earliest of the spiraeas to bloom, its pure white flowers often smother the arching branches of this graceful, deciduous shrub. It has a dense twiggy habit, often broader than it is tall, with slender downy stems. The leaves, which are narrow and shiny, about 1 inch (25 mm) long with a toothed margin, turn in autumn to shades of orange and scarlet. The flowers occur in numerous, but small, stalkless clusters of two to five flowers. Late frosts are a hazard to the early flowers of this popular shrub. Remove dead flower heads and stems if unsightly.

Spiraea x arguta
BRIDAL WREATH (U.K.), GARLAND SPIRAEA

Family: ROSACEAE
Origin: Hybrid.
Flowering time: Late spring.
Climatic zone: 4, 5, 6, 7, 8, 9.
Dimensions: Up to 6 feet (2 meters) high.
Description: One of the most effective and free-flowering of the spiraeas, bridal wreath is a hybrid of S. thunbergii and S. multiflora. It is a dense-growing, deciduous shrub with graceful, slender branches and, in habit, resembles S. thunbergii. However, its leaves are broader and it blooms later in spring so that its flowers are not so subject to damage by late frosts. To maintain a

Spiraea x arguta

tidy appearance, prune this shrub hard immediately after flowering. Alternatively, if large flowers are desired, remove dead flower heads and stems only if unsightly. Otherwise, it is very easy and rewarding to grow.

Spiraea x vanhouttei
VANHOUTTE SPIRAEA

Family: ROSACEAE
Origin: Hybrid.
Flowering time: Summer.
Climatic zone: 4, 5, 6, 7, 8, 9.
Dimensions: Up to 8 feet (approx. 2 meters) high.
Description: A hybrid from S. cantoniensis and S. trilobata, this deciduous shrub, slender and vigorous with beautifully arching branches, is one of the most commonly cultivated spiraeas. The leaves are coarsely toothed, up to 1½ inches (35 mm) long, sometimes with three to five lobes, and blue-green in color. They show off the great numbers of many-flowered clusters of blooms which smother the stems. This showy shrub may also produce good autumn color in the leaves and makes an excellent hedge. Prune after flowering by removing dead stems and flower heads.

Styrax americanus

Styrax americanus
SNOWBELL

Family: STYRACACEAE
Origin: Southeastern United States.
Flowering time: Early summer.
Climatic zone: 6, 7, 8, 9.
Dimensions: Up to 9 feet (3 meters) high.
Description: Not the easiest of plants to grow, this deciduous shrub, with its refined and graceful habit, combines well with other trees and shrubs in a mixed border. The leaves on the ascending branches are narrow, bright green, minutely toothed, and up to 3½ inches (85 mm) long. Its flowers are bell-shaped, up to ½ inch (12 mm) long, and hang by hairy stalks, either solitary or in clusters of up to four. Egg-shaped fruits about ⅓ inch (8 mm) long follow. A sandy, porous soil enriched with compost will ensure the best results. Protect from strong, cold winds. This shrub may be damaged by severe winters.

Symphoricarpos albus 'Laevigatus'
SNOWBERRY, WAXBERRY

Family: CAPRIFOLIACEAE
Origin: Cultivar.
Flowering time: Summer–autumn.

Spiraea x vanhouttei

Symphoricarpos albus 'Laevigatus'

Climatic zone: 3, 4, 5, 6, 7, 8, 9.
Dimensions: Up to 4 feet (approx. 1 meter) high.
Description: Having clusters of small, bell-shaped flowers, this deciduous shrub is mainly grown for its abundant display of fruits which appear in late summer and autumn and are retained for a long period. The fruits are round, white berries about ½ inch (12 mm) in diameter and are prized by floral arrangers for winter decoration. The shrubs, with slender, erect, downy shoots, form dense thickets of upright stems. The leaves are about 1 inch (25 mm) long. Snowberries will grow in shade, and in city and seaside environments.

Syringa vulgaris 'Madame Lemoine'
LILAC

Family: OLEACEAE
Origin: Cultivar.
Flowering time: Early summer.
Climatic zone: 4, 5, 6, 7, 8, 9.
Dimensions: Up to 15 feet (5 meters) high.
Description: This horticultural cultivar of the common lilac is grown, as are all lilacs, for its deliciously perfumed flowers. These cover the plant in great panicles, up to 8 inches (200 mm) long, of multiple blooms. The flowers are creamy-yellow in bud, opening to pure white. The leaves are heart-shaped and up to 5 inches (125 mm) long. Grow in fertile, moist soil.

Syringa vulgaris 'Madame Lemoine'

Teucrium chamaedrys
WALL GERMANDER

Family: LABIATAE
Origin: Central and southern Europe-southwestern Asia.
Flowering time: Late summer.
Climatic zone: 6, 7, 8, 9.
Dimensions: Up to 12 inches (300 mm) high.
Description: A small, erect shrub, well suited to a sunny border, *T. chamaedrys* has toothed, glossy, deep-green leaves and tiny, tubular flowers which are pale to deep rosy-purple and appear in terminal whorls. Plant in well-drained soil in a sunny position.

Teucrium chamaedrys

Vaccinium corymbosum
SWAMP BLUEBERRY, HIGHBUSH BLUEBERRY

Family: ERICACEAE
Origin: Eastern North America.
Flowering time: Early summer-mid summer.
Climatic zone: 3, 4, 5, 6, 7, 8, 9.
Dimensions: Up to 12 feet (4 meters) high.
Description: While showy autumn leaves and attractive berries are notable features of this deciduous shrub, the flowers, in clusters of small, urn-shaped blooms, are also attractive. When they open, the leaves are half-grown. The leaves are bright green and when mature are about 3 inches (75 mm) long. With autumn, they turn brilliant shades of bronze and scarlet. The comparatively large berries, about ⅓ inch (8 mm) in diameter, are black with a "blue" bloom and are sweet and edible. Larger fruits are produced on commercial cultivars. For best results, plant in a moist, acid, peaty soil.
Varieties/cultivars: 'Early Blue', 'Grover', 'Jersey', 'Pemberton.'

Vaccinium corymbosum

Viburnum japonicum

parallel veins. The flowers are produced in somewhat rounded clusters up to 2 inches (50 mm) wide, and retain a blush of pink after opening from pink buds. Hardy, this plant prefers a fertile, well-drained, sunny position.
Varieties/cultivars: 'Candidissimum', 'Nanum'.

Viburnum japonicum
JAPANESE VIBURNUM

Family: CAPRIFOLIACEAE
Origin: Japan.
Flowering time: Spring.
Climatic zone: 8, 9.
Dimensions: Up to 25 feet (8 meters) high.
Description: Sometimes seen as a small tree, this handsome evergreen shrub has glossy, leathery, dark-green leaves up to 6 inches (150 mm) long. The paler undersides are spotted and the leaf margins near the tips may be toothed. On mature plants, the small, fragrant flowers are borne in dense, rounded clusters. Small numbers of red fruits are produced and are particularly sparse on young specimens. Japanese viburnum has conspicuous, warty young shoots and relatively flat flower clusters. Plant in a sunny position in well-drained soil. It may be killed or damaged by severe winters and needs a sheltered site.

Viburnum macrocephalum 'Sterile'
CHINESE SNOWBALL

Family: CAPRIFOLIACEAE
Origin: Cultivar.
Flowering time: Late spring.
Climatic zone: 6, 7, 8, 9.

Viburnum dentatum

surfaces. In autumn they may become shining red. Produced in long-stemmed clusters measuring about 3 inches (75 mm) in diameter, the flowers are small with long, protruding stamens. The egg-shaped fruits are blue-black. A sunny position and well-drained soil are preferred.

Viburnum farreri syn. *V. fragrans*
FRAGRANT VIBURNUM

Family: CAPRIFOLIACEAE
Origin: Northern China.
Flowering time: Winter.
Climatic zone: 6, 7, 8.
Dimensions: Up to 10 feet (3 meters) high.
Description: With its very fragrant flowers opening well in advance of its foliage, this shrub is a most valuable, deciduous, winter-flowering plant. The leaves are up to 4 inches (100 mm) long, elliptic, and toothed, with conspicuous,

Viburnum farreri 'Candidissimum'

Viburnum carlesii

Viburnum carlesii
KOREAN VIBURNUM

Family: CAPRIFOLIACEAE
Origin: Korea.
Flowering time: Spring.
Climatic zone: 4, 5, 6, 7, 8, 9.
Dimensions: Up to 5 feet (approx. 2 meters) high.
Description: Since W. R. Charles, a British diplomat, discovered this deciduous plant in Korea, it has become one of the most popular of shrubs. It is a rounded bush whose leaves, downy on both sides, look dull until autumn comes, when they turn shades of yellow and red. The buds are pink and red. The flowers exquisitely fragrant. Supported by a rose-pink tube, the petals are pure white on the inside. The flower heads, produced in profusion, are hemispherical, about 3 inches (75 mm) across, and appear with the new leaves. A hardy plant, it prefers fertile, well-drained soil.

Viburnum dentatum
ARROWWOOD

Family: CAPRIFOLIACEAE
Origin: Eastern United States.
Flowering time: Late spring.
Climatic zone: 2, 3, 4, 5, 6, 7, 8, 9.
Dimensions: Up to 15 feet (5 meters) high.
Description: The common name of this deciduous shrub refers to the strong, straight basal shoots which the American Indians are said to have used for making arrows. The leaves are oval, up to 3 inches (75 mm) long, and coarsely toothed, with hairs on both

Viburnum macrocephalum 'Sterile'

Dimensions: Up to 12 feet (4 meters) high.
Description: Chinese snowball is a semi-evergreen shrub which will lose all its leaves in a severe winter. Its leaves are finely toothed, up to 4 inches (100 mm) long, and furry on both surfaces. The flowers give a spectacular display of open-faced, sterile blooms in large, globular heads up to 6 inches (150 mm) across, reminiscent of the sterile forms of *Hydrangea macrophylla*. There is some doubt as to whether the wild form, with fertile flowers, is still in cultivation. This cultivar thrives in a sunny, well-drained location.

Viburnum odoratissimum
SWEET VIBURNUM ○
Family: CAPRIFOLOACEAE
Origin: China.
Flowering time: Summer.
Climatic zone: 6, 7, 8, 9, 10.
Dimensions: Up to 13 feet (4 meters) high.
Description: This viburnum is a delightful, fragrant, deciduous tree which appears quite ordinary until in flower when it is covered with dense, terminal clusters of small, white flowers. Plant in an open, sunny position in medium to light, well-drained soil, and mulch around the base well with

organic matter to keep the ground cool in summer. This viburnum cannot withstand very dry summers or extremely cold winters, and should be positioned with some thought to protection from strong winds.

Viburnum odoratissimum

Description: This is the finest of the snowball bushes and rates very highly among the hardy ornamental shrubs. It is deciduous, with wide-spreading, arching branches. Its leaves, egg-shaped and toothed on the margins, are up to 4 inches (100 mm) long and hairy on their undersides. They color in the autumn. The conspicuous, sterile flowers are arranged in globular heads measuring up to 3 inches (75 mm) across. They are produced in a double row along the length of each stem of the previous year's growth and persist for several weeks. Make this a feature plant as it is hardy and prefers a reasonably sunny, well-drained site.
Varieties/cultivars: *V. p.* var. *tomentosum*, *V. p. t.* 'Lanarth', *V. p. t.* 'Mariesii', *V. p. t.* 'Pink Beauty', *V. p. t.* 'Rowallane'.

Viburnum plicatum

Viburnum plicatum syn. *V. tomentosum* 'Plicatum'
JAPANESE SNOWBALL ○ ◑
Family: CAPRIFOLIACEAE
Origin: China, Japan.
Flowering time: Late spring.
Climatic zone: 4, 5, 6, 7, 8, 9.
Dimensions: Up to 10 feet (3 meters) high.

Viburnum plicatum var. *tomentosum* 'Mariesii'

Viburnum plicatum var. *tomentosum* 'Mariesii'
DOUBLEFILE VIBURNUM ○ ◑
Family: CAPRIFOLIACEAE
Origin: Cultivar.
Flowering time: Summer.
Climatic zone: 4, 5, 6, 7, 8, 9.
Dimensions: Up to 8 feet (approx. 2 meters) high.
Description: A cultivar of *V. plicatum* var. *tomentosum*, the original wild species of *Viburnum*, 'Mariesii' has a much stronger tiered habit than its parent and is very free-flowering, making it a most desirable addition to the garden. Plant 'Mariesii' in a well-drained, reasonably sunny position.

SHRUBS

Viburnum rhytidophyllum

wrinkled upper surfaces and the dense felting of yellowish hairs on the undersurfaces. The flowers, which individually measure ¼ inch (6 mm) across, are yellowish-white and are gathered into large, flat clusters up to 8 inches (200 mm) wide. The red, oval fruits become black when mature. Plant in well-drained soil.

Viburnum sieboldii
SIEBOLD VIBURNUM ◐ ◑

Family: CAPRIFOLIACEAE
Origin: Japan.
Flowering time: Early spring.
Climatic zone: 7, 8, 9.
Dimensions: Up to 30 feet (9 meters) high.
Description: One of the most handsome viburnums, this deciduous shrub has a shapely, rounded form. The elliptic leaves are coarsely toothed, up to 6 inches (150 mm) long, with conspicuous veins, and while the upper surfaces are glossy, the undersides are hairy. Numerous small, creamy-white flowers are produced in rounded, open clusters up to 4 inches (100 mm) long. The distinctive oval fruits are pink, maturing to blue-black. The new leaves of spring and fallen leaves of autumn emit an objectionable smell when crushed. Plant in well-drained soil. Propagate from seed when ripe, or by layering in late winter.

Viburnum rhytidophyllum
LEATHERLEAF VIBURNUM ◐ ◑

Family: CAPRIFOLIACEAE
Origin: China.
Flowering time: Late spring–early summer.
Climatic zone: 5, 6, 7, 8, 9.
Dimensions: Up to 15 feet (approx. 5 meters) high.
Description: The hardiest of the evergreen viburnums, this shrub, which becomes as broad as it is tall, is thickly covered with narrow leaves up to 7 inches (175 mm) long. These are distinctive because of their much-

---

Viburnum tinus

Viburnum tinus
LAURUSTINUS ◐ ◑

Family: CAPRIFOLIACEAE
Origin: Southeastern Europe.
Flowering time: Late autumn–early spring.
Climatic zone: 7, 8, 9.
Dimensions: Up to 10 feet (3 meters) high.
Description: This shrub is a most popular evergreen. Its dense, bushy habit, with foliage growing from ground level, makes it an excellent informal hedge. Its glossy, oval, dark-green leaves, up to 4 inches (100 mm) long, thickly cover the stems. This valuable winter-flowering shrub can have its long flowering period extended if there are spells of mild weather. The flowers, each ¼ inch (6 mm) wide, emerge from pink buds in flat clusters about 4 inches (100 mm) across. The plant tolerates light shade and grows well in seaside locations. It may be damaged or killed by severe winters.
Varieties/cultivars: 'Eve Price', 'Variegatum', *V. t.* var. *hirtulum*, *V. t.* var. *lucidum*.

Viburnum x burkwoodii
BURKWOOD VIBURNUM ◐ ◑

Family: CAPRIFOLIACEAE
Origin: Hybrid.
Flowering time: Spring.
Climatic zone: 5, 6, 7, 8, 9.
Dimensions: Up to 6 feet (2 meters) high.
Description: This upright shrub is semi-evergreen to evergreen. It is a more vigorous grower than its parent,

---

Viburnum sieboldii

also hairy, and they and the leaves are strongly aromatic when bruised. The leaves consist of five or seven narrow leaflets up to 4 inches (100 mm) in length. Plant in autumn or spring against a wall in a sunny position. Fertile, well-drained soil is preferred.

Viburnum x carlcephalum

FRAGRANT SNOWBALL

Family: CAPRIFOLIACEAE
Origin: Hybrid.
Flowering time: Spring.
Climatic zone: 5, 5, 7, 8, 9.
Dimensions: Up to 10 feet (3 meters) high.
Description: Fragrant snowball is a splendid, compact, deciduous shrub producing large, rounded flower heads up to 5 inches (125 mm) across. The flowers are very fragrant and open from pink buds. The broad leaves are up to 4 inches (100 mm) long, shiny green on the upper surface and covered with fine hairs on the undersides. After hot summers they color to rich shades of orange and crimson in autumn. A robust grower, plant from autumn to spring in well-drained soil.

Zenobia pulverulenta

Zenobia pulverulenta syn. *Z. speciosa*

ZENOBIA, ANDROMEDA

Family: ERICACEAE
Origin: Southeastern United States.
Flowering time: Early summer.
Climatic zone: 5, 6, 7, 8, 9.
Dimensions: To 6 feet (2 meters) high.
Description: Named after Zenobia, a queen of ancient Syria, this single species of *Zenobia* is a beautiful deciduous or semi-evergreen, small shrub. The narrow leaves, up to 3 inches (75 mm) long, are covered by a conspicuous gray bloom which is more noticeable when they are young. The flowers are fragrant and bell-shaped, resembling a large lily-of-the-valley. About ½ inch (12 mm) long, they appear on whitish stems in drooping clusters. Zenobia requires a lime-free, moist soil and is an excellent companion plant for *Pieris, Leucothoe* and *Rhododendron*.
Varieties/cultivars: *Z. p.* var. *nuda*.

Viburnum x carlcephalum

Viburnum x burkwoodii

V. *carlesii*, from which it inherits its fragrant, pink-budded, white flowers. Rounded, and measuring up to 3 inches (75 mm) across, the beautiful flower heads open after the new leaves. The egg-shaped leaves are slightly toothed, up to 4 inches (100 mm) long, and a shiny, rich green on the upper surface, with grayish-brown felting on the underside. The fruits are red, maturing to black. Hardy, it prefers a well-drained but not dry soil. It is well-suited to training up a wall, where it may grow up to 10 feet (3 meters) high.
Varieties/cultivars: 'Chenaultii', 'Park Farm Hybrid'.

Viburnum x carlcephalum

Vitex agnus-castus 'Alba'

CHASTE TREE

Family: VERBENACEAE
Origin: Cultivar.
Flowering time: Summer.
Climatic zone: 8, 9, 10.
Dimensions: Up to 20 feet (6 meters) high.
Description: Chaste tree is an ornamental, deciduous shrub which can withstand sea winds in warmer regions. The fragrant flowers are small and tubular and grow in spikes up to 7 inches (175 mm) long, clustered at the ends of the erect stems. The shrub's velvety appearance is due to the short gray hairs on the undersurface of the dark-green leaves. The new shoots are

Vitex agnus-castus 'Alba'

Aesculus hippocastanum
COMMON HORSE CHESTNUT

Family: HIPPOCASTANACEAE
Origin: Northern Greece, Albania, Bulgaria.
Flowering time: Late spring–early summer.
Climatic zone: 3, 4, 5, 6, 7, 8, 9.
Dimensions: 60–120 feet (20–36 meters) high.
Description: Horse chestnut is one of the finest of all the deciduous broadleaf trees, with its handsome canopy of huge, radiating leaves, bright green in spring and turning yellow in autumn. Its wonderful spikes of white flowers flecked with red, sit up like candles in spring. In autumn children use the seeds to play the game of "conkers". The leaves create such a dense shade that nothing much will grow beneath the tree. Slow-growing, it is not fussy regarding soil type.
Other colors: Crimson.
Varieties/cultivars: 'Baumannii', A. x carnea 'Briotii'.

Amelanchier arborea

Climatic zone: 4, 5, 6, 7, 8, 9.
Dimensions: 20–35 feet (6–11 meters) high.
Description: Masses of pure white, star-shaped, fragrant flowers hanging in slender, nodding clusters bedeck this pretty tree in spring. Tender young leaves emerging as a delicate pink turn to a rich red color in autumn. In summer, birds love the clusters of sweet edible berries, which start as purplish black and later turn to red. A. laevis forms a more tree-like shape than most amelanchiers and pruning is rarely necessary. Give it extra water during dry spells. Plant it in a lime-free soil in a moist situation.

Amelanchier x lamarkii

tallest-growing of the amelanchiers, A. arborea is similar to the much smaller A. canadensis, but its pure white, star-shaped flowers are larger and hang more loosely. Deciduous, toothed leaves appear in spring from pointed buds. In summer, bunches of edible black berries hang among the foliage. Autumn changes the color of the foliage to subtle reds, oranges, and browns. This tree requires lime-free soil, with plenty of water in dry spells. It is susceptible to rust and fire-blight disease in some areas.

Amelanchier laevis
ALLEGHENY
SERVICEBERRY (U.S.A.),
SHADBLOW (U.S.A.),
SHADBUSH (U.K.)

Family: ROSACEAE
Origin: Eastern North America.
Flowering time: Spring, northern hemisphere.

Amelanchier laevis

Amelanchier x lamarkii
SHADBUSH

Family: ROSACEAE
Origin: Northern Europe.
Flowering time: Spring.
Climatic zone: 4, 5, 6, 7, 8, 9.
Dimensions: Up to 25 feet (8 meters).
Description: A most attractive deciduous tree, often confused with A. canadensis, however distinguished by the new foliage growth which is coppery-red and covered with silken hairs. The small white flowers appear in profusion, making a dramatic, if short-lived, display. It prefers a well drained, slightly acid soil and a sheltered position. Although frost resistant, it cannot withstand long periods without water.

Aesculus hippocastanum

Amelanchier arborea
SHADBLOW (U.S.A.),
SERVICEBERRY,
JUNE-BERRY (U.K.)

Family: ROSACEAE
Origin: Eastern North America.
Flowering time: Spring, northern hemisphere.
Climatic zone: 4, 5, 6, 7, 8, 9.
Dimensions: 30–50 feet (10–17 meters) high.
Description: The most vigorous and

Arbutus menziesii

Description: Every part of this tree is attractive — its almost translucent-petaled flowers which look like lily-of-the-valley, the red, round fruits that follow, and the rich red stringy bark of the trunk and branches. All three delights can be enjoyed in autumn when the tree is covered in fragrant, white flowers, blooming amid the previous year's fruit. Easily grown, this evergreen is perfect for small gardens. Enrich soil with some well-rotted compost or cow manure prior to planting, and ensure that drainage is adequate. It can be damaged by severe winters.
Other colors: Pink.

Climatic zone: 8, 9.
Dimensions: 27-40 feet (8-12 meters) high.
Description: This is one of the hardiest of the bottlebrushes and will grow in both hemispheres. The leaves, soft, downy, and pink when new, turn green at maturity and are aromatic when crushed. The flowers are actually a pale creamy-yellow and bloom in abundance. New shoots emerge from the flowering tips, which may be pruned to encourage bushier growth and longer life. These evergreen bottlebrushes grow in most soils, dry or wet.
Other colors: Pink.

Arbutus menziesii
MADRONE (U.K.), MADRONA, OREGON LAUREL

Family: ERICACEAE
Origin: British Columbia-California.
Flowering time: Spring, northern hemisphere; late winter and spring, southern hemisphere.
Climatic zone: 7, 8, 9.
Dimensions: 25-100 feet (7-30 meters) high.
Description: Often called the Californian version of the strawberry tree, this magnificent tree adds drama and beauty to gardens in many climates. In its native habitat it grows to large proportions, but in gardens it rarely exceeds 30 feet (10 meters). It bears clusters of small, white flowers similar to those of heather, which belongs to the same family. In autumn, handsome, round fruits change color from yellow to orange to red amid rich green leaves. This species can tolerate some lime though it prefers neutral to acid conditions and should be planted in any moderately rich, well-drained soil. Excellent in that it can tolerate hot, dry conditions.

Arbutus unedo
STRAWBERRY TREE

Family: ERICACEAE
Origin: Mediterranean region and southwestern Eire.
Flowering time: Autumn to early winter, northern hemisphere; late autumn, southern hemisphere.
Climatic zone: 7, 8, 9.
Dimensions: 20-25 feet (6-8 meters) high.

Callistemon salignus

Callistemon salignus
WHITE BOTTLEBRUSH, WILLOW BOTTLEBRUSH

Family: MYRTACEAE
Origin: Australia (southern Queensland-Tasmania).
Flowering time: Mid-spring-summer.

Arbutus unedo

Catalpa bignonioides
SOUTHERN CATALPA (U.S.A.), INDIAN BEAN TREE (U.K.)

Family: BIGNONIACEAE
Origin: Southeastern United States.
Flowering time: Spring.
Climatic zone: 5, 6, 7, 8, 9.
Dimensions: 30-40 feet (9-12 meters) high.
Description: Big, bold, and beautiful, southern catalpa is unfortunately not very long-lived. This exotic-looking, rounded tree on a sturdy trunk is much admired for its wonderful clusters of fragrant, white flowers spotted with yellow, and its huge, heart-shaped leaves. Its rapid growth makes it a most desirable tree for new gardens. Because it needs a lot of space, it is best planted in large gardens. It will tolerate wet and dry conditions and withstand frost. Its leaves, though attractive, have an unpleasant smell.
Varieties/cultivars: 'Aurea' (yellow-tinted foliage).

Catalpa bignonioides

✿

Description: *Chionanthus* is derived from Greek words meaning snowflower. Pure white, fragrant flowers in loosely branched clusters grow at the end of branches produced from the previous year's growth. Later, dark-blue fruits ripen on the female trees. The fringe tree, with its single trunk and spreading canopy, makes an ideal shade tree. In autumn, the leaves turn yellow and often remain on the tree, especially in milder areas. Rather slow-growing — 8 feet or so (about 2 meters) in 20 years — it likes rich, moist soils on a wind-sheltered site, in a cool, humid climate.

Chionanthus virginicus

○

tree, often shrub-like, is covered with white, fine-petaled flowers during summer. It is an ideal choice for the cool, temperate garden because of its size and its tolerance of a wide range of soils. Chinese fringe tree prefers a sunny aspect with protection from the wind.

Chionanthus virginicus
**OLD-MAN'S-BEARD,
FRINGE TREE (U.K.)**

Family: OLEACEAE
Origin: Gulf and lower Atlantic states of United States.
Flowering time: Late spring.
Climatic zone: 5, 6, 7, 8, 9.
Dimensions: 10–30 feet (3–9 meters) high.

Citharexylum spinosum
FIDDLEWOOD

Family: VERBENACEAE
Origin: West Indies, Central America.
Flowering time: Mid-summer–mid-winter.
Climatic zone: 9, 10.
Dimensions: 16–40 feet (5–12 meters) high.
Description: *C. spinosum* is conspicuous

Citharexylum spinosum

Cedrela sinensis

○

Cedrela sinensis syn. *Toona sinensis*
**CHINESE CEDAR,
CHINESE TOON**

Family: MELIACEAE
Origin: Northern and western China.
Flowering time: Summer, northern hemisphere.
Climatic zone: 6, 7, 8, 9.
Dimensions: 20–70 feet (6–21 meters) high.
Description: Given the right conditions, this deciduous tree is perfect for the larger garden. A fast-grower, it will, if carefully pruned, develop a single trunk and rounded canopy. Its huge leaves, made up of numerous leaflets, are pinkish, onion-flavored, and edible when young, turning to green in summer and yellow in autumn. Flowers hang in 12-inch (300-mm) long clusters. It needs hot summers, complete protection from winds, and excellent drainage, and is found in such diverse places as wilderness areas in Victoria, Australia, and the streets of Paris.

Chionanthus retusus
CHINESE FRINGE TREE

○

Family: OLEACEAE
Origin: China.
Flowering time: Summer.
Climatic zone: 6, 7, 8, 9.
Dimensions: 10–20 feet (3–6 meters) high.
Description: This superb deciduous

Chionanthus retusus

Clethra arborea
LILY-OF-THE-VALLEY TREE

Family: CLETHRACEAE
Origin: Madeira.
Flowering time: Late spring, southern hemisphere; late summer, northern hemisphere.
Climatic zone: 9, 10.
Dimensions: 10–20 feet (3–6 meters) high.
Description: Would that this delightful, small, evergreen tree could be grown in a wider range of climates. The nodding clusters of flowers resemble those of lily-of-the-valley, hence its name. Its glossy, elliptic leaves, 2–5 inches (50–130 mm) long, are similar to those of the rhododendron but serrated. It enjoys a mild, coastal climate and humus-rich, lime-free soils. If it is growing where autumns are always hot, dry, and long, giving time for the tender wood to harden, it may survive brief, light frosts. It develops into a multi-stemmed tree, unlike other *Clethra* which are shrub-like.
Varieties/cultivars: 'Flore-pleno' (double-flowered form).

among green trees in late winter when its own leaves turn a beautiful shade of apricot before some of them drop. Creamy-colored spikes of deliciously perfumed flowers appear in warm weather. New leaves are a glossy, bright green. Happy in most soils, it needs plenty of mulch and water in hot, dry weather. A fast-grower, it responds well to fertilizer and to pruning, which makes it an ideal plant for hedging. Plant it near the house in large containers so that the perfume, especially at night, can be enjoyed.

Clethra arborea

Cornus capitata
STRAWBERRY TREE, EVERGREEN DOGWOOD, BENTHAM'S CORNEL

Family: CORNACEAE
Origin: Himalayas, western China.
Flowering time: Summer.
Climatic zone: 8, 9.
Dimensions: 20–30 feet (6–10 meters) high.
Description: One of the many beautiful dogwoods, this small, slow-growing, evergreen species is happiest in the mildest of climates. The actual flowers are quite small, but are surrounded by four to six cream-colored bracts which are what really attract the eye. These splendid "flowers" are followed by strawberry-shaped fruits, 1–1½ inches (25–40 mm) wide, which turn from yellow to crimson. The young shoots harden into sprays of dull green, leathery leaves.

Cornus capitata

Cornus florida
FLOWERING DOGWOOD (U.K.), EASTERN DOGWOOD

Family: CORNACEAE
Origin: Eastern United States, south of Massachusetts).
Flowering time: Late spring–early summer, northern hemisphere; late spring, southern hemisphere.
Climatic zone: 5, 6, 7, 8, 9.
Dimensions: 15–30 feet (4–9 meters) high.
Description: *C. florida* is a spectacular sight when in full flower. Petal-like bracts surround the tiny, greenish flowers, which are carried on upturned twigs along horizontal branches. Very often the canopy spreads wider than the height of the tree, the main trunk dividing at an early stage of growth. The flowers are followed in autumn by scarlet fruits and red to purplish leaves. It needs excellent drainage, but will not tolerate drought conditions.
Other colors: Red, pink.
Varieties/cultivars: 'Pleniflora', *C. f.* var. *rubra*.

Cornus florida

foliage in spring, and is followed by numerous clusters of bright red "berries" in autumn. Orangy-red foliage at this time produces what looks like a tree on fire! Its single, short trunk and shapely canopy make it an excellent small shade tree, and its very sharp, slender thorns 2–2½ inches (50–65 mm) long make it a good barrier plant. It prefers cool climates and deep, rich soils.

Crataegus phaenopyrum

Crataegus x lavallei
LAVALLE THORN

Family: ROSACEAE
Origin: Hybrid.
Flowering time: Mid-spring, northern hemisphere; late spring, southern hemisphere.
Climatic zone: 5, 6, 7, 8, 9.
Dimensions: 16–25 feet (5–7 meters) high.
Description: The hardy hawthorns are all reliable for their show of spring flowers and autumn color. C. lavallei is no exception. Pretty, white flowers,

Crataegus x lavallei

Cornus kousa

Cornus kousa
JAPANESE DOGWOOD, KOREAN DOGWOOD

Family: CORNACEAE
Origin: Japan, Korea, China.
Flowering time: Early summer.
Climatic zone: 5, 6, 7, 8, 9.
Dimensions: 16–20 feet (5–6 meters) high.
Description: This small, deciduous tree is mostly grown for its summer display of white, showy bracts. It has a preference for acid soils and summer moisture. Its distinctive strawberry-like fruit in late summer and its bright autumn foliage are added features. Its size makes it suitable for small gardens.
Other colors: Pink.
Varieties/cultivars: 'Chinensis', 'Rubra'.

Crataegus crus-galli

Crataegus crus-galli
COCKSPUR THORN, COCKSPUR HAWTHORN

Family: ROSACEAE
Origin: Northeastern United States and adjacent Canada.
Flowering time: Spring.
Climatic zone: 5, 6, 7, 8, 9.
Dimensions: 13–30 feet (4–9 meters) high.
Description: Cockspur thorn lights up each spring as small clusters of tiny rose-like flowers decorate this attractive, deciduous tree. The orange to scarlet foliage provides a foil for the crimson berries in autumn. It develops a small trunk which branches low down. Formidable, sharp thorns (up to 4 inches (100 mm) in length) cover the

branches, making it an ideal barrier plant, although it will not stand much clipping. It grows best in cool climates in limy soils, and tolerates drought and pollution. In disease-prone areas, check for fireblight regularly.

Crataegus phaenopyrum
WASHINGTON THORN

Family: ROSACEAE
Origin: Southeastern United States.
Flowering time: Spring, northern hemisphere; late spring–early summer, southern hemisphere.
Climatic zone: 5, 6, 7, 8, 9.
Dimensions: 20–30 feet (6–9 meters) high.
Description: Often described as the best of the hawthorns, C. phaenopyrum is deciduous and easy to grow. Profuse, pear-like blossom sits well clear of the

Davidia involucrata

marked with a red disk, produce brick-red fruits in autumn which hang on into winter. Autumn leaf coloration varies from reddish-brown to purplish-red. Sparse, stout, dark-red thorns 2 inches (50 mm) in length on the branches make it a suitable small barrier tree, or it can be grown as a small shade tree if the lower branches are cut away from the trunk to form a partial standard. Deciduous, though in mild climatic conditions only a percentage of the foliage falls in winter.

Davidia involucrata
HANDKERCHIEF TREE, ○ ◐
DOVE TREE

Family: DAVIDIACEAE
Origin: Southwestern China.
Flowering time: Late spring–early summer.
Climatic zone: 6, 7, 8, 9.
Dimensions: 40–50 feet (12–15 meters) high.
Description: This deciduous tree is named after the nineteenth-century plant collector and missionary, Abbé Armand David. The common name refers to the conspicuous white bracts which flutter in the breeze like handkerchiefs waving. The floral display, which begins just as the tree's foliage opens, lasts for several weeks. The tree is welcome in the garden because it tolerates a wide range of climates.

Dombeya tiliacea
NATAL CHERRY, ○
WEDDING FLOWER

Family: BYTTNERIACEAE
Origin: South Africa (frost-free areas of Eastern Cape, Natal, Transvaal).
Flowering time: Autumn–winter,

233

northern hemisphere; autumn–spring, southern hemisphere.
Climatic zone: 9, 10.
Dimensions: 13–25 feet (4–7 meters) high.
Description: Like all dombeyas, this is a small tree for tropical to subtropical areas only. In autumn it becomes weighed down by what look like huge clusters of cherry blossom. These perfumed flowers later fade to a pale brown, becoming papery and persistent. Although the tree is evergreen, some of the dark-green leaves turn yellow or red in autumn. The mature tree is slim, with a rounded crown. Grow it in fertile, well-drained soils, in a warm wind-sheltered position.
Other colors: Rose-pink.
Varieties/cultivars: 'Dregiana'.

Eucalyptus citriodora
LEMON-SCENTED GUM ○

Family: MYRTACEAE
Origin: Australia (tropical Queensland).
Flowering time: Winter, southern hemisphere.
Climatic zone: 9, 10.
Dimensions: 35–65 feet (10–20 meters) high.
Description: Tall, slender, and graceful describes this popular, ornamental, evergreen eucalypt. Its elevated canopy makes this tree a marvellous feature in parks and gardens when planted in small groups. Its smooth, pale gray-pink

Dombeya tiliacea

to white bark is then really appreciated. The flowers are pretty, and its rough leaves give off a strong lemon scent when the breeze blows or when they are crushed. Grow it in well-drained sites, but give it water in dry spells. Do not spoil its shape by lopping. In cold climates it is often grown as a greenhouse pot plant for its scented foliage.

Eucalyptus citriodora

TREES

Franklinia alatamaha

Eucryphia lucida

Eucalyptus scoparia

Eugenia smithii syn. *Acmena smithii*

Fraxinus ornus

Eugenia smithii

crown in abundance. Not easy to cultivate unless conditions are just right, it enjoys cool, moist conditions. It will not endure harsh, drying winds or frosty winters. *Lucida*, Latin for bright and shiny, refers to the glossy leaves.

Eucalyptus scoparia
WALLANGARRA WHITE GUM, WILLOW GUM
Family: MYRTACEAE
Origin: Australia (N.S.W. and Queensland border).
Flowering time: Late spring–summer, southern hemisphere.
Climatic zone: 9, 10.
Dimensions: 30–40 feet (10–12 meters) high.
Description: One of the loveliest eucalypts, willow gum is grown widely in hot climates as an evergreen, ornamental, shade, or screen tree. Graceful, willowy leaves cover the slender canopy. It has attractive white flowers, and the smooth bark is a wonderful, subtle medley of white and creamy-yellow, often daubed with areas of blue and pink which intensify in color when wet. Plant it in coarse, well-drained soils, giving plenty of water in dry weather.

Eucryphia lucida
LEATHERWOOD
Family: EUCRYPHIACEAE
Origin: Australia (Tasmania).
Flowering time: Summer, northern hemisphere; late summer–early autumn, southern hemisphere.
Climatic zone: 8, 9.
Dimensions: 10–30 feet (3–9 meters) high.
Description: Native to rainforest areas of Tasmania, this slender evergreen tree is popular with bees. Leatherwood honey has a very distinctive, strong, and pungent flavor. The beautiful, delicate-looking, fragrant flowers with numerous stamens have been likened to small, single camellias, and cover the

Eugenia smithii syn. *Acmena smithii*
LILLY PILLY
Family: MYRTACEAE
Origin: East coast of Australia (Cape Howe to Cape York).
Flowering time: Late spring–summer, southern hemisphere.
Climatic zone: 9, 10.
Dimensions: 25–30 feet (7–10 meters) high.
Description: If you live in a warm climate, this evergreen tree will certainly enhance your garden. Everything comes in abundance; indeed, the Greek word *acmena* means buxom. Glossy green leaves, numerous fluffy flowers, followed by clusters of white to purplish, edible fruits keep this plant looking good all year. Prune it to form a hedge or screening plant, or allow it to grow as a tree, pruning to a single trunk. It likes well-drained soils, and plenty of water in hot, dry weather.

Franklinia alatamaha
FRANKLIN TREE
Family: THEACEAE
Origin: Georgia, United States.
Flowering time: Late summer–autumn.
Climatic zone: 6, 7, 8, 9, 10.
Dimensions: Up to 30 feet (9 meters) high.
Description: This tree, discovered close to the mouth of the Alatamaha River in 1765, was named in honor of Benjamin Franklin. It has not been seen in the wild since 1803, so all known specimens are the result of the original collection of seeds. This history makes it an interesting tree, but it is also highly ornamental. Given a hot continental summer, the 3-inch (75-mm) wide, open, cup-shaped flowers with their conspicuous yellow stamens are produced in profusion. In autumn, the large, lustrous, green leaves, 6 inches (150 mm) long, turn crimson before they fall. It requires an acid soil and cannot tolerate cold winters.

Fraxinus ornus
MANNA ASH (U.K.), FLOWERING ASH
Family: OLEACEAE
Origin: Southern Europe–Turkey.
Flowering time: Late spring–early summer.

Climatic zone: 5, 6, 7.
Dimensions: 20–65 feet (6–20 meters) high.
Description: Manna ash is grown in southern Italy and Sicily for its sap which hardens to a sugary substance called manna and is used medicinally. The tree is readily distinguished from other ashes by the showy clusters of fragrant flowers opening in late spring just after the new leaves have appeared. In its native habitat it is found growing in mixed woods, thickets, and rocky places, so the ideal place for this deciduous tree is in similar positions in large gardens for a natural effect.

Gordonia axillaris
GORDONIA, FALSE CAMELLIA

Family: THEACEAE
Origin: Taiwan, southern China, Vietnam.
Flowering time: Late autumn–early winter.
Climatic zone: 8, 9, 10.
Dimensions: 30 feet (10 meters) high.
Description: Gordonia, a close relative of the camellia, is an evergreen tree which is slow to establish. It is noted for its showy, solitary, white flowers, with their prominent stamens. The flowering cycle can last from two to three months, the fallen blooms producing a showy carpet beneath the tree. Gordonias respond equally well to full sun or dappled shade, but tolerate nothing more than light frosts — severe winters can kill them. Its soil requirements are similar to those of camellias — a light, well-drained, acid soil enriched with well-rotted compost to encourage rapid growth. The two can be grown successfully together.

Gordonia axillaris

235

Hakea laurina
PINCUSHION HAKEA, SEA URCHIN

Family: PROTEACEAE
Origin: Western Australia.
Flowering time: Autumn–winter, southern hemisphere.
Climatic zone: 9, 10.
Dimensions: 10–20 feet (3–5 meters) high.
Description: Its curious and beautiful flowers are the main attraction of this pretty hakea. The globular flower clusters, with their protruding, creamy-colored styles, look like round pincushions when fully opened. Sprays, attached to branches, make good cut flowers in autumn and winter. Give this evergreen tree a sunny, well-drained position in a dry atmosphere similar to that of its native home in Western Australia and its adopted home in California. It grows fairly quickly into a small, low-branching tree. Prune it lightly after flowering.

Hakea laurina

Hakea salicifolia syn. *H. saligna*
WILLOW-LEAVED HAKEA

Family: PROTEACEAE
Origin: Australia (coastal N.S.W. and Queensland).
Flowering time: Spring–early summer, southern hemisphere.
Climatic zone: 9, 10.
Dimensions: 10–20 feet (3–6 meters) high.
Description: Unlike most hakeas, which need well-drained soils, the willow-leaved hakea will grow in wetter conditions, often being found in good soils near permanent, running streams in its native habitat. It will tolerate some frost and is most useful in the home garden as a quick-growing, evergreen, screen plant. It has attractive, white flowers borne in showy, dense clusters. Tip-prune it regularly to keep the screen or hedge dense, but do wait until the flowers have finished. Hakeas form decorative, woody fruits after flowering, so you have to decide whether to keep these or prune the plant.
Varieties/cultivars: 'Fine Leaf'.

Hakea salicifolia

Liriodendron tulipifera
TULIP TREE, WHITEWOOD, ○
YELLOW POPLAR

Family: MAGNOLIACEAE
Origin: Southeastern United States.
Flowering time: Early summer.
Climatic zone: 4, 5, 6, 7, 8, 9.
Dimensions: 50–200 feet (15–60 meters) high.
Description: This magnificent tree,

Halesia carolina

Halesia carolina syn. *H. tetraptera*
SILVER-BELL TREE, ○
SNOWDROP TREE (U.K.), ◑
CAROLINA SILVERBELL

Family: STYRACACEAE
Origin: Southeastern United States.
Flowering time: Spring.
Climatic zone: 5, 6, 7, 8, 9.
Dimensions: 10–30 feet (3–9 meters) high.
Description: Halesias enjoy similar conditions to rhododendrons and azaleas — moist, rich, well-drained, lime-free soil. Requiring filtered sun and protection from strong winds, these plants would revel in a light, woodland setting. Easily grown, they are hardy in cold winter areas. Train them to a single stem whilst young or the plants will become too bushy. You have plenty of time for they grow slowly — about 12 feet (4.5 meters) in 15 years. In late spring, an excellent display of pendulous clusters of white, bell-shaped flowers appear just before the new leaves begin to open. The leaves turn yellow in autumn.

Description: Native to the North Island of New Zealand, the Latin name *Hoheria* is derived from the Maori name "houhere". *H. glabrata* has pale green, oval leaves with serrated margins, and fragrant white trumpet-shaped flowers occurring in terminal clusters. Grows best in organically rich, well-drained soil and is frost resistant, but drought tender. Useful as a screen or background plant, it can be propagated either by seed or from cuttings.

Liriodendron tulipifera

Hoheria glabrata

Hoheria glabrata
HOUHERIA ○ ◑ ●

Family: MALVACEAE
Origin: New Zealand (North Island).
Flowering time: Summer (northern hemisphere); late summer (southern hemisphere).
Climatic zone: 8, 9.
Dimensions: Up to 30 feet (9 meters) high.

236

which grows huge and fast on a straight trunk, can be grown in the very large garden. The handsome leaves differ markedly from any other broadleaf, looking rather like a maple leaf with the middle lobe cut off. One cultivar develops leaves that are almost rectangular. The flowers resemble tulips. Carried on the branchlet tips, these are greenish-yellow with a band of orange, and often only appear when the tree is twenty to twenty-five years old. Tulip tree prefers deep, crumbly soils and a cool, wet spring season. Deciduous, with yellow leaves in autumn, it withstands pollution.
Varieties/cultivars: 'Fastigiatum' (narrow tree, for limited space), 'Aureo-marginatum' (variegated foliage).

Magnolia grandiflora
BULL BAY MAGNOLIA
(U.K.), SOUTHERN MAGNOLIA
(U.S.A.)

Family: MAGNOLIACEAE
Origin: Florida–Texas, North Carolina, United States.
Flowering time: Mid-summer.
Climatic zone: 7, 8, 9, 10.
Dimensions: 80 feet (25 meters) high.
Description: This is a slow-growing, broad-domed, evergreen tree, with dark, glossy green leaves and spectacular, solitary, bowl-shaped white flowers. Its size, longevity, and grandeur make it very suitable for use in large-scale landscapes, such as parklands, avenues, and malls. It prefers a well-drained, sandy loam which is slightly acid. Summer moisture is essential, and frost protection is necessary when the tree is young. Prune to shape the tree and raise the crown in its early years.
Varieties/cultivars: Several cultivars are available.

Magnolia grandiflora

237

Malus baccata hybrids and cultivars
SIBERIAN CRAB APPLE ○

Family: ROSACEAE
Origin: Eastern Asia.
Flowering time: Mid-late spring.
Climatic zone: 2, 3, 4, 5, 6, 7, 8, 9.
Dimensions: 15–40 feet (5–12 meters) high.
Description: Any plant that can grow in Siberia is tough. Siberian crab apple is a beautiful tree, smothered in fragrant, white blossom in spring, and later by yellow to red fruits which remain after the leaves have dropped. It has been used by breeders since the end of the eighteenth century to yield a fair number of hybrids and cultivars. A most successful cultivar, 'Marchuria', is the first of all the crab apples to flower. The species plant is resistant to apple scab and is long-lived. It does best in cool, moist climates, and is deciduous.
Varieties/cultivars: There are many cultivars available.

Malus 'Golden Hornet'
ORNAMENTAL CRAB
APPLE ○

Family: ROSACEAE
Origin: Cultivar.
Flowering time: Mid-spring.
Climatic zone: 4, 5, 6, 7, 8, 9.
Dimensions: 13–25 feet (4–7 meters) high.
Description: Ornamental crab apple has white to palest pink flowers in spring, followed by delightful yellow fruits (¾ inch (20 mm) across) which hang on the tree into winter. Heavy crops weigh down its slender branches, creating a graceful, weeping appearance. Delicious jelly can be made from the apples. Like all other crabs, they are best pruned only when young, in this

Malus 'John Downie'

Malus baccata 'Jackii'

case to a single trunk. Thereafter flowering and fruiting are better if the tree is left undisturbed. This deciduous tree does best in cool, moist climates and good soils.

Malus 'John Downie'
ORNAMENTAL CRAB
APPLE ○

Family: ROSACEAE
Origin: Cultivar.
Flowering time: Spring.
Climatic zone: 4, 5, 6, 7, 8, 9.
Dimensions: 13–20 feet (4–6 meters) high.
Description: This crab apple is grown for its luscious fruit, which are good for eating straight off the tree or for making jam. The white flowers in spring are followed by a generous crop of bright orange and red fruits in autumn, which, if not picked, remain through the winter. Do not crowd this pretty deciduous tree among other trees. It prefers a cool, moist climate and good soils.

Malus 'Golden Hornet'

evergreen, it is best grown from seed or semihardwood cuttings in large home gardens as a background plant. **Varieties/cultivars:** 'McMahon's Golden'.

Michelia doltsopa
MICHELIA, WONG-LAN

Family: MAGNOLIACEAE
Origin: Eastern Himalayas–western China.
Flowering time: Winter–spring.
Climatic zone: 8, 9, 10.
Dimensions: 20–40 feet (6–12 meters) high.
Description: This neat, pyramid-shaped tree, with its rich green leaves is popular in many home gardens. The large, showy white flowers are fragrant and measure 4 inches (100 mm) across, with 12–16 narrow petals. Plant it as an individual in a lawn or use it as a

Michelia doltsopa

background tree. Do not plant it too near the house, because perfume from the flowers, although pleasant at first, can become rather overpowering. Fast-growing and easy to grow in mild climates, it likes a rich, well-drained soil. Sow this evergreen from seed in spring.

Oxydendrum arboreum
SOURWOOD, SORREL TREE (U.K.)

Family: ERICACEAE
Origin: Southeastern United States.
Flowering time: Mid-summer–late summer.

Melaleuca linariifolia

Melaleuca linariifolia
FLAXLEAF PAPERBARK, SNOW IN SUMMER

Family: MYRTACEAE
Origin: Australia (Queensland and N.S.W.).
Flowering time: Late spring, northern hemisphere; late spring–summer, southern hemisphere.
Climatic zone: 9, 10.
Dimensions: 16–30 feet (5–9 meters) high.
Description: A hot climate tree, snow in summer certainly lives up to its name when a cloudburst of white flowers envelops it all at once. The flowers, though otherwise similar to the bottlebrush, differ in that the stamens are joined together in groups. Birds find the honey attractive. Often developing several trunks, it is a good foil tree, and its flaky bark makes it team well with shrubby plants. It will grow in any soil, and has needle-like, evergreen leaves.

Melaleuca quinquenervia
BROAD-LEAVED PAPERBARK, PAPERBARK (U.K.), CAJEPUT TREE, SWAMP TEA TREE

Family: MYRTACEAE
Origin: Australia (east coast from Cape York to Shoalhaven).
Flowering time: Spring–late summer and intermittently.

Melaleuca quinquenervia

Climatic zone: 9, 10.
Dimensions: 27–75 feet (8–23 meters) high.
Description: So good is this tree at adaptation, it is planted worldwide for many purposes. It will grow in dry or wet ground, and in some countries it is used to stabilize swampy ground. Unfortunately, it has become too successful in Florida, where it threatens to overtake the Everglades. Its fluffy, cream flowers are similar to those of the bottlebrush, except that the stamens of *Melaleuca* are united in bundles. White, flaky bark contrasts with the dark-green leaves, with their five parallel veins. An

Oxydendrum arboreum

Climatic zone: 5, 6, 7, 8, 9.
Dimensions: 20–50 feet (6–15 meters) high.
Description: Sourwood is worth growing for its brilliant coloring in autumn, when its leaves turn a fiery red before they fall. Slender heads of fragrant flowers droop from the tips of shoots in summer, attracting birds and bees to their honeyed nectar. Belonging to the same family as rhododendrons, it enjoys similar conditions — moist, acid soil with other trees nearby, in a light glade, for example. It can be grown from seed, cuttings, or layers, but is slow-growing and dislikes polluted air.

Photinia x fraseri 'Robusta'

Family: ROSACEAE
Origin: Hybrid.
Flowering time: Spring–early summer, southern hemisphere; late spring–summer, northern hemisphere.
Climatic zone: 5, 6, 7, 8, 9.
Dimensions: 20–50 feet (6–15 meters) high.
Description: [text continues]

Photinia x fraseri 'Robusta'
RED-LEAF PHOTINIA ○

Climatic zone: 4, 5, 6, 7, 8.
Dimensions: 13–16 feet (4–5 meters) high.
Description: This handsome, evergreen shrub has white, bitter-smelling flowers which fade to brown. Carried in clusters 5–6 inches (120–150 mm) across, they appear above the upper leaves. Fleshy, green fruits follow, ripening to red in autumn. It has showy foliage — the new leaves are a shiny, coppery-red, which mature to a deep green; older leaves turn crimson in autumn before they fall. Tolerant of regular clipping which induces plenty of new growth, photinias are often used as hedging plants, or as a background foil.
Varieties/cultivars: 'Red Robin', 'Americanum'.

Prunus cerasifera and cultivars
CHERRY PLUM,
MYROBALAN CHERRY ○

Family: ROSACEAE
Origin: Southeastern Europe–central Asia.
Flowering time: Late winter–early spring.
Climatic zone: 4, 5, 6, 7, 8, 9.
Dimensions: 15–30 feet (5–9 meters) high.
Description: Flowering cherry plums really are a study in themselves, with so many beautiful varieties and cultivars bred from the species. One of the more notable ones is 'Pissardii', first noticed in the Shah of Persia's garden by the French gardener Pissardt. Its flowers are

---

Plumeria rubra

Plumeria rubra syn. *P. acutifolia*
FRANGIPANI,
GRAVEYARD TREE (Asia) ○

Family: APOCYNACEAE
Origin: Central America, Mexico, Venezuela.
Flowering time: Summer–autumn, northern and southern hemispheres; most of year in tropical areas.
Climatic zone: 9, 10.
Dimensions: 10–27 feet (3–8 meters) high.
Description: You can often smell this wonderful tree before you see it, so pervasive is its perfume. Glorious flowers, carried on stubby branches, cover the tree when in bloom. It can be grown successfully only in warmer gardens in full sun, protected from the wind.

Cuttings taken from hardened stem tips about 4–6 inches (100–150 mm) long are planted in early spring. The stems contain a milky sap. Deciduous, it is often planted as a street tree in tropical countries.

Prunus cerasifera

white to blush-pink and the foliage is purple. A further development from America produced 'Pissardii Thundercloud', with pink flowers and deep, smoky, purplish-red foliage. Others are listed below. All are deciduous, easy to grow, and do best in full sun. Their dark-colored foliage can be used, sparingly, for contrast in the garden.
Varieties/cultivars: 'Festeri' and 'Nigra' (single pale pink), 'Vesuvius' (white to blush-pink), 'Elvins', 'Rosea' (salmon-pink flowers, bronze-green foliage).

Prunus lusitanica

Prunus cerasifera 'Elvins'
CHERRY PLUM

Family: ROSACEAE
Origin: Cultivar.
Flowering time: Spring.
Climatic zone: 4, 5, 6, 7, 8, 9.
Dimensions: 10–13 feet (3–4 meters) high.
Description: 'Elvins', developed in Victoria in about 1940, is a small tree that can enhance many small gardens in cool to temperate climates. Each spring it appears as a froth of pure white flowers which, though enchanting, have a very brief life. This deciduous tree has a mass of slender shoots spreading out from a short trunk. Plant it with other blossom trees for an outstanding spring show.

Prunus dulcis

topped tree, or a formal or informal hedge or screen. Evergreen and elegant all year with glossy green foliage, there comes a bonus in spring as slender, long heads of cream, fragrant flowers appear, followed in summer by red berries that turn purplish-black. It withstands poor, chalky soils, and looks most effective in large gardens lining a driveway or screening off unattractive areas.
Varieties/cultivars: 'Variegata', 'Myrtifolia'.

backdrop of large evergreens which also provide protection.
Varieties/cultivars: *P. d.* var. *praecox*, 'Macrocarpa' (large, very pale pink to white flowers), 'Roseoplena' (double pale pink flowers).

Prunus lusitanica
PORTUGAL LAUREL

Family: ROSACEAE
Origin: Spain, Portugal.
Flowering time: Early summer.
Climatic zone: 7, 8, 9.
Dimensions: 13–40 feet (4–12 meters) high.
Description: Suitable for clipping, Portugal laurel makes an elegant round-

Prunus cerasifera 'Elvins'

Prunus dulcis syn. *P. amygdalus*
ALMOND, COMMON ALMOND

Family: ROSACEAE
Origin: Western Asia.
Flowering time: Late winter–early spring.
Climatic zone: 7, 8, 9.
Dimensions: 20–30 feet (6–9 meters) high.
Description: Almonds, which are among the very first trees to blossom, are followed soon after by the peach trees. Plant them together for an extended blooming period. The species almond is a spreading, deciduous tree, extensively grown in Sicily for commercial purposes. It grows well in a dryish climate in well-drained soils. It has been crossed with *P. persica* to produce the cultivar 'Pollardii'. Often flowering in late winter, it needs protection from inclement weather. The almond looks wonderful against a

Prunus mume 'Alba Plena'
JAPANESE APRICOT (U.K.)

Family: ROSACEAE
Origin: Cultivar.
Flowering time: Early spring.
Climatic zone: 7, 8, 9, 10.
Dimensions: 10–27 feet (3–8 meters) high.
Description: Japanese apricot flowers at

Prunus mume 'Alba Plena'

Dimensions: 3–10 feet (1–3 meters) high.
Description: Graceful at any time, this little tree is a most glorious sight in spring when it is smothered in cascades of hanging flowers. The pink buds open to a single white flower. Plant white spring in a lawn or at a focal point in the garden where it is shown at its best. Deciduous, its leaves color attractively in autumn. It likes a cool climate.

Prunus subhirtella 'Alba'
WHITE SPRING, WEEPING SPRING CHERRY
Family: ROSACEAE
Origin: Cultivar
Flowering time: Spring.
Climatic zone: 6, 7, 8, 9.

the same time as many of the almonds, but needs more protection from the elements. If planted in a cold-climate garden, place it against the warmest-facing wall. The pure white, semidouble flowers decorating this deciduous tree each winter are at their best after a summer of good sunshine. Cool, moist soil conditions are preferred, however a rich and well-drained soil that is watered consistently should produce good flowering results.

Prunus serrulata hybrids and cultivars
JAPANESE FLOWERING CHERRY

white flowers pink-tinged in bud), 'Shirofugen', 'Purpurea' (white flowers, rich purple foliage), 'Kiku-shidare Sakura' (double, clear, deep-pink flowers), 'Tai Haku', 'Fugenzo', 'Autumn Glory' (pale blush flowers), 'Ojochin', 'Ichiyo'.

Family: ROSACEAE
Origin: Japan, China, Korea.
Flowering time: Mid–late spring.
Climatic zone: 6, 7, 8, 9.
Dimensions: 13–27 feet (4–8 meters) high.
Description: The many cultivars bred from this species are mostly wide, flat-topped, small trees. Most of them flower in mid-spring, producing extremely beautiful clusters of flowers hanging from long stalks. The shiny trunks are often marked by horizontal scars and the leaves color yellow through red in autumn. Give these wide-spreading, deciduous cultivars plenty of space for best effect. They need a moist, elevated site.
Varieties/cultivars: 'Shirotae' (Mt. Fuji), 'Snow Goose' (masses of pure white flowers), 'Shimidsu Sakura' (large, double

Prunus subhirtella 'Alba'

241

Prunus serrulata 'Mt. Fuji'

Prunus 'Ukon'

Prunus 'Ukon' syn. *P. serrulata luteovirens*
JAPANESE FLOWERING CHERRY (U.K.), GREEN JAPANESE FLOWERING CHERRY
Family: ROSACEAE
Origin: Japan.
Flowering time: Mid-spring.
Climatic zone: 6, 7, 8, 9.
Dimensions: 15–30 feet (5–9 meters) high.
Description: The most unusual coloring of the flowers sets this Japanese flowering cherry apart from the others. In mid-spring the flower buds appear lime-green in color, opening to reveal pale greenish-yellow to white petals, with a hint of rose along the central rib. When leaves appear, they are a pale bronze-green which soon turns to green. Later in autumn they become a rusty-purple color. Like all cherries, this tree is deciduous, needing a moist, elevated, cool site.

Pyrus calleryana

Pyrus ussuriensis

Pyrus salicifolia 'Pendula'

Pyrus calleryana
CALLERY PEAR, CHINESE ◯
WILD PEAR, BRADFORD PEAR
(U.K.)

Family: ROSACEAE
Origin: Central and southeastern China.
Flowering time: Spring.
Climatic zone: 6, 7, 8, 9.
Dimensions: 25–30 feet (7–9 meters) high.
Description: Trouble-free and unfussy, this species grows in the wilds of China as a medium-sized, deciduous tree. Pyramidal in outline, it forms a dense, much-branched canopy and lives to a great age. Frothy sprays of attractive white flowers appear each spring, followed by small, brown fruits on slender stalks. The leaves are glossy green, turning to red in autumn. Callery pear needs full sun and occasional pruning to thin out dense, thorny branches. It tolerates lime soils and thrives even when neglected.
Varieties/cultivars: 'Bradford', 'Chanticleer'.

Pyrus salicifolia 'Pendula'
WILLOW-LEAVED PEAR ◯
(U.K.), WEEPING SILVER PEAR

Family: ROSACEAE
Origin: Cultivar.
Flowering time: Early spring.
Climatic zone: 5, 6, 7, 8, 9.
Dimensions: 15–20 feet (5–6 meters) high.
Description: Many pears grow rather too large and unruly for the average garden, but this little deciduous tree is perfect for many landscape situations. Tightly packed, small flowers in flat heads appearing in spring are followed by small, brown, inedible fruits. Long, grayish leaves, covered in a silvery down, hanging from slender, drooping branches, make this tree a perfect foil for more somber-colored plants. Planted in a white garden among flowering perennials, it adds a graceful harmony. It revels in full sun in cool-climate gardens, and is not fussy as to soil conditions.

Pyrus ussuriensis
USSURIAN PEAR, ◯
CHINESE PEAR, MANCHURIAN
PEAR

Family: ROSACEAE
Origin: Northeastern China–eastern U.S.S.R., Korea, northern Japan.
Flowering time: Spring.
Climatic zone: 5, 6, 7, 8, 9.

242

Dimensions: 40–50 feet (12–15 meters) high.

Description: Eventually growing to about 50 feet (15 meters) in height, Ussurian pear develops a broad crown on a straight trunk. It is a perfect deciduous tree for a large country garden where informality is the keynote. Flat heads of pretty, white flowers, often tinged pink in the bud, appear in spring and are followed by yellowish, round fruits. These can become a nuisance if they fall on a public footpath. The broad, shiny, green leaves turn reddish in autumn. Like all pears it needs full sun. This species is resistant to fireblight disease.

Robinia pseudoacacia

Robinia pseudoacacia

BLACK LOCUST (U.K.), FALSE ACACIA, COMMON ACACIA

Family: LEGUMINOSAE
Origin: Eastern and central United States.
Flowering time: Early summer, northern hemisphere; mid-late spring, southern hemisphere.
Climatic zone: 3, 4, 5, 6, 7, 8, 9.
Dimensions: 40–65 feet (12–20 meters) high.
Description: Now at home in many countries of both hemispheres, this tree thrives in dry soils, but casts only a light shade from its open canopy. Zig-zag branches carry bright green leaves — and thorns! Its delightful, fragrant, pea-like flowers are borne in clusters, partially hidden by foliage. Fast-growing, it is valued for its durable timber. The leaves arrive late and fall early, providing sun and shade when most needed.
Varieties/cultivars: 'Frisia', 'Inermis'.

Rothmannia globosa syn. *Gardenia globosa*

TREE GARDENIA

Family: RUBIACEAE
Origin: South Africa.
Flowering time: Spring.
Climatic zone: 9, 10.
Dimensions: 9–12 feet (3–4 meters) high.
Description: A close relative of the gardenia, this evergreen tree with its upright stems forms a small multi-branched dome. It is covered with small, bell-shaped, cream flowers in spring, followed by black, round, woody seed capsules which remain on the tree. Rothmannias like only mild climates and survive best in acid soils with summer moisture. They are usually grown for their sweet fragrance.

Rothmannia globosa

243

Salix caprea

GOAT WILLOW, SALLOW, PUSSY WILLOW

Family: SALICACEAE
Origin: Europe-southwestern Asia.
Flowering time: Late winter-mid-spring.
Climatic zone: 5, 6, 7, 8, 9.
Dimensions: 27–33 feet (8–10 meters) high.
Description: Like all willows, goat willow likes water. It is a small, shrubby, deciduous tree, loved for its pretty, furry catkins. Male and female catkins grow on separate trees. Female catkins are silky and silvery. Male catkins are larger, and silky-white, turning to yellow. More graceful and needing less space is the cultivar 'Pendula'. The male tree produces ornamental yellow catkins. 'Pendula' is usually grafted onto the species as a standard trunk about 6½ feet (2 meters) tall. Plant it near water or in boggy ground.
Varieties/cultivars: See description.

Salix caprea

Sophora japonica

○

Sophora japonica
JAPANESE PAGODA TREE, CHINESE SCHOLAR TREE

Family: LEGUMINOSAE
Origin: China, Korea, Japan.
Flowering time: Late summer.
Climatic zone: 5, 6, 7, 8, 9.
Dimensions: 40–70 feet (12–21 meters) high.
Description: Admired for its beautiful foliage, the Japanese pagoda tree has bright leaves and clusters of flowers which later form pods. The leaves of this shapely tree stay fresh-looking into winter. Grow it from seed in well-drained soil and protect the young plants from frost. The cultivar, 'Pendula', is grafted onto a standard *Sophora japonica* and develops drooping, contorted branches. It tolerates pollution.
Varieties/cultivars: See description.

Sorbus alnifolia
KOREAN MOUNTAIN ASH, WHITEBEAM (U.K.)

Family: ROSACEAE
Origin: Eastern Asia.
Flowering time: Late spring.
Climatic zone: 6, 7, 8, 9.
Dimensions: 30–50 feet (9–15 meters) high.
Description: All year round there is something to enjoy on this comely tree. In spring, the abundant, flat-topped heads of white flowers become delightful, tiny, pinkish-orange berries which remain hanging on the tree. In autumn, the broad leaves turn to a beautiful orange-brown, and in winter, the beautiful gray bark is the tree's eye-catching feature. Plant it with other deciduous trees for glorious autumn color, or against dark-green evergreens for dramatic effect. Easily grown from seed, it performs best in cool, elevated sites, and must be given extra water during hot, dry spells.

Sorbus alnifolia

Sorbus aucuparia

only the silvery-white, hairy undersides. The flowers follow, in heavily scented clusters. Bunches of abundant red fruits and russet-colored foliage glow in autumn. It prefers well-drained, lime soils and with its silvery foliage will brighten a dull corner in the garden. It makes a good coastal tree and can withstand pollution. In some areas it is attacked by leaf skeletonizers.
Varieties/cultivars: 'Chrysophylla' (yellow leaves), 'Decaisneana' (large leaves), 'Lutescens', (hairy, gray-green leaves), 'Pendula' (small, weeping tree; leaves small and narrow).

○

Sorbus aucuparia
COMMON MOUNTAIN ASH (U.K.), ROWAN TREE, EUROPEAN MOUNTAIN ASH

Family: ROSACEAE
Origin: Europe, western Asia, North Africa.
Flowering time: Summer.
Climatic zone: 3, 4, 5, 6, 7, 8, 9.
Dimensions: 20–50 feet (6–15 meters) high.
Description: The common mountain ash has ash-like leaves, made up of small leaflets and contrasting with the dramatic display of bright red berries which appear after the large clusters of cream flowers. Thriving on acid soils, but short-lived on chalky soils, it prefers a well-drained site, with plenty of mulch and water in warm, dry spells. It can be susceptible to borer in the U.S.A. In autumn the leaves produce a range of color from yellow through to red, before they fall.
Varieties/cultivars: 'Cardinal Royal', 'Asplenifolia', 'Beissneri', 'Edulis', 'Fastigiata', 'Sheerwater Seedling', 'Xanthocarpa'.

Sorbus aria

○

Sorbus aria
WHITEBEAM (U.K.)

Family: ROSACEAE
Origin: Southern and central Europe, U.K.
Flowering time: Spring.
Climatic zone: 6, 7, 8, 9.
Dimensions: 25–45 feet (8–14 meters) high.
Description: If you first see this tree in spring, you can be forgiven for thinking that it is in flower, for as the leaves open, in an upright position, they show

Sorbus domestica

Sorbus domestica
SERVICE TREE, TRUE SERVICE TREE

Family: ROSACEAE
Origin: Southern and central Europe, North Africa, western Asia.
Flowering time: Late spring.
Climatic zone: 5, 6.
Dimensions: 33–60 feet (10–18 meters) high.
Description: This deciduous tree is distinguished from the rowans by its scaly bark, often used in tanning, and by its more open and wider-spreading branches. The pretty, feathery foliage colors later than that of other service trees and the attractive, rounded or pear-shaped berries turn from green to brown in autumn. Larger than those of the common rowan, they are edible only after a frost and are used in alcoholic beverages. The winter buds of this tree are shiny and sticky. Demanding no special conditions, it is an easy tree to grow.

○

Stewartia pseudocamellia
STEWARTIA

Family: THEACEAE
Origin: Japan.
Flowering time: Summer.
Climatic zone: 7, 8, 9.
Dimensions: Up to 35 feet (12 meters) high.
Description: A spreading deciduous tree that is valued for its foliage, flowers, and attractive flaking bark. The large but delicate, single white flowers resemble camellias and require similar conditions that is, a well-drained, acid soil with plenty of mulch to keep the roots cool, and extra water in warm, dry

◑

Styrax japonica 'Fargesii'

spells. Planted in semishade with azaleas and camellias it will give a fine show of summer flowers for some weeks, long after the azaleas and camellias have finished. Autumn brings more interest as the foliage turns brilliant shades of red and orange.

Styrax japonica
JAPANESE SNOWDROP TREE, JAPANESE SNOW-BELL TREE (U.K.)

Family: STYRACACEAE
Origin: Japan, Korea, China, Taiwan, Philippines.
Flowering time: Late spring-summer.
Climatic zone: 5, 6, 7, 8, 9.
Dimensions: 10–25 feet (3–8 meters) high.
Description: This graceful little tree,

○ ◑

Stewartia pseudocamellia

when in bloom, is profusely covered with snowdrop-like, waxy, fragrant flowers. Plant it on a bank or terrace where you can look up at the flowers. Another delight is the pinkish-orange fissuring appearing between ridges in the trunk. The wide-spreading, horizontal branches carry bright, glossy green leaves through the summer, which turn yellow and red in autumn. A slow-grower, this deciduous tree likes cool gardens and well-drained but moist, lime-free soils.
Varieties/cultivars: 'Fargesii'.

Syzygium jambos

Syzygium jambos
ROSE APPLE, JAMBU, MALABAR PLUM

Family: MYRTACEAE
Origin: Tropical South East Asia, Indonesia, naturalized in West Indies.
Flowering time: Spring-autumn.
Climatic zone: 9, 10.
Dimensions: 30–40 feet (9–12 meters) high.
Description: The glossy green leaves of this evergreen are bright crimson when young, and its showy, fluffy flowers, which bloom for months, are followed by pretty, fragrant, creamy-yellow fruits, tinged with rosy-pink. Insects are attracted to the nectar-bearing flowers, and flavorsome jams and jellies can be made from the fruits. When mature, jambu forms a broad dome on a short trunk, casting a welcome, dense shade. It needs no special attention.

○

YELLOW FLOWERS

Calceolaria x herbeohybrida
SLIPPERWORT

Family: SCROPHULARIACEAE
Origin: Hybrid.
Flowering time: Late spring–midsummer.
Climatic zone: 7, 8, 9.
Dimensions: Up to 18 inches (450 mm) high.
Description: A dramatic, giant-flowering hybrid available in various shades of yellow, orange, and red, spotted and blotched in many combinations. The flowers are borne in terminal trusses, are pouch-shaped, and can reach 2 inches (50 mm) across. In the right conditions this hybrid can be treated as a biennial. Plant in moderately rich, acid soil and ensure that drainage is good. Care must be taken not to overwater as it resents waterlogged root conditions. The best display is achieved by group planting which also suits its preference for slightly crowded root conditions.

Keep the seedlings well-watered during the growing period (10 weeks) and, once they are established, mulch with well-rotted manure to keep weeds down and encourage good flower production. If the seeds are allowed to ripen on the flower and fall, they will germinate the following season.

Coreopsis tinctoria
GOLDEN COREOPSIS,
CALLIOPSIS

Family: COMPOSITAE
Origin: North America.
Flowering time: Summer.
Climatic zone: 6, 7, 8, 9, 10.
Dimensions: Up to 2 feet (600 mm) high.
Description: This self-seeding, very

hardy annual has flat, daisy-like flowers which appear at the tops of the stems. The flowers are up to 2 inches (50 mm) wide, yellow-petaled with a red-brown center, and the foliage is fern-like. Because they are so brightly colored and their stems are so long (up to 18 inches (450 mm)), coreopsis are popular with both florists and home decorators. Easily grown in most soils and conditions, it may require some support when flowering.
Varieties/cultivars: 'Nana' (dwarf), also double-flowered form.

Helianthus annuus
ANNUAL SUNFLOWER,
EVERLASTING, COMMON
SUNFLOWER

Family: COMPOSITAE
Origin: North America, Mexico.
Flowering time: Summer–autumn.
Climatic zone: 6, 7, 8, 9, 10.
Dimensions: Up to 10 feet (3 meters) high.
Description: One of the tallest of the annuals, sunflowers need to be grown in special open, sunny situations to be seen at their best. The bright yellow flowers, which may be 12 inches (300 mm) across, are borne on long, hairy stems, and face the sun. Because of their size, they are seldom used in the home, but are very suitable for large-scale

Calendula officinalis

Coreopsis tinctoria

Calendula officinalis
POT MARIGOLD

Family: COMPOSITAE
Origin: Southern Europe.
Flowering time: Summer–autumn.
Climatic zone: 4, 5, 6, 7, 8, 9.
Dimensions: 1–2 feet (300–600 mm) high.
Description: This hardy and fast-growing annual blooms over many months, bringing a real splash of color to the garden, with its bright and showy, yellow-orange flowers. Sow seeds in early spring, when frosts have finished, in an open position, in moderately rich and well-drained soil.

Calceolaria x herbeohybrida

248

arrangements in foyers and other large spaces in buildings. Both humans and birds love the mature seeds, which are not only nutritious, but also produce a valuable oil. Sunflowers will grow in any soil, but really thrive in ground that has been enriched with plenty of organic matter. Full sun and some protection from strong wind is important.
Other colors: Wine-red.
Varieties/cultivars: 'Purpureus.' Also dwarf forms to 3 feet (1 meter) high.

Helianthus annuus

Hunnemania fumariifolia
MEXICAN TULIP POPPY, GOLDEN CUP

Family: PAPAVERACEAE
Origin: Mexico.
Flowering time: Summer–autumn.
Climatic zone: 4, 5, 6, 7, 8, 9, 10.
Dimensions: Up to 2 feet (600 mm) high.
Description: The foliage of this sun-loving plant is slightly gray and feathery, making a soft background for the bright yellow, cup-shaped flowers. Up to 3 inches (75 mm) wide, these are borne on upright stems about 12 inches (300 mm) long. The petals curve inwards slightly towards the center of the flower. The soil should be moderately rich, but well-drained. It can withstand very dry summers.

Layia platyglossa syn. *L. elegans*
TIDY TIPS

Family: COMPOSITAE
Origin: California.
Flowering time: Summer–autumn.
Climatic zone: 4, 5, 6, 7, 8, 9.
Dimensions: Up to 2 feet (600 mm) high.
Description: This is an attractive garden flower for sunny situations and, although it thrives in dry climates, it does not respond in temperatures continuously over 95°F (35°C). It prefers much cooler weather. The flower stems are up to 12 inches (300 mm) long, and the individual, daisy-like flowers have a clear yellow center, a ring of yellow florets with white tips. Flowers may be up to 2 inches (50 mm) wide. Moist, rich soil and full sun will yield good results.

Helichrysum bracteatum

Helichrysum bracteatum
STRAWFLOWER, EVERLASTING

Family: COMPOSITAE
Origin: Australia.
Flowering time: Summer–autumn.
Climatic zone: 5, 6, 7, 8, 9, 10.
Dimensions: Up to 3 feet (1 meter) high.
Description: This very hardy plant is a short-lived perennial, but is usually grown as an annual. Its long stems, up to 18 inches (450 mm) high, are topped with brightly colored, paper-textured flowers that last many weeks on the plant. They are very useful for floral work, particularly as a dried specimen, when they are truly everlasting. Choose a warm, sunny, and sheltered position, and water regularly for a good flower display.
Varieties/cultivars: 'Monstrosum' (large size flowers).

Hunnemania fumariifolia

Layia platyglossa

Limmanthes douglasii

Nemesia strumosa cultivar

Mentzelia lindleyi

Limmanthes douglasii
MEADOW FOAM, POACHED EGG PLANT

●

Family: LIMNANTHACEAE
Origin: North America.
Flowering time: Late spring–summer; summer–autumn.
Climatic zone: 4, 5, 6, 7, 8, 9.
Dimensions: Up to 12 inches (300 mm) high.
Description: This low-growing plant may be used in rock gardens, or at the front of borders, preferably in moist conditions. It will not tolerate dry heat in summer. The flowers are up to 1 inch (25 mm) wide, have broadly notched petals which are yellow with a broad white tip. These show above a bed of dense fern-like foliage. Rather sensitive to cultivate, meadow foam likes open sun, but cool, moist soil. Sow in autumn or in spring.
Varieties/cultivars: 'Sulphurae'.

Mentzelia lindleyi
BLAZING STAR, BARTONIA (U.K.)

○

Family: LOASACEAE
Origin: California.
Flowering time: Summer–autumn.
Climatic zone: 5, 6, 7, 8, 9.
Dimensions: Up to 2 feet (600 mm) high.
Description: This annual has broadly-cut, toothed leaves. The flowers open flat and are the clearest shiny yellow, with slightly darker stamens. The fragrant, single-stemmed flowers are up to 2½ inches (60 mm) wide. A most versatile plant, it thrives in most soils, preferring full sun in cooler climates and good drainage.

Nemesia strumosa
NEMESIA

○

Family: SCROPHULARIACEAE
Origin: South Africa.
Flowering time: Spring.
Climatic zone: 4, 5, 6, 7, 8, 9.
Dimensions: Up to 12 inches (300 mm) high.
Description: While the individual flowers of nemesia are small (1 inch (25 mm) wide), they are produced in great quantity to give a vivid display of color. They appear on top of leafy stems. Grown closely together, the

plants form a wonderful flowering border. The flowers mature quickly, but do not persist in hot climates (i.e. in temperatures over 85°F (30°C)). They are short-lived when picked and cannot be used in floral decoration. For beautiful blooms add lots of manure or fertilizer to the soil before planting. Choose a sunny position and ensure that drainage is good.

Other colors: Pale blue.
Varieties/cultivars: 'Compacta', 'Carnival', 'Blue Gem'.

Sanvitalia procumbens
CREEPING ZINNIA

Family: COMPOSITAE
Origin: Mexico, Guatemala.
Flowering time: Summer.
Climatic zone: 5, 6, 7, 8, 9, 10.
Dimensions: Up to 6 inches (150 mm) high.
Description: This is a sprawling groundcover or trailing plant which produces clusters of bright, daisy-like flowers in midsummer. Even though the flowers are only 1 inch (25 mm) in diameter, the spreading capacity of the plant and the masses of flowers produced makes it highly suitable for use in hanging baskets in a warm situation. Seeds should be sown directly where the plant is to grow, as creeping zinnia does not transplant well. The soil should be moderately rich with good drainage.

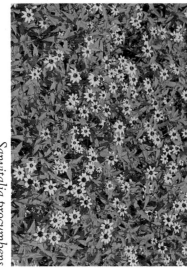

Sanvitalia procumbens

Tagetes erecta
AFRICAN MARIGOLD, AZTEC MARIGOLD, AMERICAN MARIGOLD

Family: COMPOSITAE
Origin: Mexico.
Flowering time: Summer–autumn.
Climatic zone: 4, 5, 6, 7, 8, 9, 10.
Dimensions: Up to 3 feet (1 meter) high.
Description: These tall, attractive, summer-flowering plants are among the most popular in the yellow color range. They are easily grown in average warm conditions. Each plant produces abundant, pompom-like flowers for up to two months. The stems are up to 18 inches (450 mm) long and bear large, densely petaled double flowers up to 6 inches (150 mm) wide. Not very demanding, it grows in any fertile garden soil. Water well during the growing period.
Other colors: Cream, orange, orange-red.
Varieties/cultivars: Many cultivars including 'Jubilee', 'Golden Girl', 'African Queen'.

Tagetes erecta cultivar

Tagetes patula
FRENCH MARIGOLD

Family: COMPOSITAE
Origin: Mexico, Guatemala.
Flowering time: Late summer–autumn.
Climatic zone: 4, 5, 6, 7, 8, 9, 10.
Dimensions: Up to 2 feet (600 mm) high.
Description: While the French marigold likes the sun, it prefers cooler conditions than its so-called African namesake. The plant is bushy and produces many flowers of a smaller size (up to 3 inches (75 mm) wide), which are useful for floral work and home decoration. They are usually yellow to orange with darker reddish marks towards the center, and are borne singly on short stems. Plant in an open, sunny location. Water and feed it regularly in the growing period.
Other colors: Clear orange, clear red.
Varieties/cultivars: 'Honeycomb', 'Gypsy', 'Petite Yellow', 'Petite Orange', 'Queen Sophia', 'Freckle Face', 'Cinnabar', 'Tiger Eyes'.

Tagetes patula cultivar

Tropaeolum majus
NASTURTIUM, INDIAN CRESS

Family: TROPAEOLACEAE
Origin: South America (cool mountain areas).
Flowering time: Summer.
Climatic zone: 4, 5, 6, 7, 8, 9.
Dimensions: Trailing or climbing, to 10 feet (3 meters) long. Dwarf types to 12 inches (300 mm) high.
Description: Nasturtium is a climbing or trailing plant with long stems, which may be supported on a trellis or wire fence or allowed to hang from baskets. It has unusually shaped flowers, 2½ inches (60 mm) wide with five petals opening out and curving slightly backwards. The largest petal lengthens to a spur which bears nectar. The leaves are large, flat, and are edible with a pleasant, sharp flavor. The plant prefers a sheltered position where it may persist for years. It seeds prolifically and the seeds too are edible when soft and green. They are used as a substitute for capers. Moderate to poor soils are preferable — too much fertilizer encourages foliage growth at the expense of the flowers.
Other colors: Orange to ruby-red.
Varieties/cultivars: Dwarf cultivars are 'Jewel', 'Cherry Rose', 'Whirly Bird', 'Alaska', which are all compact and non-trailing. 'Gleam' types are semitrailing and used as groundcover.

Tropaeolum majus cultivar

Calochortus venustus

Calochortus venustus

Crocus chrysanthus and cultivars

Calochortus venustus
MARIPOSA LILY

Family: LILIACEAE
Origin: North America and Mexico.
Flowering time: Early summer, northern hemisphere; summer, southern hemisphere.
Climatic zone: 7, 8, 9.
Dimensions: Up to 18 inches (450 mm) high.
Description: Mariposa lily is an American wildflower with one to three bowl-shaped flowers per stem, with patches of deep red on the stem. The flower color is very variable. The leaves are sparse and grass-like, hence the name *Calochortus*, which is Greek for "beautiful grass". Plant it in rock or native gardens and among pebble paths. It is a good choice for a newly established garden, where the soil is not too rich, but it does not like manure, frosty conditions, or very wet areas. It can be grown in pots on a sunny deck.
Other colors: White, cream, pinkish-purple, red.

Dimensions: Up to 4 inches (100 mm) high.
Description: The native form is yellow. This variable plant has produced many cultivars and is a favorite with alpine and cold climate gardeners. It provides a spectacular display in rock gardens, outdoor pots and indoor pans. Crocus forms clumps and needs little attention. Pre-cooled bulbs should be planted in semishaded areas. In their native element they thrive in enriched soils and sunny or lightly shaded positions. If plenty of water is provided a few bulbs will quickly spread and become a colorful colony in the garden.
Other colors: Blue, gold, cream, white.
Varieties/cultivars: 'Blue Pearl', 'E. A. Bowles', 'Cream Beauty', 'Warley', 'Zwanenburg Bronze'.

Crocus chrysanthus and cultivars
WINTER CROCUS

Family: IRIDACEAE
Origin: Yugoslavia to Turkey.
Flowering time: Late winter to spring.
Climatic zone: 5, 6, 7, 8, 9.

Eranthis hyemalis
WINTER ACONITE ○ ◑

Family: RANUNCULACEAE
Origin: France–Bulgaria.
Flowering time: Spring.
Climatic zone: 3, 4, 5, 6, 7, 8.
Dimensions: 4 inches (100 mm) high.
Description: Related to the buttercup, these hardy plants are best naturalized. Nestling at the base of large trees or around shrubs, they will produce flowers for up to four weeks.
Propagation is by offsets from the tubers or by seed. Both seeds and tubers need to be soaked overnight in warm water. Plant them in generous clusters in compost for a good spring display. Mice may be a problem in some areas.
Varieties/cultivars: *E.* x *tubergenii*.

253

Eucomis comosa syn. *E. punctata*
PINEAPPLE LILY ○

Family: LILIACEAE
Origin: South Africa.
Flowering time: Late summer–autumn.
Climatic zone: 7, 8, 9, 10.
Dimensions: Up to 2½ feet (750 mm) high.
Description: Dozens of flowers mass on the thick stem to form a spike, capped by a pineapple-like tuft of leaves. The name *Eucomis* comes from the Greek for "beautiful topknot". The flowers turn green with age and will bloom for several months. These sun-lovers make beautiful plants for a sheltered border. They also do well in cool greenhouses. Plant in rich, composed soil near a sunny wall protected from the wind.

Eranthis hyemalis

Fritillaria imperialis 'Lutea Maxima'

Fritillaria imperialis
CROWN IMPERIAL ○ ◑

Family: LILIACEAE
Origin: Iran–Kashmir.
Flowering time: Early spring.
Climatic zone: 5, 6, 7, 8, 9.
Dimensions: Up to 3 feet (1 meter) high.
Description: This bulb is noted for its eye-catching flower-head. At the top of an erect stem is a crown of bell-shaped flowers surrounded by a rosette of shiny leaves. *Fritillaria* has a regal form and is happy in full sun or partial shade. It requires rich, well-drained soil. Leave the bulbs undisturbed in the ground.
Varieties/cultivars: 'Lutea Maxima'.

When planted the tops of the bulbs should be well below the soil surface to give frost protection in winter. Water well in summer.
Other colors: Purple, cream.

Eucomis comosa

BULBS

Hypoxis longifolia

has good drainage. Protect from wet winter weather and frosts. Every four years the plants should be lifted and separated.

Iris danfordiae
WINTER IRIS

Family: IRIDACEAE
Origin: Turkey.
Flowering time: Winter–spring.
Climatic zone: 6, 7, 8, 9.
Dimensions: Up to 4 inches (100 mm) high.
Description: The short stems of this iris make it ideal for rock gardens, where the honey-scented, bright yellow blooms will flower for many weeks. Plant the bulbs 4 inches (100 mm) deep in well-drained soil enriched with compost. Although hardy, they need a sunny, protected position and regular fertilizing.

Iris danfordiae

Gladiolus 'Georgette'

which can spread and ruin the corms. They are best planted en masse in garden beds in good sun, protected from wind, and the smaller varieties make splendid pot plants. Gladioli are widely cultivated commercially for the cut flower trade.

Other colors: Red, white, purple, pink, lilac.

Varieties/cultivars: There are many varieties and cultivars available.

Hypoxis longifolia
STAR GRASS

Family: AMARYLLIDACEAE
Origin: South Africa.
Flowering time: Autumn.
Climatic zone: 9, 10.
Dimensions: Up to 12 inches (300 mm) high.
Description: A low-growing, spreading groundcover, *H. longifolia* is distinguished by its long, slender, glossy leaves and brilliant yellow, star-like flowers. The underside of the yellow petals is green. Grown from large tubers, it is a warm climate plant preferring a warm, sunny position in moderately rich, slightly acid soil that

Fritillaria pudica

Fritillaria pudica
YELLOW FRITILLARY, YELLOW BELL

Family: LILIACEAE
Origin: Western North America.
Flowering time: Spring.
Climatic zone: 6, 7, 8, 9.
Dimensions: Up to 9 inches (225 mm) high.
Description: Yellow fritillary is not unlike golden snowdrop. Plant it in open woodland, in rock garden pockets, and along paths and driveways. Providing it has good sunlight, perfect drainage, and very little humus, it will produce abundant offset bulbs, which should be dug up, divided, and replanted every second or third year. The bulbs should be replanted as soon as they are dug up as they can dry out very rapidly. Bunches of these yellow bells make very pretty spring floral arrangements indoors.

Gladiolus hybrids
GLADIOLI

Family: IRIDACEAE
Origin: Hybrid.
Flowering time: Summer.
Climatic zone: 7, 8, 9, 10.
Dimensions: Up to 3 feet (1 meter) high.
Description: There are over 200 species of gladioli which take their name from their sword-like leaves, the Latin *gladius* meaning sword. Miniature to giant varieties are available, with an almost endless range of forms and colors. They require some attention because of their susceptibility to virus and fungal disease

Ixia maculata

AFRICAN CORN LILY ○

Family: IRIDACEAE
Origin: South Africa.
Flowering time: Spring–summer.
Climatic zone: 8, 9.
Dimensions: Up to 18 inches (450 mm) high.

Description: A tender corm, *Ixia maculata* produces brilliant and graceful corn-colored flowers. Each long stem carries numerous blooms opening successively from the base up. The corm multiplies quickly in warmer climates and is a good choice for sunny edges and borders, where light to medium, well-drained soil is available. In colder climates, it can be successfully cultivated in a greenhouse. If pot-planting outdoors, put six to twelve corms in a large pot. *Ixia* is a very pretty plant, producing good cut flowers.

Narcissus bulbocodium

HOOP-PETTICOAT ○ ◐
DAFFODIL

Family: LILIACEAE
Origin: Spain, Portugal, France, North-western Africa.
Flowering time: Spring.
Climatic zone: 5, 6, 7, 8.
Dimensions: Up to 6 inches (150 mm) high.

Description: Hoop-petticoat daffodil has almost cylindrical leaves which are longer than the flower stems. The flowers are shades of bright yellow, with very large trumpets and six very small, narrow petals. Plant the bulbs in naturalized settings where they can be left undisturbed. The informal nature of the flower and its brilliant color make it an interesting inclusion in the spring garden.

255

Narcissus bulbocodium

Ixia maculata

Description: Jonquil is like a bunch-flowered narcissus, but with rush-like, dark green leaves. Strongly fragrant, they tend to flower earlier than daffodils. They are seen at their best in drifts under deciduous trees or naturalized in lawn areas. Jonquils are an old, familiar, hardy favorite in all gardens. Cool, moist, and well-drained soil conditions are essential for healthy growth. In warmer districts, wait until the ground has cooled in autumn before planting. Incorporate plenty of well-rotted compost.

Narcissus (daffodil)

Narcissus (daffodil)
DAFFODIL,
NARCISSUS

Family: AMARYLLIDACEAE
Origin: Southern Europe–Asia.
Flowering time: Spring.
Climatic zone: 5, 6, 7, 8, 9.
Dimensions: Up to 18 inches (450 mm) high.
Description: This is one of the biggest and most popular genera for gardeners. *Narcissus* was named after the celebrated youth who fell in love with his own image. The daffodil, with its trumpet-shaped corona surrounded by six tepals, may be naturalized, planted in clumps between shrubs, or grown in pots. Praised by poets and gardeners alike, it is beautiful indoors and out.
Other colors: White, pink.
Varieties/cultivars: The many cultivars include 'King Alfred', 'Mount Hood', 'Romance', 'Mrs. R. O. Backhouse'.

Narcissus (Tazetta hybrids)
JONQUIL

Family: AMARYLLIDACEAE
Origin: Southern Europe, Algeria.
Flowering time: Late spring.
Climatic zone: 6, 7, 8.
Dimensions: 18 inches (450 mm) high.

Climatic zone: 6, 7, 8, 9.
Dimensions: Up to 18 inches (450 mm) high.
Description: The small claw-like tubers of ranunculus are planted and then lifted in order to promote optimum flowering. Ranunculus display solitary, open, single or double flowers on erect stems. The flowers are surrounded by a mass of segmented foliage. They are most suited to being mass-planted in full sun or used in a perennial border. They are also very attractive as cut flowers. Cool, moist soil conditions are important, and bulbs will rot if planted during warm weather. The soil should be well-drained and rich in organic matter.
Other colors: White, pink, red, copper, bronze.

Narcissus (Tazetta hybrids)

Sternbergia lutea
YELLOW AUTUMN
CROCUS (U.K.), WINTER
DAFFODIL, LILIES-OF-THE-FIELD

Family: AMARYLLIDACEAE
Origin: Mediterranean Europe–Turkey, Iran, and adjacent U.S.S.R.
Flowering time: Autumn.
Climatic zone: 6, 7, 8, 9.
Dimensions: Up to 6 inches (150 mm) high.
Description: These golden-yellow flowers, which resemble crocuses and are believed by some to be the biblical "lilies-of-the-field", flourish in rocky mountain areas. They are ideal grown indoors in pots, or outdoors in rock garden pockets, or naturalized in lawns.

Ranunculus asiaticus
RANUNCULUS, TURBAN
FLOWER

Family: RANUNCULACEAE
Origin: Southwestern Asia and Crete.
Flowering time: Late spring, early summer.

Ranunculus asiaticus

Sternbergia lutea

Provided they have good sun and regular watering, they need little attention. The bulbs should be planted in sandy, well-drained soil which has had an application of compost. Lift and divide them in summer to propagate.

Triteleia ixioides

255

Tigridia pavonia

JOCKEY'S CAP LILY, MEXICAN TIGER FLOWER, PEACOCK TIGER FLOWER (U.K.)

Family: IRIDACEAE
Origin: Mexico, Guatemala.
Flowering time: Summer.
Climatic zone: 8, 9, 10.
Dimensions: Up to 18 inches (450 mm) high.
Description: These spectacular flowers look like large butterflies and can measure up to 5 inches (150 mm) across.

Tigridia pavonia

Triteleia ixioides syn. *Brodiaea ixioides*, *B. lutea*

TRITELEIA

Family: LILIACEAE
Origin: California, Oregon.
Flowering time: Summer.
Climatic zone: 7, 8, 9.
Dimensions: 12–18 inches (300–450 mm) high.
Description: This plant produces clusters of starry, yellow flowers boldly veined with purplish-brown and having six, widely expanding petal lobes. It likes a sunny, open position with light to medium, well-drained soil. It will grow in sandy or gritty soils and is useful for newly established gardens where soils are still being built up. Frosts do not bother it, but it dislikes drought, so plenty of water is needed. It does well in borders and pots.

Resting on tall, gladiolus-like stems, they are most effective planted en masse in drifts or clumps. In warmer areas, the clumps should not be disturbed for three to four years after planting. In colder climates they should be lifted annually in autumn and replanted in spring. Plant in moist, fertile soil in a sunny position protected from the wind.
Water regularly.
Other colors: Red.

Allamanda cathartica ○

Allamanda cathartica

ALLAMANDA, GOLDEN ALLAMANDA

Family: APOCYNACEAE
Origin: Guyana.
Flowering time: Summer, autumn.
Climatic zone: 9, 10.
Description: A warmth-loving, tropical vine with clear, bright yellow flowers and strong, vigorous shoots, the allamanda will decorate posts, pillars, and fences with its glossy green foliage. Rich soil, good drainage, and ample water will ensure a handsome appearance. This lovely evergreen vine is only suitable for warm tropical conditions, but makes a good addition to a warm greenhouse.
Varieties/cultivars: 'Hendersonii' (orange-yellow), 'Nobilis' (clear yellow), 'Schottii' (yellow, striped with brown).

Bignonia capreolata ○

TRUMPET FLOWER, CROSS VINE

Family: BIGNONIACEAE
Origin: Southeastern United States.
Flowering time: Spring.

Climatic zone: 8, 9, 10.
Description: This evergreen climber will grow as high as 45–50 feet (12 meters). The tendrils at the end of the branchlets cling by tiny hooks and disks, and the funnel-shaped flowers, 2 inches (50 mm) wide, are orangey-yellow, and hang in clusters. With rich, moist soil, and good drainage, this vigorous vine will quickly spread to become large and shrubby, unless trained and tied to achieve a climbing habit. It cannot withstand heavy frosts.
Other colors: Red.
Varieties/cultivars: 'Atrosanguinea'.

Billardiera longiflora

Billardiera longiflora ○

PURPLE APPLEBERRY
(Aust.)

Family: PITTOSPORACEAE
Origin: Southeastern Australia.
Flowering time: Summer–autumn.
Climatic zone: 8, 9, 10.
Description: An evergreen climber suited to moist forest conditions, the purple appleberry is a slight vine with narrow, dark-green leaves. The flowers are pale greenish-yellow with purple shading and are followed by shiny purple-blue berries which remain hanging from the slender branches for a long period. Support is needed to control its wandering habit, and it can be grown in a container up a wire or trellis. It needs well-drained soil and protection from the wind.

Bignonia capreolata

Clematis tangutica

GOLDEN CLEMATIS

Family: RANUNCULACEAE
Origin: Central Asia.
Flowering time: Summer–autumn.
Climatic zone: 5, 6, 7, 8, 9.
Description: An unusual clematis, this deciduous climber with finely divided foliage becomes a graceful, elegant vine of up to 20 feet (7 meters) high. The flowers are bell-shaped with golden-yellow petal-like sepals, 2 inches (50 mm) long and stalks 3–4 inches (75–100 mm) long. It is a vigorous vine, very hardy and free-flowering. Golden clematis needs a sunny position, but its roots must be kept cool.
Varieties/cultivars: 'Gravetye'.

Clematis tangutica

Gelsemium sempervirens ○ ◑

CAROLINA JASMINE, CAROLINA JESSAMINE

Family: LOGANIACEAE
Origin: Southeastern United States, Mexico–Guatemala.
Flowering time: Late winter–spring.

Gelsemium sempervirens

Climatic zone: 9, 10.

Description: The strong, slender branches of this dainty little evergreen vine bear small, funnel-shaped flowers about 1 inch (30 mm) across. They are bright yellow and slightly fragrant among narrow leaves. The vine looks attractive climbing up a trellis, lattice, or archway. It also makes a useful groundcover but should be kept away from children as the plant is poisonous. A hot climate plant, a greenhouse environment is essential in cooler areas.

Hibbertia scandens

Hibbertia scandens
SNAKE VINE, GOLDEN GUINEA VINE

Family: DILLENIACEAE
Origin: Australia (Queensland, N.S.W.).
Flowering time: Spring, summer, autumn.
Climatic zone: 9, 10.
Description: The shiny leaves are attractive all year on this fast-growing, but non-invasive climber. It is a versatile plant which can be grown as a groundcover, as a container plant, as a climber, over a wall or low fence, or as a trailer over a wall or low fence, or as a climber. Clear, rich yellow flowers 2 inches (50 mm) across are scattered over the vine from spring to summer. It tolerates some shade but prefers a sunny position. Very well-drained, sandy soil is essential. This is a warm climate plant which requires a greenhouse in cool areas.

Lonicera caprifolium

Lonicera caprifolium
SWEET HONEYSUCKLE

Family: CAPRIFOLIACEAE
Origin: Europe, western Asia.
Flowering time: Late spring-early summer.
Climatic zone: 5, 6, 7, 8, 9.
Description: Sweet honeysuckle is a vigorous and hardy deciduous climber with attractive foliage and masses of showy flowers that are white to deep creamy yellow, sometimes tinged with pink. The flowers are followed by orange berries. Plant in rich, well-drained soil that retains moisture well, and choose either a sunny or semishaded position offering some support to the young shoots to encourage climbing.
Other colors: Reddish-purple.
Varieties/cultivars: 'Pauciflora'.

Lonicera hildebrandiana

Lonicera hildebrandiana
GIANT BURMESE HONEYSUCKLE

Family: CAPRIFOLIACEAE
Origin: Burma, Cambodia, southern China.
Flowering time: Summer.
Climatic zone: 9, 10.
Description: Everything about this honeysuckle is big. Huge, highly-perfumed flowers 6–7 inches (150–175 mm) long changing from cream to orange-yellow hang from strong, sturdy stems. The leaves are large and glossy, up to 6 inches (150 mm) long. It grows best in good soil with plenty of water. A very vigorous climber, it needs plenty of space to grow, or regular pruning and thinning out of older branches to control its size. The stems become thick and woody when mature.

Lonicera periclymenum
WOODBINE, HONEYSUCKLE (U.K.)

Family: CAPRIFOLIACEAE
Origin: Europe, western Asia, North Africa.
Flowering time: Summer.
Climatic zone: 4, 5, 6, 7, 8, 9.
Description: A handsome climber, honeysuckle has showy clusters of fragrant, creamy flowers with pink or crimson buds. It likes temperate conditions, a moderately rich soil with good drainage, and an open, sunny position. Provide plenty of support to display this climber to best advantage. It is an excellent choice for covering a wall or trellis.
Varieties/cultivars: 'Belgica', 'Serotina'.

Lonicera periclymenum

Macfadyena unguis-cati syn. Bignonia and Doxantha unguis-cati
CAT'S-CLAW CREEPER

Family: BIGNONIACEAE
Origin: Argentina–Mexico.
Flowering time: Spring.
Climatic zone: 9, 10.
Description: This is the vine to choose when there is no support or frame available. A vigorous climber, it will cling to any surface with its dainty, claw-like tendrils. It does no damage to the surface, and can be peeled off if necessary, and grown again. Trumpet-shaped flowers, 3 inches (75 mm) wide, stand out from the evergreen foliage to form a brilliant yellow curtain in spring. Warm zones will produce rampant growth which is difficult to control. It is better grown in cooler climates. It needs a lot of sun to flower freely.

Rosa banksiae
BANKS' ROSE, LADY BANKS' ROSE, BANKSIA ROSE (Aust.)

Family: ROSACEAE
Origin: Southern China.
Flowering time: Spring, summer.
Climatic zone: 7, 8, 9.
Description: Many thornless stems, up to 20 feet (6 meters) long, make a wide base on this shrubby climber. Tiny, double, buff-yellow blooms which are delicately fragrant appear in spring or summer. A strong pergola or other support is required, or its overall size can be reduced by regular pruning and thinning. Although evergreen in warm and moderate climates, it is deciduous where the winters are cold. Because its stems are thornless, it is an excellent choice for growing over arbors or planting near paths.
Varieties/cultivars: 'Lutea' (golden yellow), 'Lutescens' (creamy yellow), 'Alba Plena' (double white).

Rosa 'Mermaid'
MERMAID ROSE

Family: ROSACEAE
Origin: Hybrid.
Flowering time: Early–late summer.
Climatic zone: 7, 8, 9.
Description: This is a popular climbing rose with large, single, open flowers, and a dense ring of yellow stamens. The flowers appear on the previous year's wood, so pruning should be selective, some old and some new wood should be retained each year. A strong-growing evergreen it will climb up into trees and hang in great festoons from the branches, or it can be tied to fences or pergolas where the lovely blooms can be seen more easily. It does not tolerate severe cold.

Rosa 'Mermaid'

Rosa banksiae

Macfadyena unguis-cati

Solandra maxima syn. S. guttata, S. grandiflora
GOLDEN CUP VINE, CUP OF GOLD

Family: SOLANACEAE
Origin: Mexico.
Flowering time: Late winter and spring.
Climatic zone: 9, 10.
Description: This rampant, evergreen vine will grow 40 feet (12 meters) high or more and grows superbly even in quite poor soils. It is tolerant of salt spray and windy positions. With good soil and adequate water it needs plenty of space. The huge, golden flowers up to 8 inches (200) mm) across are produced sporadically in winter and spring. It needs a very strong support and can cover a fence very quickly. Too heavy and thick-stemmed to be controlled by pruning, it is not suitable for a small garden. As this is a hot climate plant, a greenhouse is essential in cold areas.

Solandra maxima

Senecio macroglossus
KENYA IVY, CAPE IVY (U.K.), WAX VINE (U.K.)

Family: COMPOSITAE
Origin: South Africa (East Cape Province).
Flowering time: Winter.
Climatic zone: 8, 9, 10.
Description: As the name implies, the thick, waxy, young leaves are shaped like ivy, but, unexpectedly, the flowers are long-stalked, daisy-like, 2 inches (50 mm) wide, and in considerable numbers so they are quite showy. It is a handsome climber when growing over a low wall, or trained up a pillar. A warm and rather dry position suits it best. Protect from frost when it is young, but it becomes a little more tolerant of cold when mature. Try it in a hanging basket where the glossy leaves will look interesting all year, with the bonus of flowers in winter. In cold areas, it makes a perfect house or greenhouse plant.
Varieties/cultivars: 'Variegatum'.

Senecio macroglossus

Stigmaphyllon ciliatum
BRAZILIAN GLORY VINE, GOLDEN VINE, GOLDEN CREEPER (U.K.)

Other common names: BUTTERFLY VINE (U.K.)
Family: MALPIGHIACEAE
Origin: Tropical America.
Flowering time: Summer, autumn.
Climatic zone: 9, 10.
Description: The unusual flowers on this delightful climber hang in small clusters. The petals are fringed and appear to be on little stems, giving the golden-yellow blooms a lacy appearance. Its fast-growing, twining habit makes it useful for covering fences, lattices, or frames, or it can be used as a groundcover. The heart-shaped leaves are glossy and attractive all year. If grown in the cooler zones, this plant needs a greenhouse, but it prefers a warm, humid climate.

Stigmaphyllon ciliatum

Tropaeolum peregrinum
CANARY-BIRD FLOWER, CANARY CREEPER

Family: TROPAEOLACEAE
Origin: Peru.
Flowering time: Late summer and autumn.
Climatic zone: 5, 6, 7, 8, 9, 10.
Description: The canary creeper is a smooth-stemmed, much-branched climber, which will reach a height of 10–15 feet (3–4 meters). The flowers are bright yellow, frilled and fringed, and have a green spur holding the nectar. Ample water is needed and a frame or support to hold this graceful plant with its somewhat succulent growth. It is happy in partial shade, and should be given space to grow by itself. It does not seem to be at its best with competition from other climbers. In frost-free areas it grows as a short-lived perennial, otherwise it is treated as an annual.

Tropaeolum peregrinum

Achillea filipendulina
FERN LEAF YARROW

Family: COMPOSITAE
Origin: Caucasus, Iran, Afghanistan.
Flowering time: Summer.
Climatic zone: 4, 5, 6, 7, 8, 9.
Dimensions: 3 feet (1 meter) high.
Description: This is a most distinctive plant whose stout, leafy, erect stems bear feathery, finely divided, green leaves. The flower heads, like a yellow plate, are up to 5 inches (125 mm) across, and the foliage has a strong, spicy odor. It is a very useful perennial in borders, the flowers lasting for a long time. They can also be successfully dried. The plant needs good drainage, but the soil should be reasonably moisture-retentive. Propagate it by division in spring.
Varieties/cultivars: 'Gold Plate', 'Canary Bird', 'Sungold', 'Parker's Variety'.

Achillea tomentosa

Achillea tomentosa
YARROW

Family: COMPOSITAE
Origin: Central Europe–western Asia.
Flowering time: Summer–early autumn.
Climatic zone: 4, 5, 6, 7, 8, 9.
Dimensions: 4–6 inches (100–150 mm) high.
Description: Found on dry, sunny slopes in sandy or stony soils, this mat-forming plant is very easy to grow. It is well-suited to a rock garden or herbaceous border. The leaves are silver-gray and hairy and, if bruised, emit an aromatic fragrance. The flower heads appear in flattened clusters on long stalks and can be used for dried floral arrangements. They should be picked, tied in bunches, and hung downwards in a sheltered place. In this way they will keep their form and color. Propagate woolly yarrow by division.
Varieties/cultivars: 'Maynard Gold'.

Achillea filipendulina

Adonis amurensis
AMUR ADONIS, PHEASANT'S EYE

Family: RANUNCULACEAE
Origin: Japan, Manchuria.
Flowering time: Early spring.
Climatic zone: 4, 5, 6, 7, 8, 9.
Dimensions: 8–12 inches (200–300 mm) high.
Description: This is a pretty plant for the front of the border, with anemone-like flowers and much-divided, ferny leaves. A well-drained, fertile soil suits it best, but it should be kept consistently moist. Plant it in autumn and propagate it by division, or seed sown immediately after gathering. Germination is slow. Grow amur adonis in clumps a little distance from other plants with hungry roots.
Varieties/cultivars: 'Fukujukai', 'Nadeshiku', 'Pleniflora', 'Yatsubasa'.

Adonis amurensis 'Yatsubasa'

Alchemilla mollis

Alchemilla mollis
LADY'S-MANTLE

Family: ROSACEAE
Origin: Eastern Europe–Turkey.
Flowering time: Early summer.
Climatic zone: 4, 5, 6, 7, 8, 9.
Dimensions: 18 inches (450 mm) high.
Description: Both the leaves and the flowers of this perennial have a special beauty, making it popular with many gardeners. The soft-green leaves are rounded and downy, with radiating veins prolonged into gentle, toothed scallops. They hold drops of water like pearls. The flowers are a froth of tiny lime-green stars produced in feathery sprays which last for weeks. Lady's-mantle is the ideal foil for white or blue flowers. It can be propagated by division or seed and often self-sows if the soil remains moist.

Alchemilla saxatile syn. *Aurinia saxatile*
BASKET-OF-GOLD, GOLD DUST ALYSSUM

Family: CRUCIFERAE
Origin: Central and southeastern Europe.
Flowering time: Spring.
Climatic zone: 4, 5, 6, 7, 8, 9, 10.
Dimensions: 8–12 inches (200–300 mm) high.
Description: This bushy rock-garden plant flourishes in almost any soil, provided it is well-drained and not too

Angelica archangelica

Angelica archangelica
ANGELICA, ARCHANGEL, WILD PARSNIP ○ ◐

Family: UMBELLIFERAE
Origin: Syria.
Flowering time: Summer.
Climatic zone: 5, 6, 7, 8, 9.
Dimensions: 6½ feet (2 meters) high.
Description: Angelica is a biennial herb with yellow flowers and soft green leaves. It was said to have been given to mankind by the Archangel Michael as protection against the plague. The stems can be cooked with sugar and eaten as candied fruit. The leaves may be dried to make a tea. It may be placed among shrubs or in the herb garden. Plant it in fertile, moist, well-dug soil and protect it from the wind.

moist. Above the gray-green leaves the branched clusters of flowers are produced in profusion and, if allowed to cascade over a wall, can be most eye-catching. Water it only during dry periods and cut back quite hard after flowering to prevent it becoming woody and straggly. It is easily propagated by seed in spring or cuttings in late summer.
Varieties/cultivars: 'Citrinum'.

Alyssum saxatile

Anthemis sancti-johannis
SAINT JOHN'S CHAMOMILE ○

Family: COMPOSITAE
Origin: Bulgaria.
Flowering time: Summer.
Climatic zone: 5, 6, 7, 8, 9.
Dimensions: 1–3 feet (up to 1 meter) high.
Description: These large and beautiful daisy-like flowers, up to 2 inches (50 mm) wide, make a great splash in the garden against the elegantly lobed foliage. Nowadays the true species is rarely seen because it has cross-pollinated so prolifically with the species *A. tinctoria*. Clump-forming, it grows best in a sunny position in a well-drained soil and should be divided and replanted each spring to keep it growing vigorously. It can be grown from seed or cuttings.

Anthemis sancti-johannis

Anthemis tinctoria
GOLDEN MARGUERITE, OX-EYE CHAMOMILE ○

Family: COMPOSITAE
Origin: Europe.
Flowering time: Late summer.
Climatic zone: 4, 5, 6, 7, 8, 9.
Dimensions: Up to 3 feet (1 meter) high.
Description: This showy garden plant produces a basal clump of leaves like parsley, above which masses of daisy flowers are produced for many weeks. They were once used by the French to make a fine yellow dye. For garden purposes, the original species has been much surpassed by a vast number of improved hybrids. It does not require a very rich soil, but needs a fairly open position. Propagate it by division in spring or autumn.
Varieties/cultivars: 'Moonlight', 'Golden Dawn', 'Perry's Variety'.

Anthemis tinctoria

Arctotis x hybrida syn. Venidio-arctotis
AFRICAN DAISY (U.K.), AURORA DAISY ○

Family: COMPOSITAE
Origin: Hybrid.
Flowering time: Summer.
Climatic zone: 8, 9, 10.
Dimensions: 1–2 feet (300–600 mm) high.
Description: The numerous hybrids of this daisy vary in height, leaf shape, and color. The beautifully colored daisy flowers open only in full sunlight and the plants do best in an open, sunny position in rich, damp soil. They respond well to organic feeding and regular watering and dislike very cold weather and wet conditions. In cold climates, a greenhouse is desirable. They can be lifted and grown indoors as pot plants in winter. Keep them bushy by pinching out the growing points. They can be grown from seed.
Other colors: White, pink, red, bronze, purple.
Varieties/cultivars: Many cultivars are available.

Arctotis x hybrida

Canna x generalis

Caltha palustris

Artemisia stellerana

Buphthalmum salicifolium

Artemisia stellerana
BEACH WORMWOOD (U.K.), DUSTY MILLER, OLD WOMAN ○

Family: COMPOSITAE
Origin: Northeastern Asia.
Flowering time: Summer.
Climatic zone: 5, 6, 7, 8, 9.
Dimensions: Up to 2 feet (600 mm) high.
Description: Beach wormwood has dense heads of yellow flowers and chrysanthemum-like silvery-gray foliage which makes it an attractive perennial planted among beds of summer flowers. Unlike other *Artemisia*, it can withstand humid conditions. In general, poor, sandy soils suit it better than rich ones, but they must be well-drained and in a sunny position. Many of the *Artemisia* group are used medicinally or, like the herb tarragon, in cooking.

Description: This perennial prefers limy soils which are not too fertile. When in flower it is often staked but looks better when allowed to flop and make a large mass of narrow, dark-green leaves under the stems of the brightly colored daisy flowers. It is both drought- and frost-resistant and forms a clump about 2 feet (600 mm) wide. It can be increased by seed but is usually propagated by division in autumn or spring.

Buphthalmum salicifolium
YELLOW OX-EYE DAISY ○

Family: COMPOSITAE
Origin: Central Europe.
Flowering time: Summer.
Climatic zone: 4, 5, 6, 7, 8, 9.
Dimensions: Up to 2 feet (600 mm) high.

Caltha palustris
MARSH MARIGOLD, KING CUP, COWSLIP (U.S.A.) ○ ◐

Family: RANUNCULACEAE
Origin: Northern temperate zone.
Flowering time: Spring.
Climatic zone: 3, 4, 5, 6, 7, 8, 9.
Dimensions: Up to 18 inches (450 mm) high.
Description: This moisture-loving plant is found in nature in marshy meadows and beside streams. In cultivation, it will grow in any wet soil, but prefers a sunny site. It makes a clump of shining, rounded leaves with brownish yellow branching stems covered with single flowers filled with rich yellow stamens. This perennial looks best when planted beside water, such as an ornamental pond. Propagate it by division or by seed.

Varieties/cultivars: 'Flore Pleno' (double).

Canna x generalis
INDIAN SHOT (U.K.), CANNA LILY ○

Family: CANNACEAE
Origin: Hybrid.
Flowering time: Summer–autumn.

Climatic zone: 5, 6, 7, 8, 9, 10.
Dimensions: Up to 5 feet (approx. 2 meters) high.
Description: These cultivated varieties are all hybrids obtained by crossing three distinct canna species. They are most decorative plants, both for flowers and foliage, and suit both summer bedding and pot planting. The three-petaled tubular flowers appear on terminal racemes and are most striking. The leaves vary from pale- to dark-green to bronze and claret shades. They require enriched soil, a sunny site, and copious water during dry weather. Dead blooms should be continuously removed to ensure a long flowering period. They should be cut down to ground level in winter and the rhizomes can then be divided. Protect against frost. In cold areas, they should be lifted in autumn and replanted in spring.

Other colors: Pink, white, red, orange, speckled.
Varieties/cultivars: Many cultivars are available including 'Eureka', 'The President', 'King Humbert', 'Wyoming', 'Copper Giant', 'Bonfire', 'Brilliant', 'Coq d'Or', 'America', 'Striped Beauty'.

Centaurea macrocephala
YELLOW HARDHEAD, GLOBE CENTAUREA, YELLOW KNAPWEED (U.K.) ○

Family: COMPOSITAE
Origin: Caucasus.
Flowering time: Summer.
Climatic zone: 3, 4, 5, 6, 7, 8, 9.
Dimensions: 3 feet (1 meter) high.
Description: A well-grown plant of this species may produce between twenty

and thirty stems topped with golden flowers enclosed in brown calyxes which look like a fur coating. The rough, oblong leaves are stemless, giving the plant a very dense appearance. The flowers make excellent specimens for drying. Fertile, moist but well-drained soils seem to suit them best, although they are easy to grow in most garden soils.

Cephalaria gigantea
GIANT SCABIOUS ○ ◖

Family: DIPSACACEAE
Origin: Siberia.
Flowering time: Summer.
Climatic zone: 5, 6, 7, 8, 9.
Dimensions: Up to 6 feet (2 meters) high.
Description: This quite large perennial is best used as a background plant as it tends to be rather ungainly. It has dark-green, divided leaves and wiry stems ending in the large scabious-like flowers. The blooms are excellent for cutting purposes. It is a hardy plant needing only a normal, fertile soil to give good results. Propagate it from seed or by division in spring.

Cephalaria gigantea

Centaurea macrocephala

Cheiranthus cheiri
WALLFLOWER ○

Family: CRUCIFERAE
Origin: Southern Europe.
Flowering time: Early spring–early summer, northern hemisphere; summer, southern hemisphere.
Climatic zone: 7, 8, 9.
Dimensions: Up to 16 inches (400 mm) high.
Description: In ancient times, maidens carried these flowers during festivals and the Elizabethans called them gilloflowers, or 'yellow flowers". These popular perennials, grown as annuals or biennials, look pretty against a sunny wall in a cottage garden. Although the old-fashioned yellow and brown wallflowers are still the favorites, there are now many different colors to choose from. Flowering for several weeks, the plants are suited to beds and borders in a sunny position, protected from the wind.
Other colors: Many varied colors including red.
Varieties/cultivars: 'Harpur Crewe', 'Rufus'.

Cheiranthus cheiri

Chelidonium majus
GREATER CELANDINE, SWALLOW-WORT ○

Family: PAPAVERACEAE
Origin: Europe, Asia.
Flowering time: Late spring–late summer.
Climatic zone: 5, 6, 7, 8, 9.
Dimensions: 2 feet (600 mm) high.
Description: This rather weedy plant is best suited to a wild garden. It forms a basal rosette of quite attractive, coarsely-toothed and lobed foliage. In its second year, erect-branching stems of small flowers rise from the rosette. These stems, when broken, emit a

PERENNIALS

bright yellow, somewhat caustic juice. It self-sows readily but dislikes boggy locations and over-wet conditions. There is a semi-double-flowered form which also self-sows readily.
Varieties/cultivars: 'Flore Pleno'.

Chelidonium majus

Coreopsis lanceolata
TICKSEED, LANCE COREOPSIS ○ ◖

Family: COMPOSITAE
Origin: Eastern United States.
Flowering time: Summer.
Climatic zone: 5, 6, 7, 8, 9.
Dimensions: 2–3 feet (up to 1 meter) high.
Description: This is a short-lived perennial which thrives in any well-drained soil. If the soil is too fertile, it tends to produce more foliage than flowers. Dead flowers should be removed to keep the plant flowering constantly. Any position in the garden usually suits it, but it does not like to be disturbed and needs regular but restrained watering. It can be propagated by division in spring or autumn.
Varieties/cultivars: 'Sunray', 'Baby Sun'.

Coreopsis lanceolata

Dietes bicolor

Coreopsis verticillata

Coreopsis verticillata
THREADLEAF
COREOPSIS, TICKSEED

Family: COMPOSITAE
Origin: Southeastern United States.
Flowering time: Summer–autumn.
Climatic zone: 4, 5, 6, 7, 8, 9.
Dimensions: 2 feet (600 mm) high.
Description: This species is distinctive because of its foliage which is finely divided into thread-like segments. The daisy-like flowers, 1–2 inches (30–40 mm) wide, are produced in great profusion over a number of months, and are useful for cutting. It is easy to grow and will withstand dry conditions for a long period. Once established, it increases quite readily to form wide clumps. The usual method of propagation is by division.
Varieties/cultivars: 'Golden Shower', 'Moonbeam', 'Zagreb'.

Dietes bicolor
FORTNIGHT LILY

Family: IRIDACEAE
Origin: South Africa.
Flowering time: Summer.
Climatic zone: 9, 10.
Dimensions: Up to 12 inches (300 mm).
Description: Fortnight lily forms a spectacular clump of arching, slender, green leaves and showy, yellow flowers with brown blotches on three of the six petals. The flower, resembling iris in shape, is borne on graceful stems. Drought-resistant, it prefers a rich and well-drained soil and a semishaded position. It can be planted as a low-growing hedge which, when established, will annually self-seed to create a thick, lush clump.

Digitalis grandiflora
YELLOW FOXGLOVE ○ ◐

Family: SCROPHULARIACEAE
Origin: Southern and central Europe–western Turkey.
Flowering time: Summer.
Climatic zone: 4, 5, 6, 7, 8, 9.
Dimensions: 2–3 feet (up to 1 meter) high.
Description: This clump-forming perennial has broad, slightly hairy leaves and produces tall flower spikes of showy blooms arranged on only one side of the spike. It prefers moist but well-drained soils, rich in organic matter. All species of the *Digitalis* genus are poisonous, but they are worthy garden subjects. Yellow foxglove can be easily propagated by seed.

Doronicum cordatum syn. *D. columnae*
LEOPARD'S-BANE ○ ◐

Family: COMPOSITAE
Origin: Eastern Europe.
Flowering time: Late spring.

Digitalis grandiflora

266

Doronicum plantagineum

Climatic zone: 4, 5, 6, 7, 8, 9.
Dimensions: 1–2 feet (300–600 mm) high.
Description: An easy-to-grow perennial with heart-shaped, serrated leaves and short stems of daisy-like flowers, leopard's-bane flowers in spring with the daffodils. Partial shade is needed in hot climates, where it may become dormant. It does best in a moist soil even during its dormant period. Slugs and snails are particularly partial to the new shoots. The flowers are excellent for cutting and often a second crop is produced in autumn. Dividing the roots in spring will produce new plants.
Varieties/cultivars: 'Miss Mason', 'Madame Mason', 'Spring Beauty', 'Magnificum'.

267

Doronicum cordatum

Doronicum plantagineum
LEOPARD'S-BANE
Family: COMPOSITAE
Origin: Western Europe.
Flowering time: Spring.
Climatic zone: 4, 5, 6, 7, 8, 9.
Dimensions: 2 feet (600 mm) high.
Description: The hairy, kidney-shaped leaves of this perennial are slightly toothed and the upper ones clasp the stem. It makes a lovely contrast in the garden when planted with euphorbias and honesty (*Lunaria*). Easy to grow, it likes moist and fertile soil and the flower stems are excellent for picking. A number of hybrids have now been produced, and this species is largely passed over by gardeners in favor of the new cultivars. It can be propagated by division.
Varieties/cultivars: 'Harpur Crewe', 'Excelsum'.

Epimedium perralderianum
ALGERIAN BARRENWORT
Family: BERBERIDACEAE
Origin: Algeria.
Flowering time: Spring.
Climatic zone: 5, 6, 7, 8, 9.
Dimensions: 12 inches (300 mm) high.
Description: This spreading perennial has very attractive foliage, the shiny, rich-green leaves being bronze-tinted

when young. It forms wide clumps, with the little brown-spurred flowers appearing on wiry stems just above the leaves. Like all epimediums it can be used in the front of a border or as a groundcover under trees. It retains its leaves throughout the year. It is best propagated by division after flowering.
Varieties/cultivars: 'Fronleiten'.

Euphorbia characias var. *wulfenii*

Epimedium perralderianum

Euphorbia characias var. *wulfenii*
POISON SPURGE (U.S.A.)
Family: EUPHORBIACEAE
Origin: Eastern Mediterranean region.
Flowering time: Late winter–late spring.
Climatic zone: 8, 9.
Dimensions: 4 feet (over 1 meter) high.
Description: This is a handsome and eye-catching plant in the garden because of its unusual color. The tall, imposing flower-stems are clothed in gray-green leaves and topped with yellowish-green flowers. These decorative parts are really bracts, the flowers themselves being small and insignificant. When cut, the stems exude a milky sap which is poisonous and may irritate the skin. It prefers a relatively dry position and makes an effective color contrast with bronze foliage. Propagate it by seed in early spring or soft cuttings in summer.

Gaillardia aristata

Gaillardia aristata
BLANKET FLOWER

Family: COMPOSITAE
Origin: Central–northwestern United States.
Flowering time: Summer.
Climatic zone: 4, 5, 6, 7, 8, 9.
Dimensions: 2–3 feet (up to 1 meter) high.
Description: Blanket flower is a very showy perennial, although it is often not long-lived, especially if the soil becomes overly wet. It blooms in the first year from seed and is a parent of most of the garden forms grown today. The plant tends to be sticky and aromatic and the large, daisy-shaped flowers are excellent for cutting. It is easily raised from seed, but the many named hybrids are propagated from root cuttings. Over-fertilizing may cause the plant to collapse.
Other colors: Red, orange.
Varieties/cultivars: 'Croftway Yellow', 'Wirral Flame', 'The King', 'Ipswich Beauty', 'Mandarin', 'Dazzler'.

Gerbera jamesonii
BARBERTON DAISY, AFRICAN DAISY, TRANSVAAL DAISY

Family: COMPOSITAE
Origin: South Africa.
Flowering time: Spring-summer.
Climatic zone: 9, 10.

Dimensions: 18 inches (450 mm) high.
Description: From clumps of dark-green, lobed, and rather coarse leaves arise single, strong flower stems. The perfect shape of the bloom makes it look almost artificial. As a cut flower, it lasts a long time in water. Not particularly easy to grow, Barberton daisy prefers neutral to slightly alkaline soil that is well-drained. It can be propagated by division in autumn if the young plants are protected from frost. If grown from seed, the seed must be very fresh.
Other colors: White, red, orange, pink.
Varieties/cultivars: Many semidouble and double varieties.

Gerbera jamesonii

Hedychium gardnerianum
FALSE GINGER LILY, KAHILI GINGER

Family: ZINGIBERACEAE
Origin: India.
Flowering time: Late summer–autumn.

Climatic zone: 9, 10.
Dimensions: Up to 4 feet (approx. 1 meter) high.
Description: Growing from a large rhizome, the tall stems have paddle-shaped leaves for most of their length and are topped with an exotic flower head composed of many orchid-like flowers. The perfume is very pronounced and spicy. It is rather like a canna lily and responds to similar treatment of cutting the flowering stems back to ground level in winter. It requires a moist soil enriched with organic matter. The rhizomes can be divided in winter.

Helianthus angustifolius

Helianthus angustifolius
SUNFLOWER, SWAMP SUNFLOWER

Family: COMPOSITAE
Origin: Southeastern United States.
Flowering time: Late summer-autumn.
Climatic zone: 6, 7, 8, 9.
Dimensions: 5 feet (approx. 2 meters) high.
Description: This is an easily grown perennial with coarse, hairy leaves and stiff, upright flower stems. It prefers a moist, fairly fertile soil, but even when it is planted at the back of a border, the roots can be invasive. For this reason it should be divided at least every three years. It is closely related to the Jerusalem artichoke. It can be used as a cut flower and is propagated by division in autumn.

Hedychium gardnerianum

268

Helenium autumnale

Helenium autumnale

SNEEZEWEED, FALSE SUNFLOWER ◯

Family: COMPOSITAE
Origin: Eastern and central northern North America.
Flowering time: Late summer–autumn.
Climatic zone: 3, 4, 5, 6, 7, 8, 9.
Dimensions: 5 feet (approx. 2 meters) high.
Description: This plant is usually so covered with flowers that it requires

staking. It is very useful as a background plant, but the strong colors need to be softened by growing it with good greenery and some creamy-white flowers. It is the parent plant to several horticultural varieties. It grows in almost any soil, provided it is well-drained. Propagation is by division in autumn or spring.
Other colors: Red, orange, bronze.
Varieties/cultivars: 'Riverton Beauty', 'Riverton Gem', 'Bruno', 'Crimson Beauty', 'Wyndley', 'Coppelia'.

Helianthus × multiflorus

PERENNIAL SUNFLOWER ◯ ◖

Family: COMPOSITAE
Origin: Hybrid.
Flowering time: Late summer.
Climatic zone: 4, 5, 6, 7, 8, 9.
Dimensions: 3–6 feet (1–2 meters) high.
Description: This robust and very showy perennial performs best in moist, well-drained soils. It is a thin-leaved

plant producing tall, branched flowering stems which should be cut back after flowering to the basal clump. The wide daisy-like flowers are yellow with a large central disk. It is a plant that spreads quickly and requires regular division. It is best planted at the back of the border and will need staking. There are now many cultivars and they are propagated easily by division.
Varieties/cultivars: 'Loddon Gold', 'Soleil d'Or', 'Miss Mellish', 'Triomphe de Gard'.

Helianthus × multiflorus

Heliopsis helianthoides var. scabra

Heliopsis helianthoides var. scabra

ORANGE SUNFLOWER, ROUGH HELIOPSIS, OX-EYE ◯

Family: COMPOSITAE
Origin: Eastern North America.
Flowering time: Late summer.
Climatic zone: 4, 5, 6, 7, 8, 9.
Dimensions: Up to 4 feet (over 1 meter) high.
Description: Like most of the sunflower-type plants, this is a long-lasting perennial giving strong color to border plantings. The flowers range from single to fully double and are produced quite prolifically. It is a reasonably compact plant with very rough stems and leaves and is easily grown in most types of soil. Several garden varieties have been bred from the species. It is propagated by division in spring.
Other colors: Orange.
Varieties/cultivars: 'Light of Loddon', 'Orange King', 'Patula', 'Summer Sun', 'Gold Greenheart'.

Hemerocallis x hybrida

Hemerocallis x hybrida
DAYLILY
Family: LILIACEAE
Origin: Hybrids.
Flowering time: Spring-summer.
Climatic zone: 4, 5, 6, 7, 8, 9.
Dimensions: Up to 3 feet (1 meter) high.
Description: The elegance and charm of these plants and the range of flower colors make them an asset in any garden. Easy to grow and tolerant, they thrive in any good soil, preferably a moist one, and although each flower only lasts a day or two, the blooms open successively over a long period. The clumps of arching leaves are attractive and many turn bright yellow in autumn. The plant can be divided at any time, although spring is best, as the new growth appears.
Other colors: White, red, pink, bronze, violet, orange.
Varieties/cultivars: 'Black Cherry', 'Diva', 'Bride Elect', 'Green Magic', 'Pink Damask', 'Royal Crown'.

Iris pseudacorus
YELLOW FLAG, YELLOW IRIS
Family: IRIDACEAE
Origin: Europe, western Asia.
Flowering time: Summer.
Climatic zone: 4, 5, 6, 7, 8, 9.
Dimensions: 4 feet (over 1 meter) high.
Description: This is an aquatic iris that thrives in water or in boggy ground beside streams and ponds. It colonizes quite rapidly and large clumps can make a stunning picture, especially when associated with blue flowers. The graceful, slender foliage is attractive, and there is a variegated form with yellow-striped leaves turning green in summer. This flower is the Fleur de Lys of heraldry. It is propagated by division.
Varieties/cultivars: 'Golden Fleece', 'Variegata'.

Iris pseudacorus

Ligularia stenocephala
ROCKET LIGULARIA
Family: COMPOSITAE
Origin: Northern China.
Flowering time: Summer.
Climatic zone: 4, 5, 6, 7, 8, 9.
Dimensions: 4–6 feet (up to 2 meters) high.
Description: In its natural habitat, this perennial is found in damp mountain meadows and forests and therefore needs a deep, fertile, and moist soil. The dark-green leaves are elegant, decorative, and deeply lobed and extend up the almost black-colored stems. The spikes of daisy-like flowers look quite imposing, especially when planted near water. Hot sun can wilt the large leaves and slugs and snails are fond of them. Propagation is by division in spring.
Varieties/cultivars: 'The Rocket'.

Linum flavum
GOLDEN FLAX, YELLOW FLAX (U.K.)
Family: LINACEAE
Origin: Central and southeastern Europe.
Flowering time: Summer.
Climatic zone: 5, 6, 7, 8, 9.
Dimensions: 1–2 feet (300–600 mm) high.
Description: This woody-based species forms mounds of spoon-shaped leaves in rosettes, above which rise the wiry stems of satiny-textured flowers. Flowering will be prolonged if the faded blooms are regularly removed. It requires a well-drained soil in an open position and makes a very satisfactory rock garden plant. The usual method of propagation is by seed in spring or by cuttings in summer.
Varieties/cultivars: 'Compactum'.

Ligularia stenocephala 'The Rocket'

Lysimachia punctata

Lysimachia punctata
YELLOW LOOSESTRIFE, CIRCLE FLOWER ◐ ●
Family: PRIMULACEAE
Origin: Southeastern Europe.
Flowering time: Summer.
Climatic zone: 4, 5, 6, 7, 8, 9.
Dimensions: 3 feet (1 meter) high.
Description: This plant is best grown in a wild garden as it spreads readily and the underground rhizomes can be very invasive. It prefers moist or wet soils and usually looks good when planted near water. The spikes of brightly colored flowers, in whorls around the leaf axils, last for a considerable period without any maintenance. The clumps need to be reduced regularly, and it is propagated by division.

Linum flavum

Meconopsis cambrica
WELSH POPPY ○ ●
Family: PAPAVERACEAE
Origin: Western Europe.
Flowering time: Late spring.
Climatic zone: 6, 7, 8, 9.
Dimensions: 18 inches (450 mm) high.
Description: This delightful little plant forms clumps of ferny leaves, the papery flowers swaying above them on fine stems. It blooms for a long period and seeds readily so that the plant soon naturalizes itself. Although it seems to flourish in most conditions, it prefers a well-drained soil, rich in humus. There is a double-flowered form which does not self-seed as readily. Welsh poppy is one of the easiest of the Meconopsis genus to grow.
Other colors: Orange.
Varieties/cultivars: M. c. var. aurantiaca, 'Flore Pleno'.

Mimulus guttatus
COMMON MONKEY FLOWER ●
Family: SCROPHULARIACEAE
Origin: Western North America.
Flowering time: Summer-autumn.

Mimulus guttatus

Meconopsis cambrica

Climatic zone: 5, 6, 7, 8, 9.
Dimensions: Up to 2 feet (600 mm) high.
Description: Cool conditions are essential for this plant, although it is widely grown throughout America. The 2 inches (50 mm) long flowers are tubular, expanding to five rounded petal lobes at the mouth. Basically yellow, each flower has a red-spotted throat. Several flowers are borne on a single stem which makes the plant useful for pot culture, especially as it will flourish indoors. The soft leaves may be eaten in salads. Ideal for damp, partially shady corners.

Oenothera fruticosa

Papaver alpinum

Potentilla eriocarpa

evergreen, and the hooded flowers are formed in whorls around the stem. It is excellent in gardens by the seaside or in a border of gray-leaved plants. It will tolerate even strongly alkaline soils, but needs protection in cold winters. It can be propagated by seed or by division.

Potentilla eriocarpa
CINQUEFOIL ○

Family: ROSACEAE
Origin: Himalayas.
Flowering time: Spring–autumn.
Climatic zone: 4, 5, 6, 7, 8, 9.
Dimensions: Up to 2 inches (50 mm) high.
Description: This matt-forming groundcover spreads to 12 inches (300 mm) in width, with a dense covering of hairy, gray-green foliage and a dramatic display of showy, bright yellow flowers over many weeks. Position in an open, sunny location in well-drained, moderately rich soil. It grows extremely well in rocky soil, making a delightful addition to the rock garden.

Primula veris
COWSLIP, COWSLIP PRIMROSE (U.S.A.) ◐●●

Family: PRIMULACEAE
Origin: Europe–western Asia.
Flowering time: Spring.
Climatic zone: 5, 6, 7, 8, 9.
Dimensions: 8–12 inches (200–300 mm) high.
Description: As this species grows wild

---

close-growing, compact plant with much-segmented leaves. It needs open, well-drained soil. With a little attention, it makes an excellent pot plant. Propagate it from seed which should be fresh.
Other colors: White, red.

Phlomis russeliana
BORDER JERUSALEM SAGE ○◐

Family: LABIATAE
Origin: Turkey.
Flowering time: Summer.
Climatic zone: 5, 6, 7, 8, 9.
Dimensions: 3 feet (1 meter) high.
Description: This is a plant for a warm, well-drained position in the garden. The finely wrinkled, sage-like leaves are

Phlomis russeliana

Oenothera fruticosa
COMMON SUNDROPS, EVENING PRIMROSE ○

Family: ONAGRACEAE
Origin: Eastern United States.
Flowering time: Summer.
Climatic zone: 5, 6, 7, 8, 9.
Dimensions: 18 inches (450 mm) high.
Description: The foliage is small, narrow, and pointed and forms dark clumps, over which the stiff stems of the flowers appear. The flowers are reddish in bud before they open out into silky, cup-shaped, yellow blooms. Unlike some of the evening primroses, which belong to the same genus, these flowers remain open all day. It is a suitable plant for edging purposes or for rock garden pockets. Propagate it by seed, division, or by cuttings. It is sometimes confused with *O. tetragona*, a very closely related species.
Varieties/cultivars: 'Yellow River', 'William Cuthbertson'.

Papaver alpinum
ALPINE POPPY ◐○

Family: PAPAVERACEAE
Origin: European alps.
Flowering time: Summer.
Climatic zone: 5, 6, 7, 8, 9.
Dimensions: 6 inches (150 mm) high.
Description: The rock garden is the place for this tiny, tufted perennial with pretty four-petaled, bowl-shaped flowers. If conditions are ideal, it will often seed itself and grow in unlikely spots, especially gravel paths. It forms a

Primula veris

surroundings. The rough and wrinkled green leaves form a rosette from which the flower stems arise. This species has given rise to a number of garden varieties. It is very useful in planters or rockeries, and the clumps can be divided in autumn.
Other colors: White, red, purple, pink.
Varieties/cultivars: *P. v.* var. *sibthorpii*, 'Alba Plena'.

Primula veris
COMMON PRIMROSE, ENGLISH PRIMROSE (U.S.A.)

Family: PRIMULACEAE
Origin: Europe–western Asia.
Flowering time: Spring.
Climatic zone: 5, 6, 7, 8, 9.
Dimensions: 6 inches (150 mm) high.
Description: Common primrose is one of the best-known wildflowers in Europe, where it sometimes forms carpets of yellow in sheltered and shaded areas. It prefers moist, humus-rich soil, as found in woodland in cool, fresh meadows and open woodlands, it prefers a moist, well-drained soil, but will not tolerate dryness. The broad and wrinkled leaves form a basal rosette, and the erect stems bear drooping, bell-shaped flowers with a pleasant fragrance. It can be propagated by division in autumn or spring or from chilled, fresh seed. In ancient times an infusion of the roots and flowers was believed to have a sedative effect.
Other colors: White, pink, red, purple.
Varieties/cultivars: 'Alba', 'Aurea', 'Caerulea'.

Primula vulgaris

Primula vulgaris

Primula x polyantha 'Barrowby Gem'

Primula x polyantha syn. *P. x tommasin*, *P. x variabilis*
POLYANTHUS

Family: PRIMULACEAE
Origin: Hybrids.
Flowering time: Late winter–spring.
Climatic zone: 5, 6, 7, 8, 9.
Dimensions: Up to 9 inches (225 mm) high.
Description: These popular plants are chiefly derived from *P. veris* and *P. vulgaris*. They have coarse green leaves and bunched flower heads in a variety of colors. They will grow in practically any soil, but grow best when the soil is kept moist and decayed animal manure is dug in. After flowering, they should not be left in a hot, dry place, but dug up and replanted in cool shade. Protect them from attack by slugs and snails. They can be divided after flowering.
Other colors: White, cream, pink, red, blue.
Varieties/cultivars: 'Garryarde Guinevere', 'Pacific Giants', 'Barrowby Gem'.

Ranunculus acris 'Flore Pleno'

Rudbeckia fulgida var. *deamii*.

Rudbeckia hirta

Ranunculus acris 'Flore Pleno'
DOUBLE MEADOW BUTTERCUP, BACHELOR'S BUTTONS

Family: RANUNCULACEAE
Origin: Cultivar.
Flowering time: Late spring.
Climatic zone: 5, 6, 7, 8, 9.
Dimensions: 3 feet (1 meter) high.
Description: Derived from the common European meadow buttercup, this attractive plant forms wiry, branching stems with neat, shining, and fully double flowers. It often flowers twice in a season and is a non-invasive, clump-forming perennial. Propagation is by division in autumn or spring. This plant is poisonous.

Rudbeckia fulgida
CONEFLOWER, BLACK-EYED SUSAN

Family: COMPOSITAE
Origin: Eastern United States.
Flowering time: Summer–autumn.
Climatic zones: 3, 4, 5, 6, 7, 8, 9.
Dimensions: 2 feet (600 mm) high.
Description: A sturdy and hardy plant with rough, narrow leaves and tall stems of flowers, it looks best in bold groups. The flowers last for a long time and are

suitable for cutting. It will tolerate light frosts and most garden conditions, and does exceptionally well on heavy soils but needs plenty of water during summer. Propagation is mainly by division in spring or by sowing seed.
Varieties/cultivars: *R. f.* var. *speciosa*, *R. f.* var. *sullivantii* 'Goldsturm', *R.f.* var.*deamii*.

Rudbeckia hirta
BLACK-EYED SUSAN, CONEFLOWER, GLORIOSA DAISY

Family: COMPOSITAE
Origin: Eastern North America.
Flowering time: Summer.
Climatic zone: 5, 6, 7, 8, 9, 10.
Dimensions: Up to 3 feet (1 meter) high.
Description: Originally a short-lived perennial, black-eyed Susan is now mostly grown as a hardy annual. It is grown widely for its continuous flowering and ability to stand up to hard conditions. The flowers may be 4–6 inches (100–150 mm) in diameter

Rudbeckia nitida
BLACK-EYED SUSAN,
CONEFLOWER ◐

Family: COMPOSITAE
Origin: Southeastern United States.
Flowering time: Late summer.
Climatic zone: 5, 6, 7, 8, 9.
Dimensions: 4 feet (over 1 meter) high.
Description: The single daisy flowers with their green central cone have a certain freshness in their appearance even on a hot summer's day. This plant is good in a large garden, but can be blown about by wind so some support is necessary. The rounded, lance-shaped leaves are attractive and the flowers are

and mostly in shades of deep yellow to orange, but always with a contrasting black center. Given its height, the plant is best situated towards the rear of a border, in association with others of complementary tones. It looks spectacular mass-planted in parks and other large areas. Indoors it is also very useful for floral work. It is easily grown from seed and thrives in warm, sunny situations. Grows well in most soils and conditions, providing drainage is good.
Other colors: See Description.
Varieties/cultivars: 'Gloriosa', 'Marmalade', 'Gold Flame'.

Rudbeckia nitida

Senecio cineraria syn. Cineraria maritima

Santolina chamaecyparissus
LAVENDER COTTON ○ ◐

Family: COMPOSITAE
Origin: Mediterranean region.
Flowering time: Spring-summer.
Climatic zone: 6, 7, 8, 9, 10.
Dimensions: 1–2 feet (300–600 mm) high.
Description: The finely dissected and heavily felted foliage forms attractive mounds of silvery white, making this a most useful plant in garden borders. The leaves have a strong, aromatic odor when bruised, and the button flowers, on almost leafless stems, are useful for picking and drying. It does best in an open situation in well-drained soil. This plant is evergreen but should be cut back hard, almost to ground level in spring, to prevent it from becoming straggly. It can be propagated by stem cuttings in the summer.
Varieties/cultivars: 'Weston'.

Santolina chamaecyparissus

excellent for cutting. If grown on light soils, it needs plenty of organic matter added. Propagate it by division or cuttings in spring.
Varieties/cultivars: 'Herbstsonne', 'Goldquelle'.

Senecio cineraria syn. Cineraria maritima, Senecio maritimus
DUSTY-MILLER (U.K.), SEA RAGWORT, SILVER CINERARIA ○

Family: COMPOSITAE
Origin: Mediterranean region.
Flowering time: Summer.
Climatic zone: 7, 8, 9.
Dimensions: 2 feet (600 mm) high.
Description: The jagged, lobed leaves of this plant are felted in a silvery gray color making it a useful foil for other colors in a garden border. Like so many gray-leaved plants it grows exceptionally well near the seaside and can survive dry conditions, but not frost. Weak and exhausted growth should be removed after flowering and the plant regularly trimmed. The small, rayed flower heads appear in compound corymbs. Propagation is by cuttings or clump division in autumn, and also by seed.
Varieties/cultivars: 'White Diamond', 'Hoar Frost', 'Dwarf Silver'.

Thalictrum speciosissimum syn.
T. flavum glaucum
YELLOW MEADOW RUE

Family: RANUNCULACEAE
Origin: Europe, temperate Asia.
Flowering time: Summer.
Climatic zone: 5, 6, 7, 8, 9.
Dimensions: Up to 5 feet (approx. 2 meters) high.
Description: The handsome foliage is blue-green in color and delicately lobed and divided. The tiny flowers are formed in dense panicles on tall stems. This is a most useful plant in the garden especially in blue-and-yellow color schemes. It will grow in most types of soil, but requires good watering during dry weather and may need support to hold the flower heads high. It becomes dormant in winter and can be divided or else propagated from seed.
Varieties/cultivars: 'Illuminator'.

Thalictrum speciosissimum

Sisyrinchium striatum
SATIN FLOWER

Family: IRIDACEAE
Origin: Southern Chile.
Flowering time: Summer.
Climatic zone: 7, 8, 9, 10.
Dimensions: 2 feet (600 mm) high.
Description: The gray-green, sword-like leaves of satin flower grow in clumps similar to bearded iris and from them arise the slender spikes of flowers. The flowers fade in the afternoon. When grown in an open, well-drained location, it will freely set seed. It is usually propagated from seed.
Varieties/cultivars: 'Aunt May'.

Sisyrinchium striatum

can be quite invasive and spreads seed prolifically. The garden cultivars are less weedy and more acceptable. It grows in any good garden soil, and was once used medicinally as a poultice and a tonic. Propagate it by division.
Varieties/cultivars: 'Golden Wings', 'Goldenmosa', 'Lesdale', 'Cloth of Gold', 'Lemore', 'Golden Thumb'.

Solidago canadensis
GOLDEN ROD

Family: COMPOSITAE
Origin: North America.
Flowering time: Summer.
Climatic zone: 4, 5, 6, 7, 8, 9.
Dimensions: Up to 5 feet (approx. 2 meters) high.
Description: This species is one of the parents of the many hybrid forms of golden rod available today. It forms wide clumps and has narrow, downy leaves and broad, pyramidal clusters of flowers. A very easily grown plant, it is useful at the back of the border, but it

Solidago canadensis

Trollius europaeus
GLOBEFLOWER

Family: RANUNCULACEAE
Origin: Europe–Caucasus, Canada.
Flowering time: Late spring–summer.
Climatic zone: 3, 4, 5, 6, 7, 8, 9.
Dimensions: 2 feet (600 mm) high.
Description: This is a plant for moist, boggy soils, good for growing in a

Trollius x cultorum 'Golden Queen'

sunken garden or beside an ornamental pond. The leaves form a basal clump which gradually increases with age. In high altitudes it can take full sun, but it usually requires some protection. The flowers, which are single and solitary, are mildly fragrant. There are now a number of hybrid cultivars available. It is propagated by division in autumn or spring.

Varieties/cultivars: 'Superbus', 'Canary Bird', 'Orange Princess', 'Empire Day', 'Lemon Queen', 'Fire Globe'.

Trollius x cultorum 'Golden Queen'
GLOBEFLOWER ◐ ○
Family: RANUNCULACEAE
Origin: Hybrid
Flowering time: Summer.

Uvularia grandiflora

Uvularia grandiflora
MERRYBELLS, MOUNTAIN
MERRYBELLS, BELLWORT ◐
Family: LILIACEAE
Origin: Eastern North America.
Flowering time: Late spring.

Trollius europaeus

Climatic zone: 4, 5, 6, 7, 8, 9.
Dimensions: 2-3 feet (up to 1 meter) high.
Description: This garden form is distinct from the true species which is now claimed not to be in cultivation. The formation of the flower is a little different from other globeflowers as the inside is filled with slender, petal-like orange stamens. It requires moist, well-drained soil that is well nourished, and locks splendid beside a green lawn or a stretch of water. Propagate it by division in autumn.

Climatic zone: 4, 5, 6, 7, 8, 9.
Dimensions: Up to 2 feet (600 mm) high.
Description: This dainty woodland plant, closely related to Solomon's seal, has a thick, creeping rootstock. The narrowly oval to oblong leaves on arching stems are half unrolled as the pretty bell-shaped flowers hang from the stem. When they have faded, the leaves straighten out and remain fresh throughout summer. It needs a moist, slightly acid soil, with protection from the wind. It is easily propagated by division of the rhizomes in autumn.
Varieties/cultivars: 'Pallida'.

Verbascum phoeniceum hybrids
MULLEIN ○ ◐
Family: SCROPHULARIACEAE
Origin: Hybrids.
Flowering time: Summer.
Climatic zone: 6, 7, 8, 9.
Dimensions: 3-6 feet (1-2 meters) high.
Description: These lovely perennial hybrids are useful garden plants with a wide range of colors. From a rosette of large, gray-felted leaves, a tall flower spike arises bearing masses of small flowers. Mullein look best when grown in large numbers and at the back of a border with delphiniums and lupins. They thrive in well-drained, even poor, dry soil. Some plants may need staking if exposed to the wind. Cut them back after flowering and divide in autumn or spring.
Other colors: White, pink, mauve, bronze.
Varieties/cultivars: 'Bridal Bouquet', 'Miss Willmott', 'C. L. Adams', 'Cotswold Queen', 'Gainsborough'.

Verbascum phoeniceum

Dimensions: Up to 6 feet (2 meters) tall.
Description: This evergreen plant with its drooping stems and pendulous flowers looks attractive in a hanging basket or spilling over the edge of a large container or retaining wall. The leaves are arrow-shaped, slender, and up to 4 inches (100 mm) long. Each flower, with its yellow petals and purple anthers, is suspended by a slender stem holding a bell-shaped red calyx from which the petals unfurl to a diameter of 1 inch (25 mm). It dislikes cold climates, where a greenhouse is essential.
Varieties/cultivars: 'Variegatum'.

Abutilon megapotamicum

Abutilon megapotamicum
BRAZIL FLOWERING
MAPLE, BRAZILIAN LANTERN
FLOWER ●

Family: MALVACEAE
Origin: Brazil.
Flowering time: Summer and autumn.
Climatic zone: 9, 10.

Dimensions: Up to 7 feet (approx. 2 meters) high.
Description: This charming, warm-climate shrub is generally grown for its pendulous, bell-shaped, golden yellow flowers and handsome, long-stalked, maple-like leaves. The best position is against a warm, sunny, and sheltered wall where well-drained, moderately rich soil will help produce an abundance of flowers in summer. Water well in summer and pinch back to encourage branching and increased flower display. *Abutilon* can also be trained around a column if the conditions are warm and sheltered.
Other colors: Orange, crimson, orange-yellow, creamy yellow, yellow with purple veins.
Varieties/cultivars: 'Ashford Red', 'Boule de Neige', 'Canary Bird', 'Fireball', 'Nabob', 'Orange Glow', 'Souvenir de Bob', 'Emperor', 'Vesuvius', 'Tunisia'.

Abutilon x hybridum 'Golden Fleece'
FLOWERING MAPLE ○

Family: MALVACEAE
Origin: Hybrid.
Flowering time: Summer–autumn.
Climatic zone: 9, 10.

Abutilon x hybridum 'Golden Fleece'

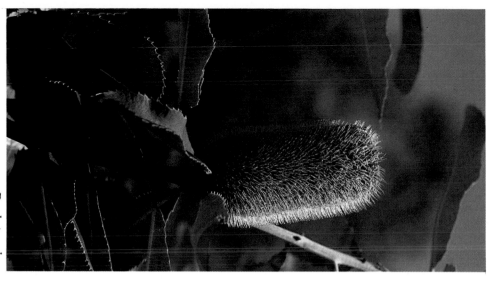

Banksia robur

Banksia robur

Berberis darwinii

279

Berberis darwinii

SWAMP BANKSIA, BROAD-LEAVED BANKSIA

Banksia robur

Family: PROTEACEAE
Origin: Australia (Queensland, N.S.W.).
Flowering time: Winter-spring.
Climatic zone: 9, 10.
Dimensions: Up to 7 feet (2 meters) tall.
Description: In its swampy native habitat, this unusual shrub, with its coarse, wide-spreading branches, grows broader (9 feet (3 meters)) than it does tall. The flowers are in dense, erect spikes, or "brushes", 6 inches (150 mm) long, yellowish-green at first, deepening to bronze-green with black stigmas. The large, elliptic leaves, 10 inches (250 mm) long, with sharp, irregular teeth on the margins, are smooth and dark green on the upper surface and rusty-red and furry on the undersurface. Prefers well-drained, heavy soil that is slightly acid.

DARWIN BARBERRY

Berberis darwinii
BARBERRY (U.K.),
DARWIN BARBERRY

Family: BERBERIDACEAE
Origin: Chile.
Flowering time: Early spring.
Climatic zone: 7, 8, 9.
Dimensions: Up to 10 feet (3 meters) high.
Description: First discovered in Chile in 1835 by Charles Darwin on the voyage of the *Beagle*, this early-flowering species is one of the finest of all flowering shrubs. The orange-yellow flowers numbering from ten to thirty, are arranged in drooping flower heads up to 4 inches (100 mm) long. It is a densely-branched shrub with the new growth arching outwards. The leaves are holly-like, three-pointed and spiny-toothed up to ¾ inch (18 mm) long, and a rich glossy green. Dark-blue-purple waxy berries make a fine autumn and winter display. A sheltered position is preferred together with well-drained soil to ensure good results.

Berberis thunbergii 'Crimson Pygmy'

BARBERRY, JAPANESE BARBERRY

Berberis thunbergii 'Crimson Pygmy'
BARBERRY, JAPANESE
BARBERRY

Family: BERBERIDACEAE
Origin: Japan.
Flowering time: Spring.
Climatic zone: 4, 5, 6, 7, 8, 9.
Dimensions: Up to 2 feet (600 mm) high.
Description: Also known as 'Atropurpurea Nana' and 'Little Favorite', this dwarf cultivar was raised in Holland in 1942. The pale yellow flowers form in small clusters and are followed by bright red berries which persist all winter. The rich reddish-purple color of the foliage intensifies as winter approaches. This charming compact shrub is excellent in rock gardens and, with its thorns, makes an impenetrable low hedge. Hardy, it needs a well-drained soil.

Buddleia globosa

Caesalpinia gilliesii

Buddleia globosa
GOLDEN HONEY BALLS, GLOBE BUDDLEIA (U.K.), ORANGE BALL TREE

Family: LOGANIACEAE
Origin: Chile, Peru.
Flowering time: Summer.
Climatic zone: 7, 8, 9.
Dimensions: Up to 15 feet (5 meters) high.
Description: This is a striking, wide-spreading, semi-evergreen shrub which is deciduous if the winter is severe. The common names describe the tight ball-like clusters of flowers which are arranged in loose clusters at the tips of the stems. They have a pronounced honey fragrance and flower for several weeks. The handsome, lance-shaped leaves, up to 8 inches (200 mm) long, are dark-green and wrinkled above, with felted, tawny hairs on their undersides. Plant in well-drained soil in a sunny position.
Varieties/cultivars: 'Lemon Ball'.

Caesalpinia gilliesii
BIRD-OF-PARADISE BUSH

Family: CAESALPINACEAE
Origin: Argentina.
Flowering time: Summer.
Climatic zone: 9, 10.
Dimensions: Up to 10 feet (3 meters) high.
Description: This is a non-prickly, straggly, evergreen shrub or small tree. The flowers, crowded thirty or forty together in racemes up to 5 inches (125 mm) long, consist of rich yellow petals from which bright red, showy stamens protrude. The cluster of stamens can be as long as 3 inches (75 mm). The new shoots are sticky and hairy and the numerous small, dainty leaflets make the foliage appear very feathery and graceful. An open, sunny position with well-drained soil fertilized with a complete plant food will ensure good results for this warm climate plant.

Cassia artemisioides
SILVER CASSIA

Family: CAESALPINACEAE
Origin: Australia.
Flowering time: Early spring–summer.
Climatic zone: 9, 10.
Dimensions: Up to 4 feet (over 1 meter) high.
Description: Compact and bushy, this attractive, evergreen shrub has beautiful silvery gray shoots and feathery foliage. The leaves are finely divided into six or eight narrow leaflets. The abundant bright yellow flowers, each about ½ inch (12 mm) in diameter, form flower heads 6 inches (150 mm) long, arising in the leaf axils. The seed pods are flat and about 3 inches (75 mm) long. Excellently adapted to hot dry conditions, this plant requires full sun and exceptionally well-drained, open, sandy soil.

Cassia artemisioides

Chimonanthus praecox syn. *C. fragrans*
WINTERSWEET

Family: CALYCANTHACEAE
Origin: China.
Flowering time: Winter.
Climatic zone: 7, 8, 9.
Dimensions: Up to 8 feet (2.4 meters) high.
Description: This deciduous shrub spreads as wide as it grows tall. The bare stems of the previous year produce

Chimonanthus praecox

exceedingly fragrant flowers during the winter months. They open to 1 inch (25 mm) across, the outer petals being a translucent greenish-yellow and the inner ones stained a purplish-brown. Cutting the flowered stems to bring the perfume indoors, is also an effective method of pruning. The short-stalked, ovalish, dark-green leaves are up to 6 inches (150 mm) long. A good wall shrub, it prefers a sheltered, sunny position in well-drained, humus-rich soil.

Varieties/cultivars: 'Grandiflorus', 'Luteus'.

Colutea arborescens
BLADDER SENNA ○ ◐

Family: LEGUMINOSAE
Origin: Southeastern Europe.
Flowering time: Early summer.
Climatic zone: 6, 7, 8, 9.
Dimensions: Up to 12 feet (4 meters) high.
Description: This deciduous shrub sometimes naturalizes too readily to be included with selected plantings, but it will succeed in many inhospitable situations as long as the soil is not too wet and the position is not too shaded. The leaves, which are up to 6 inches (150 mm) long, consist of seven to thirteen leaflets each 1 inch (25 mm) long. The bright yellow flowers are about ¾ inch (18 mm) long and are arranged in racemes of three to eight flowers. The papery and inflated bladder-like pods are about 3 inches (75 mm) long and are sometimes flushed with red. Grow it in well-drained soil.

Corylopsis veitchiana

Corylopsis veitchiana
WINTERHAZEL ◐

Family: HAMAMELIDACEAE
Origin: China.
Flowering time: Spring.
Climatic zone: 7, 8, 9, 10.
Dimensions: Up to 6½ feet (2 meters) high.
Description: A bushy, rounded, deciduous shrub, this species has slender, pointed leaves and showy catkin-like racemes of fragrant primrose-yellow flowers which create a dense display. For good results this shrub requires humus-rich, slightly acid soil and should be positioned in a semishaded, protected site. It can be propagated either from ripe seed cuttings, or by layering in spring.

Colutea arborescens

SHRUBS

Corylopsis spicata

Cytisus scoparius

and summer. Intolerant of severe winters.
Other colors: Brown, crimson, orange, scarlet, deep yellow, pale cream.
Varieties/cultivars: 'Andreanus', 'Cornish Cream', 'Dorothy Walpole', 'Firefly', 'Lady Moore', 'Lord Lambourne'.

Cytisus x spachianus

Corylopsis spicata
SPIKE WINTER HAZEL ○

Family: HAMAMELIDACEAE
Origin: Japan.
Flowering time: Spring.
Climatic zone: 5, 6, 7, 8, 9.
Dimensions: Up to 8 feet (2.4 meters) high.
Description: Spike winter hazel is a wide-spreading shrub with a subtle display of bright yellow blooms, sometimes appearing in late winter. The open, cup-shaped flowers are produced in pendant spikes up to 2 inches (50 mm) long of six to twelve flowers with hairy calyxes. The stamens are much the same length as the petals and the anthers are purple. The rounded leaves are about 4 inches (100 mm) long with grayish-green, hairy undersides supported by 1 inch (25 mm) long densely hairy stalks. Humus-rich, acid to neutral soil is preferred.

Cytisus scoparius syn. *Sarothamnus scoparius*
COMMON BROOM, SCOTCH BROOM ○

Family: LEGUMINOSAE
Origin: Western and central Europe.
Flowering time: Late spring–early summer.
Climatic zone: 6, 7, 8, 9.
Dimensions: Up to 10 feet (3 meters) high.
Description: Freely naturalizing, this

shrub grows in great numbers in many areas, where its glowing flowers can turn a whole hillside golden. It is a deciduous, erect shrub with many evergreen branches. The leaf usually consists of three leaflets about ½ inch (12 mm) long. The profuse flowers are produced singly or in pairs, and measure about 1 inch (25 mm) long. Many cultivars are available, with flower colors ranging from cream to shades of yellow with splashes of reds and browns. Although hardy, it prefers a well-drained, sunny site.
Varieties/cultivars: 'Andreanus', 'Cornish Cream', 'Golden Sunlight', 'Sulphureus', 'Firefly'.

Cytisus x spachianus
YELLOW BROOM, ○ ◑
CANARY ISLAND BROOM (U.K.)

Family: LEGUMINOSAE
Origin: Hybrid.
Flowering time: Winter–spring.
Climatic zone: 9, 10.
Dimensions: Up to 6 feet (2 meters) high.
Description: This tender, evergreen shrub has deep-green foliage with silky down beneath and rich yellow, fragrant, pea-shaped flowers in slender racemes. Often grown as a pot plant under the name *Genista fragrans*, this species prefers a light, well-drained, slightly acid soil and plenty of water during spring

Enkianthus campanulatus
ENKIANTHUS, RED- ○ ◑
VEIN BELL FLOWER, REDVEIN
ENKIANTHUS

Family: ERICACEAE
Origin: Japan.
Flowering time: Early summer.

Enkianthus campanulatus

Climatic zone: 4, 5, 6, 7, 8, 9.
Dimensions: Up to 12 feet (4 meters) high.
Description: This erect, deciduous shrub is an excellent companion for rhododendron, because they both require lime-free soil. The bell-shaped flowers, up to ½ inch (12 mm) long, are yellow to yellow-orange and streaked with red. Five to fifteen flowers form flower heads, which appear in great profusion and last on the shrub for about three weeks. The elliptic leaves, which are about 3 inches (75 mm) long with bristly, toothed margins, appear before the flowers open, and turn gold and red in autumn. The cut flowers are useful for floral decoration. Lime-free loamy soil which is well-drained is preferred.

Euryops pectinatus
GRAY EURYOPS

Family: COMPOSITAE
Origin: South Africa.
Flowering time: Spring-summer.
Climatic zone: 8, 9, 10.
Dimensions: Up to 5 feet (approx. 2 meters) high.
Description: In a warm, sunny position and well-drained soil, this half-hardy evergreen shrub will flower for months and provide constant color in the garden. The daisy-like flowers, 2 inches (50 mm) across and borne in great numbers on erect, 6-inch-long (150 mm) stems, are clustered towards the end of the branches. The leaves are up to 3 inches (75 mm) long and deeply lobed, and both leaves and stems are densely felted with gray or white hairs. Cutting the flower heads for indoor decoration

Forsythia viridissima 'Bronxensis'

---

provides sufficient pruning for this plant. In cooler climates, this plant makes an attractive pot plant for a greenhouse or patio.

Euryops pectinatus

Forsythia viridissima
GOLDEN-BELLS, SPRING BELLS (U.K.), FORSYTHIA

Family: OLEACEAE
Origin: Eastern China.
Flowering time: Spring.
Climatic zone: 5, 6, 7, 8, 9.
Dimensions: Up to 10 feet (3 meters) high.
Description: Golden-bells is normally the last forsythia to flower. The flowers, which consist of four strap-shaped petals, cover the length of the erect,

square stems in clusters of up to six. Each bright yellow flower is 1¼ inches (30 mm) wide. The leaves are lance-like, up to 6 inches (150 mm) long, and turn purple-red before they fall. Easy to grow, forsythia is effective planted in large masses with an evergreen background. Well-drained soil in a sunny position is necessary for good flower production.
Varieties/cultivars: 'Bronxensis', 'Koreana'.

Forsythia x intermedia
GOLDEN-BELLS, SPRING BELLS (U.K.), FORSYTHIA

Family: OLEACEAE
Origin: Hybrid.
Flowering time: Spring.
Climatic zone: 5, 6, 7, 8, 9.
Dimensions: Up to 10 feet (3 meters) high.
Description: This hybrid (derived from *F. suspensa* and *F. viridissima*) and its cultivated varieties are regarded as being among the most beautiful of the forsythias. So many clusters of flowers appear along the length of each stem that it seems to be a solid block of color. The flower, with its four strap-shaped petals, is about 1 inch (25 mm) wide. The branches are arching or spreading and the oblong or oval leaves, up to 5 inches (125 mm) long, are toothed or sometimes divided into three. Plant in any well-drained garden soil. Pruning every few years encourages a neater, more compact shape.
Varieties/cultivars: 'Primulina', 'Spectabilis', 'Vitellina'.

Forsythia x intermedia

Genista hispanica

Fremontodendron californicum

Fremontodendron californicum syn. *Fremontia californicum*
FLANNEL BUSH,
FREMONTIA (U.K.)

Family: STERCULIACEAE
Origin: California, Arizona.
Flowering time: Spring–summer.
Climatic zone: 8, 9.
Dimensions: Up to 20 feet (6 meters) high.
Description: Previously named *Fremontia*, this evergreen shrub is excellent as a single specimen, in groups, or espaliered. The flowers, which open flat, are up to 2¼ inches (56 mm) across and although they are produced singly from the leaf axils, they are numerous. The thick, dull green leaves are covered on their undersides with irritant hairs which easily rub off and can be painful if they get into eyes. Each leaf is up to 3 inches (75 mm) long and more or less three-lobed, with three veins radiating from the heart-shaped base. This shrub thrives in dry conditions.

Genista hispanica
SPANISH GORSE

Family: LEGUMINOSAE
Origin: Southwestern Europe.
Flowering time: Early summer.
Climatic zone: 7, 8, 9.
Dimensions: Up to 2 feet (600 mm) high.
Description: Closely allied to *Cytisus*, this small, deciduous shrub grows as a rounded, prickly mound with intertwining, prominently spined branches and hairy shoots. The stalkless leaves are less than ½ inch (12 mm) long and densely covered with silky hairs on the undersides. The flowers, about ⅓ inch (8 mm) long, are in crowded clusters of up to twelve and are produced so abundantly that they completely cover the shrub for up to two months. This plant is easy to grow in soils that are dry and infertile, although it can be damaged or killed by severe winters.

Genista tinctoria
DYER'S GREENWEED

Family: LEGUMINOSAE
Origin: Mediterranean Europe, Caucasus, Turkey.
Flowering time: Summer–early autumn.
Climatic zone: 3, 4, 5, 6, 7, 8, 9.
Dimensions: Up to 2 feet (600 mm) high.
Description: This shrub is hardy and has naturalized in many areas on poor, gravelly soils. Typically, it has many upright branches which are spineless. The pea-shaped flowers are produced in great profusion in long, terminal racemes over a long period. The narrow, oblong pods are often slightly hairy like the leaves, which are nearly ½ inch (12 mm) long. This is the best known and hardiest of the genistas, but some of its cultivars are more attractive for planting in gardens.
Varieties/cultivars: *G. t.* var. *prostrata*, 'Plena', 'Royal Gold'.

Genista tinctoria var. *prostrata*

Hamamelis mollis
CHINESE WITCH
HAZEL

Family: HAMAMELIDACEAE
Origin: Western China.
Flowering time: Winter.
Climatic zone: 5, 6, 7, 8, 9.
Dimensions: 10–20 feet (3–6 meters) high.
Description: This slow-growing, deciduous shrub or tree is perhaps the

Hamamelis virginiana
WITCH HAZEL ○ ◐

Family: HAMAMELIDACEAE
Origin: Eastern North America.
Flowering time: Autumn.

finest witch hazel in bloom and certainly the most popular. It is distinguished from the other species by the soft hair on its young shoots and the undersides of its leaves. It has large, rounded leaves to 6 inches (150 mm) long. The fragrant flowers consist of four narrow, strap-shaped petals which emerge crumpled from the buds. When fully open, they are ¾ inch (18 mm) long, reddish at the base, and a welcome sight in the cold months.
Varieties/cultivars: 'Pallida'.

Hamamelis virginiana

Climatic zone: 4, 5, 6, 7, 8, 9.
Dimensions: Up to 20 feet (6 meters) high.
Description: This deciduous shrub flowers as the leaves drop in autumn. The fragrant flowers have four strap-shaped petals which are up to ¾ inch

Hamamelis mollis

(18 mm) long, and arranged in clusters. The leaves are oval, 6 inches (150 mm) long, coarsely toothed, and turn golden yellow before they fall. This large shrub, which is the source of commercial witch hazel is occasionally seen as a small, broad-domed tree.

Hamamelis mollis

Hypericum calycinum
SHRUBBY ST. JOHNS WORT, AARON'S BEARD, ROSE OF SHARON ○ ◐

Family: HYPERICACEAE
Origin: Southeastern Bulgaria, Turkey.
Flowering time: Summer–autumn.
Climatic zone: 6, 7, 8, 9.
Dimensions: 1–2 feet (300–600 mm) high.
Description: This semi-evergreen, dwarf shrub is one of the finest of the hypericums. Spreading by stems that can take root where they touch the ground, it forms a dense mat which makes it an excellent groundcover, but it can become a nuisance if allowed to spread unchecked. The flowers, which appear over the whole of a long summer season, are up to 4 inches (100 mm) wide, occur singly or in pairs, and have numerous stamens. The leaves are oblong and up to 4 inches (100 mm) long. The plant thrives in either sun or partial shade, and in dry soils.

Hypericum calycinum

Climatic zone: 7, 8, 9.
Dimensions: Up to 2 feet (600 mm) high.
Description: Raised in France in 1887 from *H. calycinum* and *H. patulum*, this low-growing shrub does not, however, spread by rooting stems like *H. calycinum*. With its numerous arching, reddish branches it is an excellent dwarf shrub for rock gardens. The flowers, solitary or in clusters of up to five in number, are 2½ inches (60 mm) across, with conspicuous reddish anthers, and are borne over a long summer. The egg-shaped leaves, up to 2¼ inches (54 mm) long, are grayish on their undersides. Cut back to ground level if winters are harsh. A sunny, well-drained site is preferred.
Varieties/cultivars: 'Tricolor'.

Illicium anisatum

Illicium anisatum syn. *I. religiosum*, *I. japonicum*
JAPANESE STAR ANISE

Family: ILLICIACEAE
Origin: China, Japan, Taiwan.
Flowering time: Spring.
Climatic zone: 8, 9.
Dimensions: Up to 25 feet (8 meters) high.
Description: Related to the magnolia, this outstanding evergreen shrub thrives in conditions congenial to Rhododendron. It is slow-growing and aromatic and is often found in Buddhist cemeteries or near temples, where its wood is used in incense. Its lustrous, oval leaves, which are also aromatic, are thick, fleshy, deep-green, and up to 4 inches (100 mm) long. The many-petaled flowers are pale yellow, about 1 inch (25 mm) across, and appear even on young plants. This species is poisonous, and needs a sheltered site in cooler climates.
Varieties/cultivars: 'Variegatum'.

Hypericum kalmianum

Hypericum kalmianum
KALM ST. JOHNS WORT, SHRUBBY ST. JOHNS WORT

Family: HYPERICACEAE
Origin: Northeastern North America.
Flowering time: Summer.
Climatic zone: 4, 5, 6, 7, 8, 9.
Dimensions: Up to 3 feet (1 meter) high.
Description: This dense, compact, evergreen shrub exists as a native over large areas of the eastern United States and is a popular garden inclusion. The stems are pale green when young, and when mature are often gnarled with pale brown, flaky bark. Its leaves, up to 2½ inches (60 mm) long, are narrowly oblong. The flowers, almost stalkless, open wide to 2 inches (50 mm) across to display five rounded petals and a show of stamens. They appear in the axils of the leaves as solitary flowers or in groups of two or three. Plant in a sunny position, in well-drained soil.

Hypericum x moseranum 'Tricolor'

Hypericum x moseranum
GOLD FLOWER, SHRUBBY ST. JOHNS WORT

Family: HYPERICACEAE
Origin: Hybrid.
Flowering time: Summer.

Itea ilicifolia

Itea ilicifolia
HOLLY-LEAF
SWEETSPIRE

○ ◑

Family: SAXIFRAGACEAE
Origin: Western China.
Flowering time: Late summer.
Climatic zone: 7, 8, 9.
Dimensions: Up to 9 feet (3 meters) high.
Description: This handsome evergreen shrub has holly-like, spiny-toothed, broad leaves up to 4 inches (100 mm) long, which are a rich, glossy green on the upper surface and paler beneath. The pale greenish-yellow flowers, which are produced in arching, trailing, slender, catkin-like racemes up to 12 inches (300 mm) long, cover the plant in late summer. These shrubs can be used in much the same manner as hollies — in groups, as single specimens, as hedges, or combined with other plants in the shrub garden. Plant in well-drained, humus-rich soil in sun or partial shade. A sheltered position is preferred, especially in cooler climates.

Jasminum humile 'Revolutum'
YELLOW JASMINE,
SHRUBBY YELLOW JASMINE,
ITALIAN JASMINE

○

Family: OLEACEAE
Origin: Cultivar.
Flowering time: Summer–autumn.
Climatic zone: 7, 8, 9.
Dimensions: Up to 10 feet (3 meters) high.
Description: Although rather sprawling in habit, this beautiful evergreen shrub forms a more or less

rounded shape. Its deep-green leaves with three to seven leaflets, the terminal one being the longest and measuring up to 2½ inches (60 mm) long, form a splendid background for the deep-yellow, sometimes fragrant flowers. On a long tube, the spreading petals, measuring ¾ inch (18 mm) across, are arranged in clusters of six to twelve or more. This shrub is an ideal plant for a sunny, protected situation such as against a wall. It does not tolerate severe winters. Well-drained but moist soil is preferred.

arching outwards, scramble over any support. The flowers of deep-yellow open to 1½ inches (35 mm) across on a slender tube ½ inch (12 mm) long. They are often semidouble and are produced in succession over a long spring season on the 1- and 2-year-old outer stems for a length of 3 feet (1 meter) or more. The leaves, which grow opposite one another on the stems, consist of three leaflets and are up to 4 inches (100 mm) long. Well-drained, moist soil is preferred. This plant may be killed by severe winters.

Jasminum mesnyi

Jasminum humile 'Revolutum'

Jasminum mesnyi syn. *J. primulinum*
PRIMROSE JASMINE

○ ◐

Family: OLEACEAE
Origin: Western China.
Flowering time: Spring.
Climatic zone: 8, 9, 10.
Dimensions: Up to 3 feet (1 meter) high.
Description: Sometimes included among the climbing plants, this very attractive evergreen shrub has weak stems which emerge from the base and, and which open to show their petals and numerous stamens. The egg-shaped leaves, which are about 4 inches (100 mm) long with double-toothed margins, are bright green, smooth on the upper surface, and hairy on the underside. They turn yellow in autumn. Grow in any well-drained soil. It tolerates both sun and partial shade.

Kerria japonica 'Pleniflora' syn. 'Flore Pleno'
KERRIA, JEW'S
MALLOW, BACHELORS
BUTTONS (U.K.)

○ ◐

Family: ROSACEAE
Origin: Cultivar.
Flowering time: Spring.
Climatic zone: 5, 6, 7, 8, 9.
Dimensions: Up to 6 feet (2 meters) high.
Description: A cultivar of the only species of *Kerria*, this deciduous, suckering shrub has been a favorite in gardens since its introduction into Europe in 1834. Long, slender, cane-like stems from the previous year support the flowers, which are clear golden-yellow, up to 1¾ inches (42 mm) across,

Kerria japonica 'Pleniflora'

Lantana camara 'Drap d'Or'
COMMON LANTANA, YELLOW SAGE (U.K.)

Family: VERBENACEAE
Origin: Cultivar.
Flowering time: Year round.
Climatic zone: 9, 10.
Dimensions: Up to 6 feet (2 meters) high.
Description: Deep golden-yellow flowers and a more compact growth habit distinguish this cultivated variety from other *Lantana* species. Otherwise it has similar characteristics — the crushed leaves give off the familiar pungent smell, the stems are prickly, and the foliage is covered in short hairs. The leaves are oval, wrinkled, up to 5 inches (125 mm) in length, with toothed margins. The small flowers are arranged in flattish clusters of twenty to thirty, measuring up to 2 inches (50 mm) across. The black fruits which follow are mostly sterile (and do not present the same problem as the non-cultivated lantanas whose readily germinating seeds are widely dispersed by birds).

Laurus nobilis

Laurus nobilis
SWEET BAY, BAY LAUREL

Family: LAURACEAE
Origin: Mediterranean region.
Flowering time: Late spring.
Climatic zone: 7, 8, 9.
Dimensions: Up to 20 feet (6 meters) high.
Description: In cultivation since 1562, this is the true laurel that the ancients made into wreaths for poets and crowns for triumphant heroes. Because it stands

Lantana camara 'Drap d'Or'

clipping well it is today often grown beside doorways and trimmed to shape. Although in the wild it can reach a height of 40 feet (12 meters), in a cultivated garden it is well suited to large containers. The evergreen leaves are narrow, up to 5 inches (125 mm) long, a rich dark-green, and are the bay leaves much esteemed by cooks the world over. Small clusters of fragrant, yellowish flowers are followed by small berries which ripen to purplish-black. Plant in spring in moderate soil in a sunny or partially shady position. It is tolerant of some frost but may be damaged by severe winters.
Varieties/cultivars: 'Angustifolia'.

Lindera benzoin
SPICE BUSH

Family: LAURACEAE
Origin: Eastern North America.
Flowering time: Spring.
Climatic zone: 6, 7, 8, 9.

Lindera benzoin

Dimensions: Up to 15 feet (5 meters) high.
Description: Of compact habit, this is a magnificent deciduous, tall shrub. Its long leaves are aromatic when bruised. Bright green in summer, the leaves in autumn may turn a glorious butter-yellow with rich pink tints. The small flowers are petalless, their calyces being yellow-green. The berry-like fruits are red. Plant in partial shade or full sun in moist soil.

Mahonia aquifolium

Mahonia aquifolium
OREGON GRAPE, HOLLY MAHONIA

Family: BERBERIDACEAE
Origin: Northwestern North America.
Flowering time: Spring.
Climatic zone: 6, 7, 8, 9.
Dimensions: Up to 4 feet (approx. 1 meter) high.
Description: This very beautiful evergreen shrub looks attractive planted under deciduous trees. The showy flowers are produced in dense, golden-yellow clusters of racemes up to 3 inches (75 mm) long. Masses of attractive blue-black berries follow with their covering of purple bloom. The handsome leaves, up to 10 inches (250 mm) long, consist of five to nine oblong leaflets each up to 3 inches (75 mm) long with shallow-toothed margins. In autumn bronze and purple tints are added to their rich, glossy green. Grow in humus-rich, well-drained soil.
Varieties/cultivars: 'Atropurpureum', 'Moseri'.

Mahonia bealei
LEATHERLEAF MAHONIA

Family: BERBERIDACEAE
Origin: China.
Flowering time: Late winter–late spring.
Climatic zone: 6, 7, 8, 9.
Dimensions: Up to 8 feet (approx. 2 meters) high.
Description: The hardiest of the Asian mahonias and, with *M. aquifolium* and *M. repens*, the most cold-resistant, this popular evergreen shrub has stout, upright stems. The fragrant, lemon-yellow flowers are clustered into erect racemes up to 6 inches (150 mm) long. The fruits are a waxy bluish-black. The leaves are stiff, leathery, semi-glossy, deep green and up to 1½ feet (450 mm) long, with nine to fifteen round to oval leaflets each up to 4 inches (100 mm) in length. There are a few large, spiny teeth on the margins. It is adaptable to both sun and partial shade as long as a humus-rich soil is provided.

Ochna serrulata

Ochna serrulata syn. *O. atropurpurea*
BIRD'S EYE BUSH, MICKEY-MOUSE PLANT, CARNIVAL BUSH

Family: OCHNACEAE
Origin: South Africa.
Flowering time: Summer.
Climatic zone: 9.
Dimensions: Up to 10 feet (3 meters) high.

Mahonia bealei

Description: Often known as *O. multiflora*, this evergreen shrub has leathery, elliptic leaves which are up to 2 inches (50 mm) long and have sharply toothed margins and prominent midribs. The bronze-colored spring foliage is followed by the fragrant flowers, resembling yellow buttercups, about ¾ inch (18 mm) wide, which are freely produced at the ends of the many lateral shoots. The fruits which quickly follow are kidney-shaped and bright green at first, maturing to a glossy black. Their curious appearance is heightened by the enlarged, bright crimson, waxy receptacles to which they are attached. Hardy, it is easy to propagate as seedlings are freely produced.

Phlomis fruticosa
JERUSALEM SAGE

Family: LABIATAE
Origin: Southwestern Europe.
Flowering time: Summer.
Climatic zone: 7, 8, 9.
Dimensions: Up to 4 feet (approx. 1 meter) high.
Description: Jerusalem sage is a small, broad, evergreen shrub excellent for a sunny position in well-drained soil. Its many branches are densely hairy, as are the ovalish, wrinkled leaves, which are up to 4 inches (100 mm) long. The hairs on their upper surface are green, while those on the undersides are more dense and white or yellowish. The flowers, which are dusky yellow and more than 1 inch (25 mm) long, form rounded clusters at the tops of the stems. Pruning the spent flower heads will increase flowering and maintain the bush's compact shape.

Phlomis fruticosa

SHRUBS

Reinwardtia, yellow flax is a splendid small, evergreen shrub for warm, sunny, and preferably humid locations and, in warm greenhouses, makes an attractive pot plant. The bright golden-yellow, nearly circular flowers are about 2 inches (50 mm) in diameter and open wide above a slender tube. They fall quickly, but are produced in abundance over a long period. The soft, thin, narrow leaves, about 3 inches (75 mm) long, are bright green. The plant should be pruned to shape in early spring.

Ribes odoratum

YELLOW FLOWERING CURRANT, BUFFALO CURRANT (U.K.) ○ ◑

Family: SAXIFRAGACEAE
Origin: Central United States.
Flowering time: Late spring.
Climatic zone: 5, 6, 7, 8, 9.
Dimensions: Up to 12 feet (4 meters) high.
Description: Closely related to the fruiting currants and gooseberries, this ornamental, deciduous shrub is charming in bloom, when its numerous clove-scented, bright yellow, tubular flowers emerge in drooping, hairy racemes of up to ten. The racemes are 2 inches (50 mm) long. Small, smooth, black, edible fruits follow. The leaves are three- or five-lobed, smooth, though at first hairy, and measure up to 3 inches (75 mm) in length and width. They color to scarlet in autumn. Pruning after flowering produces a compact shape. A well-drained but moist soil and a sunny or partially shaded position are preferred.

Ribes odoratum

Potentilla fruticosa

Potentilla fruticosa

SHRUBBY CINQUEFOIL ○

Family: ROSACEAE
Origin: Northern temperate zone, mountains further south.
Flowering time: Summer.
Climatic zone: 2, 3, 4, 5, 6, 7, 8, 9.
Dimensions: Up to 3 feet (1 meter) high.
Description: Usually a rounded bush growing as wide as it does tall, this deciduous shrub is hardy, thrives in any soil, and has flowers like small, single roses which are displayed over a long summer season. Its erect stems bear hairy green to grey leaves divided into five to seven leaflets up to 1 inch (25 mm) long. The open-faced, bright yellow flowers, up to 2 inches (50 mm) in diameter, are numerous and showy. This shrub is the parent of several hybrids as well as producing many cultivated varieties.
Other colors: White, red, orange, cream.
Varieties/cultivars: Many cultivars are available, including 'Grandiflora', 'Katherine Dykes', 'Vilmoriniana', 'Berlin Beauty', 'Klondyke', 'Longacre'.

Reinwardtia indica syn. *R. trigyna*,
Linum trigynum

YELLOW FLAX ○

Family: LINACEAE
Origin: Northern India.
Flowering time: Winter–spring.
Climatic zone: 9, 10.
Dimensions: Up to 3 feet (1 meter) high.
Description: The most commonly cultivated of the few species of

Reinwardtia indica

290

Senecio greyi

Ulex europaeus
COMMON GORSE, FURZE, WHIN

Family: LEGUMINOSAE
Origin: Western Europe–southern Scandinavia.
Flowering time: Late winter–late spring.
Climatic zone: 6, 7, 8, 9.
Dimensions: Up to 6 feet (2 meters) high.
Description: Closely resembling the related *Cytisus*, this fiercely spiny, evergreen shrub has been known to produce flowers over the whole year, but only in dry, sandy soil in full sun and in a mild climate. The brilliant yellow pea flowers are up to ¾ inch (18 mm) long, almond-scented, and form loose to dense clusters at the ends of the branches. Young plants have three leaflets, but on older specimens the leaves are scale-like or represented by spines. Naturalized in many areas, sometimes to the point of being a pest, gorse grows well in association with heather. It is suitable for clipping as a hedge.
Varieties/cultivars: 'Plenus'.

thriving in well-drained soils in a sunny situation. The fragrant flowers measure 1 inch (25 mm) long and wide, and look like small, golden-yellow sweet peas arranged in showy, loose, terminal racemes up to 1½ feet (450 mm) long. Because its leaves are small and inconspicuous on the erect, rush-like, green stems, the shrub seems almost leafless. Prune in early spring to keep it shapely. The shrub is tolerant of moderate frost but not severe winters.

Senecio greyi
GROUNDSEL, SHRUBBY GROUNDSEL

Family: COMPOSITAE
Origin: New Zealand.
Flowering time: Summer.
Climatic zone: 7, 8, 9.
Dimensions: Up to 6 feet (2 meters) high.
Description: Considered by some the loveliest of the New Zealand *Senecio* species, this very popular wide-spreading, evergreen shrub brings soft shades of white-gray to the garden, with the young shoots, undersides of the leaves, and leaf stalks all densely covered in a felt of white hairs. The bright yellow, daisy flower heads, up to 1 inch (25 mm) wide, are arranged in broad clusters up to 6 inches (150 mm) long. The oblong leaves are up to 4 inches (100 mm) long. This shrub is ideal for seaside planting, but cannot tolerate severe winters.

Spartium junceum

Spartium junceum
SPANISH BROOM, WEAVER'S BROOM

Family: LEGUMINOSAE
Origin: Southwestern Europe.
Flowering time: Summer–autumn.
Climatic zone: 8, 9.
Dimensions: Up to 8 feet (approx. 2 meters) high.
Description: Closely related to *Cytisus* and *Genista*, this single species of *Spartium* is a wonderful seaside shrub

Ulex europaeus

Description: In the wild, silver wattle grows by permanent creeks. With its profuse flower heads of highly fragrant flowers it is a favorite in France for the perfume industry. After blooming, the tree takes on a hazy pink hue, as masses of pods hang among the silvery, feathery foliage. Fast-growing and evergreen, it is best grown in a very large, natural garden, near a running creek. It is easily grown from seed in spring, but the seed must be soaked in freshly boiled water which is allowed to cool slowly for 24 hours before sowing.

Acacia baileyana

Acacia baileyana
COOTAMUNDRA
WATTLE, BAILEY WATTLE,
BAILEY ACACIA

Family: LEGUMINOSAE
Origin: Australia, N.S.W.
Flowering time: Winter–spring.
Climatic zone: 9, 10.
Dimensions: 20–40 feet (6–12 meters) high.

Description: One of the most popular and widely grown of the acacias, Cootamundra wattle is smothered in golden balls of small, fluffy, fragrant flowers in winter. Its bluish or silvery-gray leaves consist of many, divided leaflets, producing a soft, feathery appearance. It can be grown successfully in most soils and conditions, providing drainage is excellent. Like all wattles it is fast-growing which makes it a valuable plant for new gardens for use as a screen or a shade tree. Another asset in landscaping is its role as a "nurse" plant — it fills in space and protects much slower-growing plants. In cold areas, it needs to be grown under glass. Tip-prune it after flowering, to prolong its life.
Varieties/cultivars: 'Purpurea'.

Acacia dealbata
SILVER WATTLE,
MIMOSA

Family: LEGUMINOSAE
Origin: Eastern Australia.
Flowering time: Spring.
Climatic zone: 8, 9, 10.
Dimensions: 33–66 feet (10–20 meters) high.

---

used extensively in California as a street tree, while in South Africa it has reached almost weed proportions. Profuse, fragrant fingers of fluffy flowers appear each spring. Beautiful, fast-growing, and resistant to salt spray, it will bind soil when planted on a bank, or very quickly create a screen for a new garden. *Acacia longifolia var. sophorae* is a much smaller, spreading form which will bind sand in beach gardens. Grow new plants from seed in spring, soaking them in warm water for 12 hours before planting.
Varieties/cultivars: *A. l.* var. *sophorae*.

Acacia dealbata

Acacia longifolia
SYDNEY GOLDEN
WATTLE, SALLOW WATTLE

Family: LEGUMINOSAE
Origin: Eastern and southern Australia.
Flowering time: Spring.
Climatic zone: 9, 10.
Dimensions: 10–20 feet (3–6 meters) high.
Description: At home in many warm, temperate climates, this evergreen tree is

---

Acer platanoides
NORWAY MAPLE

Family: ACERACEAE
Origin: Scandinavia, western Europe, western Asia.
Flowering time: Early spring.
Climatic zone: 3, 4, 5, 6, 7, 8, 9.
Dimensions: 50–100 feet (15–30 meters) high.

Description: Found over large areas in its natural habitat, this tree is also extensively cultivated. Attractive clusters of yellow flowers appear just before the fine, green leaves, which turn yellow briefly in autumn before falling. One of the fastest-growing of the maples, it prefers cool, moist gardens in areas high above sea level, but will withstand pollution. Because it produces a dense canopy, not much will grow beneath this tree. Plant it where shade is required, perhaps in a paved area with garden seats.
Varieties/cultivars: 'Crimson King', 'Drummondii', 'Dissectum', 'Erectum', 'Faasen's Black', 'Reitenbachii', 'Schwedleri', 'Goldsworth Purple', 'Laciniatum', 'Lorbergii'.

Acer platanoides

Acacia longifolia

292

Azara lanceolata
AZARA

Family: FLACOURTIACEAE
Origin: Chile.
Flowering time: Midsummer.
Climatic zone: 8, 9.
Dimensions: Up to 20 feet (6 meters) high.
Description: This is a neat and pretty evergreen tree covered in slender, dark green, glossy foliage. The strongly fragrant flowers are mustard-yellow, and followed by pretty, pale mauve berries. To achieve good results position in a warm, sheltered site in rich, moist soil that is slightly acid. Mulch well around the base, and ensure there is a good supply of water during summer. Avoid planting close to other species, as the roots produce a growth inhibitor.

Azara lanceolata

Azara lanceolata

Banksia serrata
RED HONEYSUCKLE, SAW BANKSIA

Family: PROTEACEAE
Origin: Eastern Australia.
Flowering time: Summer.
Climatic zone: 9, 10.
Dimensions: Up to 30 feet (9 meters) high.
Description: Banksias are a useful shrub in poor, sandy, coastal soil and are salt-resistant. The spikes of golden flowers, which look like erect cylinders, are about 6 inches (150 mm) long. The fruits are woody seed cells. The shiny

leaves are leathery, narrow, and up to 6 inches (150 mm) long, with closely toothed margins. Plant in acid, well-drained, sandy to loamy soil.

Banksia serrata

Caesalpinia ferrea syn. Poinciana ferrea
BRAZILIAN IRONWOOD, LEOPARD TREE

Family: CAESALPINIACEAE
Origin: Eastern Brazil.
Flowering time: Spring.
Climatic zone: 9, 10.
Dimensions: 33–50 feet (10–15 meters) high.
Description: The beautiful mottling of the trunk, caused by peeling bark, gives this tree the name leopard. In spring, the top of the tree is lit up with vivid yellow blossoms, and its soft, feathery foliage, reddish at first but bright green when mature, adds a touch of elegance. Ideal in the subtropical garden, it is a fairly fast grower, making a good shade tree, but needing plenty of room. It grows well in coastal areas, but not the dry inland. Grow it from seed that has been soaked for several hours in warm water.

Caesalpinia ferrea

Caragana arborescens
SIBERIAN PEA TREE, PEA SHRUB

Family: FABACEAE
Origin: Siberia, Mongolia.
Flowering time: Late spring, northern hemisphere.
Climatic zone: 3, 4, 5, 6, 7, 8, 9.
Dimensions: 15–20 feet (5–6 meters) high.
Description: The deciduous Siberian pea tree was first introduced into England in the mid-eighteenth century and has since been used as a hedge or windbreak in dry, exposed areas. The attractive yellow flowers appear in clusters from buds of the previous year. This tree is best planted in either autumn or winter, and will grow well in most soils and conditions providing drainage is adequate. Being such an adaptable plant it is often used for grafting other desirable varieties.
Varieties/cultivars: 'Lorbergii', 'Nana', 'Pendula'.

Caragana arborescens

Genista aetnensis

Grevillea robusta

Cornus mas

Cassia fistula

Dimensions: 17–27 feet (5–8 meters) high.
Description: Cornelian cherry bears profuse clusters of tiny, yellow flowers on naked branches at the end of winter, and produces pretty, bright-red, edible fruits in summer. In autumn, the leaves may turn reddish-purple before falling. Not many other trees will tolerate the conditions this tree does — dry, chalky soils, pollution, exposed situations — and also resist pests and diseases.
Often shrubby in habit, cornelian cherry should be pruned to train it as a single trunk. Grow this tree from semihardwood cuttings in late summer.
Varieties/cultivars: 'Aurea', 'Elegantissima', 'Variegata'.

Cassia fistula
GOLDEN-SHOWER (U.K.),
INDIAN LABURNUM, PUDDING-
PIPE TREE

Family: CAESALPINACEAE
Origin: Tropical India, Burma, Sri Lanka.
Flowering time: Late summer–early autumn.
Climatic zone: 9, 10.
Dimensions: 20–33 feet (6–10 meters) high.
Description: Showy, large, drooping clusters of clear yellow, fragrant flowers adorn this lovely tree for weeks on end, enhanced by the pretty, fresh-green leaves. The name "pudding-pipe" refers to the long, brown, rather ugly seed pods that hang from the branches. The seeds may be sown in spring after soaking them in warm water for 24 hours to soften their outer coating. Easy to grow in warmer gardens, pudding-pipe tree needs to be protected from frost and cold winds in borderline climates. It thrives in well-drained soils in warm, coastal environments with good rainfall. It sheds its leaves for short periods.

Cornus mas
CORNELIAN CHERRY

Family: CORNACEAE
Origin: Central and southern Europe.
Flowering time: Late winter–spring.
Climatic zone: 4, 5, 6, 7, 8, 9.

broom prefers a well-drained position and tolerates chalky soil; in some areas it is subject to fungal die-back. Grow it in spring from seed that has been soaked for 24 hours in warm water. It requires no pruning.

Grevillea robusta
SILK OAK (U.S.A.), SILKY
OAK

Family: PROTEACEAE
Origin: Australia (coastal N.S.W. and Queensland).
Flowering time: Spring, northern hemisphere; late spring–early summer, southern hemisphere.
Climatic zone: 9, 10.

Genista aetnensis
MOUNT ETNA BROOM

Family: LEGUMINOSAE
Origin: Sicily, Sardinia.
Flowering time: Summer, northern hemisphere; late spring–mid-summer, southern hemisphere.
Climatic zone: 8, 9.
Dimensions: 17–20 feet (5–6 meters) high.
Description: Imagine a landscape of black and yellow. That is Mount Etna in summer, when the broom is in full flower on the lava-blackened slopes. Loose clusters of fragrant, clear yellow, pea-shaped flowers weigh down the slender branches of this graceful, little deciduous tree. The silky, downy, sparse leaves appear somewhat silvery. This

Dimensions: 40–145 feet (12–44 meters) high.

Description: Silky oak is widely grown — as a garden tree, a street tree, a pot plant, indoors and outdoors, and as a rootstock for grafting other grevilleas. Largest of all the grevilleas, it can grow rapidly to 65 feet or more (over 20 meters) in southern hemisphere gardens, and even higher in parts of the northern hemisphere. It has yellow-orange, toothbrush-shaped clusters of spider-like flowers and deeply-lobed, feathery leaves, somewhat silvery underneath. The tree prefers warm, moist soils. Normally evergreen, it tends to become deciduous if affected by cold and drought. Protect it from frost when young. It can be grown from seed.

Harpephyllum caffrum
KAFFIR PLUM
Family: ANACARDIACEAE
Origin: Southeastern Africa.
Flowering time: Mid-late summer.
Dimensions: 33–40 feet (10–12 meters) high.
Description: Give this handsome, evergreen tree plenty of space to develop its wide canopy. The young leaves appear reddish and shiny and can be mistaken for flowers from a distance. They later become dark-green and lustrous giving the tree a rather somber appearance. Delicious jams and jellies are made from the bright, red fruits, which develop from the rather pale, greenish-yellow flowers. Plant it as a shade tree in large coastal gardens where the rainfall is high. It grows easily from large stem cuttings, 12–24 inches (300–600 mm) long in late spring.

Harpephyllum caffrum

Koelreuteria paniculata
VARNISH TREE (U.S.A.), GOLDEN RAIN TREE (U.K.), PRIDE OF CHINA TREE
Other common names: WILLOW PATTERN PLATE TREE
Family: SAPINDACEAE
Origin: Northern China, Korea.
Flowering time: Early summer.
Climatic zone: 5, 5, 7, 8.
Dimensions: 20–50 feet (6–15 meters) high.
Description: Golden rain tree grows in a wide range of climates and soils, tolerating drought, but disliking the coastal garden with its salt-laden winds. Its large, drooping clusters of yellow

Description: In a sunny, open space in the garden, this delightful, evergreen tree grows only a fraction of the height it attains in its natural habitat, where it has to fight for light. The sprays of scented yellow flowers are tubular, with five open lobes. The tree needs to be carefully positioned, because both flowers and leaves are borne towards the end of the thinnish, brittle branches. Because its branching is open and irregular, it throws little shade. Protect it from the wind by planting it either against a fence or wall, or behind a shrubbery. It enjoys warm, coastal areas and free-draining soil.

flowers are followed by long, reddish, papery pods which hang on the tree into winter, and its large, feathery leaves color well in the autumn. Developing a wide canopy when mature, it grows rapidly in warmer climates, but in cooler regions takes about 20 years to attain a height of 18 feet (5 meters). Propagate it from seed or root cuttings.
Varieties/cultivars: 'Fastigiata', 'September' (flowers in late summer).

Hymenosporum flavum
NATIVE FRANGIPANI, AUSTRALIAN FRANGIPANI, SWEET-SHADE (U.K.)
Family: PITTOSPORACEAE
Origin: Australia (northern N.S.W. and Queensland).
Flowering time: Late spring–early summer.
Climatic zone: 9, 10.
Dimensions: 20–66 feet (6–20 meters) high.
Description: In a sunny, open space in

Hymenosporum flavum

Koelreuteria paniculata

Laburnum anagyroides
COMMON LABURNUM
Family: LEGUMINOSAE
Origin: Central and southern Europe.
Flowering time: Early summer.
Climatic zone: 6, 7, 8, 9.
Dimensions: Up to 20 feet (6 meters).
Description: This charming, small, deciduous tree has a spreading shape and large, drooping clusters of bright yellow, pea-like flowers. It likes cool-climate gardens, and although it can be grown successfully in most soil types, one that is deep and moist will bring the best results. In country gardens do not position it where stock can eat it, as all parts of the plant are poisonous.

Laburnum anagyroides

Parkinsonia aculeata

Laburnum x watereri 'Vossii'

Tamarindus indica

Laburnum x watereri 'Vossii'
LABURNUM, GOLDEN
CHAIN TREE, WATERER'S
LABURNUM

Family: LEGUMINOSAE
Origin: Hybrid.
Flowering time: Late spring–early summer.
Climatic zone: 6, 7, 8, 9.
Dimensions: 20–30 feet (6–9 meters) high.
Description: This beautiful tree bears long, drooping sprays of yellow, pea-shaped flowers, and has attractive, soft foliage which consists of three leaflets on a common stalk. An avenue of laburnum, flowering vividly yellow in the spring, is an enchanting spectacle. Laburnum is deciduous and grows in almost any position in regions where the winters are cold and the atmosphere moist. All parts of the plant are poisonous so fence it off from stock.

Parkinsonia aculeata
MEXICAN PALO VERDE
(U.S.A.), JERUSALEM THORN
(U.K.)

Family: LEGUMINOSAE
Origin: Tropical America.
Flowering time: Spring.
Climatic zone: 9, 10.
Dimensions: 20–27 feet (6–8 meters) high.
Description: Growing rapidly in its early years, this elegant little tree is for

the tropical garden only. Its large clusters of yellow flowers, slightly scented, are followed by seed pods which look like a short string of beads. The soft, green, gracefully drooping branches, with their sparse foliage, cast a delicate tracery of shadow, but carry sharp thorns about 1 inch (25 mm) long. Jerusalem thorn grows well in coastal gardens or in frost-free inland gardens and tolerates alkaline soil and drought. Propagate it from seed.

Tamarindus indica
TAMARIND

Family: CAESALPINACEAE
Origin: Tropical Africa, Abyssinia, India.
Flowering time: Summer, then intermittently.
Climatic zone: 10.
Dimensions: 50–80 feet (15–25 meters) high.
Description: In India, it is believed that bad spirits take possession of anyone who sleeps beneath the dense canopy of the tamarind, so dense that nothing grows below it. Abundant, orchid-like flowers, with a delicate scent, fall to create carpets of pale yellow. A hot-

climate, adaptable tree, it grows slowly, tolerating semi-arid conditions, but preferring deep, moist soils. Grow it from seed or buy a grafted specimen for quicker flowering. It is best suited to large, coastal or country gardens. The pulp from the large seed pods is used in curries and drinks.

296

Thevetia peruviana
LUCKY NUT, YELLOW OLEANDER, BE STILL TREE ○

Family: APOCYNACEAE
Origin: Tropical America.
Flowering time: Throughout hottest months.
Climatic zone: 9, 10.
Dimensions: 10–30 feet (3–9 meters) high.
Description: With its glossy green leaves and trumpet-shaped, sunshine-yellow flowers, that bloom for much of the year but never fully open, this little tree is a welcome addition to any hot climate garden. Demanding only a sunny spot and a free-draining soil, it forms a neat dome with little or no pruning. Plant it on its own or among lush vegetation. Beware of all parts of this innocent-looking tree — they are poisonous! The hard, triangular seeds are often worn as lucky charms — hence the name, lucky nut. Grow it in the warm months from seed or cuttings.
Other colors: Salmon-orange, white.
Varieties/cultivars: 'Aurantiaca', 'Alba'.

Tipuana tipu
PRIDE-OF-BOLIVIA (U.K.), TIPU TREE, ROSEWOOD ○

Family: LEGUMINOSAE
Origin: Mountains of Bolivia, southern Brazil.
Flowering time: Late spring.
Climatic zone: 9, 10.
Dimensions: 27–40 feet (8–12 meters) high.

Tipuana tipu

Description: Growing up to 100 feet (30 meters) in the wild, the tipu is much more manageable as a garden tree. Crinkled, apricot-yellow flowers appear in late spring at the tips of the branches. Pretty, light-green leaflets growing on wide-spreading limbs form the flattened canopy which, sometimes wider than it is high, makes tipu a perfect shade tree. In the subtropics it loses its leaves for a short time only. Grow it from seed.

Thevetia peruviana

Tristaniopsis laurina syn. Tristania laurina
KANOOKA, WATER BOX (U.K.), AUSTRALIAN WATER GUM ○

Family: MYRTACEAE
Origin: Australia (coastal Victoria to Queensland).
Flowering time: Summer.
Climatic zone: 9.
Dimensions: 15–50 feet (5–15 meters) high.
Description: A most accommodating tree, Australian water gum, which grows quite large in the wild, can nevertheless be easily grown as a tub plant. Although it is found naturally by river banks, it will adapt to average rainfall conditions, but not to heavy soils. Handsome, glossy green leaves are enhanced in summer by the scented, bee-attracting flowers clustered at the leaf bases. Newly exposed bark appears in shades of pale yellow, gray, and red. Slow-growing, it makes a good shade or background tree. Grow it from seed in spring.

Tristaniopsis laurina

GLOSSARY

ACID SOIL: has a pH of less than 6, turning litmus paper red.

ALKALINE SOIL: has a pH of more than 8, turning litmus paper blue.

ANNUAL: a plant grown from seed that flowers, fruits, then dies within one year or season.

AXIL: the angle or point between a leaf and stem or branch.

BIENNIAL: a plant completing its life cycle in two years.

BRACT: a modified leaf, often at the base of a flower.

BUD: a more or less immature shoot arising from the leaf axil.

CALYX: the outer ring of the flower, consisting of sepals.

CANE: a slender woody stem that is often hollow. Bamboo and most berry fruits produce canes.

CONIFER: a plant that bears its primitive flowers and seeds in cones.

COROLLA: a collective term for sepals and petals.

CORYMB: similar to a raceme, but with the stalks of the lower florets longer than the upper ones, creating a flattened or convex head.

CULTIVAR: a selected plant form introduced into cultivation, which has some horticultural value.

DECIDUOUS: a plant which loses its leaves every year, generally referring to shrubs or trees.

DIVISION: a propagating method where perennials are separated by digging up and dividing the roots and top growth into clumps that can be replanted.

DOUBLE FLOWER: a flower with more than twice the usual number of petals, usually formed from stamens.

ELLIPTIC: describing the shape of a leaf, being in outline the shape of an ellipse.

ESPALIER: a plant which has been trained to lie flat against a wall or trellis featuring a central trunk with opposite pairs of horizontal stems.

EPIPHYTE: a plant which grows on another, using it for support without actually being a parasite, e.g., many orchids.

FAMILY: a natural grouping of plant genera with certain essential characteristics in common.

FLORET: an individual small flower that forms part of a large cluster of flowers, e.g., daisy.

GENUS: a group of species which have common features and characteristics.

GRAFTING: A propagating method where a section of one plant is inserted into the rootstock of another.

GREENHOUSE: a structure surfaced with glass or plastic sheeting which provides a sheltered environment for growing plants.

HARDENING OFF: a method of gradually acclimatising plants into a new temperature situation, usually after being reared in a greenhouse before transplanting into the garden.

HARDY: being able to withstand extremes of cold and frost, or harsh, dry conditions. Varies from zone to zone.

HUMUS: dark brown material produced after composting vegetable and animal matter.

HYBRID: the progeny of a cross between two different species.

INFLORESCENCE: the arrangement of flowers of a plant.

LANCEOLATE: describing the shape of a leaf, being like the head of a lance, tapering at each end.

LATERAL: a stem or shoot arising from a leaf axil of a larger stem.

LEADER: a shoot at the end of a main stem.

LINEAR: very narrow.

LOAM: a moderately fertile soil composed of clay, sand, and humus with a texture that is neither too sandy nor too heavy. Good loam will retain moisture and be rich in humus.

MULCH: a layer of organic material laid at ground level to help reduce weed growth and conserve soil moisture.

NATURALIZED: plants growing in areas or countries where they do not naturally occur, often escapees from gardens.

ORGANIC: material derived from living organisms. In horticulture referring to soil additives of natural orgin, i.e. animal manure, compost from decayed plant remains.

OVATE: describing the shape of a leaf, being oval or egg-shaped in outline.

PANICLE: a many-branched inflorescence.

PERENNIAL: a plant living for more than two years.

PINNATE: a compound leaf with leaflets arranged along either side of a common stalk.

PISTIL: the female section of the flower.

RACEME: a group of flowers arranged along an unbranched stem, each floret having a distinct stalk.

RHIZOME: an underground creeping root system

from which shoots and roots develop.

ROOTSTOCK: the root and base of a plant onto which sections of another plant can be grated.

ROSETTE: a group of leaves arranged in an overlapping, circular fashion.

RUNNER: aerial stems from which roots grow, forming a new plant.

SEPAL: a unit of the calyx protecting the petals.

SESSILE: used of flowers and leaves without individual stalks.

SINGLE FLOWER: a simple flower form with one ring of petals.

SPADIX: a spiked inflorescence in which the axis is fleshy.

SPATHE: a large bract, sometimes pair of bracts, enclosing the spadix.

SPECIES: a collection of individual plants essentially alike when grown in the same conditions. In horticulture and botany it is used as a form of classification.

SPIKE: similar to a raceme but having stalkless florets.

SPORE: a specialized reproductive cell usually formed asexually; the reproductive unit of ferns and fungi.

STAMEN: the male part of the plant, consisting of filament, anther, and pollen.

SUCKER: a shoot arising from the root system or base of a plant.

SYN: a plant name that has been set aside in favor of a new name.

TENDRIL: a spiraling slender shoot by which some climbing plants cling for support.

TERMINAL: at the apex or tip.

TRIFOLIATE: a leaf divided into three leaflets.

TUBER: a fleshy root or stem that stores nutrients for later use.

UMBEL: a rounded, often flattened head of flowers, the stalks of which all arise together from the tip of a stem.

UNISEXUAL: a flower of only one sex.

VAR: a variant species.

WEEPING: a shrub or tree whose branches hang in a pendulous, drooping fashion.

WHORL: a group of three or more structures encircling an axis.

X: denoting a hybrid species.

BIBLIOGRAPHY

Beckett, Kenneth A. 1983. *The Concise Encyclopedia of Garden Plants*. London: Orbis.

Clausen, Ruth Rogers and Nicolas H. Ekstrom. 1989. *Perennials for American Gardens*. New York: Random House.

Hortus Third: A Concise Dictionary of Plants Cultivated in the United States and Canada. 1976. New York: Macmillan.

Johnson, Hugh. 1973. *The International Book of Trees*. London: Mitchell Beazley.

Macoboy, Stirling. 1986. *What Flower is That?* Sydney: Lansdowne.

Moggi, Guido and Luciano Giugnolini. 1983. *Simon and Schuster's Guide to Garden Flowers*. New York: Simon and Schuster.

Readers Digest. 1984. *Guide to Creative Gardening*. London: Readers Digest.

Readers Digest. 1987. *Illustrated Guide to Gardening*. Sydney: Readers Digest

Taylor's Guides to Gardening. 1986. Boston: Houghton Mifflin.

INDEX OF COMMON NAMES

FLOWERS BY COLOR

INDEX OF BOTANICAL NAMES

INDEX OF SYNONYMS